'In our contemporary geopolitical world of transience, mass migration, and social instability; difference, opposition, and alterity play a formidable role in the fluidity and imposed re-inscription of identity. In this important and timely book, Jungian analysts, academics, and social activists perspicaciously illuminate our current plight where diverse cultural complexes saturate our social collectives vying for protectionism, exclusionary praxis, and self-security at the expense of the 'Other' living in transitional states of uncertainty with no status value. This notable contribution to post-Jungian depth psychology will make you rethink your cherished assumptions about human sociability and the logic of containment in an uncontained world based on division, nihilism, and the indeterminacy of our looming collective shadow'.

– **Professor Jon Mills, Psy.D., Ph.D., C.Psych., ABPP**; Faculty, Postgraduate Programs in Psychoanalysis & Psychotherapy, Adler Graduate Professional School, Toronto; author and editor of numerous works on psychoanalysis including *Jung and Philosophy*

'This is an innovative book of excellent and creative contributions presented at the 2018 Joint IAAP–IAJS Conference in Frankfurt on Indeterminate States. The collection of papers gives us the opportunity to reflect on states of life that are uncertain, unusual, not clearly defined, perhaps disturbing, but in some way always innovative. The book shows how analytical psychology in particular contributes to understanding and dealing with such situations and processes and helps balance indeterminate and determinate states. It is a timely book and confronts us with the most critical questions of our time. The editors did a wonderful job in assembling all these papers. I wish this publication many interested readers'.

– **Marianne Müller**, Past President IAAP; Jungian Training Analyst and Supervisor, Bern, Switzerland

'All too often conferences and the books they generate have vague and rag-bag themes with little genuine coherence. This book is the exception. Not only is the theme of liminality perfectly chosen for a psychology (Jung's) that sits squarely on the difficult interface between the opposites, but it provides the writers of the chapters of this book with an opportunity to address some of the key issues of our time. Modern post-Jungian literature is finally addressing the psychosocial dimension, and this book provides a fascinating example, with chapters on topics like the psychology of migration across borders and the phenomenology of liminal gender. Throughout the volume, the range is immense, covering as it does clinical, ethical, cinematic and sociological topics. However, what holds the book together is an abiding awareness of the transformative possibilities that can emerge out of a willingness to stay with ambiguity'.

– **Mark Saban, Ph.D.**, senior Jungian analyst with the Independent Group of Analytical Psychologists; Lecturer at the Department of Psychosocial and Psychoanalytic Studies, University of Essex, UK; author, *Two Souls Alas: Jung's Two Personalities and the Making of Analytical P*

Jungian Perspectives on Indeterminate States

In *Jungian Perspectives on Indeterminate States: Betwixt and Between Borders*, Elizabeth Brodersen and Pilar Amezaga bring together leading international contributors to analyse and interpret the psychological impact of contemporary border crossing – both literally and figuratively.

Each chapter assesses key themes such as migration, culture, gender, and identity formation, through a Jungian lens. All the contributors sensitively explore how creative forms can help mitigate the trauma experienced when one is forced to leave safety and enter unknown territory, and examine the specific role of indeterminacy, liminality, and symbols as transformers at the border between culture, race, and gender. The book asks whether we are able to hold these indeterminate states as creative liminal manifestations pointing to new forms, integrate the shadow 'other' as potential, and allow sufficient cross-border migration and fertilisation as permissible. It makes clear that societal conflict represents a struggle for recognition and identity and elucidates the negative experiences of authoritarian structures attached to disrespect and misrecognitions.

This interdisciplinary collection will offer key insight for Jungian analysts in practice and in training, psychotherapists, anthropologists, political and cultural theorists, and postgraduate researchers in psychosocial studies. It will also be of great interest to readers interested in migration, sexuality, gender, race, and ethnicity studies.

Elizabeth Brodersen, Ph.D., is an accredited Training Analyst and Supervisor at the CGJI Zürich, Switzerland. Elizabeth received her doctorate in Psychoanalytic Studies from the University of Essex, UK, and works as a Jungian analyst in private practice in Germany and Switzerland. She is currently Co-Chair of The International Association for Jungian Studies (IAJS) with Dr. Kiley Laughlin.

Pilar Amezaga, Jungian analyst, is the Founder Member of the Uruguayan Society of Analytical Psychology and Professor at the Catholic University of Uruguay. She is currently Vice President of the Executive Committee of the International Association for Analytical Psychology (IAAP) and member of the Editorial Board of the Journal of Analytical Psychology.

Jungian Perspectives on Indeterminate States

Betwixt and Between Borders

Edited by Elizabeth Brodersen and Pilar Amezaga

LONDON AND NEW YORK

First published 2021
by Routledge
2 Park Square, Milton Park, Abingdon, Oxon OX14 4RN

and by Routledge
52 Vanderbilt Avenue, New York, NY 10017

Routledge is an imprint of the Taylor & Francis Group, an informa business

© 2021 selection and editorial matter, Elizabeth Brodersen & Pilar Amezaga; individual chapters, the contributors

The right of Elizabeth Brodersen & Pilar Amezaga to be identified as the authors of the editorial material, and of the authors for their individual chapters, has been asserted in accordance with sections 77 and 78 of the Copyright, Designs and Patents Act 1988.

All rights reserved. No part of this book may be reprinted or reproduced or utilised in any form or by any electronic, mechanical, or other means, now known or hereafter invented, including photocopying and recording, or in any information storage or retrieval system, without permission in writing from the publishers.

Trademark notice: Product or corporate names may be trademarks or registered trademarks, and are used only for identification and explanation without intent to infringe.

British Library Cataloguing-in-Publication Data
A catalogue record for this book is available from the British Library

Library of Congress Cataloging-in-Publication Data
Names: Brodersen, Elizabeth, editor. | Amezaga, Pilar, 1959- editor.
Title: Jungian perspectives on indeterminate states: betwixt and between borders / edited by Elizabeth Brodersen & Pilar Amezaga.
Description: Abingdon, Oxon; New York, NY: Routledge, 2021. | Includes bibliographical references and index. |
Identifiers: LCCN 2020013080 (print) | LCCN 2020013081 (ebook) | ISBN 9780367339623 (hardback) | ISBN 9780367339630 (paperback) | ISBN 9780429323072 (ebook)
Subjects: LCSH: Emigration and immigration–Psychological aspects. | Statelessness–Psychological aspects. | Immigrants–Psychology. | Jungian psychology.
Classification: LCC JV6013 .J86 2021 (print) | LCC JV6013 (ebook) | DDC 304.801/9–dc23
LC record available at https://lccn.loc.gov/2020013080
LC ebook record available at https://lccn.loc.gov/2020013081

ISBN: 978-0-367-33962-3 (hbk)
ISBN: 978-0-367-33963-0 (pbk)
ISBN: 978-0-429-32307-2 (ebk)

Typeset in Times
by Deanta Global Publishing Services, Chennai, India

This collection is dedicated to all cross-border travellers

Contents

Notes on the contributors	xii
Acknowledgements	xvi
Copyright permissions and credits	xvii
Editorial introduction	xviii

PART I
Border, migration, and identity   1

1 Crossing physical borders and the making of identity: The case of Europe   3
   MONICA LUCI

2 Challenges to the individuation process of people on the move: Developing a sense of global citizenship   28
   ELISABETTA IBERNI

3 The Mexican-American cultural complex: Assessing the depth-psychological problems due to challenges of assimilation in American society   47
   VALERIA CÉSPEDES MUSSO

4 Hidden in plain sight: How therapists miss cultural trauma in trans-cultural white clients   63
   RACHAEL A. VAUGHAN

PART 2
Border phenomenology and gender   77

5 Ismail is now called Ebru and Lea wants to be a mechanic:
   Transgender and intercultural work as a municipal task   79
   ELENA BARTA

6 Child development and gender issues: Symbols, creativity, and
   alterity through Sandplay therapy   95
   DENISE GIMENEZ RAMOS AND JULIA KADDIS EL KHOURI

7 Bernini and the Pont Sant'Angelo: The transcendent
   hermaphrodite as symbol of individuation   108
   WILLIAM T. FARRAR, IV

8 Problems of symbolisation and archetypal processes: The case
   of male same-sex desire   127
   GIORGIO GIACCARDI

PART 3
Liminality between borders and symbol formation   145

9 An invisible magic circle: A Jungian commentary on *When
   Marnie Was There*   147
   MATHEW MATHER

10 Duality of the Japanese 'fish' symbol: Standing at the edge of
   life and death   161
   YUKA OGISO

11 Heart of Darkness: An archetypal journey to the other side   175
   MIRELLA GIGLIO

PART 4
Border crossing and individuation   189

12 Re-visioning individuation: Opening to a witness
   consciousness   191
   EILEEN SUSAN NEMETH

13	**The tension and paradox between determinate and indeterminate state: Clinical, social, and cultural aspects** TOSHIO KAWAI	**209**
14	**The consequences of freedom: Moving beyond the intermediate states of broken individualisation and liquidity** STEFANO CARPANI	**221**
15	**Vulnerability and incorruptibility: An aretaic model of the transcendent function** NICCOLÒ FIORENTINO POLIPO	**240**

Index 261

Contributors

Elena Barta, M.Phil., is a historian and educator. An intersectional and transformative approach on contemporary history, gender, sexuality, disability, race, and culture is the focus of their academic and educational work. Since 2015 they are responsible for the Coordinating Office for lesbian, gay, bisexual, transgender, intersex, and queer (LGBTIQ) issues. The office is situated within the Department for Multicultural Affairs (AmkA) in the city of Frankfurt am Main.

Stefano Carpani, M.A., M.Phil., is an Italian sociologist and Jungian psychoanalyst (CGJI Zürich) and a Ph.D. candidate at the Department of Psychosocial and Psychoanalytic Studies, University of Essex (UK). He works in private practice in Berlin (DE) and is the initiator of *The School of Dreams* and the YouTube interview series *Breakfast at Küsnacht*, which aims to capture the voices of senior Jungians. Stefano is the author of '*Breakfast at Küsnacht: Conversations on C.G. Jung and Beyond*' (Chiron, 2020) and editor of '*The Plural Turn in Jungian and Post-Jungian Studies: The Work of Andrew Samuels*' (Routldge, forthcoming 2020). His paper '*The Numinous and the Fall of the Berlin Wall*' won the Kim Arndt Award in 2019.

Julia Kaddis El Khouri, Ph.D., is a clinical psychologist and received her doctorate in Clinical Psychology at the Pontifical Catholic University of São Paulo (PUCSP). She is a member of AJB (IAAP) and a member of IBTSANDPLAY (ISST). She works as volunteer psychologist at the Transdisciplinary Outpatient Clinic of Gender Identity and Sexual Orientation (AMTIGOS-IPq/HCFMUSP).

William T. Farrar, IV, Ph.D., is the current Chair of the Division of Behavioral Sciences and Cultural Studies at Estrella Mountain Community College and the former Director of the Center for Teaching and Learning at Estrella Mountain Community College, where he teaches Research Methods, Statistics, the Psychology of Religion, and Introduction to Psychology. His earned his doctorate in Experimental Psychology at the University of California in Santa Cruz, and he has published a number of articles in psycholinguistics. In his teaching role, he has explored the role that archetypal structures can play in people's self-understanding. He is also interested in exploring how the interplay of verbal narrative and image-based semantics in archetypes can be used to communicate complex, internal psychological states and their relationship to social issues. He has been a member of IAJS since 2014.

Giorgio Giaccardi is a Jungian analyst, senior member of the BJAA, and working in private practice in London. He has written, taught, and given seminars on sexual diversity, gender identity, and the notion of symbol at Birkbeck, University of Essex and various professional Associations (bpf, SAP, AJA, WMIP). He has recently published contributions on these themes in the journal *Couple and Family Psychoanalysis* (2016) and in the BPC Magazine *New Associations* (2015). He is a member of the Advisory Group on Sexual and Gender Diversity within the British Psychoanalytic Council. His latest paper 'Unconscious Processes, Instrumental Musical and the Experience of the Sublime' was commended with the 2014 Rozsika Parker Prize and published in the *BJP* (2015).

Mirella Giglio is a psychologist in private practice. She obtained a B.A. (2007) in Psychology at PUC-São Paulo, Brazil and a Master's degree (2017) in Science of Religion (PUC-São Paulo, Brazil) with the dissertation: '*Heart of Darkness*: A symbolic expression of depression'. Her first research about depression was to see if depression has a purpose by analysing Jungian theory. This research was presented in several conferences and received a grant from Oxford University in 2016. Mirella is interested in the following topics: depression, chronic pain, symbols, and cultural expressions. Her latest goal is to use literature as a way to comprehend human beings and their life motivations.

Elisabetta Iberni, Ph.D., is an analytical psychologist born and raised in Italy, and an individual member of the International Association of Analytical Psychology (IAAP). She works bilingually (Italian/English) in private practice in The Hague, Netherlands. Between 2009 and 2016, she has been working as a clinical psychologist from a multicultural perspective in several organizations in a post-conflict setting and as human rights observer with minority groups in Kosovo. She is an active member of the Serbian Developing Group and has a Ph.D. from the Department of Psychosocial and Psychoanalytic Studies of the University of Essex.

Toshio Kawai is Professor at the Kokoro Research Center of Kyoto University. Educated in Clinical Psychology at Kyoto University and in Philosophical Psychology at Zurich where he gained his Ph.D. in 1987, Toshio Kawai received his diploma in Analytical Psychology from the CGJI Zürich in 1990, where he trained to become a Jungian analyst. He is the author of numerous articles and book chapters on cultural and collective trauma in German, English, and Japanese including 'The 2011 Earthquake in Japan: Psychotherapeutic Intervention and Change of Worldview' in *Spring Journal*, 2012. He is currently President of IAAP.

Monica Luci, Ph.D., is a clinical psychologist, Jungian and relational psychoanalyst. She has been working as a researcher, psychologist, and psychotherapist with vulnerable asylum seekers and refugees, survivors of torture, war traumas, and human trafficking in Italy and within transnational projects. She is author of several articles and presentations in conferences on the themes of trauma, collective violence, cultural studies, sexuality, and ethical issues, and the book *Torture, Psychoanalysis and Human Rights* (Routledge, 2017). She is also the winner of the 2018 Fordham Prize awarded by the *Journal of Analytical Psychology* for the article 'Disintegration of the Self and Regeneration of the Psychic Skin in the Treatment of Traumatised Refugees'.

Mathew Mather is a Ph.D. graduate of the University of Essex, where he specialised in Jung and Alchemy. He is a Lecturer at Limerick School of Art and Design, Program Director of the BSc (Hons) in Digital Animation Production and Course Director of the Certificate in Jungian Psychology with Art Therapy. Mathew regularly presents at international conferences, and has an especial interest in dream interpretation, synchronicity, art, alchemy, astrology, the environment, as well as personal and cultural mythologies. He is author of *The Alchemical Mercurius: Esoteric Symbol of Jung's Life and Works* published by Routledge and lectures in Narrative, Media Psychology, and Film Studies.

Valeria Céspedes Musso is an independent researcher and a recent Ph.D. graduate of University of Essex in Psychosocial and Psychoanalytic Studies. She is currently a training candidate at the CGJI Zürich and has recently published a book entitled *Marian Apparitions in Cultural Contexts*, Routledge, 2018.

Eileen Susan Nemeth is a Jungian analyst and psychotherapist in private practice in Zürich, Switzerland. Her work as an analytical psychologist and therapist combines her training as a Jungian analyst, dance therapist, and former dancer, teacher, and choreographer. A member of AGAP, Eileen teaches at the CGJI Zürich and ISAP, Zürich. Circling all her work is a strong focus on creativity and the integration of the body in analytical and psychotherapeutic work.

Yuka Ogiso, Ph.D., is a Research Fellow at the Well-being Research Center, Dôshisha University, Japan. She also works as a clinical psychologist at a psychiatric clinic. She was educated in the Philosophy of Religion at Tokyo University and in Clinical Psychology at Kyoto University, where she received a Ph.D. in 2013. She is author of *Jung and James: Exploration about Individuality and Universality* (Sôgensha, 2014); and co-author of *Analytical Psychology in a Changing World: The Search for Self, Identity and Community*, Lucy Huskinson & Murray Stein (ed.) (Routledge, 2014).

Niccolò Fiorentino Polipo is a psychologist registered in Italy with the Charter of the Psychologists of Lombardy and a chartered member of the British Psychological Society. He graduated in philosophy at the San Raffaele Vita-Salute University (Milan) with a dissertation on Jung, Neumann, and the new ethic. Later, he trained as a clinical psychologist at the University of Bologna and completed his placement at the Jonas Centre of Psychoanalytic Clinical Practice for New Symptoms (Bologna) and the Cyprus Institute for Psychotherapy (Limassol). He conducted different types of research, including an empirical study on the psychological well-being and attachment representations of lay and consecrated Roman Catholics (EuARe First Annual Conference 2018); an ethnobotanical study on the use of medicinal plants for physical and mental health purposes in rural Cyprus (SEPI 34th Annual Conference 2018); and a psychoeducational program on the sexualization of young girls as part of his M.Sc. in Forensic Psychology at the University of Kent.

Denise Gimenez Ramos, Ph.D., is Professor at the Post-Graduate Program in Clinical Psychology at Pontifical Catholic University of Sao Paulo. She is a member of SBPA (IAAP) and Vice President for America of ISST. She is the author of several books and articles.

Rachael A. Vaughan, MFT, is a licensed psychotherapist and Associate Professor at the California Institute of Integral Studies in San Francisco, California. She holds an M.A. in Depth Psychology from Pacifica Graduate Institute, California, as well as an M.A. in Linguistics from the University of Edinburgh, Scotland. She has studied at the C. G. Jung Institute of San Francisco. Born in Asia and raised primarily in Europe, Rachael has a lifelong, passionate interest in issues of culture, identity, and inclusion. Her teaching is informed by multiple cultural perspectives, as well as post-colonial and feminist theory. She has a bilingual therapy practice in San Francisco.

Acknowledgements

We wish to thank all those who presented and participated in the joint IAAP–IAJS Frankfurt am Main Conference on *Indeterminate States*, August 2–5, 2018 at the West end Campus, Goethe University and made this innovative, international conference such a rich and scholarly experience. Unfortunately, due to word count restrictions, we are unable to publish in this collection all the excellent research material that was offered at the conference.

We are particularly indebted and grateful to Marianne Müller, Toshio Kawai, Regina Renn, and Margaret Klenck from IAAP; Michael Glock, Camilla Giambonini, Mathew Mather, and Konoyu Nakamura from IAJS for all their generous, indispensable organizational support throughout the Frankfurt conference planning. Michael, former IAJS Co-Chair, helped to co-chair the conference, adding his warm humour, as well as contributing his IT wizardry to the submission and registration logistics and aiding the presentations throughout the conference.

We greatly appreciate the teamwork and friendly co-operation of Goethe University, Frankfurt, Campus Service, particularly Nicolas Hofmann, for all his help and engagement.

This collection forms one of the stimulating joint publishing collegial exchanges between IAAP and IAJS on cultural transitions; another is the publication edited by Murray Stein and Raya Jones, *Cultures and Identities in Transition*, from the joint conference in Zürich, 2008. This Frankfurt volume extends these themes to update the current refugee displacement crisis, including transgender border crossing within the innovative context of *Indeterminate States*.

A special thank you is extended to Susannah Frearson and Heather Evans including the Routledge copyediting and production team for their excellent support and patience.

All client and interview material presented in this collection has been anonymised to protect their identity and privacy.

All references from Jung's *Collected Works* are translated by R. F. C. Hull and edited by H. Reed, M. Fordham, G. Adler, and W. McGuire, published in the UK by Routledge and Kegan Paul and in the US by Princeton University Press.

Copyright permissions and credits

Images

Part 2, Chapter 5: Elena Barta
Images 1 & 2: by permission of the Office for Multicultural Affairs (Amt für multikulturelle Angelegenheiten), Frankfurt am Main, Germany.

Part 3, Chapter 10: Yuka Ogiso
Figures 4 & 5: National Diet Library Digital Collection, Japan

Part 4, Chapter 12: Eileen Nemeth
Image 1: by permission of the National Archives, New York City, USA.
Image 4 of migrants: by permission of Keystone/EPA/Nake Batev; Depeschen Agentur, Germany.

Editorial introduction

Elizabeth Brodersen and Pilar Amezaga

This innovative collection of chapters from the 2018 joint IAAP–IAJS conference at Goethe University, Frankfurt am Main, Germany reflects upon the topic of *Indeterminate States* within an inter-disciplinary Jungian/post-Jungian framework attached to migration, border phenomenology, and identity formation. The material deals with intrapsychic, depth psycho-analytical perspectives as well as outer psycho-social, political aspects that necessitate migration. This international event was the first in Frankfurt am Main to introduce Jungian thought to a global audience.

Frankfurt am Main, a city 'betwixt and between' borders

Hillman (2018, pp. 17–26) stresses that the soul of a city is concerned with *emotional memories* often attached to the *experience of tragedy*. Each city as a *momento mori* signifies the remembrance of particular dark episodes in its history reminding us of the mortality of life within its buildings, street names, and memorial statutes (ibid, p. 23). In the case of Frankfurt am Main, the names of Second World War Holocaust victims from Frankfurt are engraved on the walls of central-city park-houses and on more than 1,500 so called 'stumbling stones', made of metal and inserted into the pavements. Frankfurt's long and complex multicultural trading and financial history beginning with the Romans in the area of the *Römer* and outside Frankfurt (Limes/Saalburg) during the first century AD certainly makes Frankfurt an appropriate venue for interiorising conflicting cultural values in the analysis of strong emotions attached to indeterminacy as a 'betwixt and between' border phenomenology caught in historical upheaval.

Singer asks (2010, p. 1): 'Are the souls of our cities' inhabitants lost or dehumanised in the overwhelming scale and complexity of human life?' Singer further asks: 'And what of a city's own soul? Is it overlooked and buried, along with its neighborhoods and histories?' Having lived through all its historical trans-cultural stretching of its borders first-hand, the city experienced the sudden closing of its borders during the Third Reich with its brutal emphasis on nineteenth and twentieth-century 'scientific' theories of racial purity and Aryan aestheticism (cf. Picot, 2001), which annihilated the vibrant cultural and economic contribution of the Jewish people living in Frankfurt who saw themselves primarily as Germans. The closed-border ideology of the Nazis under National Socialism eliminated Communists, Jews, and Roma people based on their alleged 'aberrant' physicality, and all mental and physically handicapped people as 'impure anomalies' of nature (see Brodersen, 2019, pp. 66–75; Thomä, 2007, pp. 75–100 on biophysical factoring such as body shape and 'twisted' facial features attached to 'others').

After the Second World War, Frankfurt am Main, as part of the occupied American Zone, experienced democratic values, neo-liberalism, and ordo-capitalism developed during the 1950s (Freiburg School) that replaced Nazi ideology and later mixed with mid-eastern European post-communist values after German unification with the collapse of the Berlin Wall in 1989. Frankfurt is a culturally and ethnically diverse city, with a large proportion of its population, including young people, having a migrant background. Between 1947 and 1949, the Frankfurt Rhine Main area resumed its open border, stretching its city's limits to include large numbers of ethnic German refugees expelled from their former homelands in Eastern Europe as retaliation for Nazi brutal territorial aggression. In support of victims of war-torn zones, such as the Balkans during the 1990s, and the recent Syrian and Middle East refugee crises, Frankfurt am Main plays an effective international role at the crossroads of Europe in offering shelter and food, also as safe passage to other destinations. In May 2017, Goethe University established the first Chair in Holocaust Studies in recognition of Frankfurt's long and respected Jewish history which includes Frankfurt's election of Ludwig Landmann, the first German Jewish mayor in 1924.

Frankfurt am Main is the birthplace of the German cultural icon and polymath, Wolfgang von Goethe (1749–1832), ostensibly an ancestor of Jung, who later moved to Weimar. As Frankfurt's rich intellectual Jewish history still impacts Frankfurt's educational system, medical research, and cultural events (see Freimüller, 2020; Seeman & Bönisch, 2019), Jung's alleged antisemitism has led to a devaluation of analytical psychology in psychoanalytical circles in Frankfurt and is taken seriously at Goethe University, the home of the Frankfurt School of Critical Theory. Formed during the 1920s and 1930s by Jewish intellectuals such as Horkheimer, Adorno, Marcuse, Benjamin, Fromm, and furthered by Habermas and Honneth, Critical Theory emphasised the role of recognition, inter-subjectivity, psychoanalysis, and social change. The University of Frankfurt, later named Goethe University, founded in 1914, marks the establishment of the first civic university in Germany; today the university exemplifies Frankfurt's long, complex history to remain an intellectual, independent, 'free' city.

The joint IAAP–IAJS Frankfurt conference material on *Indeterminate States* is an attempt to reintroduce the value of analytical psychology to Frankfurt am Main. The theme *Indeterminate States* is already well represented at Frankfurt's *Institute for Social Research*, which developed from the original Frankfurt School of Critical Theory and continues its emphasis on analysing the socio-political factoring behind forced migration, lack of a sustainable political identity as the 'other', reflected in ethnic minority injustices, gender inequalities, and commodity fetishism (cf. Wiggershaus, 1994, on the history and the diverse aims of the Frankfurt School).

The Frankfurt conference venue was chosen specifically to further interdisciplinary Jungian scholarship within these ever-pressing socio-political areas of human rights and offers a unique forum for presentations as symbolic *liminal spaces* moving across borders into unchartered territory, likened to the difficulty of working with 'shadow', intergenerational, unconscious, individual/cultural complexes attached to acknowledging the rights and the identity of the 'other' culture, race, and gender (see Part 2, Chapter 5, by Barta on Frankfurt as one of the first German municipals to engage constructively with complex cross-cultural, cross-gender issues).

The more recent Jungian/post-Jungian focus on pluralism, analysis, and political activism (cf. Samuels, 2001, 2015; Kiehl, Saban, Samuels, eds., 2016) also reflects certain psychosocial/political activism of the Frankfurt School. Briefly, (as an in-depth comparison between analytical psychology and Critical Theory needs more space than we can offer here) a core theme addressed by Honneth (1988; 1996; 2012) stresses that the struggle for *recognition* best characterises the fight for emancipation by individuals or social groups, and represents the negative experience of domination imbued in authoritarian systems (cf. Adorno, et. al., 1950) that foster racism and misrecognitions (cf. Mills, 2019a). To come to terms with such negation of subjective forms means to be able to transform socio-political reality and points to the crucial role moral recognition the 'other' plays in grounding inter-subjectivity (Mills, 2019b). Mills (2019b, pp. 17–28) notes that Honneth's recognition theory in its rational approach, however, does not take into sufficient account unconscious, intergenerational trauma that fosters dysrecognition and refutation of the 'other' and can blunt inter-subjective empathy. Mills (2019c, p. 242) and Carpani (Part 4, Chapter 14 in this collection) suggest that closer interdisciplinary research co-operation between contemporary psychoanalysis, that includes the Jungian approach to unconscious processes, and Critical Theory would be mutually beneficial.

Habermas' (1996) work to include the 'other' in political legitimacy needs not be a fixed one, but open to explore modernity's globalised multiplicity of cultural forms (Shabani, 2003, pp. 172-174). Similar to Jung's concept of individuation which stresses the need to outgrow old authoritarian, one-sided, blocking, parental mechanisms of control, Critical Theory does not 'fetishize' knowledge either, considering it functional to ideological critique, the right to dissent, and the pursuit of social emancipation. Critical Theory's transcendence of the methodological problem of 'theory/practice' through emphasising their fluid interconnectedness is similar to Jungian concepts of symbol formation and individuation albeit with different emphases on unconscious processes (see Jung, 1918, para. 38, on the role of the unconscious as a *living* creative matrix that manifests through symbols that transform energy).

What kind of border as 'skin' develops and stretches to allow sufficient traffic to pass between the ego and the unconscious? The material presented here explores transformation within (and outside) archetypal affective theory to differentiate nomadic, border*land* traffic (c.f. Bernstein, 2005) as an indeterminate *continuum* towards re-recognition and re-description. Chapters in this collection, particularly in Part 1 by Luci, Iberni, Musso, and Vaughan all examine cross-borders migration and the psycho-political problematic effects of securing a viable identity.

Indeterminacy

The term indeterminacy and, by association, indeterminate states, refers both to common scientific and mathematical concepts of uncertainty and, by implication, to another kind of indeterminacy deriving from the nature of definition or meaning (cf. Broad, 1934). Philosophers and scientists generally try to eliminate indeterminacy from their arguments, or hide it from view (cf. Hardin, 2008, p. 59) since anything indeterminate is deemed unquantifiable and untestable. This relates to Popper's (1961) earlier discussion of falsifiability in his works on the scientific method (cf. Maxwell, 1972). Popper argues that reliable conclusions can only be drawn from replicable experiments, based on the proper evaluation of past evidence, since in order to establish observer agreement scientists must be able to quantify experimental evidence. Ciprut (2008, p. 346), however, proposes that indeterminacy is foremost an ontological phenomenon and relates to the development of free will and inter-subjectivity as an alternative to fixed, deterministic, causal factoring, which has proved inadequate in the study of chaotic realms and complex and natural social systems. This view is shared by Guyer (2008, p. 41–45) who suggests that indeterminacy and freewill are modern problems to distinguish them from the ancient, outgrown concept of fatalism. The reception of quantum mechanics reveals that while statistical laws can be formulated, the behaviour of individual members of a system is indeterminate and random. Quantum indeterminacy thus undermines the universal validity of determinism and creates room for a concept of freedom to choose between alternatives despite antecedent historical factors (Guyer, 2008, pp. 44–45). Hardin (2008, p. 65) suggests that social indeterminacy is a set theoretical choice theory rather than of physical possibilities, whereas Honderich (1988, p. 66) maintains that indeterminacy satisfies because it enhances a view of humans as morally responsible and as originators who are free to choose the outcome of their actions. Without free will, humans are diminished as playthings to external causes and their moral agency undercut. Jung (1921, para. 533) sees indeterminism as less influenced by outer events and more from creative ideas springing from the unconscious, thus giving the subject more independence and freedom towards outer objects.

Indeterminacy defined by Mills (2019d) is a 'state of undifferentiated immediacy' and consists of whatever we designate as a contradiction or an alterity, remaining incomplete as an indeterminate *openness*. This definition fits well to Jungian experiential work with symbols described as living, *unfixed*, unconscious structures open to new energetic arrangements. Indeterminacy, in the context of the Frankfurt conference material, values speculative cognitive fluidity capable of reimagining new states that are *coming into being*, moving from one reference point to another in a *liminal* state, as yet quantifiably undefined and unknowable.

The chapters in this collection thus use *indeterminate* intuitive thinking that corresponds to Jung's definition of *indirect*, symbolic thinking (1911–1912/1952, paras. 4–54) as compared to directed, hierarchical, abstracted thinking (logos) applied to generalised scientific observation. The inclusion of *indirect* thinking pertaining to the personal and collective unconscious psyche gives room for inter-subjectivity and pluralist, affective responses that have the creative ability to transform energy through symbol formation. Jung and Jungian analysts such as Adams (2001, 2004, pp. 2–19) use imagination, through amplification, as a *directed* analytical tool to sharpen affective images and bring them into legitimate ego and collective analytical discourse. Such intense immediacy and agency that qualify complex affective states would be lost if transferred to generalised scientific objectivism (James, 1890, p. 53; Jung, 1957, para. 531).

Holding the tension of the opposites

This collection ties together a key Jungian concept of 'holding the tension of the opposites' as an Indeterminate State, not fixed in a specific identity, whether cultural, racial, or gendered within the innovative work on complex theory. The chapters reflect our increasingly global migration and mixing between cultures, races, and the sexes, which mirror the way we work with our own unconscious 'shadow' complexes. Are we able to hold these indeterminate states as creative *liminal* manifestations pointing to new forms, integrate the shadow 'other' as a responsible choice to allow sufficient cross-border migration and fertilisation as permissible?

Van Gennep (1960) suggests that *liminality* belongs to inter-structural phenomena attached to *rites of passage* as a transitional, transformative process and has shown that all rites of transition are marked by three phases: separation, margin, and aggregation. The first phase of separation comprises symbolic behaviour signifying the painful detachment of the individual or group from an earlier fixed point of containment; during the second phase of margin, described as the intervening liminal period, a person passes through a realm that has few or none of the attributes of the past or the coming state. Turner (1964, pp. 234–238) calls it the *anomalous, liminal* stage of 'betwixt and between' where a person is structurally if not physically *invisible as dead* having no status value, clothes, property, or kinship position, until the third phase is consummated in accordance with the inculcation of new societal and ethical norms.

This is a complex and difficult process as it triggers and activates our own unconscious complexes, personal and cultural, in terms of securing a viable sense of self-identity. Can we stand the process of 'not knowing' as we cross our own safe borders and move into new developmental terrain whereby we question the tenets of safe and determinist belief systems? (See Part 3 with chapters by Mathers, Giglio and Osigo; Nemeth and Kawai from Part 4).

The symbol

Jung positions the *symbol* as the mediatory product that develops from 'holding of the tension of the opposites' between the conscious and unconscious opposing positions, combining both opposites in its resolution as *the transcendent function* and creating new cross-border forms capable of restabilising the ego. Jung describes symbols as deriving from unconscious activity (1923, paras. 825): 'From the activity of the unconscious there now emerges a new content, constellated by thesis and antithesis in equal measure and standing in complementary relation to both'. He continues (para. 826): 'Sometimes it seems as though the stability of the unborn individuality were the decisive factor, sometimes as though the mediatory product possessed a superior power …' Out of this activity emerges a *living third form* that is neither a combination nor a rejection of the two. Trapped energy is released by the creation of a new gradient.

Jung further explains (1923, para. 828) that the transcendent function does not denote a metaphysical quality but facilitates the transition from one attitudinal value to another. The living symbol is the 'very stuff of the psyche, transcending time and dissolution … and its configuration by the opposites ensures its sovereign power over all the psychic functions'.

Recent interdisciplinary research on symbol formation (Mithen, 1999; Lewis-Williams, 2002; Renfrew and Morley, 2009; Colman, 2016) all speculate that human ability to create symbols constitutes a *continuum* that dates back to the Upper Palaeolithic era (ca. 40,000 years). Mithen (1999) argues that this ability derives from the development of *cognitive fluidity*, capable of recombining knowledge through 'mapping across domains', by allowing social, technical, and natural history knowledge domains to cross-over and become integrated. Cognitive fluidity expresses itself as the 'emergence of representational re-description' in order to solve complex, life-threatening problems in highly uncertain environments and find new creative solutions. (See chapters from Part 4 by Nemeth, Kawai, Carpani, and Polipo on that complex difficulty.)

Migration across borders: Problems of identity and recognition

Cognitive fluidity is a highly relevant skill needed by migrating peoples into Europe and the US from different ethnicities, religions and languages as a result of globalization, the increase in national political protectionism, and populism. It also reflects the recent need (even among school children) to cross-over from a binary sexual identification into an indeterminate sexual orientation. Turner (1964, p. 237) suggests that movement across borders into liminality encourages the return to *prima materia* as undifferentiated raw material, expressed by creative images of androgyny and the breakdown of binary sex distinctions. This is particularly evident in LGBTIQ and other forms that stress *difference* from past gendered parental roles. Do the sexes (male/female) remain polarised out of fear of creating new forms of reproduction through the painful and difficult process of separation imbued in ritual liminality, or do same sex parents (male and female) nurture their young because they have distanced themselves from the tenets of monotheistic gender ideals and created new forms of sexual identity and specificities? (See Part 2 with chapters from Barta, El Khouri and Ramos, Farrar, and Giaccardi)

These chapters reflect the recent work of Singer and Kimbles (eds.) 2004; Kimbles (2014); and Rasche and Singer (eds.) (2016) on cultural complexes, cultural diversity, and *phantom narratives* amongst multiple 'soul' manifestations of people who are forced to traverse 'foreign' borders due to the painful cultural trauma, environmental disasters, war, scapegoating, torture, and loss of land and personal history, leaving their roots behind them. The experience of the loss of cultural identity and recognition when moving into new terrains is well documented, through the work of Amezaga and Gelsi, 2012; Wirtz, 2014; Sauer, 2014; Hill, 2014; Gudaite, 2014; Auestad, 2017; Luci, 2017; Tenenbaum, 2018, and others. From the perspective cultures facing influxes of migrants and refugees, Volkan (2017, p. 100–101) explores the fear of accepting newcomers using the concept of *border psychology* which fits well as a concept presented in this collection of chapters. He suggests that migrants and refugees represent the 'other' who threatens psychological as well as physical borders, both perceived as protecting group integrity, identity, and cohesion from disintegration and loss of collective cultural values.

The theme of Indeterminate States has particular relevance for Jungians (academics and analysts) not living in their country of origin and speaking another language, not their mother tongue. It speaks to analysts and psychotherapists working with traumatised clients not of their culture, and influences how Jungian training programmes are established by emphasising diversity over the need for cultural sameness and conformity. How does the psyche incorporate the 'other' in a creative mixing of cultural and racial histories, language and gender specificities quite foreign to its own? How we navigate such Indeterminate States as we cross-over from the known as 'safety/perfection' into the new terrain of 'risky/imperfect' is the key into the psychological opening up and crossing over into new complex and creative forms. The crossing over into new spaces feels like a death process as the spaces in transit (past and present) are caught between two status values that as yet belong to neither (cf. Shalit, 2018). This *emergent* phenomenon, however, can promote change through movement and action by allowing borders to develop that let sufficient traffic pass between the ego and the unconscious. (See Vaughan in Part 1 presenting client cases caught in migration between cultural values.)

Chapter parts

The conference chapters deal with all the above aspects in different forms and are divided into four main parts: Part 1 addresses the socio-political aspects of *border, migration, and identity* with chapters by Monica Luci, Elisabetta Iberni, Valeria Cespedes Musso, and Rachael Vaughan. Luci takes European identity in an innovative case study as an *unheroic heroic* intergenerational cultural complex and addresses the role that terrorism and migration play in the making of a new European identity; Iberni explores the specific challenges of people on the move and how their move stretches their plasticity at the border to achieve greater adaptability. She uses the term *rhizome phenomenology* to illustrate and link Indeterminate States. Musso examines cross-border responses to pertinent psycho-social questions concerning Mexican-American group identity that remains varied and indeterminate. Vaughan identifies the clinical, non-visible areas of unconscious cultural complexes in transcultural white patients who have suffered the trauma of migration due to personal and political dislocation.

Part 2 examines the theme of *border phenomenology and gender* from chapters by Elena Barta, Julia Kaddis El Khouri and Denise Gimenez Ramos, William T. Farrar, and Giorgio Giaccardi. Barta describes the work of the first department in Germany, established in 1989 in Frankfurt, and their intersectional awareness of LGBTIQ, migration issues, and those peoples' inclusion and acceptance. El Khouri and Ramos use Sandplay as a way of working with psychodynamic liminal spaces of children with gender incongruence. Farrar suggests through the art of Bernini that the *rebis*, a two-headed bisexual being, may represent a false *coniunctio* and the use of the one-headed hermaphrodite is a better image to represent the transcendent function. Giaccardi examines the problems of an inadequate anima symbolisation in *male same-sex desire* in the search for a more personal and individuated relationship to one's interiority and sexual agency.

Part 3 explores *liminality between borders and symbol formation* within indeterminate states as a way of recombining the opposites in new creative structures through chapters by Mathew Mather, Yuko Osigo, and Mirella Giglio. Mather explores the symbol of the magic circle (mandala) in the acclaimed Japanese film (2014) *When Marnie Was There*. Osigo focusses on the ubiquitous symbol of the fish with its duality of 'above and below', likening it to the twin fishes of Mercurius and Christ. She illustrates the theme through the use of a Japanese short story called *Dream Carp*. Giglio depicts Marlow from Conrad's *Heart of Darkness* as the cross-border traveller, to illustrate the world of liminality, crossing borders, intra-physically as well as physically, as a journey into the dark world of Hades, associated with symbolic death.

Part 4 examines *border crossing and individuation* through chapters by Eileen Susan Nemeth, Toshio Kawai, Stefano Carpani, and Niccolo Fiorentino Polipo. These show how cultural complexes pertaining to the 'other' are triggered and witnessed through cross-border migration. Nemeth emphasises the need to witness, reflect, and experience the complexities of an ever-moving, indeterminate, metamorphosing world that promotes inclusivity. Kawai questions the *efficacy of indeterminacy* and the development of individuation in therapeutic relationships with ASD patients who lack a determinate subject capable of holding tension. Carpani differentiates between individualisation and individuation and advocates building better bridges between sociology and unconscious processes, particularly Jungian, to promote a freer yet more stable core identity within the modern development of socio-political indeterminate liquidity. Polipo stresses the importance of holding the creative tension between vulnerability and incorruptibility in the individuation process by re-evaluating the ethics of Jung and Neumann.

References

Adams, M. V. (2001). *The mythological imagination*. Putnam, CT: Spring Publications.
Adams, M. V. (2004). *The fantasy principle, psychoanalysis of the imagination*. Hove, UK/New York, NY: Brunner-Routledge.
Adorno, T., Frenkel-Brunswik, E., Levinson, D.J., Sanford, N., et al. (1950). *The authoritarian personality*. London/New York, NY: Verso, 2019.
Amezaga, P. and Gelsi, P. (2012). 'The official story of Uruguay: cultural complexes in what was and was not included'. In P. Amerzaga, P. Gelsi, et al., (eds.), *Listening to Latin America, exploring cultural complexes in Brazil, Chile, Columbia, Mexico, Uruguay and Venezuela*. Series editor T. Singer. New Orleans, LA: Spring Journal Books, pp. 211–231.
Auestad, L. (ed.) (2017). *Shared traumas, silent loss, public and private mourning*. London: Karnac.
Bernstein, J. (2005). *Living in the borderland; the evolution of consciousness and the challenge of healing trauma*. London/New York, NY: Routledge.
Broad, C. D. (1934). *Determinism, indeterminism, and libertarianism, an inaugural lecture*. Cambridge, UK: Cambridge University Press.
Brodersen, E. (2019). *Taboo, personal and collective representations, origin and positioning within cultural complexes*. Abington, Oxon/New York, NY: Routledge.
Ciprut, J. V. (2008). 'Good God! Is every something an echo of nothing?'. In J. V. Ciprut (ed.), *Indeterminacy: the mapped, the navigable, and the uncharted*. Cambridge, MA: The MIT Press, pp. 345–348.
Ciprut, J. V. (ed.) (2008). *Indeterminacy: the mapped, the navigable, and the uncharted*. Cambridge, MA: The MIT Press.
Colman, W. (2016). *Act and image: the emergence of symbolic imagination*. New Orleans, LA: Spring Journal Books
Freimüller, T. (2020). *Frankfurt und die Juden: Neuanfänge und Fremdheitserfahrungen 1945-1990*. Göttingen: Verlag Wallstein.
Gudaite, G. (2014). 'Restoration of continuity: desperation or hope in facing the consequences of cultural trauma'. In G. Gudaite and M. Stein (eds.), *Confronting cultural trauma, Jungian approaches to understanding and healing*. New Orleans, LA: Spring Journal Books, pp. 227–242.
Guyer, P. (2008). 'Indeterminacy and Freedom of the Will'. In J. V. Ciprut, (ed.), *Indeterminacy: the mapped, the navigable, and the uncharted*. Cambridge, MA: The MIT Press, pp. 41–57.
Habermas, J. (1996). *The inclusion of the other: studies in political theory*. C. P. Cronin and P. De Greiff (eds.). Cambridge, MA: The MIT Press.
Hardin, R. (2008). 'Indeterminacy and basic rationality'. In J. V. Ciprut, (ed.). *Indeterminacy: the mapped, the navigable, and the uncharted*. Cambridge, MA: The MIT Press, pp. 59–78.

Hill, J. (2014). 'Dreams don't let you forget. Cultural trauma and its denial'. In G. Gudaite and M. Stein (eds.), *Confronting cultural trauma, Jungian approaches to understanding and healing*. New Orleans, LA: Spring Journal Books, pp. 31–46.

Hillman, J. (2018). *City & soul* (revised ed. R. J. Leaver). Thompson, CT: Spring Pubs.

Honderich, T. (1988). *Mind and brain, a theory of determinism*, Vol 1. Oxford: Clarendon Press.

Honneth, A. (1988). *Social action and human nature*. Cambridge: Cambridge University Press.

Honneth, A. (1996). *The struggle for recognition. The moral grammar of social conflict.* Cambridge, MA: MIT Press.

Honneth, A. (2012). *The I in the We: studies in the theory of recognition*. Cambridge, UK: Polity Press.

James, W. (1890). *Principles of psychology*. Vol. 2. New York, NY: Dover Publications.

Jung, C. G. (1911-1912/1952). 'Two kinds of thinking'. In *Collected works*, Vol. 5, *Symbols of transformation* (2nd ed.). London: Routledge and Kegan Paul, paras. 4–46, 1995.

Jung, C. G. (1918). 'The role of the unconscious'. In *Collected works*, Vol. 10, *Civilisation in transition* (2nd ed.). London: Routledge and Kegan Paul, paras. 1–48, 1991.

Jung, C. G. (1921). 'Indeterminism versus determinism'. In *Collected works*, Vol. 6, *Psychological types* (2nd ed.). London: Routledge and Kegan Paul, paras. 531–535, 1989.

Jung, C. G. (1923). 'Definitions'. In *Collected works*, Vol. 6, *Psychological types* (2nd ed.). London: Routledge and Kegan Paul, paras. 672–844, 1989.

Jung, C. G. (1957). 'The undiscovered self'. In *Collected works*, Vol. 10, *Civilization in transition* (2nd ed.). London: Routledge and Kegan Paul, paras. 488–588, 1991.

Kiehl, E., Saban, M., and Samuels, A. (eds.) (2016). *Analysis and activism, social and political contributions of Jungian psychology*. London/New York, NY: Routledge.

Kimbles, S. (2014). *Phantom narratives. The unseen contribution of culture to psyche*. New York, NY/London: Bowman & Littlefield.

Lewis-Williams, D. (2002). *The mind in the cave*. London: Thames and Hudson.

Luci, M. (2017). *Torture, psychoanalysis and human rights*. London/New York, NY: Routledge.

Maxwell, N. (1972). *Philosophy of science. A critique of popper's view on scientific method*. London: University College London Archive.

Mills, J. (2019a). 'Recognition and *pathos*'. *International Journal of Jungian Studies*, 11, 1–22.

Mills, J. (2019b). 'Dysrecognition and social pathology: new directions in critical theory'. *Psychoanalysis, Culture and Society*, 24 (1), 15–30.

Mills, J. (2019c). 'Contemporary psychoanalysis and critical theory: a new synthesis'. *Critical Horizons*, 20 (3), 233–245.

Mills, J. (2019d). 'Psyche as inner contradiction'. *Continental Thought and Theory: A Journal of Intellectual Freedom*, 2 (4), 71–82.

Mithen, S. (1999). 'Symbolism and the supernatural'. In R. Dunbar, C.Knight, and C. Power, (eds.), *The evolution of culture: an interdisciplinary view*. Edinburgh: Edinburgh University Press, pp. 147–169.

Picot, A. (2001). *The pure society, from Darwin to Hitler*. D. Fernbach (Trans.). London/ New York, NY: Verso, 2009.

Popper, K. (1961). *Poverty of historicism*. London: Routledge and Kegan Paul.

Rasche, J. and Singer, T. (eds.) (2016). *Europe's many souls Exploring cultural complexes and identities*. New Orleans, LA: Spring Books.
Renfrew, C. and Morley, I. (eds.) (2009). *Becoming human, innovations in prehistoric material and spiritual culture*. Cambridge, UK/New York, NY: Cambridge University Press.
Samuels, A. (2001). *Politics on the couch*. London: Profile Books.
Samuels, A. (2015). *A new therapy for politics?* London/New York, NY: Routledge.
Sauer, G. (2014). 'Cultural trauma in modern Germany'. In G. Gudaite and M. Stein (eds.), *Confronting cultural trauma, Jungian approaches to understanding and healing*. New Orleans, LA: Spring Journal Books, pp. 181–192.
Seeman, B., and Bönisch, E. (2019). *Das Gumpertz'sche Siechenhaus- ein >Jewish Place> in Frankfurt am Main. Geschichte und Geschichten eine jüdischen Wohlfahrtseinrichtung*. Frankfurt am Main: Brandes and Apsel Verlag GmbH.
Shabani, O. A. P. (2003). *Democracy, power, and legitimacy. The critical theory of Jürgen Habermas*. Toronto/London: University of Toronto Press.
Shalit, E. (2018). *The human soul (lost) in transition at the dawn of a new era*. Ashville, NC: Chiron Press.
Singer, T. (ed.) (2010). *Psyche and the city: a soul's guide to the modern metropolis*. New Orleans, LA: Spring Journal.
Singer, T., and Kimbles, S. (eds.) (2004). *The cultural complex, contemporary Jungian perspectives on psyche and society*. Hove/New York, NY: Brunner Routledge.
Tenenbaum, S. (2018). 'Borders of belonging'. In O. Gozlan (ed.), *Current critical debates in the field of transsexual studies*. London/New York, NY: Routledge, pp. 145–157.
Thomä, D. (2007). 'The difficulty of democracy: rethinking the political in the philosophy of the thirties (Gehlen, Schmitt, Heidegger)'. In W. Bialas and A. Rabinbach (eds.), *Nazi Germany and the humanities. How German academics embraced Nazism*. London: Oneworld Publishers, pp. 75–100.
Turner, V. W. (1964). 'Betwixt and between: the liminal period in rites de passage'. In W. A. Lessa and E. Z. Vogt (eds.), *Reader in comparative religion, an anthropological approach* (4th ed.). Harvard: Harper Collins, pp. 234–243.
Van Gennep, A. (1960). *Rites of passage*. Chicago, IL: University of Chicago Press.
Volkan, V.D. (2017). *Immigrants and refugees. Trauma, perennial mourning, prejudice and border psychology*. London: Karnac.
Wiggershaus, R. (1994). *The Frankfurt School, its histories, theories and political significance*. M. Robertson (trans.). Cambridge, UK: Polity Press.

Part I

Border, migration, and identity

Chapter 1

Crossing physical borders and the making of identity

The case of Europe

Monica Luci

Introduction

This chapter aims to analyse the problem of the making of identity and the role that crossing physical borders may play. The question of identity, a subject traditionally reflected in social sciences, is reframed here in terms of analytical psychology, and these two fields are ideally put in dialogue with each other.

Identity has to do both with the inner and outer world. Dynamics of the inner world can be described through the concepts of analytical psychology, but a particular emphasis is placed here on the outer world: non-human objects, space, and environment, which have a role, it is stated, in identity formation. Not only human objects but external space – the environment – and non-human objects are consciously and unconsciously invested and have a role in defining our belonging and sense of self. After having set some theoretical foundation of this discourse in psychoanalysis and analytical psychology, European identity is taken as a case study. This chapter addresses the question of the role of migration and terrorism in the making of a new European identity as the *enactment* of two opposite poles of a European *cultural complex of an unheroic heroine*. Looking at migration and terrorism as two poles of a complex characterised by the experience of bodily violence, the crossing of physical borders, the clash and meeting of two cultures or groups, and the concern for security and self-protection, this analysis intends to throw a new light on the processes implied in the making of identity.

Identity: a brief review of key questions

The diversity of ways in which the term *identity* is employed in social sciences makes it difficult to define it once and for all. The concept has an even much longer history in Western philosophy, which deals with very different meanings of the term. Such complexity of history and meanings cannot be addressed here for space reasons. However, it is important to be aware that these philosophical meanings of identity, in the sense of singularity, individuality, or self-sameness, may structure the ongoing discussion on identity in social sciences, and in particular, in psychology and psychoanalysis (for a review on this topic, see Sollberger, 2013).

"Identity" is a word sometimes used as synonymous with self which *bridges between the psychic and social worlds*. Many understandings of identity start with the presupposition of the existence of a reciprocal relationship between self and society. The self cannot be separated from society, because self can only exist and be meaningful in its relationship with other selves or entities, and in turn society has powerful influence on the self (for a review about theories on identity formation, see Cinoğlu & Arikan, 2012).

Stets and Burke (2003) believe that we can separate theories of identity into three different categories: the ones that explain identity within a group's membership (here the group has prevalence on individuals); the ones that explain identity through the roles that one occupies in the group (here the role is the mediator between social and individual dimensions); and the ones that explain identity from a more personal perspective (here individual characteristics and needs have prevalence on the group).

In Western philosophy, there is a shifting emphasis on individual and group prevalence to explain identity. The notion of identity as an individual feature is historically linked to the idea of the sameness of the self, since Descartes's *Discours de la Méthode* (1637). The cognising self (*res cogitans*), certain of its existence through its own acts of cognition (*cogito ergo sum*), became the warranty against an ambiguous and deceptive world of things (*res extensa*). This warranty was valid only on the condition that the ego remained the same, that is, identical. This was the guarantee for the possibility of knowing the world. However, this idea of an identical self was robustly challenged, among others, by poststructuralist deconstruction. Michel Foucault analysed the subject not as the source and foundation of knowledge but as itself a product or effect of networks of power and discourse (1979, p. 35) and so created and controlled by group and collective dynamics.

A different perspective on identity and self is introduced by Damasio, whose studies introduce the body as a basis for the primordial sense of self (Damasio, 2000, p. 154). Self-identity begins as a feeling within us, because emotionality precedes rationality in the development of consciousness. In other words, the primordial form of self-consciousness is not 'I think therefore I am' but 'I feel therefore I am' (Damasio, 1994). For Damasio the sense of self is progressively built out of three main stages: the *protoself*, the *core self*, and the *autobiographical self*. The *protoself* is the stepping-stone required for the construction of the core self: it maps, moment by moment, the most stable aspects of the organism's physical structure. It generates primordial feelings about the existence of the living body independently of how objects engage it or not. The *core self* is concerned only with the 'here' and 'now': it is a transient entity re-created for each object with which the brain interacts. According to Damasio, the organism (body and brain) interacts with object, and the brain reacts to the interaction. Rather than making a record of an entity's structure, the brain actually records the multiple consequences of the organism's interaction with the entity (2010, p. 132). The *autobiographical self* goes beyond the here and now of the core self, even though it cannot exist without the core self; it grows and consolidates across the lifetime of an individual (Damasio, 1999; 2010). It is the intellectual and self-created part of the self: we are both the author and the main character in this internal story of who we are as a story perpetually open to revision.

For the complexity of our contemporary understanding, identity and self seem not to exist in the singular. Whereas identity was once defined by sameness and unity, both qualities have given way to difference and plurality, an idea particularly akin to contemporary psychoanalysis, in which the self is depicted as fragmented, not unitary since its origin (Bromberg, 1998, p. 186, p. 256, p. 311; Mitchell, 1991, pp. 127–139), essentially fluid, multiple (Gergen, 1991; Rosenberg, 1997), paradoxical (Jung, 1921, para. 789; 1928a, para. 274; 1954, paras. 430–432), and 'protean' (Lifton, 1993). For Mitchell, the self is a constellation of meanings organised around relationships involving a way of being with others, a person in relation to other persons, resulting in a plural and multiple organisation of self around different images and representations of self and object (Mitchell, 1991, p. 131). Similarly, Bromberg writes that the psyche does not arise as a compact whole that becomes fragmented as a result of a pathological process. 'It is a structure that originates and continues as a multiplicity of self-other configurations ... that maturationally develop a coherence and continuity that comes to be experienced as a cohesive sense of personal identity' (1998, p. 181). However, this cohesiveness is a developmentally acquired adaptive illusion. Jung's model of self is paradoxical in itself (Luci, 2017a, pp. 98–100): besides a dissociative model of personality expressed in the complex theory, Jung formulated a theory of integration and unity of self through its archetype. In Jung's works, the self is depicted at the same time as centre and circumference of the psyche (Jung, 1928b, paras. 399–405). The nature of the Jungian self remains inherently out of reach but it can be grasped as 'experience' thanks to symbols of numinous nature (the king, the prophet, the hero, geometrical structures, etc.) producing a sense of wholeness that is self-validating.

Stets and Burke (2000), social identity theorists, define the self as a dynamic entity with the ability to interpret and reinterpret its environment and eventually transform itself: identity would be a product of this reflexive activity. Here a particular tension arises between the idea of an innate, stable identity and the 'postmodern' construction of identity as an amalgam of multiple incoherent and unstable centres of self.

Similarly, but with stronger emphasis on groups, Symbolic Interaction tradition in sociology tends to see the self as a product of the mind, which is created during interactions with social institutions and target groups that are used as reference points for the mind to evaluate its social environment, interpret the interaction, and then use the outcome to re-evaluate and, if necessary, change itself. One of its greater influences was G. H. Mead, and its theories about the relationship between self and society (1934). In this context, target groups or significant individuals become the major source for inspirations to the self. *Thus, identities are meaningful after an interaction of some sort with other identities.*

It is helpful here to distinguish two inseparable aspects of identity for the relationship between the individual and social dimensions: *structure* and *agency* (Stets & Burke, 2003, pp. 132–150). *Structure* represents the external and structural factors that are influential over identity. It refers, for example, to the impact of institutions on groups that exist in a society: individuals do not have absolute control or even choice over their behavioural options in society and there are sanctions for violators. However, when we start thinking about the *agency* aspects we realise that agents do feel freedom of choice. Agents do often realise that when using their imagination and creativity they can choose any behavioural option they desire. The only condition that they need to fulfil is to be within the borders of the structure. Actually, this is where we start seeing the original practices of revolutionary individuals, those who *go beyond borders* and change the structure.

Identity in analytical psychology

How can we think of identity in terms of analytical psychology? Along the lines of the investigations of social sciences, identity seems to be a self-defining narrative that derives from a process of mutual relationship between an individual ego complex, the self, and the groups to which the person feels belonging to, resulting in a perception of self as close to a group and distant or separate from other groups. It is not structure, although related to the structure of the self and the group, but more the result of a process. Identity has a changing nature and is influenced by internal and external pressures and needs.

The inner actors implied in identity may be the ego complex, the self, and two mediating inner agencies, Persona and anima; the first two agencies, ego and self, are more related to *structure*, and the second two, Persona and anima, more relate to *agency*. A fifth actor is also implied in identity dynamics: the Shadow that plays its part in the dynamics of these agencies as opposite or what is outside consciousness and rejected, the inferior, the undifferentiated, the primitive, the dark parts of personality (Jung, 1917, n. 5 para. 103).

According to Jung, the ego complex is made up of representations that constitute the centre of consciousness and make the individual experience oneself as identical and continuous (1921, para. 706). As such, the ego seems to be the structure more related to identity as a conscious self-definition. As a complex of conscious representations, the ego contains everything that the subject knows about itself, that is, all those characteristics of its way of being that are in agreement with the principles, ideals, and values of the social context in which the subject recognises itself (Pieri, 1998, p. 389). In this sense, its function is close to that of the Cartesian *cogito*. However, in analytical psychology the ego is also understood as a mediating force between consciousness and unconsciousness as well as the individual and the collective. In this sense, the individual psyche is constantly referring to the external world and the internal world, and in referring to these the ego utilises two precise psychological functions that are complementary: Persona and anima (Jung, 1921, para. 804).

Persona is the prominent representative of the external collective psyche in the personality; a psychic structure and a sub-personality that is in a changing relationship to the ego, the image that the individual shows to the world, the role or the social status of the individual in the relationship with the cultural and social world, and the individual's adaptation to the collective, the whole of attitudes, feelings, thoughts of an individual in his relationship to the conscious and unconscious collective psyche (Jung, 1928c, para. 246). In its being the awareness of the relationship of the individual with objects, the world of things, and society, the term becomes a metaphor of the immobility of the mask to which, during the acting, the theatrical actor had to be able to match the mobility of his face. It indicates, for each individual, his access or integration into the world and, simultaneously, his distance or differentiation from the world (Jung, 1921, paras. 801–802).

Anima is a term that represents the attitude of the psyche towards its inner life, the character through which the individual addresses their unconscious. It is a functional complex or sub-personality able to connect consciousness and the unconscious and to make parts of the psyche achieve differentiation and integration among themselves (Jung, 1921, paras. 803–806). We can say that anima is the border zone and contact zone between the ego complex and all that is 'other' than itself. If anima is conscious, then inner and outer worlds are distinct and consciousness and unconscious differentiated and in relationship to each other. Anima is a threshold that allows an objective and fertile exchange between the ego complex and the self and between the self and the world. However, in order for the anima to function consciously, a fight with personal and collective Shadow must have been accomplished. In the early works, the Shadow appears essentially as the unaccepted side of the personality, the set of tendencies and characteristics, attitudes and desire that are unacceptable for the ego complex, and a set of poorly differentiated (or undifferentiated) functions of the individual psyche (synonymous with personal unconscious) (1911–1912/1952a, para. 267; 1917, para. 103, n. 5). In subsequent works, the Shadow becomes charged with collective meanings, the image of one of the multiple archetypes of the collective unconscious to intertwine with the themes of *evil* (1934a, para. 189). In these later works, the Shadow expresses one of the multiple archetypes of psychic life which, lying in the collective unconscious, is activated in relation to the current needs of the individual's consciousness: the 'radical evil' and instinctive drives, archaic and undifferentiated, irrational and destructive aspects of individual destiny, tendencies contrary to the historically dominant cultural canon, against which consciousness and will fight and reconcile (Jung, 1946, paras. 444–457). The conscious connection with the Shadow is also what enables anima to function in a differentiated way.

The possible connection between Persona and anima makes evident the passage between the received structuring of the collective elements transmitted by a certain culture and the choice of structuring the same elements (Jung, 1921, paras. 800–4; 1928d, paras. 304, 309). Therefore, this is the passage and the exchange between the condition of factuality, for which the individual adapts to its environment, and the condition of the possibility of assuming critically the culture in which it finds itself and being itself a producer of culture (what we called before *structure* and *agency*). In this sense, the Persona can be a porous mask allowing a circular relationship between individual and culture. In this case, identity is not just a taking in of structural elements of the outer world (for example, coming from the group) into the person's inner world, but a reworking of material critically assumed and adjusted to the individual personality, which in turn is able to act on the structure of the outer world with a sense of agency. What Jung failed to fully develop is the bi-directional exchange between group and individual psyches that modify their reciprocal structure and sense of agency.

Space, body, borders, and identity formation

Being rooted in space: human and non-human environment

The point I am going to make in this section is that the formation of identities has to do with a definition of one's own self achieved through a variety of relational processes with other subjects, and between subjects and material objects, that bind together individual and collective dimensions.

More in particular, I am going to state here that identification (from Latin *idem*, the same + *facere*, to make) (Oxford Dictionary of English, 2010, pp. 868–869) deals with the correspondence to a body and its occupation of a space as a source of rootedness and experience. This is linked to the earliest phases of development of an individual. According to object relation theory, self-awareness is constructed through one's own relationship with other subjects or better, (human) objects, in the language of these theories, that satisfy the child's needs. A group of these theorists, in particular, Donald Winnicott (1960, p. 592), Esther Bick (1968, 1986), and Didier Anzieu (1989, 1990), tend to emphasise touch as when the infant's skin comes into physical contact with other (human) objects. The earliest experiences of this tactile encounter (generally called, 'the mother's touch') are regarded as the occasion for the earliest experiences of self, for they provide the infant with the required experiences of containment and integration to stabilise the frenzied impulses that otherwise overwhelm the infant, granting them the capacity to gather themselves together into a more coherent self. Importantly, these experiences continue throughout life. The quality of the infant's containing experiences is thought to establish the template for all future object relations, and thereby determines both the manner and extent to which a person is able to relate to human objects within their environment, and subsequently use those experiences in the elaboration of themselves.

However, and this is important for the main argument here, not only do human objects have a role in the formation and transformation of a sense of self, but also the environment, the objects, and subjects that inhabit the environment; all have a role in the formation and stabilisation of a sense of self, and therefore, one's identity. Huskinson (2018, p. 123) emphasised that mimetic identifications with human and non-human objects, whether the mother or the physical environment or its objects or a combination of them, are implied in the creative transformations of the self. The mergers and separation of the self vis-a-vis its human and non-human objects are essential to the construction of personal identity and group identity.

The physical space we inhabit is invested with conscious thought and unconscious phantasy, both the human-built environment and natural environment. Some architectural theorists studied the way we 'project our psyche into space' creating ourselves as subject, and the 'curious exchange', the conversation, that takes place between the human body and buildings (Huskinson, 2018, pp. 22–63). Something similar was experienced by Jung as a child in his garden with the large stone, where Jung's awareness of his identity shifted between himself and the stone such that at any one time he took himself to be the boy sitting on the stone or the stone upon which he was sitting. This was among a series of childhood games Jung invented, in which he imagined himself in a "secret relationship" with an object, a play in which Jung experienced a dialogical other within himself, a motif that continued in what later became his "No. 1 and No. 2 personalities" (Jung, 1961/1989, pp. 20–34).

We might expand this discourse by imagining that also members of a group invest conscious and unconscious thought, emotions, and shared projections in the human and non-human (natural and built) environment as part of a normal process of development. We are embedded in a matrix of conscious and unconscious links between our inner and outer worlds as individuals and group members. And, with few exceptions (Huskinson, 2018; Brodersen & Glock, 2017; Tacey, 2009), the role of the non-human environment has been widely disregarded by psychoanalysis and analytical psychology, so far.

Donald Winnicott was the first theorist to use the term 'nurturing environment' and 'holding environment' but referred it to the bond between mother and baby. And sometimes he referred to the mother as 'environment' (1960, p. 593). Winnicott grasped, to some extent, the fact that the development of self has to do with processes that happen in a space and in relation to objects through his idea of 'transitional object' or 'transitional space', which he postulates in order to explain how our earliest experiences of the mother informs our capacity to play imaginatively with objects and our environments in later life (Winnicott, 1953, pp. 91–93). The psychodynamics with the transitional object show that an object can be imbued of qualities of the subjects, and the environment can play the role of transitional space in which to negotiate ourselves throughout life.

The Jungian psychologist J. W. T. Redfearn in his essay 'When are things persons and persons things?' (1982) notices the interplay between human and non-human objects and the way our psyche play with them, sometimes using human others as material objects and sometimes using material objects as persons. In this latter case, material objects are used not only as targets of projections but as multidimensional wholes containing both human and non-human qualities.

Bodies and borders

The body and 'bodily margins' – the skin – have a crucial role in ego and self formation and, thereby, in identity formation. Although Freud laid the ground for a psychology of the body by declaring that the ego be 'first and foremost a bodily ego', a mental 'projection of the surface of the body' (Freud, 1923, p. 26), he did not develop further the implications of this claim. Esther Bick (1968) was one of the first to discuss the crucial role of the skin for 'binding together' the infant's sensations. Bick is known for asserting ideas on the proto-mental functions of the skin that help to organise one of the most primitive sensations of being held together passively, without which we would be prey to the deadly anxiety of falling apart. In this sense, the skin of which the new-born has experience is an amalgamation of the skin of the child and of that of the mother, an amalgam created through manipulation. The internalisation of this function, according to Bick, provides the infant with the primitive notion of a bodily boundary, of dimensionality, of a subdivision and, at the same time, a container, a necessary precursor of the splitting and those projective and introjective mechanisms, which contribute to supporting the schizo-paranoid and depressive positions hypothesised by M. Klein. Significant for our investigation is Bick's suggestion that any object, including a non-human object, can facilitate the infant's containment, despite the touch of the mother's skin as the 'optimal object'. Whatever the material source of the infant's containing experience—human or non-human—it is 'experienced concretely as skin' (Bick, 1968, p. 484).

Winnicott also points out that in early stages the baby's body has no borders: the sense of border, the perimeter that delimits it and distinguishes an interior from an exterior, is acquired in relation to another (1960, p. 592; 1962, p. 59, 1970), through the contact with the mother's hands and handling (Winnicott, 1971). Winnicott outlines the development of the child's mind through the interaction with the mother 'environment' to reach the capacity of playing with the transitional object and, later in life, transitional phenomena. Such intermediate area of human experience is between inner reality and the outside world, and makes use of illusion for creative coexistence of primary creativity and objective perception based on reality (Winnicott, 1953; 1971). The transitional phenomena allow both containment and separation and are important in developing porous skin boundary (me and not me) capable of allowing material to pass through it in an open exchange.[1] And this is a crucial acquirement for the capability to regulate closeness and difference towards others and others' identity.

The psychoanalyst Didier Anzieu (1989, 1990) developed similar ideas to Bick and Winnicott. Anzieu sees the body's surface – its skin – as a crucial constituent of the mind's structures and functions. Before the development of the cognitive ego, or 'thinking ego', as he terms it, the infant depends on something called a 'skin ego', which performs the maintenance of the infant's sense of self through its 'containment', 'protection', and 'inscription' (Anzieu, 1994, pp. 195–203). Anzieu defines the skin ego as a mental representation of the experience of the body surface used by the infant's emerging ego in order to construct itself as a container capable of containing psychic contents (1989, p. 61). The skin ego is not available to the infant from birth: the new-born baby has a rudimentary notion of where its body ends and the body of the other begins, but this is gradually achieved in response to stimuli impinging on the surface of its skin. These stimuli lead the infant to construct a mental image of itself as a container that is capable of holding its experiences together (Anzieu, 1989, p. 61).

Although this function of the skin draws back during development, while psychic functions differentiate, it is highly unlikely that it fades completely. It is much more reasonable to think that the sensations it works through continue their vital role in shaping identity, such that we continue to relate to objects, things, and other people through our imaginative perception of them, and experience ourselves as if to merge with them, with 'shared skin'. Whilst Anzieu discussed this phantasised union of the self and other in the context of relationships between people, we can also apply it to our relationships with non-human objects and group experiences. When we perceive a building or a monument imaginatively, we identify with its containing forms, and experience ourselves as if merged with it and inscribed by it. This is what I called before the investment of space and object of conscious thought and unconscious phantasy.

The concept of 'identity' in analytical psychology inscribes itself into this line of thinking. In analytical psychology the term 'identity' denotes an unconscious conformity between subject and object, oneself and others, and it is the basis for identification, projection, and introjection. It is what Jung conceptualised as *participation mystique*: borrowing the term from the anthropologist Lévy-Bruhl, to conceptualise a state of unconscious identity between the individual and the environment (or others) without awareness of being in such a state, "the primordial unconscious state" (Jung, 1921, para. 781). This expression is to indicate also all those cases in which the subject cannot be clearly distinguished from the object but is tied to it in a basic relationship of partial identity.

According to Jung, the concept of *participation mystique* is also correlated to that of *abaissement du niveau mental*, the effects of which are: (1) the loss of entire sections of personality normally in control; (2) the production of dissociated fragments of personality; (3) the disruption of the normal logic thinking; (4) a reduced sense of responsibility; (5) an incomplete representation of reality and inadequate emotional reactions; and (6) a lowering of the consciousness level allowing the unconscious contents to penetrate as autonomous invasions. Negative aspects of this state, such as confusion, identity loss, or panic, often appear dominant (Jung, 1957, para. 122; 1921, paras. 741–742).

Thus *l'abaissement* triggers a restriction of conscious personality and, at the same time, compensates this latter with characteristic unconscious phenomena, like *reveries*, that paradoxically may also have the effect of an enlargement of personality (Jung, 1934b, para. 215). This is because the *participation mystique has the power to break down inner psychic boundaries, as well as those between a person and the object world*. This breakdown of structures is essential to any qualitative personality change and change in the social domain.

Psychological and social phenomena connected to trauma have much to do with these identity states and breakdown of structures. After trauma, the old psychic structures that created past meanings are blown to pieces and if such a breakdown involves a very large area of the self the damage to the ability to create meaning can be extensive. Thus, the breakdown of structures is often linked to a breakdown of the symbol formation ability of mind. This latter cannot be found or created in a condition of boundlessness, lack of containment, and collapsed psychic space (cf. with the concept of *states of twoness* and 'splintered reflective triangle' Luci, 2018, pp. 25–49). Generally, states of identity follow trauma, because such states allow the self to reorganise and recreate some sense of boundaries that are essential to carry out basic psychic processes. In a state of identity stereotyped and preformed (archetypal) meanings emerge. These meanings are primitive and sometimes dysfunctional, but able to orientate basic behaviours in the face of outer danger and inner disorganisation. They create a barrier in face of the overwhelming psychic contents and processes of trauma. For these reasons, the slow process of recovery from trauma involves processes that happen in liminality and involve the phenomena linked to the 'psychic skin', for example the working through of traumatic contents on the bodily margins, or the interpersonal phenomena of the 'shared skin' between therapist and patient (see Luci, 2017b) or the search for 'group skin'. And liminality emerges as a crucial theme in the social phenomena analysed in the following paragraph, i.e. terrorism and refugees, where trauma, as something that pushes social actors towards liminality, is protagonist.

Study case: the European identity

Contemporary Europe offers an interesting case study in the relationship between 'crossing borders and the making of identities'. However, as prelude to this argument we need to ask whether there is such a thing as a European identity and, if so, what is that identity composed of? The issue is controversial and debated. Many arguments are in favour and many are against it. I will explore more in depth the arguments that look for a continuity among the European identities.

A founding myth

The history of Europe, as narrated in many variants of the founding myth of Europe by Greek and Latin poets, begins with the Phoenician Princess Europa, daughter of Agenor, King of Tyre in Lebanon, gathering flowers with her companions at a beach near Tyros. The beautiful lady is seduced into riding a lovely white bull, Zeus in one of his amorous metamorphoses. He abducts the girl across the sea and, in the shape of an eagle, rapes her under a willow or a plane tree on the island of Crete. Europa gives birth to three sons, Minos, Rhadamanthus, and Sarpedon, all three of them founders of empires (Rasche & Singer, 2016).

Littlejohns and Soncini (2007, pp. 24–25) detect three aspects that are particularly remarkable about this foundational myth: 1) Europe is mythically represented as female, and she will remain a woman also in later representations, when the fragile girl will be transformed into a queen endowed of authority and armed power; 2) an emphasis is positioned by the myth on borders and margins. The myth of Europa is not set at the centre of Europe, but takes place at its outer margins: Europa comes from Asia Minor and is taken to Crete, an outpost of Europe; and 3) the definition of the borders of Europe is completely blurred, and even the origin of the name is not clear, if Hellenic or Semitic: *the incarnation of Europe is not truly European.*

Another interesting account about ancient Europe is the one made by Marija Gimbutas' work (1989). Through the interdisciplinary method of archeomythology, Gimbutas sheds new light on the archaic feminine civilisation, a Goddess-oriented civilisation, that flourished between 7000 and 3500 BCE, and lived in peace and in harmony with nature and with a high degree of economic, social, and sexual equality, its goddess-centred art exhibiting a striking absence of images of warfare and male domination. Later, this culture was invaded by aggressive Indo-European nomads from the Russian steppes, who worshipped a lightning God, Perun, The Striker. The domination was not merely geographical: corporate, military, and family structures were taken over by hierarchical, patriarchal, Indo-European values, that work even today as enculturing tools for contemporary males, living embodiments of the Lightning God: Zeus-type bosses, generals, and fathers wishing to establish their own realm over which they are the absolute ruling divinities, through possession, domination of space and centrality.

Did a European identity exist in the past?

The question of the existence of a European identity in the past is at the centre of a complex historiographic debate. Dawson (1956, p. 24) writes,

> Europe is not a natural unity, like Australia or Africa; it is the result of a long process of historical evolution and spiritual development. From the geographical point of view Europe is simply the north-western prolongation of Asia, and possesses less physical unity than India or China or Siberia; anthropologically it is a medley of races, and the European type of man represents a social rather than a racial unity. And even in culture the unity of Europe is not the foundation and starting-point of European history, but the ultimate and unattained goal, towards which it has striven for more than a thousand years.

In approaching such an issue, we cannot forget that in the history of Europe there is a factor of 'particularity' that followed the collapse of Charlemagne's empire that determined a situation where each king wanted to reign over his own kingdom. This plurality of kingdoms led to competition which formed the core of the European political dynamic for a long time. Slowly, Europe invested in a political model, that of the Nation State, which substituted that of the city (for which Athens provided the model) and that of the Empire (embodied by Rome). This led to the formation of Nations through the history of kingdoms, first of all France and England, to the national revolutions of 1830 and 1848, the Italian and German unifications, etc. (Chopin, 2018, p. 3). This competition was at the foundation of the European dynamism, and led to rivalry and conflict that characterised the history of Europe in modern and contemporary times.

However, some historians emphasise that there are reasons to think of a European identity as springing from a shared past. Focussing on a definition of identity as a non-exclusive background feeling of membership and a sharing of some values, according to them, it can be argued that Europe had an identity or identities in the past, to which many Europeans have felt a degree of allegiance at various times, although not intended as it is conceived today. According to Chopin (2018, p. 3), during modern history, a certain number of elements such as Church and feudalism – the Court, the town, religious orders, universities – provided some unity to European culture. For the high middle Ages, Robert Bartlett makes a strong case about the 'Europeanization of Europe' between 950 and 1350 that, according to him, occurred through the spread of homogeneous Latin-Christian cultural elements, administrative practices, and institutionalised education from the core European regions (France, Germany, and north of Italy) of the former Carolingian empire to more peripheral regions (1993, pp. 269–91). James Joll (1990) focuses instead on the Roman Empire, Christianity, the Enlightenment, and industrialisation as key influences on the European experience, shared at least in part by enough of Europe to act as a defining cultural heritage for the continent. During the Renaissance a renewed European awareness emerged, thanks to the 'discoveries' of the New World: not only the American continent, but also travels to Africa and Asia sparked new feelings of identity within the European continent, portrayed in visual material for instance in cartography, and in drawings, prints, paintings, and sculptures (Wintle, 2009). These images were widely circulated in Europe and portrayed a Europe positively valued, embodying superiority over the other continents in many respects (power, culture, war, etc.), a supremacist identification with a dominating family of nations characterised by a high level of 'civilisation', an argument that was used to rationalise the colonisation of non-white people during 18th and 19th century (see Pichot, 2001). However inappropriate that idea may seem today, European intellectual elites during the Enlightenment assumed internationally such identification. Edmund Burke remarked that 'no European can be a complete exile in any part of Europe' (in Hay, 1968, p. 123), and Voltaire could see Europe as a 'great Republic', sharing political ideas, religion, and law (Hazard, 1965, p. 463). It seems that intellectual Europe had a clear self-image by the time of the Enlightenment, and a strong sense of its shared cultural heritage.

Of course it remains a question of definition of what kind of 'European identity'. The identity of the past cannot be treated as a prototype, blueprint, or prehistory of the European Union today, without becoming nonsense. Instead, it can be stated that at various times in the past there have been periods in which many Europeans in many areas of Europe have shared certain key unifying experiences that could act as a defining heritage for a feeling of belonging to the same large group. On some occasions, however, some of these unifying experiences were also opportunities to differentiate national particularities (see the break of England from Europe as early as 1536 with the dissolution of the monasteries and its rejection of patrilineal Roman papal power in secular affairs.)

Some scholars think that there has always been such a duality at the heart of European identity, between a common culture and belonging on one hand, and political fight and fragmentation on the other hand, and this duality continues in the present day (Barnavi, 2008; Jaume, 2009).

What kind of identity today?

Does this generalised feeling of supranational Europeanness still exist today? The emphasis here seems to concentrate on culture as shared heritage that gives meaning to the European identity. Michael Wintle (2009) noticed that most of Europe has a common 'Indo-European' linguistic heritage and a common religion, Christianity. Although the splitting of state and religion is at the foundation of contemporary European democracies, and the importance of religion in Europe has today radically diminished in people's lives and in the public and political life of states, its part in Europe's past has been a defining one (even now, the influence of Christian Democrat parties in Europe should not be underestimated). In the various forms of art and high culture there is a richly varied but recognizably European tradition that Jurgen Habermas has proclaimed as something that can serve as the 'common denominator' in the future of Europe (Wintle, 2009).

The type of Europeanness being retraced has no finite characteristics: it is constantly changing over time and space, as culture changes, and is experienced differently – in varying degrees – in different areas and nations of Europe. It is partial and nonexclusive, because it is not saturating cultural or political identity. Sometimes the United Kingdom has been very much a part of this Europe and had a symbiotic relationship with Europe being shaped by it or it shaping Europe (see Simms, 2017), and sometimes it has been less so. Being an island, for example, it never felt part of a landlocked Europe, having more opportunity to expand its borders through seafaring (Moffat, 2002). Even today, Britain has equal trade affiliation with its old Commonwealth connections, as with Europe; and, while writing, it is in the process of leaving the European Union. Hungary has experienced a debate for 300 years about whether it is or wants to be part of Europe (Andor, 2000). Russia has shifted from being in and out in many historical situations, and the debate about its position has been going on over the last 500 years (see Malfliet & Verpoest, 2001, pp. 71–132). Many in Central and Eastern Europe saw 1989 as the occasion for the region's 'return to Europe', in the words of Vaclav

Havel (Shahin & Wintle, 2000, p. 18). The borders of Europe, especially in the East, are anything but stable, and they move all the time.

It is essential to grasp that this kind of European identity is emphatically not the same as the collective identity from which a state – especially a nation state – derives its political legitimacy. It is substantially different in the quality: it has *not* to do with the kind of national identity which generates patriotism, the bond of blood and land, duty to country, and jingoism that usually can be found in that kind of identity. However, it still seems to exist. On the other hand, it is clear that the nation is still the vital framework of political reference for most Europeans, and although an absolute majority of Europeans has a dual sense of identity, both national and European, their nationality comes first in their identification (see Eurobarometer[2] Standard 84 Survey, Autumn 2015).

Territory

From a geographical point of view, Europe's borders are delimited by seas in the north, the west and the south, but there is no obvious geographical limit to the European project in the east. When viewing the geography of the European institutions the picture becomes very complex and kaleidoscopic: the Organisation for Security and Cooperation in Europe (OSCE) includes 57 countries; the Council of Europe has 47 members (including Russia and Turkey). Moreover, the continued enlargement of the European Union looks more like a process of indefinite extension than a process of definition of a territorial framework. In this regard, it seems particularly important to find the absence of the word 'territory' from the Union's founding legal texts and from its primary law (Chopin, 2018). Territory is a term mainly associated with the States, but not to the Union. Instead 'area' is a term extremely present in Europe's primary and secondary law. Beyond the territories of the Member States, the European Union seems to be typified by areas which have specific functions: money, free-trade, security, justice, and so on. This series of interconnected functional areas leads to differentiated types of integration and to a segmented, geometrically variable area made of the internal market (28 Member States, 27 after Brexit); the Economic and Monetary Union (19 members); and the Schengen Area (22 Member States and 4 Associate States) (Bertoncini, 2017). This extreme differentiation creates a degree of legal, political, and institutional complexity.

Values

The EU is founded on a community of values set down in the treaties: the respect of human dignity, freedom, democracy, equality, the rule of law, and the respect for Human Rights are all mentioned in the preamble of the Treaty on European Union, while pluralism, non-discrimination, tolerance, justice, solidarity, and equality between men and women are mentioned in Article 2 of TEU. It now seems possible to speak of a core of European values that bring together part of Europe and comprise the base of a joint political identity. However, another work of synthesis of these European Values Surveys shows that Europe has not undergone a process of progressive matching of values in time, apart from those mentioned in the treaties. In fact, whether we talk of family, social life, politics, work policy, or religion, diversity stays very strong between north and south, east and west.

To summarise,

1) Europe has a founding myth based on a feminine character, whose story is liminal (it develops at its margins). However, its history is also marked by an aggressive, centralising and dominating male spirit.
2) Europeanness seems to exist in a sense of belonging based on key experiences shared in the past, that created, to a certain extent, a common culture.
3) There is a complex contemporary European identity based on *a core set of values written in its founding texts* widely shared in principle: freedom, security and justice without any internal borders, pluralism, non-discrimination, tolerance, solidarity, and equality between men and women; but *other values are extremely varied* and not homogeneous among populations and they seem not to tend to homogeneity.
4) The EU *is not rooted in a definite territory* but in shifting 'areas', according to functional or organisational needs and fields of interest that may change over time; the *majority of people is identified first with their nationality and then with European identity*.

All these aspects seem to be at the base at the same time of European strength, hold, and fragility.

'How unheroic Europe is!' writes Luigi Zoja (2017, p. 315), secular, peaceful, reasonable, based on the economy, and for this reason opposed by extreme right and extreme left. The tragic history of the 20th century with two World Wars seems to have warned Europe (but not national states!) from nationalisms, their rhetoric of heroes, sacrifices, and the close link between territory and nations, at least for a while, in favour of a wider perspective. One of the etymologies of the word 'Europe' is εὐρύς (eurús), 'wide, broad' and ὤψ (ōps, gen. Ὠπός, ōpós) 'eye, face, countenance', hence their composite Eurṓpē would mean "wide-gazing" or "broad of aspect", as Rasche (2016, p. 15) reminds, a 'princess with bright shining eyes'.

A *cultural complex of an unheroic heroine* seems to be a core of this loosely identified, weak, but still emerging European identity.

The European cultural complex of an unheroic heroine

This section advances the idea that European identity as a continuous process is presently dealing with the cultural complex of an unheroic heroine enacted in the contact zone between the ego and the other, with participation from counter-identitarian heroes who cross or threaten to cross its physical borders.

Cultural complexes are in Singer's words: 'emotionally charged aggregates of ideas and images that tend to cluster around an archetypal core and are shared by individuals within an identified collective' (Singer & Kaplinski, 2010, p. 25). The concept of a cultural complex fills a gap in analytical psychology, between the idea of a collective unconscious based on archetypes and the individual psychology. When we use the concept of cultural complexes to organise the psychological history of a culture, we can readily see that cultural memory belongs not just to the individuals residing in the culture but also to the culture itself, which generates its own emotional fields. These fields of course operate through the psyches of individuals to achieve their effects.

We have seen that Europe has no *strong* identity. On the other hand, the identity of European nations is and was often built through national wars with neighbour countries, human sacrifices, and monumentalism of those collective sacrifices that established a close bond between a people, a culture, and a territory. That history was widely founded on mythical themes of national heroes, characters, human sacrifices and battles, armed and cultural ones, the rhetoric of several -isms that built the history of different national groups. The only *strong* motive that in recent times seemed to keep together so many different countries, cultures, traditions, and nations in Europe seems to be the memory of and the lessons learned from the two World Wars: the awareness that rivalry among nations, nationalisms, and paranoid fears can result in millions of deaths, war crimes, starvation, economic crisis, widespread human suffering, and the supreme value of building an area of peace, respect for human rights, freedom, equality, and democracy. This awareness constitutes a fragile, unstable, and probably, at certain historical times, an abstract motive for identification.

In this sense, the European identity is heroic in Jungian terms, since it emerged as an individuating, unifying, and self-conscious political principle. In analytical psychology, the hero is the image of individual excellence, the prodrome of the constitution of the individuality of each and, therefore, through which the ego passes through the conquest of its own identity and self-consciousness. Erich Neumann (1949) has abundantly documented this myth as the prototype of the mature self, struggling to break free from the dominance of unconscious forces. This depends on the awakening of the ego that is experienced as a progressive activation of one's own self-consciousness; the ego finds itself through differentiation from the maternal matter, the latter understood as the original unconscious state, the starting point, the Great Mother, symbol of psychic fusion and the co-presence of all indistinct psychic parties.

The contact zone between the ego and the other

Robert Schuman, speaking in Strasbourg on 16 May 1949, stated: 'The European spirit signifies being conscious of belonging to a cultural family and to have a willingness to serve that community in the spirit of total mutuality, without any hidden motives of hegemony or the selfish exploitation of others'. However,

Europe is not so innocent. It constructed itself through a century of colonisation and military interventions in different continents, substantially changing the political, economic, and cultural balance of many regions of the world according to its own political and economic interests. Now, it is receiving the middle- and long-term effects of those interventions, with migration coming from the same areas of former colonies or where military interventions or economic exploitations were carried out, changing the life of ethnic groups, countries, tribes, and communities. People who immigrated and are immigrating to Europe, because the instability and difficulties of different aspects to living in their origin country, pose some true challenges to Europe. In this sense, they create some 'contact zones' between European identity and its Other, in which the European identity is confronted (Luci, 2017c).

The main argument here is that the European cultural complex of an unheroic heroine is presently made through contact with the opposite poles of the cultural complex of hero, 'a threatening other', the *terrorist* (*a group hero*) and 'an exposed other', the *asylum seeker* (*an individual hero*) both characterised by the experience of bodily violence, inflicted and endured, through the clash and meeting of two cultures or groups, the destructive or desperate crossing of physical borders, the increasing concerns for security, self-protection, the need of mutual recognition. This argument is confirmed by numbers provided by the *Eurobarometer* of Spring 2018, from which it emerges that the two main concerns of European citizens are immigration and terrorism (while at the national level, their main concerns are unemployment, health, and social security).

The violent crossing of borders by a threatening other, the terrorist

The terrorist is a group hero. In the terrorist mind, collective reasons and logics have prevalence over individual motives. Worries and enthusiasms are focused on society as its whole, on cultural, social bonds with his/her society, cultural and religious group. This supremacy of group that might be the reply to the social call for unity for defensive purposes (see the idea of group defence mechanisms in Singer, 2003), a monolithic state of mind ('united we stand') produces a precise style of relationship characterised by a phantasied kind of vertical protector–protected relationship. Relationships are modulated according to the need of fusion with peers (brothers) and/or to the need of protection by someone in a powerful position (God). Ruth Stein's pioneering study (2009) on suicidal terrorism argues that most Islamic extremists undertake destructive and self-destructive actions not out of blind hatred, nor even for political gain, but to achieve an explosive merger with a transcendent awesome Father, God. According to her, the extremists would be thus motivated more by their vertical love for God than the hatred of the infidel. The contemporary Islamic terrorists would kill 'God's enemies' to express their intoxication with and complete submission to the God-idea.

The prevalence of collective reasons and spaces over individual ones is proved by the recurrence of the theme of sacrifice in the rhetoric of religious and state powers. The English word *sacrifice* is derived from sacred; it is a ritual in which the sacrificial victim is destroyed in order to achieve a desired relation between the individual who makes the sacrifice and the deity to whom the offering is made and on whose good will the individual depends. Colman (2000) suggested that this is the archetypal situation that characterises a totalitarian power, in which there is an archetypal relationship between a devouring father and his sons within a context of splitting the parental couple (syzygy). From the perspective of the inner world, this is an omnipotent defence against infantile dependence on the mother, which is expelled and excluded from such a devouring relationship. It is a state of total projective identification between father (God or any other idealised unifying principle) and son, with terrorists living inside the stomach of Chronos with no access to the maternal feminine and no possibility of escape.

Brodersen (2016, pp. 20–27) proposes an interesting analysis in which climate, natural environment, and topography play a crucial role in how we envisage male authority and its 'divine' right. Hu, the Welsh sun god is warm, bright but temperate, not hot or authoritarian like the Egyptian sun god Osiris/Ra, thus offering more democratic in-between spaces (rain, wind, and cloud) for individuating, co-operative possibilities between the sky and the earth. The feminine is an active, separating force herself, not needing permission or blessing from the sun god to create life. Keeping in mind Gimbutas' line of thought (1989), and combining it with reflections developed so far, the Islamic god that claims the son's life sacrifice is burning, authoritarian, high up, abstracted, and perfectionist, which is the reason why terrorists have to blow themselves and 'others' to contact him. This kind of god reflects the physicality of the burning sun that dries up new growth. There is no third, intermediate border/skin dialogue to express differences. The feminine is dominated and subjugated in such terrain that is hot, dry, with little rain, water, streams, or vegetation.

Writing on religious fundamentalism, Stein (2009) comments on noticing that monotheism, which sanctifies a single, integrative entity, may be the source of a violent, homoerotic, self-abnegating father–son relationship. This kind of love is far from being simply a love of God; rather it has the character of reverence and fear, and a desire for a God who manifests Himself through absoluteness and unconditionality. When the Father as legislator and protector assumes the traits of a primitive, inexorable figure, He becomes the object of a certain kind of desire. This desire is a type of love that is marked by its dissociated tone and its secret, alienated intimacy. Stein calls this "vertical mystical homoeros" (2003).

Those who seek combat in order to penetrate others violently, or who aim themselves as missiles to obliterate enemies, or who take lascivious delight in the fantasy of terrorising and liquidating others are not reacting to an imminent threat, but have created a neosexual, or perverse, strategy to avenge archaic injury and depredation in that dominating transcendence (Piven, 2006). The lack of connection and recognition between father and son is compensated through such a vertical relationship of possession by the (idea of the) father and this destructive merger with the other that produces an explosion of borders.

If terrorism can be imagined as possession by the archetypal Spirit father, the challenge for Europe and its unheroic identity is restoring a horizontal principle in the relationship with the terrorist, or his group, in which there is the possibility of a recognising father–son relationship.

The crossing of borders by an exposed other, the asylum seeker

The asylum seeker is an individual hero, and as such their initial condition is one of fragility (the abandoned child), a motive that very often characterises the myth of hero:

> Abandonment, exposure, danger, etc. are all elaborations of the child's insignificant beginnings and of his mysterious and miraculous birth. This statement describes a certain psychic experience of a creative nature, whose object is the emergence of a new and as yet unknown content.
> (Jung, 1940, para. 285)

This lack of protection is the one that literally characterises the condition of asylum seekers, fleeing when they cross national borders and facing natural or human dangers during their often long and perilous journeys. Very often this hero is represented by a journey and portrayed while travelling. In myths and legends, the hero typically travels by ship, fights a sea monster, is swallowed, struggles against being bitten or crushed to death, and after arriving inside the belly of the whale, like Jonah, seeks the vital organ and cuts it off, thereby winning release. This is a good illustration of the fact that the birth and development of consciousness is truly a heroic adventure.

In addition, asylum seekers' bodies are often like living geographical maps where the violence of world politics is inscribed: they often bring the marks of war, violence, rapes, tortures, beatings, starvation. The journey can present violence, extortions, and slavery carried out by state actors or private criminal subjects, possible imprisonment for a number of reasons, long marches, and shipwrecks. Asylum seekers flee from social contexts where no safe place is offered for their lives to develop. They cross European borders in search of that safe place. And the first reaction urged is the one of the Good Mother, to nurture, to protect, to warm, to defend, to save in the sea. However, they can also be perceived as threats and the Terrible Mother is also there with her destructive forces, when this protective function is denied, and the concave space of the Mediterranean, the boat, the cradle and the bed, and house is transformed into the terrible concave space of a grave or a devouring sea.

The theme of fracture and expulsion from the land of fathers and the community of brothers refers to a male principle, and the issue of exclusion from the social contract transforms the land from female to male, with the father as 'representative of laws and order'. Fathers, according to Neumann (1949, p. 172), 'from the earliest taboos to the most modern juridical systems … hand down the highest values of civilization'. The refugee status is permeated by this feeling, exclusion from the political and social fabric of the original group. Often this happens after a confrontation with what Neumann calls the archetype of the Terrible Father, which manifests itself through an instinctive and uncontrollable phallic aggression, or as a destructive monster (a transfiguration of the power of the Great Mother), the Earth Father: state violence, torture, rapes, experiences related to war and imprisonment. 'For she [the Great Mother] is the instinctual ruler of the unconscious, mistress of animals, and the phallic Terrible Father is only her satellite, not a masculine principle of equal weight' (Neumann, 1949, pp. 185–187).

From a legal perspective the refugee status restores a relationship with a state that guarantees, at least in principle, safety and justice, in a sense, repairing the wound inflicted by the Earth Father; on the other hand, the exile as a category of the soul seems to exclude in itself the possibility of a reparation and condemns one to perpetual *nostalgia* (*nóstos* = coming back + *algos* = pain; *nostalgia* = the suffering of the person who wishes to go home), with a perpetual desire of merger with the Good Mother, source of nurture, protection and warmth (Luci, 2016, p. 41).

If asylum-seeking is linked to persecution by the Earth Father, the aim of Europe while addressing this kind of migration should be that of guaranteeing a safe space where a life is returned its dignity and can develop. The etymology of the term 'asylum' (*a-sylon*) refers to a space which is 'not violable'. And it is this inviolability that asylum seekers desire, to enter a sacred space, a *temenos*, becoming the subject of a universal law that Europe would like to see itself respect.

The line of development of individuation suggests that once asylum seekers have returned to the womb of the Good Mother, Europe, for nurture and protection, they may gain strength and transform enough to separate and individuate (cf. Jung, 1911–1912/1952b, paras. 332–334); they are called to practice some kind of existential 'return', more often symbolic and personal than literal and collective (see Luci, 2016, pp. 51–53), to fight the absolutism of the terrible monistic father. How this is accomplished in practice depends on individual and collective stories and personal characteristics, and the working through of personal meanings.

Conclusions

Europe is struggling in the grip of its cultural complex of an unheroic identity, confronted with archetypal themes of the opposite poles of the cultural complex of a feminine hero. In this sense, when Europe addresses the issues of terrorism and immigration, it deals with its main central complex. How to keep the EU unheroic in order to develop and save its own identity, avoiding to stiffen its internal identitarian boundaries and its external physical borders? How to avoid falling back into those identification processes that had a big part in the making of 20th century tragedies, connected to the societal states of nationalism, fascism, Nazism, and communism, that would push a monolithic 'identity' against the 'threatening others'? How can Europe maintain its respect for human rights to protect the 'exposed others' without feeling overwhelmed and recognise the 'threatening others' without feeling swept away by their own actions? These challenges are not incidental; they spring from the core unconscious source of the European identity itself, through its complex of an unheroic heroine. The way the European Union will address these challenges will, in all probability, determine its future existence or its collapse into renewed forms of nationalisms.[3]

Notes

1 Cf. Luci, 2017b, pp. 232–234 on the development of a porous skin; and Ziegler, pp. 63–73 on skin irritation, cutting, and its psychosomatic symbolism.
2 Eurobarometer is a series of public opinion surveys regularly conducted on behalf of the European Commission since 1973. They address a wide variety of topical issues relating to the European Union throughout its member states.
3 As I am writing the last few lines of this chapter, *Der Spiegel*, the German weekly magazine, has published on its cover Carola Rackete's face with the title 'Captain Europe'. Carola is 31 years old woman, Captain of the ship 'Sea-Watch 3', belonging to a German NGO. She challenged the nationalistic Italian politics of Matteo Salvini, Minister of Interior, who closed the Italian ports to ships carrying asylum seekers rescued in the Mediterranean Sea with a law based on 'national security'. Carola saved 42 people from a shipwreck and waited several days for permission to dock at a safe harbour in Italy (Lampedusa). After many days of waiting and because of critical conditions with migrants on the ship, she decided to force the entry to the Italian coasts and was arrested by police, and then released by the judge for preliminary investigations (with the reason that saving lives is not a crime but a duty and carrying survivors of a shipwreck is not a threat to national security). In any event, she will have to face a trial with heavy charges of crimes related to illegal immigration. She crossed illegally national borders according to present Italian laws, while complying with international law and the law of sea and fully respecting basic values set out in the European social model. Carola has large eyes and a broad face, like the beautiful mythical girl Europa. With simplicity and without using heroin tones, she made a heroic gesture. She wrote the history of Europe at its margins, geographical (the Mediterranean) and social (migrants). She is in fact Captain Europe!

References

Andor, L. (2000). *Hungary on the road to the European Union: transition in blue.* Westport, CT/London: Praeger.
Anzieu, D. (1989). *The skin ego: a psychoanalytic approach to the self.* New Haven, CT: Yale University Press. English Trans.
Anzieu, D. (ed.) (1990). *Psychic envelopes.* London: Karnac Books.
Anzieu, D. (1994). *Le Penser: du Moi-Peau au Moi-Pensant.* Paris: Dunod.
Barnavi, E. (2008). 'Identité'. *Dictionnaire critique de l'Union européenne.* Paris: Armand Colin.
Bartlett, R. (1994). *The making of Europe: conquest, colonization and cultural change – 950–1350.* London: Penguin Books.
Bertoncini, Y. (2017). 'EU 60: re-founding Europe. The responsibility to propose: differentiated integration and the EU: a variable geometry legitimacy'. Retrieved at https://www.iai.it/sites/default/files/eu60_7.pdf.

Bick, E. (1968). 'The experience of the skin in early object relations'. *International Journal of Psycho-Analysis*, 49, 484–486.

Bick, E. (1986). 'Further considerations on the function of the skin in early object relations'. *British Journal of Psychotherapy*, 2, 292–299.

Brodersen, E. (2016). *Laws of inheritance: a post-Jungian study of twins and the relationship between the first and other(s)*. London/New York, NY: Routledge.

Brodersen, E., and Glock, M. (eds.) (2017). *Jungian perspectives on rebirth and renewal: phoenix rising*. London/New York, NY: Routledge.

Bromberg, P. M. (1998). *Standing in the spaces: essays on clinical process, trauma, and dissociation*. Hillsdale, NY: The Analytic Press.

Chopin, T. (2018). 'Europe and the identity challenge: who are 'we'?'. *European Issues*, 466, 19 March 2018. Retrieved at https://www.robert-schuman.eu/en/doc/questions-d-europe/qe-466-en.pdf.

Cinoğlu, H., and Arikan, Y. (2012). 'Self, identity and identity formation. From the perspectives of three major theories'. *International Journal of Human Sciences [Online]*, 9 (2), 1114–1131.

Colman, W. (2000). 'Tyrannical omnipotence in the archetypal father'. *Journal of Analytical Psychology*, 45, 521–539.

Damasio, A. (1994). *Descartes' error: emotion, reason, and the human brain*. New York, NY: Avon Books.

Damasio, A. (1999). 'How the brain creates the mind'. *Scientific American*, 281 (6), 74–79.

Damasio, A. (2000). *The feeling of what happens: Body, emotion and the making of consciousness*. London: Heinemann.

Damasio, A. (2010). *Self comes to mind: constructing the conscious brain*. New York, NY: Pantheon Books.

Dawson, C. (1956). *The making of Europe; an introduction to the history of European unity*. New York, NY: Meridian Books.

Descartes, R. (1637). *Discourse de la Méthode. Introduction par E. Faguet*. Paris: Nelson.

European Commission. (2015). 'Standard Eurobarometer 84, Report'. Autumn 2015. Retrieved at https://ec.europa.eu/commfrontoffice/publicopinion/index.cfm/ResultDoc/.../71806

European Commission. (2018). 'Standard Eurobarometer 89, Report'. Spring 2018. Retrieved at ec.europa.eu/commfrontoffice/publicopinion/index.../83548

European Union. (2012). 'Consolidated version of the treaty on the European Union'. *Official Journal of the European Union*, 326/01 (26 October 2012. 13–46. Retrieved on https://eur-lex.europa.eu/resource.html?uri=cellar:2bf140bf-a3f8-4ab2-b506-fd71826e6da6.0023.02/DOC_1&format=PDF

Foucault, M. (1979). *Power, truth, strategy*. Sydney: Feral Publications.

Freud, S. (1923). 'The ego and the Id'. In J. Strachey et al. (Trans.), *The standard edition of the complete psychological works of Sigmund Freud*, Volume XIX. London: Hogarth Press, pp. 12–68.

Gergen, K. (1991). *The saturated self: dilemmas of identity in contemporary life*. New York, NY: Basic Books.

Gimbutas, M. (1989). *The language of the goddess*. London: Thames and Hudson.

Hay, D. (1968). *Europe: the emergence of an idea*. Edinburgh: Edinburgh University Press.

Hazard, P. (1965). *European thought in the eighteenth century*. Harmondsworth: Penguin.

Huskinson, L. (2018). *Architecture and the mimetic self: a psychoanalytic study of how buildings make and break our lives*. London and New York: Routledge.

Jaume, L. (2009). *Qu'est-ce que l'esprit européen?* Paris: Flammarion, Champs essais.
Joll, J. (1990). *Europe since 1870: an international history.* London: Pengin Books.
Jung, C. G. (1911–1912/1952a). 'The origin of the hero'. In *Collected works*, Vol. 5, *Symbols of transformation* (2nd ed.) London: Routledge and Kegan Paul, 1995.
Jung, C. G. (1911–1912/1952b). 'Symbols of the mother and of rebirth'. In *Collected works*, Vol. 5, *Symbols of transformation* (2nd ed.) London: Routledge and Kegan Paul, 1995.
Jung, C. G. (1917). 'The personal and collective unconscious'. In *Collected works*, Vol 7, *Two essays on analytical psychology* (2nd ed.) London: Routledge and Kegan Paul, 1990.
Jung, C. G. (1921). 'Definitions'. In *Collected works*, Vol 6, *Psychological types.* (2nd ed.) London: Routledge and Kegan Paul, 1989.
Jung, C. G. (1928a). 'The function of the unconscious'. In *Collected works*, Vol. 7, *Two essays in analytical psychology* (2nd ed.) London: Routledge and Kegan Paul, 1990.
Jung, C. G. (1928b). 'The mana-personality'. In *Collected works*, Vol. 7, *Two essays in analytical psychology* (2nd ed.) London: Routledge and Kegan Paul, 1990.
Jung, C. G. (1928c). 'The persona as a segment of the collective psyche'. In *Collected works*, Vol. 7, *Two essays in analytical psychology* (2nd ed.) London: Routledge and Kegan Paul, 1990.
Jung, C. G. (1928d). 'Anima and animus'. In *Collected works*, Vol. 7, *Two essays in analytical psychology* (2nd ed.) London: Routledge and Kegan Paul, 1990.
Jung, C. G. (1934a). 'Psychological aspects of the mother archetype'. In *Collected works*, Vol. 9i, *The archetypes and the collective unconscious* (2nd ed.). London: Routledge and Kegan Paul, 1990.
Jung, C. G. (1934b). 'A review of the complex theory'. In *Collected works*, Vol. 8, *The structure and dynamics of the psyche* (2nd ed.) London: Routledge and Kegan Paul, 1991.
Jung, C. G. (1940). 'The psychology of the child archetype'. In *Collected works*, Vol. 9i, *The archetypes and the collective unconscious* (2nd ed.). London: Routledge and Kegan Paul, 1990.
Jung, C. G. (1946). 'The fight with the shadow'. In *Collected works*, Vol. 10. *Civilisation in transition* (2nd ed.) London: Routledge and Kegan Paul, 1991.
Jung, C. G. (1954). 'On the nature of psyche'. In *Collected works*, Vol. 8, *The structure and dynamics of the psyche* (2nd ed.). London: Routledge and Kegan Paul, 1991.
Jung, C. G. (1957). 'The visions of zosimos'. In *Collected works*, Vol.13, *Alchemical studies* (2nd ed.) London: Routledge and Kegan Paul, 1981.
Jung, C. G. (1961/1989). *Memories, dreams, reflections.* Jaffe A. (ed.), New York, NY: Vintage Books.
Lifton, J. R. (1993). *The protean self: human resilience in an age of fragmentation.* Chicago, IL: University of Chicago Press.
Littlejohns, R., and Soncini, S. (2007). *Myths of Europe.* Amsterdam: Rodopi.
Luci, M. (2016). 'Inner and outer travels: analytical psychology and the treatment of refugees'. *Quadrant*, XLVI (2), 35–55.
Luci, M. (2017a). *Torture, psychoanalysis and human rights.* London/New York, NY: Routledge.
Luci, M. (2017b). 'Disintegration of self and the regeneration of 'psychic skin' in the treatment of traumatized refugees'. *Journal of Analytical Psychology*, 62 (2), 227–246. doi: 10.1111/1468-5922.12304.

Luci, M. (2017c). 'The salience of borders in refugees' experience: violation of bodies, transgression of national boundaries, and threatened identities in the Mediterranean'. *Paper presented at IAAP Conference, Analysis and Activism: More Social and Political Contributions of Jungian Psychology*, Prague, Czech Republic, 1st–3rd December.

Luci, M. (2018). 'The splintered reflective triangle in bystanders, perpetrators and victims of torture'. In E. Brodersen and M. Glock (eds.), *Indeterminate states: spaces 'betwixt and between'*. London and New York: Routledge, Freebook, pp. 25–49.

Malfliet, K., and Verpoest, L. (2001). *Russia and Europe in a changing international environment*. Leuven: Leuven University Press.

Mead G. H. (1934). *Mind, self, and society from the standpoint of a social behaviorist*. Chicago, IL: University of Chicago Press.

Mitchell, S. A. (1991). 'Contemporary perspectives on self: toward an integration'. *Psychoanalytic Dialogues*, 1, 121–128.

Moffat, A. (2002). *The sea kingdoms: the story of celtic Britain and Ireland*. London: HarperCollins.

Neumann, E. (1949). *The origins and history of consciousness*. Mythos: The Princeton/Bollingen Series, 2014.

Angus Stevenson (Ed.) *Oxford dictionary of English*. (2010). Oxford: Oxford University Press.

Pichot, A. (2001). *The pure society: from Darwin to Hitler*. Transl. David Fernbach. London: Verso, 2009.

Pieri, P. F. (1998). *Dizionario Junghiano*. Torino: Bollati Boringhieri.

Piven, J. S. (2006). 'Narcissism, sexuality, and psyche in terrorist theology'. *The Psychoanalytic Review*, 93 (2), 231–266.

Rasche, J. (2016). 'Introduction'. In J. Rasche and T. Singer (eds.), *Europe's many souls: exploring cultural complexes and identities*. New Orleans, LA: Spring Journal Books, pp. 15–31.

Rasche, J., and Singer, T. (eds.) (2016). *Europe's many souls: exploring cultural complexes and identities*. New Orleans, LA: Spring Journal Books.

Redfearn, J. W. T. (1982). 'When are things persons and persons things?'. *Journal of Analytical Psychology*, 27, 215–37.

Rosenberg, S. (1997). 'Multiplicity of selves'. In D. Ashmore and Lee Jussim (eds.), *Self and identity: fundamental issues*. New York, NY: Oxford University Press, pp. 23–45.

Shahin, J., and Wintle, M. (2000). *The idea of a united Europe. Political, economic and cultural integration since the fall of the Berlin Wall*. London: Macmillan Press.

Simms, B. (2017). *Britain's Europe: a thousand years of conflict and cooperation*. London: Allen Lane.

Singer, T. (2003). 'Cultural complexes and archetypal defenses of the group spirit'. In J. Beebe (ed.), *Terror, violence and the impulse to destroy*. Einsiedeln, Switzerland: Daimon Verlag, pp. 191–209.

Singer, T., and Kaplinsky, C. (2010). 'Cultural complexes in analysis'. In M. Stein (ed.), *Jungian psychoanalysis: working in the spirit of C. G. Jung*. Chicago, IL: Open Court Publishing Company, pp. 22–37.

Sollberger D. (2013). 'On identity: from a philosophical point of view'. *Child and Adolescent Psychiatry and Mental Health*, 7 (1), 29. doi: 10.1186/1753-2000-7-29.

Stein, R. (2003). 'Vertical mystical homoeros: an altered form of desire in fundamentalism'. *Studies in Gender and Sexuality*, 4 (1), 38–58.

Stein, R. (2009). *For love of the father: a psychoanalytic study of religious terrorism*. Stanford, CA: Stanford University Press.
Stets, J. E., and Burke, P. J. (2000). 'Identity theory and social identity theory'. *Social Psychology Quarterly*, 63 (3) (September), 224–237.
Stets J. E., and Burke P. J. (2003). 'A sociological approach to self and identity'. In M. R. Leary and J. P. Tangney (eds.), *The handbook of self and identity*. New York, NY: Guilford Press, pp. 128–152.
Stevenson A. (ed.) (2010). *Oxford Dictionary of English*. Oxford: Oxford University Press.
Tacey, D. (2009). 'Mind and earth'. *Jung Journal: Culture and Psyche*, 3 (2), 15–32. doi: 10.1525/jung.2009.3.2.15.
Winnicott, D. W. (1953). 'Transitional objects and transitional phenomena—a study of the first not-me possession'. *International Journal of Psycho-Analysis*, 34, 89–97.
Winnicott, D. W. (1960). 'The theory of the parent-infant relationship'. *International Journal of Psycho-Analysis*, 41, 585–595.
Winnicott, D. W. (1962). 'Ego integration in child development'. In W.D. Winnicott (ed.), *The maturational processes and the facilitating environment. Studies in the theory of emotional development*. London: Karnac Books. pp. 56–63.
Winnicott, D. W. (1970). 'On the basis for self in body'. In C. Winnicott, R. Shepherd, and M. Davis (eds.), *Psycho-analytic explorations*. London: Karnac, 1989, pp. 261–83.
Winnicott D. W. (1971). *Playing and reality*. Harmondsworth: Penguin, 1985.
Wintle, M. (2009). *The image of Europe: visualizing Europe in cartography and iconography throughout the ages*. Cambridge: Cambridge University Press.
Ziegler, A. J. (1983). *Archetypal medicine*. Woodstock, CT: Spring Publication, Inc.
Zoja, L. (2017). *Paranoia. The madness that makes history*. Abingdon, Oxon/New York, NY: Routledge.

Chapter 2

Challenges to the individuation process of people on the move
Developing a sense of global citizenship

Elisabetta Iberni

Introduction

In a globalised world increasingly dominated by the perverse rules of neoliberal markets and advanced capitalism, the phenomenon of migrations dramatically highlights the massive structural differences and inequalities that are generated by this system (World Migration Report, 2018). Goods and information can move without restrictions across the globe in a much less problematic way than people. In fact some people are entitled to fully enjoy the right of freedom of movement across borders (Art. 13b of the United Nations Universal Declaration of Human Rights, 1948/2015), while others are pushed to a condition of inferiority and denied enjoyment of the same right. In the contemporary world, subjects embody their bio-psycho-social power (Lehman, David, Gruber, 2017) while being embedded in specific historical, economic, and political circumstances. The human consequences of globalisation have been described by the Polish philosopher Zygmunt Bauman, who observed how 'the reality of modernity is contributing to individualization and fragmentation instead of unifying' (1998, p. 2), and since we are always on the move, physically or psychologically, humans experience more profound psychological effects than ever before (Bauman, 1998, p. 18). The construction of their identity unfolds in a mutual dialogue, shaped by personal experiences occurring in a certain psychosocial realm and in a process of co-construction with others (Mead, 1934; Erikson, 1956). Media and their language can powerfully influence the social and cultural realm so as to frame and actualise the identity of people on the move by applying categorical distinctions. Thus, often these categories are taken as object of academic and empirical research to improve the quality of social and clinical interventions targeting individuals and families on the move. If not carefully examined these assumptions might grasp only a partial understanding of the subjective experience of these people.

Aiming to unpack and trespass the rigid boundaries drawn between these categories, I will use the lens of analytical psychology, together with concepts extracted from the mainstream of relational psychoanalysis (Mitchell, 1988; Bromberg, 2011) and inter-subjective theory (Benjamin, 1998, 2004, 2005;

Orange, 2009). I aim to observe the subjective experience of these groups across a continuum dimension by indicating four main common aspects: 1) the archetypal experience of home; 2) the impact of potentially traumatic life events; 3) identity and belonging; 4) individuation. Jung conceived the process of individuation as a series of synthetic movements between Ego and self in order to achieve a sense of wholeness. In his writings, Jung described the movement towards self-realisation mostly as an inner personal project, moving from a rather aristocratic position than looking through the political collective and democratic realm (this point is discussed by prominent post-Jungians such as Samuels, 1993). Individuation and the shaping of the sense of identity cannot take place in a vacuum but implies belonging to a wider relational and external matrix. In a sense, individuation refers always to engendered bodies and encompasses the process of raising political awareness of one's own position in the collective life.

In order to fill this conceptual gap and to integrate the Jungian theoretical framework, I propose using the idea of 'rhizome' introduced by Deleuze and Guattari (1980/1987) and further elaborated by the post-humanist philosopher Rosi Braidotti, who created the notion of 'nomadic subject' (2011a, 2011b). I suggest this conceptual association by drawing on the immanent and non-dualistic view of mind and body endorsed by Jung (for a discussion on Spinoza's influence on Jung's work see Shamdasani, 2003), as he illustrates discussing his idea of psychoid archetype, cosmic unity, unus mundus and synchronicity (Jung, 1952), Deleuze's thinking and further the 'nomadic thought' are solidly grounded in the materialist monism, rejecting the fallacious Cartesian division between mind and body. Both Jung and Deleuze borrowed from Spinoza and Bergson a vitalist materialism position that allows extending consciousness beyond human rationality, embracing even inorganic matter (Shamdasani, 2003). Another conceptual point of convergence between Jung, Deleuze, and the theory of the nomadic subject refers to the immanent quality of desire. Jung embraces a teleological view where individuation is foreseen as the constant movement towards the achievement of the totality and wholeness of the self; while in the latter's the desire corresponds to an 'ontological force of becoming' (Braidotti, 2011b, p. 2).

Exploring in depth the connections of Jungian psychology with postmodern philosophy (Hauke, 2000; Jones, 2007), and, in particular, to debate the affinity between Deleuze's interpretation of analytical psychology and the points of contact between Jung and his philosophy, is beyond the scope of this paper (such interconnections have been addressed only by a few authors such as: Main, Henderson, McMillan, 2019; Kerslake, 2007; Jenkins, 2017). In particular, McMillan (2018, p.10) has conducted a thorough analysis of Jung's key original ideas with the tools of Deleuzian thought and debated the anti-foundational criticism posed by different post-Jungian authors (Brooks, 2011; Colman, 2015, 2017). According to McMillan (2018, p. 11), different concepts have been marginalised to minimise the foundationalist epistemology adopted by Jung and the consequent dualism that has important ethical implications in clinical practice. In this paper, I argue that using the lens of Deleuzian and nomadic philosophy to re-read Jung's definition of individuation can provide useful tools to overcome the liberal individualism discourse implicit in its historical definition, and explore an alternative connection to the relational and feminist psychoanalysis. Deleuzian philosophy and nomadic thought rely on the major insights offered by psychoanalysis pointing to the capacity of thought processes to follow a self-organising structure in a dynamic manner, while at the same time being single and multiple, independent and interconnected (Braidotti, 2001b: 6), such as archetypal action patterns and emergent structures (Hogenson, 2009).

Geographical dislocations represent an existential condition involving a growing number of subjects. Moving to new places and relocating can present specific challenges in achieving individuation and a coherent sense of identity as it requires the capacity to face tensions between opposites, such as: local versus global culture, familiarity and strangeness, integration and marginalisation. Drawing on the notion of transcendent function (Jung, 1958, para. 145), this paper explores the possibilities of creating a third symbolical dimension, embedded in the matrix of relational experiences and conditioned by specific social legal and political constrictions that can emerge from the meaningful encounter of individuals and new environments. In this direction, people on the move can become carriers of diverse and original values and mediate between distant symbolic and cultural worlds. I attempt to describe this third meaningful dimension by formulating the concept of 'global citizenship' as a psychological state of mind drawing on three main ideas. The first is Jung's notion of the individuation process (Jung, 1939a; Stein, 1998; Samuels, 2001, 2017), re-interpreted through the Deleuzian philosophical lens. The second source is Hannah Arendt's ideas of 'world' and 'worldliness' (1958) and Smith's (2007) argument on the 'cosmopolitan virtue' involving the adoption of a self-reflexive mode of being in the world, the cultivation of a heightened care or feeling for the world, and the ability to adopt certain skills in the manner of our disclosures to the world. The third concept is Benjamin's idea of 'thirdness' (2004), as a space of inter-subjective acknowledgement and mutual recognition with another.

A hierarchy of lexicon describing people on the move

In his major work *The words and the things*, Michel Foucault (1966, 1975) adopted the methodological approach of discourse analysis to show the power that language has to control habits, practices, and politics in society. Deconstructing terms of common use permits unveiling concepts and meanings influencing social perception, but, at the same time, concealing the structural relationships between different actors and inequalities in the distribution of bio-socio-political power. A contemporary hierarchy of lexicon classifies different groups of people on the move. The term *refugee*, as defined in the 1951/2015 Refugee Convention, refers to

> any person who, owing to a well-founded fear of being persecuted for reasons of race, religion, nationality, membership of a particular social group or

political opinion, is outside the country of his/her nationality and is unable, or owing to such fear, is unwilling to avail himself/herself of the protection of that country.

(Article 1: 1)

Another related term refers to internally displaced persons: 'people forced to flee their homes but never cross an international border'. The semantic expression asylum seeker describes 'persons who flee their own country and seek sanctuary in another country, and apply for asylum – the right to be recognized as a refugee and receive legal protection and material assistance. An asylum seeker must demonstrate that his or her fear of persecution in his or her home country is well-founded'. The common meaning of migrant/immigrant is 'a person who moves from one place to another in order to find work or better living conditions' (Oxford Dictionary, 2017).

These definitions reveal how the process of drawing a linear, imaginary, and steady line between 'refugees' and 'migrants' is derived from the original motivation of the migration, forced in the case of perceived threat, or voluntary in the case of pursuing better economic opportunities. This distinction featured dramatically during the latest European 'migration crisis' in 2015. Empirical research has demonstrated that these 'dominant categories fail to capture adequately the complex relationship between political, social and economic drivers of migration or their shifting significance for individuals over time and space' (Crawley, Skleparis, 2018, p. 14). With stronger criticism, other scholars define this process 'categorical fetishism' (Apostolova, 2015), which aims primarily to justify policies of exclusion and containment (Gupte and Mehta, 2007, p. 65). The ontological reality of many people is far more complex: people can shift between and across categories both in their country of origin and as they travel through space and time. Climbing up in the hierarchy of the lexicon, defining people on the move, we find migrants and expats. Both terms are loaded with different meanings and refer to different semantic and symbolic networks. According to the Oxford Dictionary (2017) 'an expatriate (often shortened to expat) is a person temporarily or permanently residing in a country other than their native country'. Another term used as synonym to 'expat' is *global nomad*, 'a term applied to people who are living a mobile and international lifestyle. Global nomads aim to live location-independently, seeking detachment from particular geographical locations and the idea of territorial belonging' (Richard & Wilson, 2004, p. 4).

Again, the process of bounding these categories is important, because such language can (in some cases) be used as a political tool. The category of migrants plays a crucial role in the rise of nationalism in response to fears surrounding job security across the globe. The migration debate featured dramatically in the Leave campaign for the EU referendum in UK in 2016, as well as in Donald Trump's election. As globalisation is under siege from across the political spectrum (Broad, 2016), defining different people crossing borders to seek employment responds to needs for protection from the threat of losing an advantaged socio-economic position. The words 'migrant' and 'expat' have different origin and meaning; however, they are often applied interchangeably. On the one hand, expats are identified with educated, rich professionals working abroad, while those in less privileged positions are deemed foreign workers or migrant workers. Thus, extending the term 'expat' to everybody can hide unequal socio-economic and political realities. Moreover, the word 'expat' can be used with a subtle racist connotation to refer to white people (Koutonin, 2015). According to Koutonin 'immigrants' is a term set aside for 'inferior races', arguing that often the extension of the use of the category of 'expat' or 'global nomads' to all people can aim at diminishing the weight of ethnicity and nationality and the power of socio-economic structures to influence the mobility and the conditions of others and allow 'white people to deny that they enjoy the privileges of a racist system'.

Reflecting on the accuracy of these definitions and of the boundary process behind the creation of the three categories of people described above is a useful exercise. These dominant categories conceal rather than reveal the dynamic processes with which migration is increasingly associated, but also tend to bias and to orient the focus of policy making, academic research, and therapeutic intervention for health practitioners.

The academic and scientific psychological research focused on refugees in the last there decades concentrated on the experience of trauma, Post-Traumatic Stress Disorder (PTSD) (Arroyo & Eth, 1986), and lately also on the concept of resilience (Bonanno et al, 2004; Wilson & Drozdek, 2004; Yehuda, 1995). As Fassin and Rechtman (2009) have observed, over the last three decades, trauma victims have become culturally and politically respectable, and trauma has developed from a clinical syndrome to an 'unassailable moral category'. Of note, the ground-breaking work of Renos Papadopoulos (Papadopoulos, 2007, 2009, 2011) has provided an alternative epistemological framework introducing the concept of Adversity-Activated Development (AAD) to explore the experience of refugees and asylum seekers in depth. He focused on aspects often neglected by the mainstream, which tend to medicalise and pathologise human suffering. Papadopoulos refers to the positive developments that are a direct result of being exposed to adversity and to the process of meaning-making of the negative experiences that allow individuals to find new strength and experience transformative renewal. He observes what 'seemingly paradoxical outcome may create awkward moral dilemmas and complexities when mental health professionals work with such refugees, as one does not wish to focus on the positive outcomes of despicable acts of political violence' (2007, p. 307).

The dominant discourse on migration psychology (Tilburg, v. M. et al., 2005) focuses on several key words: homesickness, adjustment, adaptation, cultural shock (Oberg, 1960), and acculturation stress. The latest represents a concept that has been empirically described according to a four-category model indicating different psychosocial strategies: assimilation, integration, separation and marginalisation (Sam, 1995, p. 240). The dominant discourse on the pathways of psychological adjustment and life among 'expats' and 'global nomads' is not informed by a comparably extensive body of empirical evidence, although a few pieces of research have shown that 'expats' suffer from more anxiety and depression than people in settled locations. The seminal work of Ruth Van Reken on third culture kids (TCKs) (Pollock, Van Reken, 2009) is one of the best examples of qualitative research targeting this group. According to these authors, TCKs are persons raised in a culture other than their parents', or the culture of the country named on their passport, where they are legally considered native, for a significant part of their early development years and therefore are exposed to a greater variety of cultural influences. The term can refer to both adults and children, as the term 'kid' points more to an individual's formative or developmental years, but in order to reflect on such extension of the concept the term *adult third culture kid* (ATCK) was coined. This brief summary, far from exploring exhaustively such a complex topic and intentionally does not take into consideration the remarkable works of ethnopsychoanalysts (Devereaux, 1978; 1980; Nathan, 1986). The overview aims to sketch out the lines of scientific and clinical theoretical models' that seem to frame conceptually realities and experiences constrainted dictated by structural social, economic, and political circumstances.

The discourse on trauma and its psychopathological consequences tends to remain pivotal when studying and treating groups of people who most probably will have to live their lives in temporary camps without having an opportunity to resettle successfully to another place (UNHCR, 1951/2018). Acculturation stress represents a concern not only for psychologists and health professionals, but overall for policy makers and for the entire society in their efforts to identify more effective strategies to include in the societal fabric migrant workers relocating in a new country. On the other hand, identity and self-development seem to be fundamental themes in the discourse on 'expats' and 'global nomads', starting from their infancy, as many children are no longer faced with the realities of a mono-cultural upbringing, but becoming globally mobile students due to e.g. intercultural marriages or parents' occupational or educational choice abroad. In these cases, the cross-cultural encounter is thought to have the power to positively impact identity development in such a way that it may be constituted of multiple cultures (Pollock & Van Reken, 2009, p. 40). Such children may feel that they do not belong to just one culture; hence they are becoming citizens of the world, sort of cultural sponges where elements of each culture blend into one divergent identity (Pollock & Van Reken, 2009, p. 13). In this paper, I argue that the sense of 'being citizens of the world' might represent a potential state of mind inherent to the psychological development of people on the move more in general.

A common theoretical framework for people on the move

Drawing on the literature review discussed above, I try to select common aspects characterising the subjective psychological experience of different groups of people on the move. These elements are: 1) the experience of *home*; 2) the impact of potentially traumatic events; 3) identity development and sense of belonging; 4) individuation and global citizenship. By blending these ingredients, the experience of people on the move can be described by different patterns that emerge on a common continuum.

Home

Home represents an archetypal experience (Williams, 2018) reflecting a natural and adaptive inclination to increase the sense of safety and security, by creating a stable and predictable environment and by feeling connected to other significant relatives. The definition of the term home refers to the etymology of the old German *Heim* and refers to 'the place where one lives permanently, especially as a member of a family or household' (Oxford Dictionary, 2017). The instinct of creating a nest to give a concrete space where to organise life is common to several animal species; for human beings the meaning of home extends to the larger community, a geographical space, such as village, hometown, home-country, homeland. 'Home is where we start from' stated Winnicott (1960a, 1960b), meaning that the sense of our self is deeply rooted in our original relational experiences within the family matrix. Through the lens of object relations theory, home could be defined as an inner space where our self-objects, experiences, and memories are collected in an atmosphere of familiarity, with a shared cultural understanding, regardless of the mono or multi-ethnic environment we live in. The motivation or urge to leave home, and to explore beyond the familiar is a key component discriminating the three groups described above, which I would rather call 'fuzzy sets'. This motivation refers primarily to the 'degree of freedom from fear and lack of favourable conditions and livelihood condition that people are facing at the moment they take the decision to leave their home'. Leaving home because of war, conflict, discrimination, or lack of access to basic services and human rights implies a specific ontological condition. On the other hand, undertaking a diplomatic career that requires relocating to a different posting every four years entails a different experience. For many refugees and asylum seekers, the experience of leaving home could mean being displaced in a temporary accommodation for months or years. Home tends to become idealised as much as the experience to build up a new home is impeded by external circumstances (Papadopoulos, 2011). On the other extreme of the spectrum, global nomads face a continuous series of relocations, changing places, accommodations, cultures and relations' networks of significant persons that can create a sense of disorientation and confusion, as if home never existed in the outer nor inner reality.

The impact of potentially traumatic life events

Traumatic events are a constant variable of the human condition. However, it is important to clarify that the concept of trauma is multidimensional: it describes an event (see the A criterion of PTSD in DSM 5), in the sense in which Whitehead (2004) meant the term as 'a fact that unfolds the total effects in many directions'.

In other words, it can be said that nothing else, neither internal nor external, but trauma belongs to reality, a reality whose best definition is the pragmatic 'Real is what does' (Jung, 1933, paras. 742-748). Empirical research (Roberts et al, 2010) shows how several conditions, such as age, gender, and ethnicity, can affect subjective perceptions and the attribution of meanings to an event, therefore determining the construction the meaning of the traumatic experience.

People on the move can experience a wide range of potentially traumatic experiences, prior to, during, and after their change of location. On a psychological level, Papadopoulos (2007, p. 15) adopted the term 'nostalgic disorientation' to describe the state of mind of refugees and forced migrants who are missing their home. On the other hand, 'global nomads', especially children and adolescents, report to occasionally suffer of an inner sense of 'homelessness' and feelings of being 'rootless' as they never had the opportunity to establish a sense of home (Pascoe, 2006). Overall, relocating implies a real loss and therefore can be held into account as holding a certain traumatic impact. Trauma has a disruptive impact on the sense of an individual's psychological integrity and triggers dissociative defensive mechanisms, especially when it involves interpersonal nature. From the perspective of relational psychoanalysis, the impact of this overwhelming experience can seriously affect the psychic fabric by destroying one's capacity to create connections among states of mind, reducing the 'reflective function' (Fonagy & Target, 1997) and generating personality disorders (Liotti, 2005). Anticipating contemporary views of relational psychoanalysis and inter-subjectivity theory, Jung recognised that dissociability is a natural tendency of the psyche. However, Jung acknowledged its devastating potential when confronted with extremely abusive circumstances, and hinted at how this might develop into complexes and sub-personalities (Redfearn, 1985). Jung frequently termed complexes 'splinter psyches' (1934a, para. 203) which may possibly develop into 'alternate personalities', each with consciousness, memories, and specific adaptive functions that promote the existence of the individual as a whole.

Identity development and sense of belonging

Writing in 1912, William James distinguished between 'I', the self as knower and doer, and 'me', or myself as known or experienced. Identity is related to the individual's 'selfsameness and continuity in time', and the others' recognition of these qualities also. The self includes a material, a social, and a spiritual dimension. The construction of the self-identity can take place only within a matrix of affective relationships with significant others, an important aspect described in relational psychoanalysis (Winnicott, 1960a, 1960b; Mitchell, 2000; Fonagy & Target, 1997). Refugees, migrants, and global nomads cope with the common challenge of dealing with changes, between places, languages, familiar faces, beloved friends, any points of reference, culture, and so on. Quoting Bauman's (2005, p. 2) use of liquidity as a metaphor, when he observes that 'liquid life is a precarious life, lived under conditions of constant uncertainty', it is possible to say that people on the move have more fluid lives and deal with the effort of maintaining a solid self-identity, having to negotiate their sense belonging and intimacy within a new context. Adopting a conceptual framework to understand some specific aspect of the subjective experience of people on the move might provide a useful tool for clinical practice.

Aiming to construct a conceptual framework to understand some specific aspect of the subjective experience of people on the move, I will try to integrate the idea of the multiplicity of self-experiences as described by Jung and the notion of *rhizome* as discussed by Deleuze (2001). As mentioned above, Jung not only considered that the psyche has a natural tendency to splitting off; he assumed that partial components of the personality could be autonomous and empowered as events, which depend on the typical organisation of the psyche, visualised 'like a chain of islands or an archipelago' (Jung, 1954, para. 387). According to Jung's perspective, the real mystery is rather how the psychic identity can be maintained, which is a recent evolutionary conquest relying on the enduring integrative work of the ego complex. Redfearn (1977, 1985) extended the Jungian notion of self and noted that Jung used the word 'self' to describe a totality, or mainly to point to 'not-me' force which is usually not experienced clearly by the conscious 'I'. For Jung, the self is placed over the Ego, often overlapping with the subjective 'I'. The Ego is, for Jung, a complex, as complexes remain largely unconscious, like sub-selves affecting consciousness and behaviour but, most of the time, avoiding a direct relationship with the 'I'. Redfearn (1985) referred to the self as a migratory self, migrating 'hither and thither to various locations in the total personality, like the spotlight at a theatre picking up first one actor then another, or, even more pertinently, like a pilgrim on his journey of life visiting one place, then another, in his universe' (1985, p. xii). Redfearn considers that the looseness of the 'I' in its attachment to the various 'sub-personalities' of the individual results in a readier migration of the 'I-feeling' between the different sub-personalities. Moreover, the multiplicity of the self-experience is an idea theorised by object-relation psychoanalysts who have noticed the influence of the relational matrix and inter-subjective dialogue, as well as the harmful impact of interpersonal trauma (Bromberg, 1998; 2011).

Here I see that the notion of rhizome created by Deleuze and Guattari (1980/1987) as a useful complement to the Jungian intuitions about the multiplicity of the experiences of Ego and self. This conceptual integration might allow a better articulation of the process of identity in general but especially for people with a movable life. The notion of the rhizome offers multiple ways of engaging in and making sense of the fluidity and fragmentary nature of belonging and identity. A rhizome as 'a subterranean stem is absolutely different from roots and radicles. Bulbs and tubers are rhizomes' (ibidem, 1980/1987, p. 7). Deleuze (2001) specify that the notion of the rhizome is symbolic in both theory and research that allows for multiplicity, interconnection, and fluidity in making sense of belonging and identity, whereby no one 'theory' and/or 'method' can be said to have priority. It affords a way of considering the complexly overlapping layers of theories, philosophical underpinnings, multiple identities, cultures, and belongings, which continuously evolve and interlink with a variety of concepts and ideologies. They describe the notion of rhizome as based on four principles: the first defines the rhizome is its connectivity: 'as is the potato, or any structure in which each point is necessarily connected to each other point, in which no location may become a beginning or an end, yet the whole is heterogeneous'. (Deleuze and Guattari, 1980/1987, p. 7). Jung describes the capacity of the self to producing connections in these terms: 'The self is relatedness. ... The self only exists inasmuch as you appear. Not that you are, but that you do the self. The self appears in your deeds and deeds always mean relationship' (Jung 1935-39, para. 73). The second principle common to both the rhizome and the Jungian self is their *multiplicity*. Deleuze labels the rhizome as a 'multiplicity' rather than a 'multiple', wresting it from any relation to 'the One' (Deleuze and Guattari, 1980/1987, p. 8). For Jung, the subjective experience has a migratory quality. Because the Ego complex is subject to natural dissociation, unity is a mere illusion, and has to relate with many other complexes negotiating sometimes power positions.

The third principle shows the complementarity between the two concepts and is called the *asignifying rupture* (Deleuze and Guattari, 1980/1987, p. 9) 'against the over signifying breaks separating structures or cutting across a single structure. A rhizome may be broken, shattered at a given spot, but it will start up again on one of its old lines, or on new lines'. Jung defines the trauma at the basis of the complex creation. The rhizomatic conjunction '... and ... and ... and ...'. (Deleuze, 2001), as the rhizome has no beginning or end and it's always an *intermezzo* (in-between), echoes Jung's definition of transcendent function and in particular of the *conjunctio* unifying opposite meanings in a third meaningful symbolic dimension (Jung, 1946; 1970).

The fourth principle of *de-territorialization* considers that the rhizome likewise resists structures of domination, such as the notion of 'the mother tongue' in linguistics, though it does admit to ongoing cycles of what Deleuze refers to as 'deterritorializing' and 'reterritorializing moments' (1980, p. 3). In analytical psychology, the Ego moves continuously from and towards the self throughout the individuation, or as described by Fordham, the self develops through a constant process of de-integration and reintegration (Fordham, 1985), in order to achieve unity and wholeness.

Upon this reflection, I suggest we apply the Deleuzian philosophical lens to observe psychic dynamics between Ego and self, and to consider the nature of individual identity as *rhizomatic*, thus open to developing across new directions. This seems to be in line with the idea of subject conceptualised by Deleuze and Guattari in *A Thousand Plateaus* (1980/1987) as an open, complex 'agency-assemblage' that is ineluctably characterised ('virtually', if not 'actually') by a rhizomatic and multiplicitous structure (every subject always already being 'a crowd'). Following the four principles of the rhizome mentioned above, the *rhizomatic identity* is characterised by the quality of *relatedness* (connectivity) and the capacity to create meaningful relationships nurturing different aspects of the self. A second aspect is the *multiplicity* of self-experiences and the possibility for different 'sub-personalities' to cohabit. A third focus refers to the process of *conjunctio* (Jung, 1955/1956: 653) or the psychic capacity to synthesising opposite and discordant instances and needs, creating the *third* as meaningful dimension. A fourth facet of the *rhizomatic identity* is related to the subjective 'deterritorialization' indicating the multiple 'virtual' possibilities that may be actualised under certain conditions, offering opportunity for the subject to develop along 'nomadic' 'lines of flight'. Jung adopted the term individuation to describe the lifelong process of self-realisation, and to discover and experience meaning and purpose in life fulfilling one's potential.

Individuation and global citizenship

Throughout their entire path of individuation, especially if moving started in their childhood, refugees, migrants, and global nomads can face several questions lingering constantly in their mind. For instance, in consequence of frequent shifts of cultural frames and transition processes 'the child's passport country [may] not any longer indicate the heart's cultural belonging and it can disrupt the balance between cultural belonging and identity forming' (Pollock & Van Reken, 2009, p. 46). Trying to remain tied to their family and community origins, persons relocating in another country might experience painful moral dilemmas between values, principles, and ways of adapting to the new situation. From an inner point of view, interpersonal trauma, due to both personal and political experiences (for instance loss or collective violence) might lead to disabling states of mind not accessible to the ego consciousness and interfering with the possibility of a healthy psychosocial adaptation. Becoming a 'psychological 'in-dividual', that is, a separate, indivisible unity or 'whole' (Jung, 1939b, para. 490) may be perceived as a burden. Jung (1934a; 1934b) stressed that individuation requires the integration of both collective and personal elements by a conscious intention to change and transform. Therefore, a successful individuation depends upon the interplay and synthesis of opposites. According to Fordham's developmental model (1985), individuation begins in infancy and continues throughout life in a continuous movement of de-integration and re-integration, echoing Jung's idea that 'there is no linear evolution; there is only circumambulation of the self. Uniform development exists, at most, only at the beginning; later everything points towards the centre' (Jung, 1961, p. 188).

Stein (1998) described three main stages of individuation: a) the containment/nurturance (i.e., the maternal, or in Neumann's terminology the 'matriarchal') stage; b) the adapting/adjusting (i.e., the paternal, or, again in Neumann's terminology, the 'patriarchal') stage; and c) the centring/integrating (in Neumann's terminology, the individual) stage. During the last decade, different post-Jungian authors have given special attention to the psychosocial, cultural, and political factors influencing the individuation process. In recent years, Samuels (1993, 2001, 2017) introduced a vigorous 'political turn' into the mainstream of Jungian psychoanalysis. His research with other clinicians has revealed a strong interest in improving the way political and collective perspectives are integrated into responsible, relational clinical work. In this direction, the concept of rhizomatic identity as a conceptual tool useful to understand at clinical level, a possible subjective individuation experience in people on the move within the limits imposed by their environmental circumstances. The differences between Jung's and Deleuze's conception of the 'whole' have been discussed by Jungian scholars (Main, Henderson, and McMillan [2019]), the former viewing the individual as a closed system, while the latter theorises the subject as an open, complex 'agency-assemblage' (Deleuze and Guattari, 1980/1987: 4). In this paper, I consider the individual as relational by nature and, therefore, only able to self-develop within a matrix of different relationships. The multiplicity of experiences attached to belonging can trigger deep conflicts and symptoms that can be successfully overcome in virtue of the *transcendent function* preforming its self-regulatory quality of the psyche, experienced as a new standpoint of 'renewed power towards new goals' (Jung, 1921, paras, 827-828). The emergence of a meaningful third dimension can represent a crucial creative moment when an individual realises that he/she has the possibility of belonging to somewhere *in-between*, becoming conscious about their condition of inhabiting hybridity.

In my clinical practice, people on the move may experience an internal condition which refers to a drive towards the 'perpetually unfixed and the unfixable identity' (Bauman, 2005, p. 31) and belonging. Hybridity reminds us of Agamben's definition of a 'hyphen', a symbol of liminality, in-betweeness and threshold. In his words, the hyphen is the dialectic of both separation and connection in the sense that 'it unites only to the degree that it distinguishes and distinguishes only to the degree that it unites' (2003, p.153). Together with the sense of identity, the experience of home is often described as a hybrid place, scattered in time and spaces. The creation of a unifying symbolical image of the world as a common space to live in and to belong, therefore as a home, represents a possible answer to these dilemmas. As its psychological counterpart, a state of mind of global citizenship can emerge as a positive result of the transcendent function supporting the individuation process. Literally, a 'global citizen' is considered a 'person who is aware of and understands the wider world and their place in it. They take an active role in their community, and work with others to make the planet more equal, fair and sustainable' (Oxfam, 2015/2018). Originally, the idea of a global citizenship was conceived as a necessary complement to a utopic political project, to establishing a global or cosmopolitan democracy (Archibugi, 2004). Principles of justice should be applied in global contexts, including principles pertaining to the distribution of economic and social goods. To better describe the concept of psychological global citizenship, in relation to the capacity of an individual to hold the tensions generated by a liminal condition and to embrace the world feeling at home, I adjoin the original definition of the term 'worldliness' introduced by Arendt (1958), and the idea of cosmopolitan virtue inspired by Smith (2007).

Hanna Arendt defined as 'worldliness', or the capacity of living together in the world:

> The world ... is not identical with the earth or with nature, as the limited space for the movement of men and the general condition of organic life. It is related, rather, to the human artefact, the fabrication of human hands, as well as to affairs, which go on among those who inhabit the man-made world together.
>
> (1958, p. 52)

Being a global citizen implies the will of assuming the world as a co-creation of realities that takes place primarily among human beings. Developing Arendt's thought, Smith (2007, p. 38) points to mentalisation as a key feature of the cosmopolitan virtue, in his own words 'a self-reflexive mode of being in the world, the cultivation of a heightened care or feeling for the world, and the ability to adopt certain skills in the manner of our disclosures to the world'.

I suggest that psychological global citizenship can emerge as a possible result of the creative action of transcendent function. It represents a meaningful inner space of 'thirdness', symbolised by the world, serving as a conjunction not only between different internal (and conflicting) self-experiences, but also inhabited by a multitude of other people. Global citizenship entails, on the one hand, the possibility for an individual to acknowledge at the same time the multiplicity of self-experiences and its uniqueness, as well as the capacity of mutual recognition with others. I refer to the concept of thirdness derived from relational psychoanalysis and inter-subjectivity theory (Stolorow 1997, 2006; Benjamin, 1998, 2004, 2009), defined in terms of a relationship in which each person experiences the other as a 'like subject,' another mind who can be 'felt with,' yet has a distinct, separate centre of feeling and perception (Benjamin, 2004, p. 5). As this two-way directionality might be difficult to grasp, the *third* might provide 'a vantage point outside the two' (Aron & Benjamin, 1999).

Throughout their individuation process, people on the move can develop a sense of psychological global citizenship, feeling the right to live in the world and connected with different communities, places, and cultures. This state of mind can appear in virtue of the recognition of one's self-multiplicity and identity at the same time, if suitable conditions are given to develop the capacity of mentalisation to hold the 'one in the third and the third in the one' (Benjamin, 2004). As individuation takes place within a determined relational and historical matrix, it is important to reflect on how unequal psychosocial, environmental, socio-economic, legal, and political structures can impact negatively or positively the process to become a citizen of the world for individuals and families.

People on the move or 'nomadic subjects' (Braidotti, 2011b) might become valuable mediators between different cultures and convey a sense of inter-connectedness between people. Their psychological mind-set as global citizens tends to confer a pluralistic interpersonal attitude towards the collective life. Samuels

(2001, p. 176) defines pluralism as 'an attitude to conflict that tried to reconcile differences without imposing a false resolution on the conflict or losing sight of the unique value of each position'. He clarified that pluralism differ from multiplicity and in social and political terms from 'multiculturalism as it attempts to hold unity and diversity in balance, keeping the tension between the One and the Many'.

Conclusion

In this chapter, I have reflected on the psychological conditions faced by people on the move, focusing on three major categories: refugees, migrants, and 'expats'. Drawing on Deleuze's (2001) idea of rhizome and the Braidotti's (2011a, 2011b) notion of nomadic subject, I integrated and re-interpreted the Jungian concepts of self-development and multiplicity to construct a conceptual framework to understand their specific subjective experiences. The process of individuation and construction of an integrated self might be experienced as a real challenge for people on the move, with the risk of being unable to create meaningful connections between different self-experiences, and developing personal and cultural complexes possibly producing alienated parts of self or 'marginalized identities' related to a sense of non-belonging and uprootedness (Pascoe, 2006). The idea of a rhizomatic identity can offer a useful tool to grasp the complexity of the subjective experience of hybridity and liminality faced by people on the move, although embodied in different socio-economic conditions. The transcendent function can support the process of individuation by eliciting the feeling of being at home in the world accompanied by its psychological counterpart, a sense of global citizenship. This conceptual approach may be seen as providing different advantages.

Firstly, it can offer a useful heuristic and complementary tool for analytical psychologists who aim to better understand certain specific intra-psychic and relational dynamics common among 'people on the move'. Secondly, on a theoretical level, the revision of the Jungian conceptualisation of subjectivity through the lens of Deleuzian philosophy can inform an ethical approach adopted within the therapeutic and psychosocial settings. It raises the attention of social and health workers about the complexity and multiplicity of the subjective experiences of people on the move, bearing in mind the psychological continuous dimension ranging from the polarity of trauma, to resilience and self-development. A third possible implication of the present framework refers to the educational function of teaching global citizenship to prevent racism and discrimination and to raise awareness of the need for political co-operation between nation-states to achieve overarching collective goals. This potential use derives from the original link between global citizenship and the utopic political project of cosmopolitanism, which requires commitment to both global solidarity and global cultural diversity. Global solidarity considers the need for democratic nation-states' political representatives to pursue global and regional, rather than exclusively national, interests (Habermas, 2001, pp. 111–12), following Rawls' 'natural duty of justice' (Rawls,

1972). Cosmopolitanism attempts to protect global cultural diversity arguing in favour of 'an obligation of care and stewardship for other cultures' and 'dialogue with other cultures' (Turner, 2002, p. 57–58). Re-thinking the subjective experience as multiple and unique may reflect the contemporaneity of Jungian psychology and its transformative power also in the direction of political action.

References

Agamben, G. (2003). *Homo sacer. Sovereign power and bare life.* Stanford, CA: Stanford University Press.
Archibugi, D. (2004). 'Cosmopolitan democracy and its critics: a review'. *European Journal of International Relations*, 10 (3), 437–473.
Apostolova, R. 2015. "Of Refugees and Migrants: Stigma, Politics, and Boundary Work at the Borders of Europe." *American Sociological Association Newsletter*, September 14
Arendt, H. (1958). *The human condition*, 2nd ed. London: The University of Chicago Press.
Aron, L., and Benjamin, J. (1999). *Intersubjectivity and the struggle to think.* Paper presented at the Spring meeting Division 39 of the American Psychological Association, New York, NY.
Arroyo, W., and Eth, S. (1986). 'Children traumatized by Central American Warfare'. In R. Pynoos, and S. Eth (eds.), *Post-traumatic stress disorder in children*, Washington, DC: American Psychiatric Press, pp. 101–120.
Bauman, Z. (1998). *Globalization: the human consequences.* New York, NY: Columbia University Press.
Bauman, Z. (2005). *Liquid life.* Cambridge: Polity.
Benjamin, J. (1998). *Shadow of the other: intersubjectivity and gender in psychoanalysis.* New York, NY: Routledge.
Benjamin, J. (2004). 'Beyond doer and done to: an intersubjective view of thirdness'. *Psychoanalytic Quarterly*, 73 (1), 5–46.
Benjamin, J. (2005). 'From many into one: attention, energy and the containing of multitudes'. *Psychoanalytic Dialogues*, 15, 185–201.
Benjamin, J. (2009). 'A relational psychoanalysis perspective on the necessity of acknowledging failure in order to restore the facilitating and containing features of the intersubjective relationship (the shared third)'. *International Journal of Psychoanalysis*, 90, 441–450.
Bonanno, G. A. (2004). 'Loss, trauma, and human resilience. Have we underestimated the human capacity to thrive after extremely aversive events?'. *American Psychologist*, 59, 20–28.
Braidotti, R. (2011a). *Nomadic subjects. embodiment and sexual difference in contemporary feminist theory*, 2nd ed. New York, NY: Columbia University Press.
Braidotti, R. (2011b). *Nomadic theory. the portable Rosi Braidotti.* New York, NY: Columbia University Press.
Broad, M. (2016). 'Why is globalization under attack?'. Retrieved on 28 November 2018 at https://www.bbc.com/news/business-37554634. Accessed on 20 June 2018.
Bromberg, P. (1998). *Standing in the spaces: essays on clinical process, trauma, and dissociation.* London: Psychology Press/New York, NY: Francis and Taylor.
Bromberg, P. M. (2011). *The shadow of the tsunami: and the growth of the relational mind.* New York, NY: Routledge.

Brooks, R. M. (2011). 'Un-thought out metaphysics in analytical psychology: a critique of jung's epistemological basis for psychic reality'. *Journal of Analytical Psychology*, 56, 492–513.
Colman, W. (2015). 'Bounded in a nutshell and a king of infinite space: the embodied self and its intentional world'. *Journal of Analytical Psychology*, 60 (3), 316–335.
Colman, W. (2017). 'Soul in the world: symbolic culture as the medium for psyche'. *Journal of Analytical Psychology*, 62 (1), 32–49.
Crawley, H, and Skleparis, D. (2018). 'Refugees, migrants, neither, both: categorical fetishism and the politics of bounding in Europe's 'migration crisis'. *Journal of Ethnic and Migration Studies*, 44, 48–64.
Deleuze, G. (2001). *Pure immanence: essays on a life.* A. Boyman (Trans.). New York, NY: Zone Books.
Deleuze, G., and Guattari, F. (1972). *Anti-oedipus: capitalism and schizophrenia.* R. Hurley, M. Seem, and H. Lane (Trans.). Minneapolis, MN: University of Minnesota Press.
Deleuze, G., and Guattari, F. (1980/1987). *A thousand plateaus: capitalism and schizophrenia* (B. Massumi, Trans.). Minneapolis: University of Minnesota Press.
Devereaux, G. (1978). *Ethnopsychoanalysis: psychoanalysis and anthropology as complementary frames of reference.* Berkeley, CA: University of California Press.
Devereaux, G. (1980). *Basic problems of ethnopsychiatry.* Chicago, IL: University of Chicago Press.
Erikson, E. (1956). 'The problem of ego identity'. *Journal of the American Psychoanalytic Association*, 4, 56–121.
Fassin, D., and Rechtman, R. (2009). *The empire of trauma an inquiry into the condition of victimhood.* Princeton, NJ: Princeton University Press.
Fonagy, P., and Target, M. (1997). 'Attachment and reflective function: their role in self-organization'. *Developmental Psychopathology*, 9 (4), 679–700.
Fordham, M. (1985). *Explorations into the self.* The Library of Analytical Psychology, Vol 7. London: Academic Press.
Foucault, M. (1966). *Les Mots et les Choses Une archéologie des sciences humaines.* Paris:Gallimard.
Foucault, M. (1975). *Survelleir et punir. Naissance de la prison.* Paris: Gallimard.
Gupte, J., Mehta L. (2007). 'Disjunctures in labelling refugees and oustees'. In J. Moncrieffe and R. Eyben (eds.), *The power of labelling: how people are categorised and why it matters.* London: Earthscan, pp. 64–79.
Habermas, J. (2001). *The postnational constellation: political essays.* M. Pensky (Trans.). Cambridge, UK: Polity Press.
Hauke, C. (2000). *Jung and the postmodern: the interpretation of realities.* London: Routledge.
Hogenson, G. B. (2009). 'Archetypes as action patterns'. *Journal of Analytical Psychology*, 54 (3), 325–337.
James, W. (1912). 'Does consciousness exist?'. In *Essays in Radical Empiricism*, New York: Longman Green and Co., pp. 1–38.
Jenkins, B. (2017). *Eros and the economy: Jung, Deleuze, sexual difference.* London/New York, NY: Routledge.
Jones, R. (2007). *Jung, psychology, postmodernity.* London: Routledge.
Jung, C. G. (1921). 'Definitions'. In *Collected works*, Vol. 6, *Psychological types* (2nd ed.). Princeton, NJ: Princeton University Press.

Jung, C. G. (1933). 'Realty and surreality'. In *Collected works*, Vol 8, *The structure and dynamics of the psyche* (2nd ed.). Princeton, NJ: Princeton University Press.
Jung, C. G. (1934a). 'A review of the complex theory'. In *Collected works*, Vol 8, *The structure and dynamics of the psyche* (2nd ed.). Princeton, NJ: Princeton University Press.
Jung, C. G. (1934b). 'Archetypes of the collective unconscious'. In *Collected works*, Vol.9i, *The archetypes and the collective unconscious* (2nd ed.). Princeton, NJ: Princeton University Press.
Jung C. G. (1935–39). *Nietzsche's Zarathustra: notes on the seminar given in 1934–1939*. Princeton, NJ: Princeton University Press, 1988.
Jung, C. G. (1939a). 'A study of the process of individuation'. In *Collected works*, Vol.9i, *The archetypes and the collective unconscious* (2nd ed.). Princeton, NJ: Princeton University Press.
Jung, C. G. (1939b). 'Conscious, unconscious, and individuation'. In *Collected works*, Vol.9i, *The archetypes and the collective unconscious* (2nd ed.). Princeton, NJ: Princeton University Press.
Jung, C. G. (1946). 'The psychology of the transference'. In *Collected works*, Vol. 16, *The practice of psychotherapy* (2nd ed.). Princeton, NJ: Princeton University Press.
Jung, C. G. (1952). 'Synchronicity: an acausal connecting principle'. In *Collected works*, Vol. 8, *The structure and dynamics of the psyche* (2nd ed.). Princeton, NJ: Princeton University Press.
Jung, C. G. (1954). 'On the nature of the psyche'. In *Collected works*, Vol. 8, *The structure and dynamics of the psyche* (2nd ed.). Princeton, NJ: Princeton University Press.
Jung C. G. (1955/1956). 'The Conjunction'. In Colleted Works, Vol. 14. *Mysterium Coniunctionis*. Princeton, NJ: Princeton University Press.
Jung, C. G. (1958). 'The transcendent function'. In *Collected works*, Vol. 8, *The structure and dynamics of the psyche* (2nd ed.). Princeton, NJ: Princeton University Press.
Jung, C. G. (1961). *Memories, dreams, reflections*. London: Fontana Press.
Jung, C. G. (1970). *Collected works*, Vol. 14, *Mysterium coniunctionis*. Princeton, NJ: Princeton University Press.
Kerslake, C. (2007). *Deleuze and the unconscious*. London: Continuum.
Koutonin, M. R. (2015, 13 March). 'Why are white people expats when the rest of us are immigrants?' *The Guardian*. Retrieved on 28th November at https://www.theguardian.com/global-development-professionals-network/2015/mar/13/white-people-expats-immigrants-migration.
Lehman, B. J., David, D. M., and Gruber, J. A. (2017). 'Rethinking the biopsychosocial model of health: understanding health as a dynamic system'. *Social and Personality Psychology Compass*, 11 (8), 1–17.
Liotti, G. (2005). *La dimensione interpersonale della coscienza*. Firenze: Carocci.
Main, R., Henderson, D., and McMillan, C. (eds.) (2019). *Jung, Deleuze and the problematic whole*. London: Routledge.
McMillan, C. (2018). 'Jung and Deleuze: enchanted openings to the other: a philosophical contribution'. *International Journal of Jungian Studies*, 10 (3), 184–198. doi: 10.1080/19409052.2018.1505236
Mead, G. H. (1934). *Mind, self and society: from the standpoint of a social behaviorist*. Chicago, IL: University of Chicago Press.
MitchellS. A., 1988.
Mitchell, S. A. (2000). *Relationality: from attachment to inter-subjectivity*. Cambridge, MA: Harvard University Press,..
Nathan, T. (1986). *La folie des autres: traité d'ethnopsychiatrie clinique*. Paris: Dunod.

Oberg, K. (1960). 'Cultural shock: adjustment to new cultural environments'. *Missiology: An International Review*, 7 (4), 177–182.
Orange, D. (2009). 'Toward the art of the living dialogue: between constructivism and hermeneutics in psychoanalytic thinking'. In R. Frie and D. Orange (eds.), *Beyond postmodernism: new dimensions in clinical theory and practice*. New York, NY: Routledge, 2009.
OXFAM. (2015). *Education for global citizens*. London. Retrieved on 28th November at https://www.oxfam.org.uk/education/who-we-are/what-is-global-citizenship.
Papadopoulos, R. K. (2009). 'Extending Jungian Psychology. Working with survivors of political upheavals'. In G. Heuer (ed.), *Sacral revolutions: cutting edges in psychoanalysis and Jungian analysis*. London: Routledge, pp. 192–200.
Papadopoulos, R. K. (2011). 'The umwelt and networks of archetypal images: a Jungian approach to therapeutic encounters in humanitarian contexts'. *Psychotherapy and Politics International*, 9, 212–231.
Pascoe, R. (2006). *Raising global nomads*. Vancouver: Expatriate Press Limited.
Pollock, D. C., and Van Reken, R. E. (2009). *Third culture kids: growing up among worlds*. Boston, MA: Intercultural Press.
Rawls, J. (1972). *A theory of justice*. Oxford: Oxford University Press.
Redfearn, J. W. T. (1977). 'The self and individuation'. *Journal of Analytical Psychology*, 22 (2), 125–141.
Redfearn, J. W. T. (1985). *My self, my many selves*. London: Karnac.
Richard, G., and Wilson, J. (2004). *The global nomad: backpacker travel in theory and practice*. Toronto: Channel View Publications.
Roberts, A. L., Gilman, S. E., Breslau, J., Breslau, N., and Koenen, K. C. (2010). 'Race/ethnic differences in exposure to traumatic events, development of post-traumatic stress disorder, and treatment-seeking for post-traumatic stress disorder in the United States'. *Psychological Medicine*, 41 (1), 71–83.
Sam, D. L. (1995). 'Acculturation attitudes among young immigrants as a function of perceived parental attitudes toward cultural change'. *The Journal of Early Adolescence*, 15 (2), 238–258. doi: 10.1177/0272431695015002004
Samuels, A. (1993). *The political psyche*. London: Routledge.
Samuels, A. (2001). *Politics on the couch: citizenship and the internal life*. London: Routledge.
Samuels, A. (2017). 'The "activist client": social responsibility, the political self and clinical practice in psychotherapy and psychoanalysis'. *Psychoanalytic Dialogues*, 27 (6), 678–693.
Shamdasani, S. (2003). *Jung and the making of modern psychology: the dream of a science*. Cambridge: Cambridge University Press.
Smith, W. (2007). 'Cosmopolitan citizenship: virtue, irony and worldliness'. *European Journal of Social Theory*, 10 (1), 37–52. doi: 10.1177/1368431006068755
Stein, M. (1998). *Transformation: emergence of the self*. College Station, TX: Texas A&M University Press.
Stevenson, A. (ed.) (2017) *Oxford English Dictionary*. Oxford: Oxford University Press.
Stolorow, R. (2006). *Intersubjectivity theory and intersubjective systems theory*. In R. Skelton (ed.), *The Edinburgh international encyclopaedia of psychoanalysis*. Edinburgh: Edinburgh University Press.
Stolorow, R. D. (1997). 'Dynamic, dyadic, intersubjective systems: an evolving paradigm for psychoanalysis'. *Psychoanalytic Psychology*, 14, 337–346.

Tilburg, V. M., and Vingerhoets, J. J. M. (eds.) (2005). *Psychological aspects of geographical moves: homesickness and acculturation stress*. Amsterdam: Amsterdam University Press.

Turner, B. S. (2002). 'Cosmopolitan virtue, globalization and patriotism'. *Theory, Culture and Society*, 19, 45–63.

United Nations High Commissioner for Refugees. (1951). 'Refugee convention'. Retrieved on 28th November at https://www.unhcr.org/1951-refugee-convention.html.

United Nations High Commissioner for Refugees. (2018). 'The global report'. Retrieved on 28th November at https://www.unhcr.org/the-global-report.html.

United Nations Universal Declaration of Human Rights. (2015). United Nations Universal Declaration of Human Rights'. Retrieved on 28th November at http://www.un.org/en/udhrbook/pdf/udhr_booklet_en_web.pdf.

Whitehead, A. N. (2004). *The concept of nature*. Amherst, NY: Prometheus Books, 2, 34.

Williams, R. (2018). *Jung: the basics*. London: Routledge.

Wilson, J. P., and Drozdek, B. (2004). *Broken spirits: the treatment of traumatized asylum seekers, refugees, war and torture victims*. New York, NY: Brunner-Routledge.

Winnicott, D. (1960a). 'The theory of the parent-child relationship'. *International Journal of Psychoanalysis*, 41, 585–595.

Winnicott, D. (1960b). 'Ego distortion in terms of true and false self'. In D. W. Winnicott (ed.), *The maturational process and the facilitating environment*. London: Hogarth Press, 1965.

Yehuda, R., Boisoneau, D., Lowy, M. T., and Giller, Jr. E. L. (1995). 'Dose–response changes in plasma cortisol and lymphocyte glucocorticoid receptors following dexamethasone administration in combat veterans with and without posttraumatic stress disorder'. *Archives of General Psychiatry*, 52, 583–593.

Yehuda, R., Halligan, S. L., and Grossman, R. (2001). 'Childhood trauma and risk for PTSD: relationship to intergenerational effects of trauma, parental PTSD, and cortisol excretion'. *Development and Psychopathology*, 13, 733–75.

Chapter 3

The Mexican-American cultural complex

Assessing the depth-psychological problems due to challenges of assimilation in American society

Valeria Céspedes Musso

Introduction

A few months before I moved to Germany, a colleague of mine said that I would soon be calling myself an 'American'. My colleague and I, both American but of Mexican descent, identified ourselves as Mexican or Latino. Indeed, living overseas has forced me to re-assess my ethnic identity as a light-skinned Latina and my own assimilation in my new country. This process led me to wonder how these questions were addressed within my own community. Is there a psychological complex surrounding identity and assimilation in the Mexican-American community? A number of studies have tackled various problems and aspects surrounding assimilation into American society by Mexican-Americans, or Americans of Mexican origin (Johnson, 1998; Lazear, 2007; Vasquez, 2010). What can be gleaned from this literature is that Americans of Mexican ancestry assimilate at a slower pace than other groups in the United States. This research has mainly focused on the socio-political, economic, and even the linguistic aspects of the problem of assimilation. In this paper, I will analyse the specific Mexican-American complex from an analytical psychological perspective, keeping in mind the question: where does this cultural complex stem from? Thomas Singer defines the *cultural complex* as 'emotionally charged aggregates of ideas and images that tend to cluster around an archetypal core and are shared by individuals within an identified collective' (Singer & Kaplinsky, 2010, p. 24). Moreover, cultural complexes operate in the personal and collective psyche and 'tend to be repetitive, autonomous, resist consciousness, and collect experience that confirms their historical point of view' (Singer and Kimbles, 2004, p. 6). The cultural complex allows us to understand and analyse the psychology of group conflict (ibid, p. 2) as well as historical traumas stemming from the group's ancestral roots. The ancestry of a group does not always coincide with the land in which people from a cultural group were born and raised, as indeed is the case for many Mexican-Americans. Yet, the conflict and trauma associated with the group's ancestral roots may follow them to their new land,[1] potentially, as I argue below, causing problems of adaption to the new society.

Part 1: Mexican-Americans: a brief history

An estimated 35 million Americans of Mexican origin represent the largest population of Hispanics in the United States,[2] with a high concentration residing in the Southwestern states. Mexican-Americans have ancestral roots in parts of the U.S. territory that once belonged to Mexico (Novas, 2007, p. 49). With the signing of the Treaty of Guadalupe Hidalgo – an agreement signed in 1848 between Mexico and the United States which ended the Mexican War – Utah, Nevada, Wyoming, New Mexico, Arizona, parts of Colorado, and California became part of the U.S. (ibid, p. 74). The old Mexican-American adage: 'We didn't cross the border. The border crossed us' refers to the geographic implications of the Treaty of Guadalupe Hidalgo. Scholar of Latino and Chicano studies, Elizabeth Coonrod Martínez (2007), states that literature on Mexican-Americans 'possesses the additional sense of occupation, and experience of evidencing the production of a people who have long-resided in an area that has come to be called "America" and the United States' (p. 12). This sense of 'occupation' perhaps stems from this historical moment when the initial contact between many Mexicans and the American society was involuntary, and as Joan W. Moore (1970) argues, the Mexican-American experience is one of conquest and colonialism.[3] The feeling of occupation becomes acute after the Mexican-American or Chicano movement of the late 1960s. However, before this period, Mexican-Americans were trying to assimilate into American society.

To understand the Mexican-American assimilation experience, we have to take a look at the historical relationship between Mexican-Americans' experience of race and identity and Anglo-Americans. According to historian Neil Foley (1998), many Mexicans had learned whiteness or 'whitening' before coming to the U.S. (1998, p. 56). Foley states that a complex hierarchical racial system in Mexico was formed – whites, Indians, and Mestizos – and Mestizos had an awkward position in this hierarchy, often hated by the Spanish and shunned by the Indians for being part Spanish (ibid, p. 56). After centuries of race-mixing or *mestizaje*, the Mexican government started to classify its citizens into different categories associated to the three aforementioned racial groups. Mestizos who were able to identify as Spanish distanced themselves from the Indians, thereby imitating Europeans and fostering 'the belief in the supremacy of European white culture over native Indian culture' (ibid, p. 56). This culture of racial separation between 'white' Mexicans and 'Indian' Mexicans was brought over to the United States from Mexico, and Mexican-Americans were mortified when Anglo-Americans made no effort to distinguish between the two categories (ibid, pp. 56–57). In 1933, for example, the Mexican consul in Dallas protested that one of its citizens was jailed 'with negro prisoners instead of with the Anglos' (ibid, p. 57). Before the development of the civil rights consciousness of the 1960s, being classified as Mexican was disfavoured in the United States (Johnson, 1998, p. 186). Mexican-American organisations like the League of United Latin American Citizens (LULAC) constructed new identities as 'Spanish American' or 'Latin American' in order to arrogate to themselves the privileges of whiteness (1997, p. 55). In the 1930s and 1940s, middle-class Mexican-Americans began to call themselves 'Spanish' and insisted on their whiteness; however, due to race-mixing with indigenous populations, Mexicans were by and large not regarded as 'white' and 'denied most of the rights and privileges that whiteness bestowed' (ibid, pp. 56–58).

It was during the 1960s Civil Rights era that a new generation of Mexican-Americans, called Chicanos and Chicanas, or politically aware Mexican-Americans, rejected the accommodationist strategies of the previous generations and 'sought empowerment through "brownness" and the return, symbolically at least, to Aztlan, the heritage of their Indian past'; moreover, Chicanos accused LULAC members and conservative Mexican-Americans of running away from their brownness (Foley, 1998, p. 65). It was at this time that several activists like Cesar Chavez advocated for the extension of labour rights to agricultural workers, many of whom were of Mexican origin and were systematically exploited, and others demonstrated and demanded that their Mexican identity and heritage be recognised and respected (Novas, 2007, p. 113).

In the 2010 U.S. Census, 44.3% of people of Mexican descent wrote, in reply to the question on their race, either 'Mexican' or 'mestizo' under the 'some other race' category, by-passing the other race categories such as white, black, Asian, American Indian, etc. (Buriel, 2012, p. 293). According to scholar of Latino Psychology Raymond Buriel, the choice of a non-white racial category may be related to a person's phenotype due to *mestizaje* which can range from 'very dark to very light with degrees of indigenous American Indian physical features' (ibid, p. 293). Moreover, Buriel argues that research on Mexican-Americans should take into account phenotype, and that outcome in the study of social acceptance, depression, and perceptions of prejudice and discrimination may vary 'due to the value and social privilege placed on light skin color in society' (ibid. p. 293). According to Jessica M. Vasquez, who studied the lives of middle-class, third-generation Mexican-Americans, 'Latinos in the United States predominately self-identify as "Hispanic" and/or "Latino" *in addition to* their national origin, but do not self-identify as "American"' (2010, p. 48, italics in original). In addition, Vasquez states that despite Mexican-Americans' increasing identification with Anglo-American culture, they 'do *not* lose their identity as a distinctive ethnic group as did many Euro-American immigrants by the second or third generation' (ibid, p. 48, italics in original). This is probably due in part to the continuous immigration flows from Mexico, or 'immigrant replenishment', 'which heightens the salience of race in the minds of immigrants and native-born alike' (ibid, p. 48). The diversity among Mexican-Americans – mixture of race, immigration and generational status, culture, education, political outlook, etc. – allows some Mexican-Americans to integrate easier than others, specifically those with lighter skin colour (ibid, p. 48). Indeed, research shows that white Mexican-Americans earn more money, attain a higher level of education, and report less incidences of discrimination than their darker-skinned counterparts (Buriel, 2012, p. 293).

Since the Treaty of Guadalupe Hidalgo, the issue of phenotype continues to follow Mexican-Americans into the 21st century, despite the (unsuccessful) assimilation efforts made by those in the last century to be accepted as white. It can be argued that the issue of assimilation is closely linked to people's phenotype and behind it lays the struggles, pain, frequent rejection, and even perhaps the trauma of a culture. It forms part of the cultural complex of this group, but it did not originate in the American Southwest, even though it is part of the narrative. It can be traced much earlier, specifically with the vicissitudes surrounding the lives of Doña Marina and Hernan Cortez, the symbolic parents of this newly formed race.

Part 2: A depth-psychological perspective on the cultural complex

Almost 500 years ago, there were no Mexicans, and therefore neither were there Mexican-Americans. At an ancient Aztec ceremonial site, the Plaza de Las Tres Culturas in Mexico City, an inscription can be read on a monument with the following text:

> On this site on the night of August 13, 1521, heroically taken by Cortez, valiantly defended by Cuahutemoc, it was neither defeat nor victory, but the painful birth of the Mexican people.
>
> (Buriel, 2002, p. 292)

Mexicans and Mexican-Americans are predominately a mestizo or hybrid population made up of 'interminable blending of Indian and Spaniard' that began in 1519 when Hernan Cortez set foot in Mexico (in ibid). According to the limited historical documentation available on Doña Marina, she came from a Mexican indigenous tribe. She was either sold or given away as a child (Petty, 2000, p. 121). Doña Marina became Herman Cortez's interpreter and mistress during the conquest of Mexico. She was given to Cortez as a young woman as a gift from local Indian leaders. Marina proved useful to Cortez as she spoke Spanish, Mayan, and Nahuatl. Paintings and accounts of Marina show that she was always by Cortez's side and that her skill as a translator helped him defeat Montezuma, 'furthering the cause of the Spanish conquest in Mexico' (ibid, p. 122). Out of their sexual relationship, Marina gave birth to a son, Martin, making him the first Mexican mestizo. Sometime after Martin's birth, Cortez gave her to one of his captains to marry.

Doña Marina, also known as Malinche or Malintzin (the latter being her indigenous name), was blamed for the conquest due to her complicity with Cortez, who conquered the indigenous population and destroyed their culture (Wyatt, 1995, p. 248). As Cherrie Moraga (1986) states, '[e]ver since, brown men have been accusing her of betraying her race, and over the centuries continue to blame her entire sex for this "transgression"' (1986, pp. 174–75). Moreover, she is slandered as La Vendida, a sell-out to the white race and La Chingada, meaning the 'fucked one' (ibid). Cortez, the father of the mestizo race, is often also seen in a negative light. Cortez and the Spanish conquistadores were responsible for the brutalisation of the native Indian population and enforced religious conversions (Novas, 2007, p. 52). Moreover, Cortez offered the early colonist *encomiendas* or grants that afforded them ownership and control over native land and as many as 20,000 native people to cultivate the land, a system which essentially constituted the codification of slavery in Mexico (ibid). Doña Marina and Herman Cortez make up the parental images of the new race. One way of examining these parental images is in relation to the *coniunctio*: by doing so, it is possible to paint a picture of Mexican Americans' psychological state. According to Andrew Samuels (1993) in *The Political Psyche*, the image of the father and mother suggests '*a self-regulated diagnostic of the person's psychopolitical state at any moment*' (p. 167, italics in original). The image of the copulating parents is a metaphor for a *coniunctio oppositorum*, Latin for conjunction of opposites (ibid, p. 168). Jung derived the concept of the *coniunctio* from alchemy symbolising the union of opposites of the internal state of being, the marriage of which can birth about a new attitude or ego position; he described the *coniunctio* as 'the gradual transformation of the archetype into a psychological process which, in theory, we can call a combination of conscious and unconscious processes' (Jung, 1951, para. 297). Samuels characterises it with the Freudian term of primal scene. When the primal scene is reflected as fertile – that is, the projection of it – it is vital, and the 'psyche is trying to express its multifarious and variegated nature – and also its oneness and integration' (ibid, p. 168). Conversely, if the primal scene is one-sided it can be disharmonious, reflecting a pattern of exclusion and defeat (ibid, p. 167). We have two parents who represent the origins of the Mexican/Mexican-American mestizo, and both are negative or bad parental images – the mother is perceived as the betrayal and the father as the destroyer. This union can be seen as marking the initial trauma of Mexican-American ancestral roots. Furthermore, it can be argued that the parental images reflect a disharmonious state, and perhaps due to this imbalanced *coniunctio*, it may have had psychological implications for people of Mexican origin particularly in the adaptive patterns of their environment.

Out of the Mexican-American movement of the 1960s, the myth of Aztlán was created. This cultural myth is a conceptual construct representing the lost homeland of Mexican-Americans and 'said to be the Aztecs' place of origin' (de Alba, 2004, p. 117). In Alicia Gaspar de Alba's article 'No Place like Aztlan', she states,

> An imaginary homeland ... is not a place, but a conceptual *space* that only perpetuates our "non-existence" ... rather than locate us bodily in the land base that we claim as our place of origin, it dislocates our identity from that place, and leaves our bodies out of the equation of signifiers that connect our multiple and diverse "moments of presence"
> (ibid, p. 135, italics in original).

Aztlán is not a physical place where one can travel to. However, it was a necessary myth created during a period of political and social unrest in the United States, and a time when Mexican-Americans needed to forge an identity rooted in the American Southwest. The creation of the myth of Aztlán was a psychological need that compensated the lack of rootedness and *home*. There is a famous saying within the Mexican-American community which expresses this sentiment: 'we are neither from here, nor from there'; that is, they don't belong or feel at home neither in the U.S. nor in Mexico. In Renos Papadopoulos' (2002) work on refugees, he identifies the 'deep sense of nostalgic yearning' for restoring the loss of home (p. 15). Although Mexican-Americans are not classified as refugees, I think diaspora groups share this and other similar afflictions. Papadopoulos describes nostalgia as the hurt, pain, sickness, and suffering that a person experiences in wanting to go home (ibid). He says that the

> absence of home creates a gap in refugees which makes them feel uncontained and they then look around to fill the gap, to make up for that loss, to re-create the protective and containing membrane of home ... *de facto*, most homes provide a continuity that enables co-existence between many opposites ... [t]he function of home is important in minimizing or even avoiding archaic and fundamental forms of splitting
>
> (ibid, pp. 16-17).

Perhaps there is an archaic or fundamental split in the collective unconscious of Mexican-Americans rooted in the symbolic union of the parental images. The projection of the archetype of home on Aztlán may reflect the feminine or mother aspect. According to de Alba (2004), '[a]s a lost land, Aztlán is a metaphor for the vanquished Indian mother – the raped, abject mother iconographed by La Malinche' (p. 121).

In Mario Jacoby's (1985) *Longing for Paradise*, Jacoby analyses the image of Paradise, and he interprets it 'as an image symbolic of shelter and security with the embracing, supporting, nurturing Maternal'; moreover, it 'represents a longing for the unitary reality which precedes the development of each individual consciousness' (Jacoby, 1985, p. 194). The 'unitary reality' embraces mother and infant, and Jacoby states that the infant does not perceive the mother as a 'separate, independent entity' (ibid, p. 27). Erich Neumann characterises this as the pre-conscious stage of infancy, and that the idea of Paradise is linked to this stage, as he states,

> With the emergence of the fully-fledged ego, the paradisal situation is abolished; the infantile condition, in which life was regulated by something ampler and more embracing, is at an end, and with it the natural dependence on that ample embrace
>
> (Neumann, 1993, pp. 114–115).

The paradisal 'primal unity' is lost when the infant begins to realise that the mother is an independent 'object' (Jacoby, 1985, p. 31). Studies on infant development have showed the important role of the mother in the early stages of infancy, such as Melanie Klein's theory of 'parts objects' of the mother, and D. W. Winnicott's double function of the mother, 'object mother' and 'environment mother'.[4] According to Jacoby,

> From the standpoint of Analytical Psychology, ... the entire early phase of unitary reality and the primal relationship occurs under the dominance of the mother archetype ... we are dealing here with the experience of 'the Maternal' itself, the archetypal disposition and need to experience those things which are generally ascribed to the realm of the Maternal. The child experiences the Maternal long before it grows aware of the individuality of its own personal mother (1985, p. 35).

Jacoby and Neumann seem to suggest that the idea of Paradise exists in the preconscious stage of the individual, and that the symbiotic relationship between mother and infant which existed in the early phase, reflect yearnings and nostalgia of this initial paradisal unity. Jung traces this idea to the early image of the archetypal dream of paradise, or Golden Age, 'where everything is provided in abundance for everyone, and a great, just, and wise chief rules over a human kindergarten' (Jung, 1972, p. 85). Of course, the primal relationship is between a real mother and child and the theory is applied clinically to individuals. However, applying this theory on the collective and symbolic relationship between Mexican-Americans and Doña Marina may be worthwhile exploring. In fact, collective trauma may be passed down from one generation to another, an idea that has been explored by Lawrence Alschuler (2006). In *The Psychopolitics of Liberation*, Alschuler presents the concept of the 'soul wound'. Citing the work of Eduardo and Bonnie Duran's study on the psychology of Native Americans and the implications of the conquest of America, Alschuler states that the traumas from the past are transmitted intergenerationally, deepening the 'soul wound' from the initial trauma that took place at the time (p. 72). According to Alschuler, a traumatic historical event, such as a colonial conquest, is a wounding experience that enlarges an existing cultural complex that, in turn, becomes a vehicle for collective memory and emotions, carrying over many generations. When a renewed trauma activates the cultural complex, members of the group experience 'intense collective emotions' (in Alschuler, p. 75).

The projection of Aztlán may reflect the suffering and pain of the non-containing American environment, perhaps adding to the initial trauma of the non-containing negative mother image of Doña Marina/Malintzin. Well-being and security are needed in the primal relationship, and it is dependent on the maternal care of the person in charge (Jacoby, 1985, p. 43). Jacoby (1985) states that disturbances of the primal relationship 'are characterised in greater or lesser degree by a predominance of the archetypal "terrible mother" image, resulting in the rejection of one's "own inner vitality and mistrustful isolation from their environment"' (ibid, p. 46). As I mentioned earlier, historically Mexican-Americans pushed hard to be accepted as part of the white race. But due to their phenotypic diversity, Mexican-Americans were difficult to classify and the dominant culture never accepted them as white. The indigenous brown skin mother is a shadow aspect of the Mexican-American cultural complex as well as part of the shadow of white Americans. For the Mexican-Americans, the dark mother blocks access and entrance to the Anglo/European American world, and as a Great Mother symbol, Malintzin, maintains her rule 'preventing her offspring from achieving independence' (Neumann, 1963, p. 68). She holds on tightly like the devouring Coatlicue, the Meso-American serpent and the symbol of the instinctual in its collective, impersonal, prehumanity, the chthonic, and the feminine. She keeps her offspring in the dark and in the old world of the Aztec kings and queens, a world in need of constant blood sacrifice and dismemberment in exchange for life and rebirth; a princess herself,[5] it is as if she is saying 'do not dishonour me'. The terrible mother aspect, Malintzin, places metaphorically 'el nopel en la frente', or the cactus on the forehead, a Mexican phrase connoting that one's appearance prevents assimilation into the Anglo world, the symbol of the cactus representing Mexican culture. Only light-skinned Mexican-Americans are able to escape the wrath of the terrible mother and gain access to the American dream.

For white Americans, the shadow aspect of the dark/brown skin is projected onto the Mexican-American. In his study of racial divisions of white and black Americans and drawing on the work of Frantz Fanon (1968) on colonial oppression, Walter Odajnyk (1976) describes white racism as 'collective shadow projections that influence Black's self-image, a part of their oppressed consciousness' (pp. 82–83). Moreover, '[m]embers of shadow-bearing groups are usually demoralized and depressed' (ibid). To the psychological undifferentiated person who remains unconscious of his shadow, there will always be a need to make enemies (ibid, p. 78). Being forced to carry the shadow side of the dominant culture, black Americans came 'to hate and despised [themselves] and so cooperated in [their] own deprecation and subjugation' (ibid, p. 83). According to Neil Foley (1998), to the average white person in America 'race mixing was a menace to the purity of the Nordic race' and Spaniards mixing their blood with Indians and Africans 'removed themselves from the domain of whiteness' (Foley 1998, p. 57). Historically, white Americans perceived black Americans as unintelligent, primitive, sub-human, and inferior to whites. Mexican-Americans have been perceived as lazy, uneducated, dirty, and as criminals. This perception has been further amplified under the Trump era. Trump's view of Mexican immigrants as 'rapists', 'drug-dealers', and 'bad hombres' has affected Mexican-Americans. Discrimination has increased in the past two years, and since his election, their overall well-being has been adversely affected (Ritter and Tsabutashvili, 2017). For example, one Mexican-American woman reported that while taking money from the ATM she was asked if she was an American citizen. Others claimed they were asked if they spoke English. As a group, Mexican-Americans are not fully American; they are kept as 'Other' both from the terrible mother and from the shadow of white Americans.

There is another aspect of Doña Marina as the terrible mother that is more commonly known. In this manifestation, she is seen as the betrayer of the indigenous race. According to Octavio Paz, the Mexican writer and poet, Doña Marina is the representation of the violated Mother and the Conquest. He states,

> Doña Marina becomes a figure representing the Indian women who were fascinated, violated, or seduced by the Spaniards. And, as a small boy will not forgive his mother if she abandons him to search for his father, the Mexican people have not forgiven La Malinche for her betrayal
>
> (1967, p. 77).

On Independence Day of 1861, Mexican politician and writer, Ignacio Ramirez 'reminded the celebrants that Mexicans owed their defeat to Malintzin – Cortes's whore' (in Alarcón 1989, p. 58). Being called a malinche is used as an insult,[6] and according to Norman Alarcón (1989), '[a]mong people of Mexican descent ... anyone who has transgressed the boundaries of perceived group interests and values often has been called a *malinche* or *malinchista*' (Alarcón 1989, p. 60, italics in original).

There is anger and deep hatred towards the indigenous mother for her complicity in the destruction and fall of the Aztec civilisation. As Alarcón (1989) states, 'Malintzin may be compared to Eve, especially when she is viewed as the originator of the Mexican people's fall from grace and the procreator of a "fallen" people' (Alarcón 1989, p. 58). The paradisal world of Aztec civilisation fell, conquered and destroyed by an invader and foreigner. Perhaps this perspective points to a miscegenation taboo from the point of view of people of Mexican descent, albeit an unconscious one. From the writings of Bernal Díaz del Castillo, Cortez's loyal lieutenant, we know that the Mexican city of Tenochtitlan was described as glorious for its beauty, cleanliness, and good organisation. Bernal Díaz recalled feeling astounded when he first entered Tenochtitlan,

> We saw all those cities and villages built in the water, and other great towns on dry land, and that straight and level causeway leading to Mexico. ... These great towns and pyramids and buildings rising from the water, all made of stone, seemed like an enchanted vision. ... Indeed, some of our soldiers asked whether it was not all a dream. ... It was all so wonderful that I do not know how to describe this first glimpse of things never heard of, seen or dreamed of before.
>
> (in Boone, 1994, pp. 16–17)

Aside from the ritual human sacrifices (Townsend, 2009, p. 19), Bernal Díaz seems to describe a wonderous and enchanted world where stones were 'whitened' and 'polished'. Tenochtitlan was a type of Garden of Eden, and the entry of the Spanish along with their diseases, mistreatment, and exploitation of the people and land forever destroyed this paradisal world. For the Mexican psyche, the Spanish represent the end of purity and innocence, and *mestizaje* is a reminder of the mixing of the one true race of the paradisal land with the contaminated and invading European. Similar to the negative image ascribed to Eve, Doña Marina has been viewed as treacherous and a sell-out over the centuries. Out of her betrayal was born a race marred with conflict and suffering, a people who navigate the world in hopes of recovering the lost paradise. As Mario Jacoby (1985) states: the 'longing for freedom from conflict, suffering and deprivation is an eternal human dream of great emotional power. It is the dream of total happiness, embodied in almost all cultures in the myth of Paradise' (p. vii). For the cultural complex of the Mexican mestizo, this is their myth of Paradise, marking at the same time the initial psychic pain and trauma of a culture. The negative mother is also perceived as weak, as she is seen as 'fascinated' and 'seduced' by the Spaniards and by Cortez who, after Doña Marina is no longer of use to him, passes her off to one of his subordinate captains. The relationship between the primal parents is unequal and imbalanced; that is, the *coniunctio* is reflected as imbalance and disharmonious. If the parental relationship had been historically perceived as loving and equal and the fall of Tenochtitlan had not happened brutally as it did, perhaps the psychic trauma created from this event would have been avoided.

Part of the cultural complex is the longing for the restoration of the paradisal city of Tenochtitlan; in psychological language, it is the recovery of innocence after trauma. In *Trauma and the Soul* (2013), Donald Kalsched discusses how trauma creates an interruption of the normal processes which allows 'an embodied, true self' come into being (p. 19). By applying developmental objects–relations and attachment theory, Kalsched argues that 'good enough' mothering (D. W. Winnicott's phrase) allows the infant to mediate 'descent from omnipotence to the reality principle, from innocence to experience', resulting in a 'growing ego-strength' and by becoming 'a self as a coherent unit or whole person' (ibid, pp. 17–18). Trauma constitutes a loss of soul or a dis-integrated personality due to the trauma's prevention of the indwelling of the soul into the body, and Kalsched argues that the 'soul cannot thrive and grow in the fragmented personality'; instead, it creates a second world or a 'mytho-poetic matrix for the soul' (ibid, pp. 17–19). Trauma survivors report feeling 'broken' or that their innocence is lost forever; yet Kalsched states that their 'vital spark' can be recovered (ibid, pp. 19–20).

A detailed discussion of the possibility for Mexican-Americans of recovering innocence and the 'vital spark' of the collective is beyond the scope of this paper. However, the next part looks at the contemporary psychological implications of colonial trauma originating from the ancestral past of Mexican-Americans. Against the psychological theoretical background presented, I wonder if the initial psychic pain and trauma of the cultural complex of Mexican-Americans is projected onto the United States. I hypothesise that under the current U.S. Administration which has been hostile towards people of Mexican descent, the bad father image, replacing the original father image of Cortez of the *coniunctio*, is now represented by President Trump. In the next part, I present a small set of in-depth interviews all of which were conducted during the course of 2018.

Part 3: Interviews

The approach I use for the qualitative interviews derives from a psycho-social research methodology that has been used in the recent works of Brodersen (2016), Roper (2003), and Currie (2010), to name a few. This interview methodology assigns a high degree of importance to oral history and to the 'usefulness of narrative forms as opening new research avenues', thereby allowing for 'a collaborative, *horizontal* inter-subjective relationship between the researcher and the researched' (Brodersen, 2016, p. 106, italics in original).

In this part, I introduce and discuss interviews with four adults of Mexican descent, three from California and one from Texas. Three of the subjects are second generation Mexican-Americans, that is, born in the U.S. from foreign parents, while the fourth subject is a third generation Mexican-American. Two of the participants are female and two are male. As agreed with the subjects, their identities will not be disclosed. All interviews were conducted via FaceTime during the second half of 2018 and lasted approximately 70 minutes. Each person interviewed was asked a series of questions directly relating to their personal experience growing up as Mexican-American in the United States.

Prior to conducting the interviews, I hypothesised that Mexican-Americans would feel alienated by the dominant culture under the Trump administration. However, the results of the interviews suggest the contrary: all the interviewees reported feeling accepted by the dominant culture despite the projection of otherness onto them.

There was phenotypic diversity within the interviewee sample. When asked about their racial identity, two of the four interviewees, who we will refer to with the fictional names of 'Veronica Lopez' and 'Sergio Hernandez', identified as Mexican or Latino, while the other two identified as white. A third subject, who we will refer to as 'Tom Gomez', identified himself racially as white, but said that he was ethnically Mexican. The fourth subject, who we will call 'Rebecca Munoz', also identifies as Mexican or Latino, but she also states that she identifies as white due to her European background. Both Tom Gomez and Rebecca Munoz reported that they were 'not perceived as Mexican'. Tom Gomez stated that he can pass as white or Arab, while Rebecca Munoz has been perceived as Swedish or, more generically, as a person with European background. Sergio Hernandez and Veronica Lopez reported that they were 'perceived as Mexican' or Latino. It was not a surprise that some of the interviewees had experienced discrimination due to phenotype. Both of the male interviewees reported experiencing direct discrimination, while Veronica Lopez claims she has personally witnessed discrimination against Mexicans. For example, Tom Gomez was once called a 'beaner', a derogatory word used against Mexicans. Sergio Hernandez described a time when he was pulled over by a border patrol agent while on his way to Disneyland. The agent asked to search his car for drugs, and feeling that he could not refuse him, Sergio Hernandez got out of the car and allowed him to search it. When the search was over, Sergio Hernandez asked the border patrol agent if he had pulled him over because of the way he looked. The border patrol agent said that his appearance was not the reason, but Sergio Hernandez was convinced that he was singled out from the other drivers on the road.

All four interviewees acknowledged the tense political climate under President Trump and the hostilities towards Mexicans which emerged with the Trump presidency. However, despite this political environment, it did not seem to deter them from embracing their American identity in some form. Rebecca Munoz stated that she identifies as Mexican-American, but identifies as American when travelling outside of the U.S. At first, Veronica Lopez was hesitant to identify herself as an American. When asked where she is from, she stated that she typically replies that she is 'from LA [and] my family is from Mexico'. Tom Gomez responded that the Mexican and American culture are 'ingrained in me I can't separate the two.' It seems the interviewees are able to navigate both the Mexican and American community. Jessica M. Vasquez (2010) describes this as 'flexible ethnicity' or 'the ability to navigate different social worlds, that is, mainstream U.S. culture and a Mexican-oriented community' (p. 58). According to Vasquez, flexible ethnicity is common for many third-generation Mexican-Americans (ibid). The capacity for all four interviewees to navigate both worlds may be due to them being 'structurally assimilated' (education and occupation) and 'linguistically assimilated' (language) (Gordon 1964). Tom Gomez stated that his acceptance in the U.S. has not been affected because as he says, 'I don't fit into the stereotypes that someone might use to discriminate against me … I think if I were darker skin, if I wasn't as educated, if I didn't speak the way I speak … things would be different'. Veronica Lopez says that she feels fully accepted and this is due in large part to her level of education. Even though all the interviewees reported that they felt accepted in American society, on the question of feeling integrated in the U.S., two of the interviewees could not separate the American culture from the Mexican one. Tom Gomez: 'Do I feel fully American? No, because I'm not. Just by virtue of having a Mexican heritage and growing in the Mexican culture. There is always that part of me that is not fully American.' Rebecca Munoz stated that she feels a part of both the American and Mexican culture.

Conclusion

The results of the qualitative research were surprising. I theorised that a Trump presidency would have created 'intense collective emotions' and reactivated the cultural complex of Mexican-Americans, pushing them towards alienation, and in doing so, projecting the negative-father image onto President Trump. By doing so, there would have been a move towards the indigenous Mexican mother in some manifested form, similar to the creation of the Myth of Aztlán during the Mexican-American movement of the 1960s. Instead, all of the interviewees reported feeling accepted in American society and self-identified as American; in turn, at least psychologically, rejecting or going against the primal mother, Malintzin. It is possible that there is not a constellation in the cultural unconscious – at least not yet. At the same time, the sample size of the pool of interviewees is very small, thus not necessarily representative of the general population of Mexican-Americans, such that the qualitative research may not reflect the full extent of the overall anger felt by Mexican-Americans (Pantoja, 2018). Nonetheless, the interviews provide some interesting insight, which deserves to be further investigated. While the interviewees self-identified as American, at the same time they do not feel completely American, and they acknowledge and embrace their Mexican culture. Perhaps Mexican-Americans have learned to cope with the projection of otherness onto them by the dominant culture as a result of having embraced their ancestral roots. Rebecca Munoz stated that she feels she can embrace her Mexican culture because she sees that the majority of Americans, particularly recent immigrants from countries other than Mexico, have a 'dual-background'; that is, they embrace their American culture as well as their culture of origin. Perhaps there is a new Zeitgeist prevailing in the U.S. that allows for one's cultural agency. In her book *Borderlands/La Frontera* (1987), Gloria Anzaldúa creates a 'mythos' of mestizaje by challenging enforced paradigms established through conceptual metaphors and by consciously trying to change them. This involved Anzaldúa having a confrontation with Coatlicue in the unconscious. Subsequently, this process 'allows one to reclaim one's voice and instinct in order to name a source or potential source of oppression, even within one's own psyche' and thus freeing the individual from the colonised inner self (Aigner-Varoz, 2000, p. 59; Anzaldúa, 1987).

I have taken a speculative approach in my analysis of the cultural complex of Mexican-Americans. The question addressed is complex, and the ideas explored in this paper may need to be further expounded and expanded on, aspects such as the amplification of the parental images, specifically Cortez, miscegenation taboo, and the recovery of innocence. There is vast scholarly work on assimilation and Mexican-Americans, and it is my hope that the depth-psychological analysis presented here will contribute to provide further insights on aspects previously neglected in the interpretation of these problems, thus representing a valuable complement to this scholarship.

Notes

1 Jungian analyst Luigi Zoga (2004) has written on the cultural complex of Latin America, pointing to the historical meeting between Cortes and Montezuma; and a complex whose origins stem from the abuse and resulting trauma inflicted by Cortes and the Spaniards against the Aztecs. Zoga writes, 'From a psychological point of view, what has happened is beyond remedy or repair. It will transmit itself to what remains of Montezuma's life, to his subjects, and, to an extent that is probably underestimated, *to his descendants*, in what has become s truly monstrous cultural complex' (p. 88; italics not in original). I argue that Montezuma's descendants include Americans of Mexican descent.
2 United States Census Bureau. 'Facts for Features: Hispanic Heritage Month 2017.' RELEASE NUMBER CB17-FF.17. August 17, 2017.
3 In her article, Moore (1970) identifies three types of colonialism experience by Mexican-Americans in the states of California, New Mexico, and Texas and how

variations of colonialism in these 'culture areas' effects political participation and organisation.
4 Melanie Klein *The Psychoanalysis of Children*. New York: Dell, 1976; D. W. Winnicott *The Maturational Process and the Facilitating Environment*. New York: International University Press, 1965.
5 Some historians assert that Marina was an 'Indian princess', see Petty, 2000.
6 As a recent example, during the show *Futbol Picante*, which airs on ESPN, one of the TV sportscasters was outraged at how Mexican player Javier Hernández had been treated by the Manchester United coach. But sports journalist José Ramón Fernández sided with Manchester United. That's when the co-host threw the insult: perhaps Fernández was a *malinchista*, which means a traitor to one's own people, someone who prefers a foreign culture over his own. The comment spread throughout the world. One person said, 'I used to respect him, but he has turned into a crazy old malinchista!' (NPR, 2015).

References

Aigner-Varoz, Erika. (2000). 'Metaphors of a mestiza consciousness: Anzaldúa's borderlands/la frontera'. *MELUS*, 25 (2), 47–62.
Alarcón, Norman. (1989). 'Traddutora, Traditora: A Paradigmatic Figure of Chicana Feminism. *Cultural Critique*, The Construction of Gender and Modes of Social Division. (Autumn, 1989). No.13, 57–87.
Alschuler, Lawrence R. (2006). *The Psychopolitics of Liberation: Political Consciousness from a Jungian Perspective*. New York, NY: Palgrave Macmillian.
Anzaldúa, Gloria. (1987). *Borderlands/La Frontera: the new mestiza*. San Francisco, CA: Aunt Lute Books.
Boone, Elizabeth Hill. (1994). *The Aztec world*. Jeremy A. Sabloff (ed.). Washington, DC: St. Remy Press and Smithsonian Institution.
Brodersen, Elizabeth. (2016). *Laws of inheritance: a post-Jungian study of twins and the relationship between the first and other(s)*. London/New York, NY: Routledge.
Buriel, Raymond. (2012). 'Historical, social-cultural, and conceptual issues to consider when researching Mexican American children and families, and other Latino subgroups'. *Psychosocial Intervention*, 21 (3), 291–303.
Currie, G. (2010). *Narratives and narrators, a philosophy of stories*. Oxford/New York, NY: Oxford University Press.
de Alba, Alicia Gaspar. (2004). 'There's no place like Aztlán: embodied aesthetics in chicana art'. *CR: The New Centennial Review*, 4 (2), 103–140.
Fanon, Frantz. (1968). *The wretched of the Earth*. New York, NY: Grove Press.
Foley, Neil. (1998). 'Becoming hispanic: Mexican-Americans and the faustian pact with whiteness'. In Neil Foley (ed.), *New directions in Mexican American studies*. Austin, TX: University of Texas Press.
Gordon, Milton Myron. (1964). *Assimilation in American life: the role of race, religion, and national origins*. New York: New York University Press.
Jacoby, Mario A. (1985). *Longing for paradise: psychological perspectives on an archetype*. Translated by Myron B. Gubitz. Boston, MA: Sigo Press.
Johnson, Kevin R. (1998). 'Melting pot or ring of fire: assimilation and the Mexican-American experience'. *Berkeley La Raza Law Journal*, 10 (1), P.227.
Jung, C. G. (1951). 'The psychology of the child archetype'. In *Collected works, Vol. 9i, The archetypes of the unconscious* (2nd ed.). Princeton, NJ: Princeton University Press, 1991.

Jung, C. G. (1972). *Man and his symbols*. London: Aldus Books.
Kalsched, Donald. (2013). *Trauma and the soul: a psycho-spiritual approach to human development and its interruption*. London/New York: Routledge.
Klein, M. (1976). *The psychoanalysis of children*. New York, NY: Dell.
Lazear, P. Edward. (2007). 'Mexican assimilation in the United States'. In George J. Borjas (ed.), *Mexican immigration to the United States*. Chicago/London: The University of Chicago Press.
Martinez, Elizabeth Coonrod. (2007). 'Resistance, revolution, and recuperation: the literary production of the Mestizo/Mexican-American/Chicano'. In Carlota Caulfield and Darién J. Davis (eds.), *A companion to US Latino literatures*. Rochester, NY: Tamesis.
Moore, Joan W. (1970). 'Colonialism: the case of the Mexican-Americans'. *Social Problems*, 17 (4), 463–472.
Moraga, Cherríe. (1986). 'From a long line of vendidas: chicanas and feminism'. In Teresa de Lauretis (ed.), *Feminist studies/critical studies*. Bloomington, IN: Indiana University Press.
Neumann, Erich. (1963). *The great mother: an analysis of the archetype*. Translated by Ralph Manheim (2nd ed.). Princeton, NJ: Princeton University Press.
Neumann, Erich. (1993). *The origins and history of consciousness*. Translated by R. F. Hull. Princeton, NJ: Princeton University Press.
Novas, Himilce. (2007). *Everything you need to know about Latino history*. New York, NY: A Blume Book.
Odajnyk, Walter V. (1976). *Jung and politics: the political and social ideas of C. G. Jung*. New York, NY: New York University Press.
Pantoja, Adrian. 'Latino voters will turn anger into action in the 2018 congressional midterm elections'. In *Latino Decisions*. July 30, 2018.https://latinodecisions.com/blog/latinos-voters-will-turn-anger-into-action-in-the-2018-congressional-midterm-elections/
Papadopoulos, Renos. (2002). 'Refugees, home, and trauma'. In R. K. Papadopoulos (ed.), *Therapeutic care for refugees: no place like home*. London: Karnac.
Paz, Octavio. (1967). *The labyrinth of solitude*. Translated by Lysander Kemp. 1961. London: Penguin.
Petty, Leslie. (2000). 'The 'dual'-ing images of la malinche and la virgin de Guadalupe in Cisnero's *The House on Mango Street*'. *Melus*, 25 (2), 119–132.
Ritter, Zacc, and Tsabutashvili, Dato. 'Hispanics' emotional well-being during the Trump Era'. In *Gallup*. August 17, 2017.
Roper, M. (2003). 'Analysing the analysed: transference and counter-transference in the oral history encounter'. *Oral History*, 31 (2), P. 33. Oxford: Oxford University Press.
Samuels, Andrew. (1993). *The political psyche*. London/New York, NY: Routledge.
Singer, Thomas, and Kimbles, Samuel L. (2004). 'Introduction'. In Thomas Singer and Samuel L. Kimbles (eds.), *The cultural complex: contemporary Jungian perspectives on psyche and society*. London/New York, NY: Routledge.
Singer, Thomas, and Catherine Kaplinsky. (2010). 'The cultural complex'. In Murray Stein (ed.), *Jungian psychoanalysis: working in the spirit of C. G. Jung*. Chicago, IL: Open Court Publishing, pp. 23–37.
Townsend, Richard F. (2009). *The Aztecs*. 3rd ed. London: Thames & Hudson.
United States Census Bureau. 'Facts for features: Hispanic Heritage Month 2017'. RELEASE NUMBER CB17-FF.17. August 17, 2017.
Vasquez, Jessica M. (2010). 'Blurred borders for some but not 'others': racialization, 'flexible ethnicity', gender, and third generation Mexican American identity'. *Sociological Perspectives*, 53 (1), 45–71.

Winnicott, D. M. (1965). *The maturation process and the facilitating environment*. New York, NY: International University Press.

Wyatt, Jean. (1995). 'On not being la malinche: border negotiations of gender in Sandra's Cisneros's 'Never Marry a Mexican' and 'Woman Hollering Creek'. *Tulsa Studies in Women's Literature*, 14 (2), 243–271.

Zoga, Luigi. (2004). 'Trauma and abuse: the development of a cultural complex in the history of Latin America'. In Thomas Singer and Samuel L. Kimbles (eds.), *The cultural complex: contemporary Jungian perspectives on psyche and society*. London/ New York, NY: Routledge.

Chapter 4

Hidden in plain sight
How therapists miss cultural trauma in trans-cultural white clients

Rachael A. Vaughan

Introduction

There is a widespread tendency, at least in the United States, where I practice and teach, to assume that white people are free of ethnicity. Indeed, the experience of many American whites seems to *be* the experience of no ethnicity: they have never reflected on it, and don't see themselves as having it. Ethnicity—and culture along with it—is projected onto so-called People of Colour (DiAngelo, 2018; Irving, 2014; Lee, 1994; Lee, 2003; Wise, 2004).

In the Multicultural Counselling classes I teach at the California Institute of Integral Studies in San Francisco, my white students frequently describe themselves as being like white bread: tasteless, without texture. They perceive themselves as having no culture at all. They tend to be monolingual in English, and either they don't know where their ancestors came from, or in a somewhat desperate fetishisation of origin, they recite such a mix of ancestry that it becomes meaningless. Such as 'I'm one-eighth Scots, one-eighth Latvian, one-sixteenth Portuguese …'. There's a self-deprecation and regret in their narrative of lost origins, which is greatly saddening to witness. These white American students seem culturally lost.

The shedding of ethnicity and cultural specificity in American whites was, of course, by no means accidental (Guess, 2006). Photographs of people arriving at Ellis Island—the first point of disembarkation into the US in the early twentieth century—show people in their traditional national and regional costumes.[1] They are wearing tall lace bonnets, embroidered vests, astrakhan coats, and tribal jewellery. The price of admission to the middle class in the US at that time was the loss of all of that ethnic inheritance. If the immigrant sacrificed his or her culture, changed their name, had sufficiently pale skin, and acquired enough money, they could become reclassified as white.

Because this elision of ethnicity and culture is so widespread among American whites, and because Americans tend to centre their own world-view, most assume that the experience of white people from 'the rest of the world' (Derrida, 1991) mirrors theirs.[2] Thus, the ethnic and cultural specificity of trans-national, non-American whites goes under the radar in general in the US, and the therapy consulting room is no exception: the cultural experience of white clients is often not so much ignored as foreclosed on by the therapist's assumption that only clients of colour would have cultural material to explore.

Dr Salman Akhtar—an American Freudian born in India—mentions this in a videoed presentation on the Trauma of Dislocation (Akhtar, 2007), in which he discusses his analysis of an Irish Australian who moved to the US, and whose accent changed according to the memories she was discussing. He remarks that no other analyst had noticed the cultural layer of her experience, or her migration trauma—because they had simply classed her as white, and therefore did not consider anything else as relevant.

Cultural complexes

I came to realise all this personally when I arrived in the US as an immigrant myself. It was difficult to find the words to cogently express the fact that my internal experience was different from the experiences described by white Americans, until I came across the related concepts of the cultural complex and the phantom narrative in the work of Samuel Kimbles and Thomas Singer (Kimbles, 2014; Singer and Kimbles, 2004). These concepts enabled me to conceptualise my different experience as the result of the fact that I participate in a different set of cultural complexes, with a different set of phantom narratives.

Cultural complexes are similar to personal complexes in that they consist in 'emotionally charged aggregates of ideas and images ... [clustered] around an archetypal core', but unlike the personal complex, they are shared by people within an identifiable group (Singer and Kaplinsky, 2010). This idea of the cultural complex builds on Joseph Henderson's work on the cultural unconscious, itself defined as a layer of historical memory lying between the collective unconscious and the 'manifest pattern' or 'collective ego' of the culture (Henderson, 2010).[3] Individuals within ethnic and cultural groups share an unconscious layer, within which are shared complexes that represent the memory of the group. Like personal complexes, the cultural complexes tend to form around traumas, but in this case they are collective traumas.

Cultural complexes have a few specific characteristics. First, they manifest in powerful affect and reactive behaviour. Second, they are hard to make and keep conscious. Third, they accumulate experiences that validate their point of view and so create a set of self-affirming ancestral narratives. Fourth, they give rise to simplistic, black and white, often self-righteous attitudes, and of course these get worse the more strongly they are activated. And finally, rooted as they are in primordial ideas about what is meaningful, they are very hard to reflect upon and resist (Singer and Kaplinsky, 2010).

Samuel Kimbles builds on the cultural complex with his concept of phantom narratives—the 'unthought knowns' that move autonomously in the psyche, mediating between collective memory and the individual unconscious (Kimbles, 2014). He refers, for example, to the phantom narratives of slavery in the

American unconscious. All Americans—black, white, and brown—are haunted by these phantom narratives, just as the phantom narratives of the Holocaust and the Nazi occupation of Germany continue to haunt the souls of Germans whose parents were not even born at that time.

As a British woman born at the very tip of the tail-end of the British empire in Hong Kong, my psyche has been populated with phantom narratives of empire—with all the cringe-worthy colonial nostalgia that sells so well in movies like *Out of Africa* and *Best Exotic Marigold Hotel*. The Second World War is also profoundly woven into the British psyche (Cashford, 2016). Like my mother and grandmother, who survived the Second World War and nine years of subsequent food rationing in England, I save everything: leftover food, jars, brown paper bags, rubber bands, string, seeds, and pieces of fabric. Making do feels like a home-front triumph, despite the fact that I was born 17 years after the end of the war. But it goes further back than that. As Jung said, 'We are very far from having finished completely with the Middle Ages, classical antiquity, and primitivity, as our modern psyches pretend' (Jung 1961, p. 236).

Paul Kingsnorth has written convincingly that the divide between Saxons and Normans is still alive in the UK today, a thousand years after the Norman Conquest in 1066 (Kingsnorth 2017, pp. 180–187). He notes that commoners still drink beer, while the more wealthy drink wine, and still like to spend their holidays in France. Likewise, the split between England and the Celtic nations continues to make lumps in the British sauce. As a Scots friend of mine once announced, while we were watching the Triple Crown rugby championship: 'I'm no nationalist: I don't care who beats the English'. My own undying sympathy for under-dogs, my resistance to authority, and my scepticism of anything told to me by anyone in management came down my father-line, and are Welsh to the core.[4]

Recognising the significant influence of the multiple cultural components active within the psyche is important. Not just personally for purposes of individuation, but also collectively. Becoming conscious of such culturally determined characteristics, beliefs, and behaviours can facilitate personal differentiation from the cultural complexes, as well as inter-cultural understanding.

The notion of white people not having ethnicity is part of a presentation of whiteness-as-the-norm which *has* to be unpicked and deconstructed (Guess, 2006). This is, of course, a political project, perhaps even an activist one. But it is also a valid therapeutic project. This paper presents three vignettes of work with white clients, whose cultural specificity was an important key to their identity and their relational capacity. In each case, working out culturally related trauma was a crucial element in the therapy. In all three cases, these were foreigners in the US, but they could just as easily have been seen in Europe.

Three vignettes

The vignettes presented in the rest of this paper will illustrate intergenerational cultural trauma, collective cultural trauma, and personal cultural trauma.[5] But they also illustrate the importance of foregrounding cultural experience in treatment with *all* clients, since much of what we call psychopathology results from our acculturation into ways of being that are contextually defined as normal but that systematically frustrate the organismic needs of an embodied, emotional, mammalian creature, for example, acculturation into gender, or acculturation into being a productive, good, and obedient worker. In the US especially, the heroic ego reigns supreme, causing havoc intra-personally, relationally, collectively, and ecologically (Spector, 2010).

Unpicking culture can be enormously helpful in restoring a sense of sanity, agency, normalcy and choice, as well as being helpful in restoring the ego–Self axis (Edinger, 1992) by enabling the client to contact instinctual and imaginal parts of themselves that have hitherto been denied. It can also root us somewhere, restore a sense of lineage and locality, and a concomitant sense of belonging in the world.

On the collective level, with white supremacy on the rise on both sides of the Atlantic, it seems urgent to restore ethnic specificity to whites. We need to decentre, deconstruct, and dissolve the monolith of white identity in order to open any possibility of a potential space between the rigid binary racial categories we have now. The splitting that is at the root of whiteness inevitably induces constellation of an Other and projections of that Other onto non-whites.[6] Sam Kimbles points out (2014) that ignorance of our cultural identity and specificity is not just a not-knowing, but instead involves a *process* of blanking out, of silence, of not seeing, that allows whites to avoid collective responsibility for our privilege and its disowned shadow aspects, which have led to racial hatred, colonialism, economic inequality, and a host of other problems[7] that are now coming home to roost.

The first vignette concerns inter-generational trauma:

Michelle

This first case concerns a blond, blue-eyed, young Belgian woman, whom I will call Michelle. Michelle was participating in a Tavistock-style group I was running at the California Institute of Integral Studies. It was the kind of group where the facilitators are merely there to help model inter-personal dialogue and mediate interactions where necessary, but where the rules emerge from the group itself. Such groups present a rich field for investigating shadow processes of all kinds, as well as for practicing communicating about and across differences. The only ground-rules are that we communicate with integrity and compassion, and that we talk about what is happening here and now, rather than about things outside the room.

We do this for 45 solid hours, spread over several weeks, which creates a very intense experience. Half-way through the process, after about 25 hours, Michelle's group got stalled in a detailed, somewhat heated debate about the rules. For about two hours, they discussed seemingly trivial questions about how long break-times should be and whether they should wait for people who arrived late. When groups become side-tracked into endless discussions like this, it can mean that the members are collectively avoiding speaking about something else, flogging a red-herring to avoid the elephant in the room. I was aware of this possibility, but I decided to let the process run.

Michelle made eye contact with me several times over the course of the two hours and finally turned to me with some intensity and said, 'Why won't you just intervene and set the rules? It would be so much easier'. I opted for a policy of optimal frustration, and replied, 'I know, it's so frustrating'. Ten minutes later, she urged me once again to simply set the rule. Again I replied, this time with a grin, 'I know, it's super-frustrating, isn't it?' I sensed some tension was building, and I did not want to dissipate it. Shortly after that, our group session was over and we dispersed.

The next week Michelle spoke first. She said that she had been so distraught by the rules conversation, and in particular by my repeated refusal to set a definitive rule—which she had perceived as cruel in a figure of authority—that she could not sleep that night. Finally, she got out of bed and journaled about it. Over the following days she had continued to sit with her feelings, as she was being trained to do, until she finally had a key insight.

Michelle was Jewish, although her family no longer practiced Judaism. They had changed their name after the Second World War, in order to pass as Christians. As she incubated the feelings that had arisen with greater and greater force during the group's extensive interaction about the rules, she realised that, as well as frustration, she was feeling fear and rage. Suddenly, she recalled something she had read a few years before, while researching the history of some of her family members who had been murdered at Auschwitz. She had read that one of the key features of Auschwitz was the lack of clearly defined rules. Prisoners at Auschwitz could not stay safe by obeying the rules, because there weren't any. One could be killed for any infraction, without knowing it was an infraction. It was random and cruel and twisted. She had felt all of this during the group, mainly directed at me.

When Michelle had this realisation, she felt extremely relieved. She realised that hyper-vigilance about social rules, and making an effort to always stay within them had been a feature of her life up until then. She had always fawned on authority figures, paying close attention to their desires, obeying their demands to the letter, and simultaneously resenting and mistrusting them. Suddenly all of that paradoxical behaviour made sense, as did her reaction to me and the group.

Michelle's case provides an example of what Marianne Hirsch has called 'post-memory'—the phenomenon by which people relate to powerful, often traumatic events of which they have no personal experience but which happened to generations preceding theirs and were transmitted to them so deeply that they function almost as real memories (Hirsch, 2008). The post-memory of Auschwitz had profoundly affected Michelle. Subsequent to this realisation she seemed to become more relaxed in the group, and felt more at home there.

The fact that the reality of trans-generational trauma is recognised in French-speaking culture, in the field of *psycho-genéalogie*, may have helped Michelle to metabolise this experience. *Psycho-genéalogie*—or genealogical psychology—proposes that traumas that have never been metabolised get passed down in families as a *present absence*, conspicuous by somatisations, illnesses, symptoms in the body and untimely deaths, and it seeks to excavate them with the idea that once they are restored to consciousness, they can be resolved (Canault 1998; Schutzenberger, 1998). Michelle's extreme somatic response to something apparently trivial, but in fact deeply significant within her own psyche, both at the familial and at the cultural level, was the clue to the continuing presence of the ghosts of her murdered relatives in her psyche.

The second vignette concerns personal participation in collective cultural trauma:

Sal

Sal consulted me for relationship issues and general discontent with his career. He had a rebellious streak related to a negative father complex, balanced by a great deal of *puer* charm which made him seem younger than his age: he was smart, funny, entertaining, and flirtatious, and suffered from the eternal adolescent's classic 'fear of being pinned down' (Von Franz 1970/2000, p. 2). Sal's English was flawless, and the presence of another culture within him was only revealed by his equally flawless pronunciation of Spanish place-names around the Bay Area. When he referred to '*Tiburòn*' or '*Embarcadero*' they sounded like far-away locations in Latin America. I asked him about that, and he told me that he had been raised in Chile until his late teens, but had attended an international school, hence his perfect English.

Sal had lived a life of few responsibilities until his forties, when, faced with economic realities, he decided to settle down and get a job. He was working through this hero's journey when Donald Trump was elected president of the US. Over the next few weeks all my foreign clients talked about their fear of the way the US seemed to be heading politically, and all of them discussed leaving. So I did not notice anything special when Sal also expounded at length about the right-wing turn the country was taking, and his misgivings about it, or when he debated with himself about whether or not he should leave 'before it's too late'.

Over the next weeks, however, he reported arguments at work and discontent with his boss. Generally his tone was defiant and angry. He told me story after story about his father's authoritarianism and he spoke scornfully about Trump, seemingly linking the two. These patterns did not attenuate. Finally, one day, when he had been ranting for a few minutes about the government, it occurred to me to ask whether he thought his strong feelings had anything to do with the fact that he was raised under Pinochet's regime. I expected an off-hand 'yeah maybe' but he responded immediately and vehemently, 'Yes, I've lived under a dictatorship, I remember tanks in the street and armed soldiers …'. And for the rest of the session he poured out memories. They were a conduit into the collective trauma of his country, and they underlay, reinforced, and hid behind the father complex that had resulted from his personal history.

After this we were able to address his issues with authority more directly and with less resistance. He was able to reflect on his own defiance and gained some perspective on it. If I had not heard his accent, and asked about it, and if I had not known a little of the history of Chile and the recent demise of Pinochet (in 1990), I would not have thought to ask. I would have assumed his issues with authority were due purely to his father complex, and it would not have occurred to me to look for a significant, and mutually reinforcing interplay between his father complex and collective cultural trauma. As Jung stated,

> A collective problem, if not recognized as such, always appears as a personal problem, and in individual cases may give the impression that something is out of order in the personal psyche. The personal sphere is indeed disturbed, but such disturbances need not be primary, the consequence of an insupportable change in the social atmosphere. The cause of the disturbance is not to be sought in the personal surroundings but rather in the collective situation. Psychotherapy has hitherto taken this matter far too little into account.
> (Jung 1961, p. 233)

The cultural complex intersects with and adds weight to the personal complexes, bound up as it is with our deepest issues of identity and belonging, represented by our core values. Acknowledging the cultural complex therefore facilitates work on the personal material. But more importantly, if we take the cultural layer into account, Sal's compulsive rebellion becomes importantly recast, not as pathology, but as *resistance*; a resistance that is part of a grand and doomed narrative of anarchy, socialism, and a people's revolution crushed by force. A resistance that went underground and smouldered there in a tragic-romantic phantom narrative that continues to make it hard for Sal to advance in his career because he cannot join the ranks of management. To do so would make him a traitor to the cause. Reframing Sal's apparent failure to mature as resistance to participation in a collective narrative of oppression was important in giving meaning to his suffering, and restoring his sense of agency over the events of his own life (Afuape, 2011). After we were able to surface the issue of the collective, Sal went on to take US citizenship, buy a house and settle down, albeit still complaining.

The third vignette is one that illustrates personal migration trauma:

Virginia

Virginia was a British woman in her early forties. She was born in South Africa, and as a child had spoken Xhosa. Her family left South Africa when she was four years old, and she had no memory of that early time. As a little girl she suffered from separation anxiety. Her father was an officer in the British army, and so the family moved every few years to a different country, but they never went back to Africa.

It is obvious already that there is significant migration trauma here. The tendency is to assume that small children can be moved around without them really noticing, and that they will be just fine in their new circumstances. But, in fact, that is simply not the case. Dr Salman Akhtar has shown how migration engenders a continual subliminal stress on the migrant, not because of the loss of beloved people, but because of the difference in *environment*. In one's home country, one learns an *average expectable environment*, which includes such things as air temperature, humidity, smells, sounds, colours, shapes of buildings, languages, the way people look and dress, the presence or absence of animals, and so on. When one moves to a different place, the background becomes foregrounded because the environment does not correspond to what we subliminally expect. All the small details cause mini-ruptures. We are continually unconsciously scanning for—and not finding—the familiar, and this process becomes a cumulative stress (Akhtar, 2007).

Thirty-five years or so after leaving Africa, Virginia came into therapy with a supervisee of mine because she was struggling to leave her relationship with a Nigerian man she had been with for three years. Like her, he was an international traveller, the son of a diplomat, and a highly cultured person. Like her, he had left Africa as a small child, when his family had moved to the US. She felt 'met' by him on a level she didn't often find. However, eventually the attachment trauma in both of them took its toll. She described him as emotionally and verbally abusive, and indeed the interactions she described seemed to indicate unusual levels of antagonism, but she was unable to leave the relationship. In session after session, she related how she obsessed over whether to leave, when to leave, how to leave, or whether not to leave at all.

One day, when she was describing some charged interaction they had had, she excused what the therapist felt was plainly bad behaviour by saying she thought this was due to a difference in culture. Feeling concerned about her co-dependence and her acceptance of what he would characterise as mistreatment, the therapist responded, 'But you don't have to adjust to his culture'. To his surprise, and it turned out, to hers, she burst into tears, and sobbed for the rest of the session. 'No-one has ever said that to me', she said. 'I have spent my life adjusting to other peoples' cultures'. Despite this flash of catharsis, neither the therapist nor the client took the issue of culture any further.

A few weeks after that she left the boyfriend, but months later she was still processing what had happened, and was still unable to understand why she had had such difficulty leaving. Eventually, about a year later, she had a dream, in which she went to the man's house, which was shuttered and dusty, somewhat dilapidated although grand, and found him outside in the garden. The soil was rich and red, like African soil, and he greeted her, saying, 'Look, I have to show you, I'm growing sorghum'. In waking life the client was an avid gardener, while the man was not. In the dream, she felt envious of his plants, and thought, 'He doesn't even like gardening. Why aren't I growing sorghum?' She related this dream to her therapist, who observed that of course he was growing sorghum while she was not: 'It's his culture, not yours,' said the therapist. At this the client felt angry, misunderstood, and very sad.

Several weeks later, after pondering on the dream extensively—and particularly on her intense reaction to the therapist's comment—she realised that she had been unable to leave her lover because to do so felt like leaving Africa all over again. In being with him she had felt as though something she had deeply missed and longed for was being restored to her. The trauma of the loss of Africa was something that had directed her entire life—even to her career as an immigration lawyer defending asylum seekers and deportation cases—despite her having no conscious memory of it. This realisation finally brought her resolution. She felt more able to separate the man himself from what he represented. She still loved him, but was able to resolve not to re-enter the relationship.

This client had suffered the trauma of migration described by Salman Akhtar, but there is perhaps another level to this story, underlying the personal migration trauma. If, as Jules Cashford (2016) has claimed, the cultural complex of empire is still operating in the British psyche, we can ask ourselves how it too participated in this client's experience.[8]

A colonial upbringing imposes a radical schism on any child, particularly at the moment of entry into puberty. Prior to that, race in a colony is a relatively unmarked category, with little significance in the everyday lives of very young children. When small, a child is likely to be reared by native servants, and is generally allowed to play with native children. He or she often speaks the native tongue, and has access to native places and occupations. In post-puberty however, I suggest that race becomes the primary signifier (Evans, 1996). When the child reaches puberty, he or she is required to enter adulthood, which simultaneously requires entry into race.[9] In order to enter the white race, the child is required to split off any and all aspects of him/herself that were contextually linked to the indigenous world, including play, sensuality, and innocent friendships with People of Colour.

This schism forces a white child to split off much of its humanity—the *eros* pole of the *eros/logos* duality, in order to enter into its role as coloniser. It is this schism, and the splitting it necessitates, that allows and indeed creates the cruelty with which the natives are oppressed within the colonial system. The colonial education of whites forces them away from an authentic identity, into an alienated, dominator identity. We can see the effect of this in the recent US policy of separating children from their parents at the border with Mexico—a profoundly inhumane policy that could only be tolerated by people who have split off their own humanity.

Virginia had left Africa when she was still a young child, and she had felt the loss of its smells, colours, music, languages, food, and people very keenly. After leaving Africa, her family went to live in Denmark, which she had experienced as cold, dreary, dark, and unfriendly. Africa then became enshrined in her psyche as the symbol of happiness, innocence, and love. As an adult, she had resisted the process of colonial enculturation, becoming an advocate for the oppressed. You could say the defence of 'undoing' had directed her life. But it was a life of *logos*, with a concomitant yearning for the long-lost realm of *eros*.

When she had met her lover, she had felt the split resolve within her. It felt, she once said, like divine forgiveness. It was only when she realised all of this that she was able to parse out the different strands of her experience, and distinguish the reality of the relationship from what it represented. Now she could exchange melancholy for mourning, integrate what had been lost in an internal rather than external *conjunctio*, and move on.

Conclusion

Extrapolating from the work done with these clients, I have learned that it can be useful to attend to a few specific things when working with clients through a cultural lens. First of all, let me quote John Beebe, who wrote:

> In Jungian analytic work, which is always about the exploration of complexes, one does not necessarily recognize that the knot one is trying to untie may be a cultural complex. Like any other complex, the cultural complex creates internal conflict; occasions anxiety, anger, and depression; governs the outer situations that are brought to the therapy for counsel; shapes the transference in the therapeutic interaction; and structures the imagery of the patient's dreams. Since these complexities affect the individual, and any person who comes into the emotional field that surrounds the individual, we often assume that they belong solely to the subjective nature of that individual person. Yet, they can represent culture operating at the level of the individual. By following a careful clinical method, a therapist can unmask the intrusion of a cultural complex into the unconscious life of the patient.
>
> (Beebe, in Singer and Kimbles, 2004, p. 223)

I suggest some ways to do that:

Firstly, we can listen for words in a foreign language, or more subtly, shifts in accent that can reveal the different geographies and epochs of a trans-national life.

Secondly, we can watch for shifts in the body. Sometimes when I ask people about a lost home, I see their entire physiology shift. Their posture changes, the rhythm of their gestures becomes more fluid, their skin colour changes, their eyes sparkle; they become more alive. Sometimes there is wistfulness, a slight collapse of grief, an edge to the voice that creeps in, when people talk about one place or another. Hopefully, we can help them integrate lost cultures and left-behind selves with the current self-that-lives-here, and in so doing, restore a sense of wholeness, belonging, and peace.

Thirdly, we can be attentive to the fine details of how people get hooked by news, politics, or other ostensibly rational external-world events. The events that trigger us on the outside often resonate with our own unresolved trauma—there is usually a perfectly reasonable justification for the emotion, but the intensity of it reveals that something more is in play: a complex has been constellated.

One example is Sal, activated by the election of an extreme right-wing candidate. Another is Michelle, deregulated by a lack of clear rules.

Fourthly, as Jungians, when working with dreams we need to be aware of particular geographies, as well as culturally related symbols, so we can foreground these to see what associations arise, such as, for example, the red earth and the sorghum in Virginia's dream.

I hope these short vignettes will inspire clinicians to consider the hidden cultural aspects of the lives not only of trans-national white clients, but all clients. This is important, not just for the individual, but also for the collective. In a time of mounting racial and cultural conflict, based on splitting, scapegoating, and over-simplification, we *need* cultural complexity, inter-sectionality, hybrid identities, bilingualism, and *métissage*. In the words of Amin Maalouf:

> Each of us should be encouraged to accept his own diversity, to see his identity as the sum of all of his various affiliations, instead of as only one of them raised to the status of the most important, made into an instrument of exclusion and sometimes into a weapon of war. Especially in the case of those whose culture of origin is not that of the society they live in, people must be able to accept a dual affiliation without too much anguish… [for] the ability to live easily with their various allegiances is essential not only for their own fulfilment, but also for the peace of the society of which they are part.
>
> (Maalouf 1996/2012, p. 160)

Notes

1. https://publicdomainreview.org/collections/portraits-of-ellis-island-immigrants/
2. In fact, cultural values and expectations can be very different between the US and other predominantly white cultures, in which whiteness was not constructed in the same way as it was in the US (Guess, 2006). The fact that we speak a common language—English—can mask the fact that ideas about individual freedom, equality, gender, friendship, love, work, the social contract, and the meaning of life can have very different meanings as they are translated from one culture to another—even when those different cultures are predominantly white.
3. The 'collective ego' is my metaphorical term for the 'manifest pattern of the culture' described by Henderson.
4. For examples, see Thomas, 2000; Llewellyn, 1939.
5. All names and identifying information have, of course, been changed for confidentiality.
6. Jessica Sherman, personal communication, 2018.
7. Sam Kimbles, personal communication, July 2018.
8. This process of acquiring whiteness remains highly relevant to the construction of whiteness today, at least in some parts of the Western world including America, where the current white supremacist backlash can, I believe, be at least partially explained by the splitting-off process I describe.
9. By this, I do not just mean entry into *a* race, but entry into race per se. In other words, entry into adulthood is a racialised experience.

References

Afuape, T. (2011). *Power, resistance and liberation in therapy with survivors of trauma.* London, UK: Routledge.

Akhtar, S. (2007). *The trauma of dislocation.* Video presentation. Sourced at https://vimeo.com/16828641.

Canault, N. (1998). *Comment paye-t-on la faute de ses ancêtres: L'inconscient transgénérationnel.* Paris, France: Desclée de Brouwer.

Cashford, J. (2016). 'Britain: autonomy and insularity in an island race'. In Joerg Rasche and Thomas Singer (eds.), *Europe's many souls: exploring cultural complexes and identities.* New Orleans, LA: Spring Journal Books.

Derrida, J. (1991). 'Geopsychoanalysis: "... and the rest of the world"'. *American Imago,* 48 (2), 199–231.

DiAngelo, R. (2018). *White fragility: why it's so hard for white people to talk about racism.* Boston, MA: Beacon Press.

Edinger, E. F. (1992). *Ego and archetype.* Boulder, CO: Shambhala.

Evans, D. (1996) *An introductory dictionary of Lacanian psychoanalysis.* London, UK: Routledge.

Guess, T. J. (2006). 'The social construction of whiteness: racism by intent, racism by consequence'. *Critical Sociology,* 32 (4), pp. 649–673.

Henderson, J. (1990). *Shadow and self.* Wilmette, IL: Chiron Publications.

Hirsch, M. (2008). 'The generation of postmemory'. *Poetics Today* 29 (1) (Spring 2008), pp. 103–128.

Irving, D. (2014). *Waking up white: and finding myself in the story of race.* Plano, TX: Elephant Room Press.

Jung, C. G. (1961). *Memories, dreams, reflections.* Toronto, ON: Random House.

Kimbles, S. (2014). *Phantom narratives: the unseen contributions of culture to psyche.* Lanham, MD: Rowman & Littlefield.

Kingsnorth, P. (2017). *Confessions of a recovering environmentalist.* London, UK: Faber and Faber.

Lee, Mun-Wah. (1994). *Color of fear.* (Documentary film.) Berkeley, CA: Stir Fry Seminars.

Lee, Mun-Wah. (2003). *Last chance for Eden.* (Documentary film.) Berkeley, CA: Stir Fry Seminars.

Llewellyn, R. (1939). *How green was my valley.* London, UK: Michael Joseph.

Maalouf, A. (1996/2012). *In the name of identity: violence and the need to belong.* New York, NY: Arcade Publishing.

Schutzenberger, A. A. (1998). *The ancestor syndrome: transgenerational psychotherapy and the hidden links in the family tree.* London, UK: Routledge.

Singer, T., and Kaplinsky, C. (2010). 'Cultural complexes in analysis'. In Murray Stein (eds.), *Jungian psychoanalysis: working in the spirit of C. G. Jung.* Chicago, IL: Open Court Publishing Company.

Singer, T., and Kimbles, S. L. (2004). *The cultural complex: contemporary Jungian perspectives on psyche and society.* London, UK: Routledge.

Spector, B. (2010). *Madness at the gates of the city: the myth of American innocence.* Berkeley, CA: Regent Press.

Thomas, R. S. (2000). *Collected poems, 1945–1990*. Newhaven, CT: Phoenix Press.
Von Franz, Marie. (1970/2000). *The problem of the puer aeternus*. Toronto: Inner City Books.
Wise, T. (2004). *White like me: reflections on race from a privileged son*. Berkeley, CA: Soft Skull Press.

Part 2

Border phenomenology and gender

Chapter 5

Ismail is now called Ebru and Lea wants to be a mechanic

Transgender and intercultural work as a municipal task

Elena Barta

Introduction

The contemporary field of transgender and transcultural work is something that mostly exists outside of the academic world, drawing ideas and conclusions from various disciplines and theories and at the same time providing practical food for theoretical thought. Within LGBTIQ and specifically transgender, intersex, and queer theory and work in Germany, psychoanalysis and psychotherapy are often only associated with the pathologisation of people beyond the gender binary.

Mental health institutions have a long history of theoretically and practically sanctioning people that cross society's norms, describing them as sick and delusional.

In Germany, trans*people[1] still have to provide two psychiatric reports in order to legally change their gender marker. The interviews for these records often cross into very intimate spheres and are seen as unnecessary both by transgender people and professionals who work in that field. This article will not focus on psychoanalysis or mental health topics, but rather give examples of what transgender and transcultural work can mean on a practical level. It will explore the following questions: How does the theoretical debate around gender and culture translate into the everyday life of those *in-between* genders, races or cultures? What terms are being used to describe and analyse a diverse society? How can psychoanalysis learn from the way the city of Frankfurt am Main works with cultural and gender diversity? How can a city support and work with communities that face multiple oppressions? What does this mean for individuals and communities who are not captured by binaries (male/female, German/migrant, etc.)?

To answer these questions it is crucial to look at the concepts and terms that lie behind diversity policies in the municipality. Therefore, the first part of the article will give a short overview of the special situation Frankfurt is in, regarding cultural and national diversity. The second part will focus on the understanding of terms and concepts around gender diversity, which are being used by the coordination unit for LGBTIQ topics and their meaning for the practical field.

The third and last part contains three different examples of transgender work in the municipality over the last year. I want to look specifically at the situation of children and young adults, but also at other vulnerable groups, such as homeless transgender people, to emphasise the role of an intersectional perspective. To conclude, I would like to give you an insight in the German debate around a third gender option, because it is an intriguing example of a state of being *in-between* that I would argue is now leaving the state of uncertainty to some extent.

Interculturality in the city of Frankfurt am Main

Frankfurt is one of the bigger cities in Germany and has roughly 724,500 inhabitants. It is located within the wider metropolitan area of Rhein-Main, which is characterised by a very high mobility on different levels. If we look at public transport, mobility means that there are a lot of commuters coming into Frankfurt, doubling the number of people within the city walls during the day. If we look at the inhabitants, we can see a very high degree of diversity on all social levels. This also includes a high diversity in different districts. Although there are certain districts with a higher percentage of people with German citizenship than others, there are no cultural or ethnically 'separated' districts. If we take citizenship, which is something that is a lot easier to put in a chart compared to cultural or national identity, we can see how diverse the population is (see Figure 5.1). Although there a few more people with Italian (7.15%) than with Austrian (1.32%) passports, the population comes from all over the world. In 2015, the city had inhabitants with almost every possible citizenship (Amt für multikulturelle Angelegenheiten, 2017).

Within the German discourse of integration there was and still is a long debate over what constitutes a non-German identity or a multicultural identity. As identity is something that is not easily caught in quantitative research, the concept of

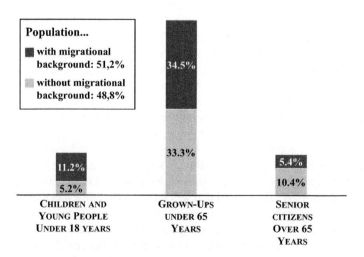

Figure 5.1 Citizenship of Frankfurt's inhabitants in 2015

Ismail is now called Ebru   81

migration background (or in German: *Migrationshintergrund*) is the one that is most commonly used and referred to in the practical field. The term originated from the state's need to quantify its inhabitants. Before its introduction, German statistics only distinguished between people with a German citizenship and people without it. In the current city's statistics 'people with migrational background' means people who are migrants or people whose parent or parents are migrants. In Germany this describes roughly one-fifth of the population. If we apply this definition of migrational background to the citizens of Frankfurt, we can see an interesting balance (see Figure 5.2).

Frankfurt has an almost equal amount of population with (51.2%) and without (48.8%) migrational background, and even more interesting, it has an almost equal balance between what are considered young and old people. The population

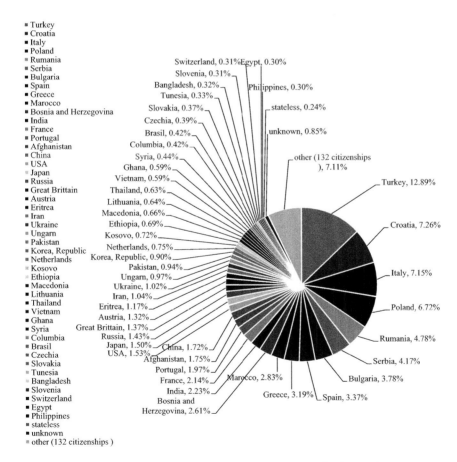

Figure 5.2 International breakdown of population with migrant background

under 18 years accounts for 16.4% and the population over 65 years 15.8% of the total population.

This definition is used to show the exclusion of migrants from well-paid jobs, higher education, etc. on a quantitative level. These numbers help to argue for inclusive policies, but they often lack the description of the many ways in which institutional racism, for example, towards black Germans work. Besides statistics *Migrationshintergrund* has become the 'standard' way of describing someone who is perceived and treated as not *originally German* and/or from *German descent*, and therefore carries great symbolism. One's migrational status is more than a question of citizenship; it becomes something cultural and is something that no matter how much an individual is integrated or assimilated will never disappear. One's *Migrationshintergrund* sort of lingers in the background, always waiting to be revealed.

The Office for Multicultural Affairs (AmkA)

Knowing that the majority of Frankfurt's inhabitants have a migrational background is one of the reasons why we understand intercultural work as a municipal task for the whole city. The Office for Multicultural Affairs (*Amt für multikulturelle Angelegenheiten*, or AmkA) is Frankfurt's way of answering questions that arise from living in a multicultural city. It was founded in 1989 by decision of the municipal administration, at a time of a very different discourse around integration and transcultural work. At the beginning of the office's work, integration was seen as something that we would now describe as assimilation. Migrants were seen as a mere workforce and expected to leave Frankfurt after a couple of years on the labour market, hence the derogatory but at the time officially used term *Gastarbeiter* (guestworker). The idea was for them to assimilate into German culture without participating in decision making processes. This assimilation discourse of the 1960s–1990s painted a picture of people entering an otherwise culturally homogenous group, which is interesting because historically Frankfurt has always been a dynamic city with debates around citizenship since the early Middle Ages.[2]

Nowadays, we understand integration or intercultural work as a communal task that focuses on the whole population. Inclusion is seen as a process of mutual understanding instead of assimilation of one group into another. The task of AmkA as a municipal authority is to promote and support the various ethnic groups in Frankfurt in living together constructively. The Office proclaims that successful integration will have been achieved once all residents of Frankfurt, regardless of origin and background, shape the future of the city together. Equal opportunity and equal participation are basic principles for this. AmkA develops focused integration measures, supports the networking of institutions that deal with integration, and promotes tolerance and understanding between residents. Migration is seen as a social reality and the office works with a long-term perspective. This can mean that AmkA works with community organizations, getting their input and insight while working on integration policies within the municipality. The office has around 40 employees that work in three main departments: the Department of Administration, the Department for Fundamental Work and Anti-discrimination, and the Department for Integration and Intercultural Communication.

The project *Mama lernt deutsch* (Mum's learning German) is an example from the Department of Communication. It is one of the longest-running projects with an intersectional perspective. It acknowledges that migrant women have a harder time learning German especially if they are mothers. Women who have children, no matter if in a relationship or as single parent, are more often in charge of taking care of them than men. At the same time, there are not enough kindergartens in Frankfurt to accommodate their needs, making it hard for women with unstable working conditions to get a kindergarten that ought to give places to children, when both parents are at work. Instead of just providing a language teacher, the project therefore also provides childcare. The courses are held in schools or child day-care centres (see Amt für multikulturelle Angelgenheiten, 2018a). This project is so successful precisely because it looks at the concrete barriers mothers face and provides pragmatic measures that make exactly the right difference. This was only possible because the project managers asked the right questions, saw the long-term perspective and the specific situation of mothers.

AmkA is also active in providing an academic foundation for multicultural work. One recent example is the study *Cultural Sensitivity in Psychosocial Services (Interkulturelle Öffnung der psycho-sozialen Dienste)* that was conducted in 2018 and published by the office (Amt für multikulturelle Angelegenheiten, 2018b). It is a project that acknowledges the fact that migrants use mental health institutions less then German citizens. The study looked at 60 psychosocial services and worked out in which areas the services could become more sensitive to the issues of migrants. The study stated, for example, that some of the services needed to rethink the ways people in need get their first contact with them. Solutions could be to offer counselling in different languages or being available online.

Another distinguishing feature in comparison to other cities' integration policies is that AmkA has been the Anti-discrimination Office (*Antidiskriminierungsstelle*) of the city since 1993.

In 2003, Frankfurt am Main was the first city of in Germany to issue Anti-Discrimination Guidelines (ADR) for complaints by citizens against city offices and operations. This was a major step in preventing discrimination through municipal authorities.

Queering the city – the coordination unit for LGBTIQ topics

The coordination unit for lesbian, gay, bisexual, transgender, intersex, and queer (LGBTIQ) topics is situated in the Department of Fundamental Work and Anti-discrimination.

The unit was formed by a decision in the municipal council, but its concrete concept was written within the Department of Multicultural Affairs. The two part-time employees started their work in November 2015.

The Coordinating Unit drafts concepts and strategies to improve the life of LGBTIQ people on a structural level. This means, for example, that I advise NGOs, companies, and the municipality when they want or are willing to be more open to LGBTIQ topics. This can be something broad like creating awareness for heteronormativity in advertising or something concrete like helping a company facilitate the transition of one of their employees.

The coordination unit stimulates, coordinates, and develops activities and actions to reduce discrimination and violence against LGBTIQ people. A recent and also intersectional example for this is a small poster campaign we did together with the lesbian-gay working group of the city's violence prevention body. The project started because, during the European Summer of Migration in 2016, Frankfurt welcomed refugees and asylum seekers and, shortly before the annual pride parade, voices in the gay community grew louder asking for an anti-hate-crime campaign towards asylum seekers. In their perception, refugees are per se violent against LGBTIQ people, and they couldn't imagine that some of the refugees were themselves LGBTIQ people or had fled their countries exactly because of different political ideas. On the other hand, the city learned of LGBTIQ people facing discrimination and violence within emergency refugee shelters. As a coordination unit, we advised taking a multidimensional perspective and looking at the specific needs of each group without reinforcing stereotypes. In the end – and with the help of a lot of different volunteers – the executive department for refugee management opened an emergency refugee shelter for gay and trans* people that is run by the local AIDS-relief association *AIDS-Hilfe Frankfurt*. The poster campaign became an LGBTIQ violence prevention campaign using the terms lesbian, gay, trans*, bisexual, intersex, and queer in six different languages. It was not addressing refugees, but the whole society in Frankfurt, which is in any case a multilingual society. The posters are now hanging in emergency shelters, as well as in police offices and LGBTIQ community centres, and make it clear that the city will not tolerate violence against LGBTIQ people. This example shows that the coordination unit also stimulates, coordinates, and reflects upon municipal activities in order to improve the life quality of LGBTIQ people. To do so we are placed between the municipal bodies, the LGBTIQ communities, and the wider public.

In order to systematically work with LGBTIQ topics, the coordination unites defined areas of action, such as education – from kindergarten children up to universities – or health, where we look at psychological as well as physiological health. The fields of action cover almost every aspect of life, while we intentionally focus on the more marginalised areas and make sure we hold an intersectional perspective. In the field of sports, for example, we make sure that the lesbian and the gay sports associations are known, and we advertise their activities on our websites, because sports is an area where a lot of people are afraid of coming out and where homo- and transphobic slurs are very common. At the same time, we support these associations in making their activities more inclusive. The lesbian sport clubs for example started a program that is free for refugee women. In order to support their project, the coordination unit put them in contact with a monthly meeting of lesbian and bisexual migrants, where they could meet women who are interested in their offer.

Transgressing the binary

Before giving concrete examples of transgender work in a municipality, I would like to define the term transgender. Every academic discipline has their theories and models to explain gender and the different statutes of being or not being one gender. Following queer theory (see Foucualt, 1976, Butler, 1990, de Lauretis, 1991) I assume that the gender binary is made by people, that it is imaginary but also real. What reality *is*, how we *do* or *undo* gender, and how identity is formed is something that is debated throughout such diverse fields as neuroscience, history, and, of course, psychoanalysis. The coordination unit draws from all of these fields in order to stimulate change within professions. For example: when working with medical professionals, I like to use medical historical references as this is where my personal expertise (history) and theirs (medicine) meet. When explaining to them how gender can be *imaginary but also real*, I ask medical staff how they define gender, but also how gendered aspects of bodies are portrayed in their training manuals nowadays. I argue that the way that genitals are portrayed, how they are simplified and which parts of them are visible, shapes our idea of genitals and gender. The historian Thomas Laquer managed to extract a variety of health manuals from the Middle Ages showing correct anatomical images of genitals in a very different cultural frame. In his book *Making Sex* (Laquer, 1990) he shows anatomical drawings of vaginas by Andrea Visalius from 1611 (see Figure 5.3).

From the way they are drawn, it becomes clear that Visalius believed that the vagina and the penis are inherently the same, one facing inward, the other facing outward. We now know that this isn't true, but nevertheless we have to acknowledge that Visalius didn't make any mistake. His drawings show just how much his perception of gender mattered in his research. Showing medical staff these historic models helps them understand that perception matters even in fields that are seen as objective. Medical staff find themselves in a profession with very real consequences for people's realities. To encourage them to critically think about gender and their gender norms can help intersex kids to live a normal life instead of being surgically altered to fit the medical definition of male and female.[3]

In my practical work around transgender issues, when training kindergarten teachers, for example, detailed theories or medical models are less important. I find that it's more useful for their work with children to talk about ways of working with a diverse society rather than asking why and how people are diverse. In order to give them a theoretical frame of gender, sexuality, and bodies whilst also showing them that no model will ever sufficiently explain gender, I mostly work with pop-cultural references.

86 Elena Barta

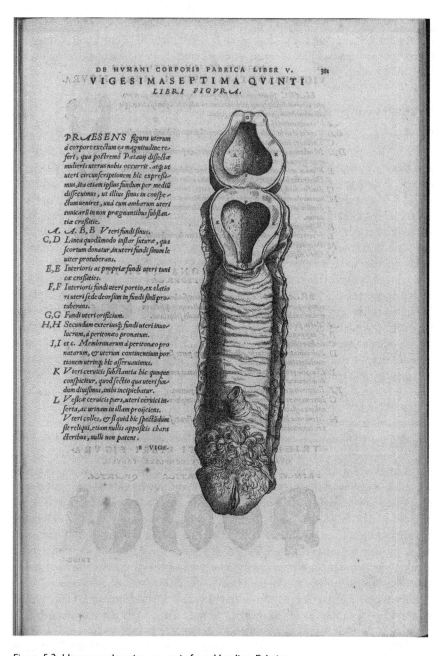

Figure 5.3 Uterus and vagina as penis from Vesalius, Fabrica

The trans umbrella (Mays & Reiff Hill, 2014), an infographic that is widely shared in social media for educational purposes, shows how diverse and big the term trans is by putting all associated terms and identities under a literal umbrella. It explains transitioning from one binary gender to another (female to male, male to female, transsexual), but also in terms of talking about people that queer or refuse gender (agender, intergender, bigender, genderqueer, etc.). It also shows that the perception of gender is intertwined with cultural narratives: the concept of Hijras in India or the Native American two-spirit are connected to a specific cultural framework but are still part of a global trans* community.

This framework becomes apparent in my day-to-day work in the field of migration and asylum policies. Many European countries want some sort of proof of an asylum seeker's transgenderness in addition to proof of a very specific form of persecution, meaning persecution by state authorities. This often clashes with the self-identification, the words, and concepts non-western trans* people use but also with the ways they are oppressed. A person who is not conforming to gender roles and who has been severely beaten by family members without help from local authorities will still face problems arguing their case if the country has no law against 'homosexual conduct', 'wearing clothes of the opposite sex', etc. In addition, translators are often unaware of subcultural terms and/or ashamed to translate stories, making it very hard for LGBTIQ people to get asylum without the help of specialised lawyers and local activists.

When I talked with kindergarten teachers about this model they quickly started to discuss if drag kings and queens – whose transgenderness is mostly on a stage performance level – are truly trans*. As much as I understand their wish for a clear distinction between cisgender and transgender, I can't give it to them. What I give them instead is a second, very different but also very popular model, the Genderbread Person (Killerman, 2015) (see Figure 5.4).

It's a catchy model that tries to explain very complicated elements of gender in one picture. The most important aspect is the theoretical separation between gender expression, gender identity, attraction, and sex. Although this is all combined and interconnected in one individual, the model helps the kindergarten teachers to see the differences but also the similarities between figures like the Austrian drag queen Conchita Wurst and children in their care. It is important for them to see that, on the one hand, kids need diverse gender roles, toys, etc. in order to develop, and that a girl who wants to be a mechanic is no less of a girl. At the same time, it is crucial for them to understand that other kids in their care have a gender identity that does not match their assigned gender and that transgender kids might need different support or changes in the structure of the kindergarten. This model helps to shift the discussion from question like 'where is the line between transgender and cisgender?' and 'how do I know if a kid is transgender?' to a professional understanding of supporting the identity development of a child without knowing the outcome. Support in this case can range from making sure the kindergarten has diverse books on its shelf, to guiding parents and kids and teaching a fluid understanding of gender.

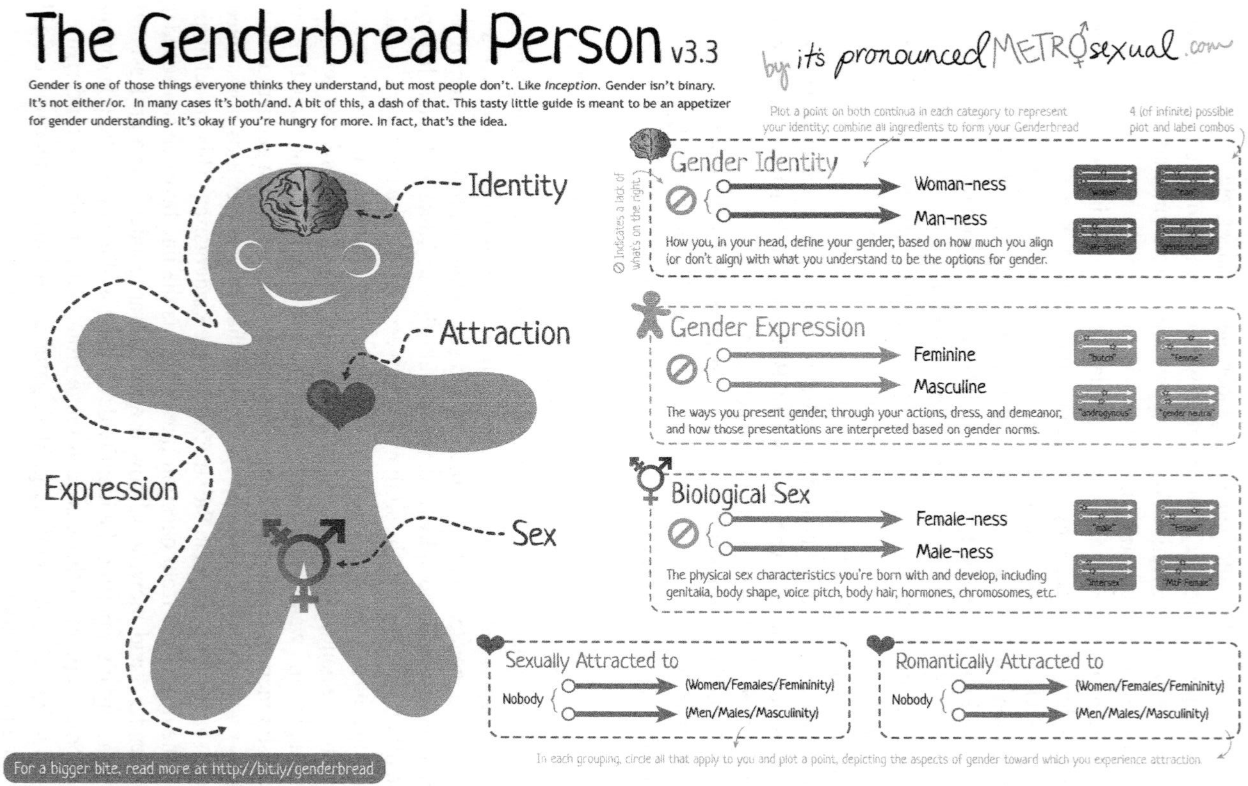

The Genderbread Person v3.3
by it's pronounced METROsexual .com
Gender is one of those things everyone thinks they understand, but most people don't. Like Inception. Gender isn't binary. It's not either/or. In many cases it's both/and. A bit of this, a dash of that. This tasty little guide is meant to be an appetizer for gender understanding. It's okay if you're hungry for more. In fact, that's the idea.
Identity
Attraction
Expression
Sex
Plot a point on both continua in each category to represent your identity; combine all ingredients to form your Genderbread
4 (of infinite) possible plot and label combos
Indicates a lack of what's on the right
Gender Identity
Woman-ness
Man-ness
How you, in your head, define your gender, based on how much you align (or don't align) with what you understand to be the options for gender.
Gender Expression
Feminine
Masculine
The ways you present gender, through your actions, dress, and demeanor, and how those presentations are interpreted based on gender norms.
Biological Sex
Female-ness
Male-ness
The physical sex characteristics you're born with and develop, including genitalia, body shape, voice pitch, body hair, hormones, chromosomes, etc.
Sexually Attracted to
Nobody
(Women/Females/Femininity)
(Men/Males/Masculinity)
Romantically Attracted to
Nobody
(Women/Females/Femininity)
(Men/Males/Masculinity)
In each grouping, circle all that apply to you and plot a point, depicting the aspects of gender toward which you experience attraction.
For a bigger bite, read more at http://bit.ly/genderbread

Figure 5.4 The genderbread person v3.

Transgender work in practice: Schools and suicide in trans* teens

Working on transgender issues in a municipality can have a variety of forms. To better understand what it means to stimulate activities and actions to reduce violence against trans* people and/or include trans* people, I would like to give three examples of projects or counselling that I was able to give in the last year. They touch on the topic of youth and schools, homelessness, and law and jurisdiction.

When we look at transgenderness or genderqueerness in children and young adults, there is not a lot of material to help young people figure themselves out, nor is there much research or pedagogical material outside an English-speaking context. In 2017, I was contacted by a school where a transgender student committed suicide. They had another suicide by an LGBTIQ student the year before and decided that they wanted to become more inclusive. I got together with *gewaltfreileben* – which translates to 'live non-violently' – a project that offers counselling for queer people who suffered violence, because I knew that they often encountered the topic of suicide. There are no specialists in LGBTIQ youth suicide, so we organised a staff training ourselves, and wanted to make sure that the teachers got a few essentials from the training. There is almost no available data on mental health of young trans* people in Germany, let alone in Frankfurt. We used US-American (Mustanski, et al., 2010) and Canadian studies (Bauer, et al., 2013) to explain the higher risk of suicide in LGBTIQ and specifically transgender teens, while making sure they understood that the teenagers' transgenderness was not the cause of the mental health issues; rather, it formed one aspect of being perceived as 'the other', causing what we would call minority stress and the implication that one's idea of self will never be able to exist. For the teachers, it was less important to understand every specific aspect of being transgender, but rather to see how and where they could make sure LGBTIQ teens felt less excluded and othered. This is specifically important because trans* teens have to struggle with internalised transphobia and a transphobic environment: The German Youth Institute asked almost 5,000 young LGBTIQ about their experience with coming out: more than 70% percent were afraid of being rejected by their peers (Krell & Oldemeier, 2015). Thinking back to school environments, where children often only know their parents and school friends, this is a rather high number.

The situation of being aware of one's otherness and the process of coming out to oneself and to others is a period of time that is especially hard for LGBTIQ teens, and one that in the case of transgender or gender-diverse youth is quite long. Most of them have their coming out around 18, mostly after graduating from high school. Combined with the fact that trans youth are often aware of their otherness before their lesbian, gay, and bisexual peers, this means that trans people spend between three and seven years in a state where their outer and inner identities are radically different from each other (Krell & Oldemeier, 2015).

In the teacher training we discussed how they could empower the students' resilience. We talked a lot about creating a supportive social environment which also includes very concrete measures, like thinking about ways to install gender neutral toilets and changing rooms that are suitable for everyone. We also discussed how often students are gendered during their school life and that creating an inclusive environment means letting the kids develop gender identities while giving them emancipatory gender roles to see and test. Integral part of good anti-discrimination prevention is having a concrete contact person. No matter if that person is ever really contacted, their mere existence shows LGBTIQ students that grown-ups care. The thing that matters most is information; no matter how a teacher or social worker perceives a kid's transgenderness, they should know all the possibilities that they have in their resources to empower the kids. A good example is the use of a new name in school records. A lot of school administrations are afraid to change the records before a legal adoption of a new name or gender. For the kids it's an important part of their social transition before embarking on the long and stressful legal route. A change of school records is legally not a problem in Germany; it cannot be classified as fraud because the students won't gain an advantage from having school records that differ from their IDs. However, although the lawyer Maria Sabine Augstein wrote a known essay on the question (Augstein, 2013), it is still something that almost every parent of a trans* kid has to fight for.

Homelessness of trans* people

Another aspect from my practical work is the topic of LGBTIQ homelessness and its specific impact on trans* people. The status of being in-between legal genders or societal perceptions of gender becomes a serious wellbeing concern when we talk about housing and homelessness. The legal process for transgender people in Germany to change their gender marker is a rather long process that includes two psychiatric reports that can cost up to 2,500 Euro. If we look at homeless people in Frankfurt, a lot of the more vulnerable people are migrants from Eastern Europe who cannot apply for welfare benefits. One can easily imagine that going through a legal or medical transition is often beyond a person's capacities. Homeless shelters, on the other hand, are often divided by gender, and the staff are not trained to assist trans* people in the complicated transition process. This can leave trans* people in a vicious circle of not being able to go through with a transition and needing it to have access to other important aspects of life support like emergency shelters. Older trans* people, who have their inner and/or outer coming-out in their thirties or forties, can find themselves with partners, kids, or families who don't want to accept them. If they are then not accepted in their work environment, they often lose their job or end up in precarious work. This change of social status, along with a lack of connection to an LGBTIQ community, can easily lead to homelessness. When we look at trans* youth we see a different phenomenon: because of unaccepting parents, these young people often face a specific form of homelessness, where they are not formally homeless but spend their nights surfing from one friend's couch to another, almost invisible to traditional homeless assistance. As with almost all topics of diversity, the risk of homelessness becomes higher the more one individual is 'othered' – this can include not having the right papers and therefore not being entitled to a bed in a homeless shelter or being without health care and therefore relying on self-medication instead of a monitored hormone replacement therapy.

In 2018 a local emergency shelter asked for advice in taking in a trans* woman. They were in need of concrete information on legal procedures and local trans* groups to professionally counsel their client, but they also needed to reflect on their role and their own stereotypes in order to successfully support their client. Being able to guide the staff members through this process was a great opportunity for the coordination unit, which could only occur because the staff members were already aware that the transgenderness of their client was a key part of her homelessness. This awareness needs to be part of their education as social workers, but also included in the official guidelines of social care units in order to reach all homeless trans* people.

Being in-between: Is a legal third gender enough?

As a last example, I would like to describe aspects surrounding the ongoing debate on a third gender option in Germany. Initially, the demand for a third option came from intersex awareness groups, who rightfully claim that their bodies and identities do not fit into the medical definition of male and female. Many experts in the field hoped that having a legal third gender marker would prevent young intersex kids from cosmetic surgeries in order to make their genitalia appear more male or female. After years of debate, including a complete hearing before the German ethical board, the law concerning gender markers was changed in 2013, saying: 'If the child cannot be assigned male or female the registry entry has to be left empty' (PStG §22).[4] Although falsely described by the media as a third option, this isn't one, because, as you can imagine, having no gender marker makes it almost impossible to navigate public bathrooms or even online shopping. The campaign group *Dritte Option* brought an individual case to the Constitutional Court. In October 2017, the court ruled that the legislature has to enact new provisions by the end of the year that either chooses to dispense of gender in civil status for everyone or give a positive gender option for people outside the male/female binary.

Throughout 2018, while we wait for a new law to be written, many debates are ongoing both within NGOs and within the municipality. The phrasing of the constitutional court ruling also allows an interpretation where a new law could give trans* people, specifically non-binary people, a legal gender marker. Genderqueer or non-binary people are more than in an indeterminate state or in-between genders. The German translation of in-between – *dazwischen* – gives it a slightly different meaning as the prefix 'da' translates to here, 'being present': being present in-between. Bearing this in mind, we have to ask if the possibility of non-binary people having their own gender marker will make their gender identity less in-between. Will they leave the state of uncertainty on a societal level or will it be a purely legal change? How can a society think of this group of people without using in-between symbols? To give an example: in the English-speaking world the singular use of the pronoun 'they' is more or less established. In German, as in many other languages we still play around with language options than cannot leave the gender binary. German genderqueer and nonbinary people use constructions like si_er (s_he) where the underscore symbolises the in-between. It can never transgress the binary. In this sense the Spanish system of using amig@s (instead of amigas and amigos) gives it a more complex symbolism, because the male o and the female a are intertwined and create a letter that is both male and female. The use of the letter x (as in Mx. instead of Mrs./Mr.) uses a third letter outside the gender binary, symbolising a sort of rejection of the binary but also using the international code for a third gender (instead of m/f).

To turn the question around: What possibilities for diverse bodies and minds could we create by using inclusive language, images, and buildings? How could we start talking about and doing gender in more than three boxes? What if we translate this flexible and playful use of language to other areas of society? These questions will most likely not be solved by a third gender marker in German passports. Nonetheless, the debate in parliament has brought forth a number of documentaries, articles, artwork, etc. that create awareness for intersex and transgender issues in a way that was deemed impossible five years ago.

Conclusion

At the beginning of the article I stated that gender is imaginary but has a very real materiality. Transgender and transcultural work can therefore never only be on a symbolic level, because it works with people's realities. The people I work with and their lives transgress and change the way society perceives culture and gender. They, as much as everyone in the practical field, need academic research and debate, because it nurtures and enriches argument. At the same time, a queer perspective within psychoanalysis and especially psychoanalytical practice can be a crucial part of an individual's understanding of their fluid gender identity as something that is not sick or delusional, but as something that merely is one lens of a complex kaleidoscope. On a municipal level, this means keeping an intersectional perspective whenever working on LGBTIQ topics, making sure to distinguish between stereotypes (Muslim migrants are homophobic, trans* people are mentally ill, etc.) and power relations within society (racism/ableism/classism/sexism within the LGBTIQ community, conservative perceptions within religious communities, pink washing, etc.). We can do this by supporting marginalised positions in their self-organization (e.g. funding community centres where black LGBTIQ people can meet), guiding institutions within but also outside the LGBTIQ community to become more inclusive (e.g. training a school board on trans* issues), creating awareness in the wider public through events where people with different perspectives speak without tokenising them (e.g. inviting a deaf historian to talk about LGBTIQ history because that's their field of expertise). This together with a strong and diverse LGBTIQ community and medical, legal, etc. professionals who reflect on LGBTIQ topics can create an environment where people who transgress gender and cultural binaries can strive and help shape a new understanding of diversity.

Notes

1. The term trans* people is referring to transgender, transsexual, transqueer, and any other individual whose gender identity is neither male nor female.
2. Frankfurt had a vibrant Jewish community in the Middle Ages, with material evidence from 1272. In 1460, Frankfurt city council decided to settle the Jewish population in a district of their own. The Judengasse in Frankfurt developed into one of the most important centres of Jewish life in Europe.
3. For more information on intersex I recommend the Network of Intersex Organizations (OII) and their member organisations, see https://oiiinternational.com/.
4. *Personenstandsgesetz §22.* [Online] Available at: https://dejure.org/gesetze/PStG/22.html (Accessed 08 November 2018).

References

Amt für multikulturelle Angelegenheiten. (2017). *Frankfurter integrations- und diversitätsmonitoring.* Frankfurt am Main: Magistrat der Stadt Frankfurt am Main.
Amt für multikulturelle Angelgenheiten. (2018a). *Vielfalt bewegt Frankfurt.* [Online] Available at https://www.vielfalt-bewegt-frankfurt.de/en/angebote/mums-learning-german (accessed 09 September 2018).
Amt für multikulturelle Angelegenheiten. (2018b). *Vielfalt bewegt Frankfurt.* [Online] Available at https://www.vielfalt-bewegt-frankfurt.de/de/studie (accessed 05 December 2018).
Augstein, M. S. (2013). *Zur situation transsexueller Kinder in der Schule vor der offiziellen (gerichtlichen) Vornamensänderung.* [Online] Available at https://www.trans-kinder-netz.de/files/pdf/Augstein%20Maerz%202013.pdf (accessed 08 November 2018).
Bauer, G., Pyne, J., Francino, M. C., and Hammond, R. (2013). 'Suicidality among trans people in Ontario: implications for social work and social justice'. *Service Social,* 59(1), 35–62.
Butler, J. (1990). *Gender trouble.* New York, NY: Routledge.
City of Frankfurt am Main. (2018). *Office for Multicultural Affairs – AmkA.* [Online] Available at https://www.frankfurt.de (accessed 10 September 2018).
de Lauretis, T. (1991). 'Queer theory: lesbian and gay sexualities'. *Differences: A Journal of Feminist Cultural Studies,* 3 (special issue), pp.iii–xviii.
Foucualt, M. (1976). *The history of sexuality, volume I.* London: Allen Lane.
Killerman, S. (2015). *The genderbread person v3.3.* [Online] Available at https://www.genderbread.org/ (accessed 08 November 2018).
Krell, C., and Oldemeier, K. (2015). *Coming-out - und dann...?!.* München: Deutsches Jugendinstitut e.V.

Laquer, T. (1990). *Making sex. Body and gender from the Greeks to Freud.* Cambridge: Harvard University Press.

Mays, J., and Reiff Hill, M. (2014). *The gender book.* Houston, TX: Marshall House Press.

Mustanski, B., Garofalo, R., and Emerson, E. (2010). 'Mental health disorders, psychological distress, and suicidality in a diverse sample of lesbian, gay, bisexual, and transgender youths'. *American Journal of Public Health,* 100(12), 2426–2432.

Chapter 6

Child development and gender issues
Symbols, creativity, and alterity through Sandplay therapy

Denise Gimenez Ramos and Julia Kaddis El Khouri

Introduction

This study discusses aspects of child development, both in theory and in practice. It presents, more specifically, a discussion about children who exhibit feelings of gender incongruity without manifesting any disorders of sexual development (e.g., congenital adrenogenital disorder, androgenic insensitivity syndrome, etc.). The motivation to develop this theme arose from inquiries and reflections from Sandplay analytical work with children and adolescents, but also from the conversations with their parents and educators during orientation sessions.

A clinical case is presented to illustrate the symbolic evolution in a Sandplay therapy process, and the identity of the patient is protected according to professional standards of privacy. We believe that the non-rational and preverbal experience offered by the Sandplay method favours access to deeper layers of the psyche, involves the patient immediately in a creative and meaningful experience, and enables contact with emotions and latent conflicts that can be reactivated, intensified, expressed, and integrated.

A child who feels incongruent between his/her gender identity and his/her biological sex may present clinically significant distress, social and cognitive impairment, or other important difficulties in other areas of life. Such psychic suffering may also provoke symptoms such as emotional vulnerability, aggression, depression, anxiety, as well as difficulty in the socialisation and learning process, among other symptoms. Traumatic stress reactions, major depression, generalised anxiety, substance abuse, social phobia, eating disorder, and suicide risk have also been identified in adolescents and adult trans, especially in the former (Moleiro & Pinto 2015).

Despite the growing understanding of sexual diversity and trans identities, we are still conditioned to a binary and heteronormative model that dictates our way of experiencing sexuality and experiencing life. In the words of Colling and Sant'ana 2014, p. 264, our translation), 'the way we think about the world in a dichotomous way creates a framework that categorises people into a logic that excludes a diversity of existences that are between one pole and another, subjectivities that enjoy precisely the position between a place'.

This discussion intends to reflect, from the principle of alterity, on how a child that presents gender issues can manifest him or herself in a more complex and creative form and in line with the emerging paradigms. We believe that the experience of continence, the teleological approach, and the possibility of evoking new potentials, experienced in the Sandplay analytical setting, facilitates the elaboration of psychic complexes and stimulates the constellation of structured and unifying symbols, resulting in the strengthening of the child's personality and, therefore, the possibility of existing more fully in their singularity and integrity.

We hope, by developing this discussion, to contribute to the understanding of new paradigms of a world in constant transformation.

The symptoms

According to Coelho and Sampaio (2014), the greater the disagreement with the body due to the incongruity between the psychological sex and gender to which one belongs, the greater the suffering. Hence, the importance to build a complex approach to understand gender identifications since their construction also involves bodily and unconscious processes. For Arán (2012, p. 67, our translation) 'these identifications are made throughout life, especially in early childhood, from the affective and corporal encounter with the other, which is always inscribed in a certain culture that transmits values and reiterates the norms of gender'.

Coelho e Sampaio (2014) also draw attention to how the experience of childhood and adolescence can be marked by feelings of discomfort, inadequacy, conflict, and discrimination, both in the family circle and in the school and work environment. Therefore, 'the feeling of inhabiting a foreign body that accompanies the transsexual person from birth, as well as the instinctual arrangements that cause the inner conflicts and, later, the social ones, loaded with prejudice, no doubt conferred to them a particular psychic functioning, but not pathological' (Cecarrelli, 2014, p. 59, our translation).

From a Jungian perspective, we understand that these symptoms can be interpreted as arising from a significant conflict encompassing the Self–ego–persona axis, directly affecting the child's ability to experience the challenges inherent to the phases of his or her development. Thus, we agree with Lima Filho (2002) when he affirms that environmental and historical factors exert important influences on the way the archetypal path will be realised, frustrated, or made difficult.

Many changes occurred in social organisation during the twentieth century, culminating in gender identity issues. 'One of these new paradigms – no doubt, one of the most fruitful and popular – was the idea of gender or the split of the concept of sex at different levels' that was born from the feminist movement in the 1960s (Benedetti 2005, p. 26, our translation).

The transgender movement challenged the binary and heteronormative model, bringing a greater understanding about the conceptions of body, gender, and sexuality, which resulted in a complex differentiation between gender identity, gender role, sexual orientation, and biological sex.

Intervention

It is important to note that there is no single symptomatology, neither a specific mode nor a homogeneous psychological structure that characterises transgenderness, nor a single model of functioning, but a diversity of expressions of subjectivities of transgender people. Like any cisgender person, whose gender identity is congruent to the biological sex, there are neurotic, psychotic, or perverse people, and 'no construction/typology can designate the transsexual in a precise place, pre-established within the theoretical space' (Ceccarelli, 2014, p. 59, our translation).

Thus, the therapeutic process with trans patients should transcend the binary references of femininity and masculinity, so that a person can express him or herself in a more spontaneous way in terms of cultural traits defined as masculine and feminine. For the so-called 'affirmative therapies' the focus is on the exploration and self-discovery of potentials, taking into consideration how this affects the patient's relationship with the other and in life. In the case of children, therapy should also involve educational work with the parents, mainly concerning the depathologisation of the trans condition, and overcoming the mourning of the designated gender in relation to the biological sex of their children, so that they can offer, in fact, the support that the child needs to unlock his or her real gender potential (Stiegitz, 2010; Vancer, Ehrensaft & Rosenthal, 2014).

For Jungians authors, as we are going to explore below, the notion of transgenderness opens up new possibilities and greater versatility of expression of the masculine and feminine principle, in any person cis or trans, and with any sexual orientation (Samuels, 1984; Kaylo, 2009; Johnson, 2015).

The Jungian perspective

A review of the literature reveals the absence of a coherent theory in Jungian psychology that takes into account the complexity and variety of expressions of sexuality. At the same time, Hopcke (1991) reminds us that discussing the theme without relating it to the archetypes of the collective unconscious would make it impossible to touch a deeper level of the soul.

Mackenzie (2006, p. 12) explains, from a Jungian perspective, that the understanding of the emerging-mind theory suggests that gender sense, like other aspects of the mind, emerges very early in development and from a self-organised process involving the body, the brain, and the cultural environment of an individual. Gender feelings, from this perspective, would be an emergent aspect of the mind and the experience of the body would be the key to the emergence of the gender.

For Singer (1995), the human psyche consists of many different dualities that need to be kept in balance; however, we verify that the idea of embodying these qualities in the consciousness and in the body, as a form of self-recognition, still raises controversial questionings. It is also important to note that contemporary studies that deal with human development have increasingly valued the intrinsic connection of body and mind in the development process. Byington (2013, p. 17, our translation) draws attention to the fact that 'Jung devoted many pages of his work to assert that psyche and matter are interconnected and inseparable. To demonstrate this inseparability, he created the concepts of unus mundus, psychoid, and synchronicity'. For Jung, 'mind and body are presumably a pair of opposites and, as such, the expression of a single entity' (Jung 1926, para. 619).

Mackenzie (2006) also elucidates how neuroscience values the importance of the body and biological processes in terms of incorporating the emerging experiences of the mind, embodying gendered feelings elaborated in the conscious dimension of the mind. Such considerations, although synthetic from psychosomatic points of view, are significant in the understanding of the processes experienced by the individual. Thus, for Marsman (2017) a more contemporary transgender discussion represents changes in the individual and collective dimension for understanding sexuality and gender identities. According to the author, 'its emergence represents a collective shift towards a new or more differentiated way of experiencing and expressing sex and gender, a movement of world soul' (Marsman, 2017, p. 679).

It is also important to underline the importance of the relational perspective of Jungian practice, valuing the intersubjective space of the therapeutic relationship when the countertransference dimension is included as part of the complex parallel processes of the body and mind system, and of the potential for change during psychotherapy (King, 2012).

Finally, the influence of the feminine and the masculine archetypes on identity and sexual orientation has been extensively discussed; however, we are now increasingly questioning how the archetype of androgyny may act as the synthesising force of these polarities also in the body and in the behavioural dimension of a person.

The analytical work with children

One of the fundamental aspects of the analytical work with children is to help them name their experiences, organise them, and signify them, taking into account the stages of their development in working through conflicts and stimulating their own resources in the course of ego development. However, according to Byington (2013, p. 23, our translation) when a 'structuring function undergoes a disorder that is not properly elaborated, a fixation occurs, which may be circumstantial or chronic'. According to the author, this is when defences can start to operate as the basis of the shadow or, in order words, the pathology.

Analysis helps the child to re-signify the facts, that is, to re-direct their life experience. With the developing ego and the capacity for non-formal abstraction, the child needs to concretise the images and fantasies that inhabit their psychic universe. They express the direction of their psyche without necessarily knowing how to name/conceptualise the experiences that provoke their emotions and feelings, while contacting archetypal energies throughout their life that can cause changes in the relation between the inner and the outer world (Horschutz, 2008).

A child needs physical and emotional security, cognitive stimulation, and interpersonal experiences to fully develop. The prototype for the ego's phallic impulsive force moving in consciousness is found at the birth of the hero prospectively toward the father, independent of gender identity. The hero recapitulates ontogeny as an archetypal image that is activated when the child's ego has assumed a heroic position in relation to the Primordial Parents. This position in relation to the Great Mother and the battle of the ego for freedom is directed against it (Neumann, 1991).

Hence the importance of offering a 'free and protected' space to facilitate personality development and the self-realising tendency, since the Sandplay process stimulates a creative regression that allows healing, provided there are adequate conditions (Weinrib, 1993).

According to Neumann (2008), it is from a dialogue between the conscious and the unconscious that the child begins to experience more naturally the gradual process of 'spiritual development', that is, of the enlargement of consciousness, made possible by the entry of the vertical axis – *Logos* – in the process of structuring their personality. Consequently, the normal course of development is re-established, its expression is reflected in an improvement in cognitive performance, concentration, and socialisation of the child, thus approaching the ideal ego-integral-positive state, that is 'able to assimilate and to integrate qualities, even when negative or unpleasant, of the internal and external worlds, such as deprivation, pain, etc' (Neumann, 1991, p. 51).

Some criteria are essential to evaluate the evolution of analytical work with children, namely: a) the structuring of the ego as well as its connection with the Self; b) the self-regulating process and the realising tendency of the Self; c) the restoration of the normal course of development; d) the development of autonomy, self-confidence and self-perception; e) sociability, sensitivity, joy, lightness; f) the performance of cognitive functions: concentration, memory, reasoning, etc; g) creative expression, intuition, imagination; and h) adaptive capacity, resilience, etc.

After discussing the various factors involved in child development, we can conclude that this movement is not linear and homogeneous, but complex and multifactored since it depends on internal factors, the environment and the relationship with the parents or substitutes as facilitators of the process of introjection and projection of these dynamics. We explain below why Sandplay therapy is understood as enabling a space for re-signification and possible restoration of the psychodynamic aspects of the child when a disturbance occurs in the course of their development.

Sandplay therapy

The Sandplay analytical setting is considered to be a creative space that promotes a playful experience as a way of connecting to the Self to achieve self-regulation and psychic transformation.

Ruth Ammann (2004) explains that it is within the creative, free, and protected space of Sandplay, encompassing the physical and psychological dimension, that internal and external realities unify, facilitating access to the deep layers of the unconscious and activating self-regulating psychic forces. The creative experience enables the expression of contents that cannot yet be expressed verbally, since diffuse and less linear awareness is best expressed through images, feelings, and intuition. We believe that giving to the low capacity for abstraction, the child needs to concretise images and fantasies that inhabit their psychic universe, expressing the direction of the psyche without necessarily knowing how to name/conceptualise the experiences that provoke feelings and emotions. In alchemical language the *temenos* or the therapeutic setting represents the alchemical vessel that contains the secret of metamorphoses (Chevalier and Gheerbrant, 2006).

Ammann (2004) also clarifies that the psychological mechanism of 'creative regression', stimulated by the experience of Sandplay, offers the way for the transformation of deep and unconscious complexes. Thus, under the proper conditions of the setting and the *temenos* of the therapeutic relationship, the self-regulating tendency can be activated, allowing unconscious images to be vitalised. Moreover, the Jungian teleological approach treats the symbolic image as a possible activator of psychic forces, giving them a proper meaning within the psychic process, hence the importance of the amplification method for Jungian analytic work. When a child objectifies contents of their unconscious, the internal images can operate together with the conscious as 'this living being appears outwardly as the material body, but inwardly as a series of images of the vital activities taking place within it' (Jung, 1926, para. 619).

In the creative setting or *temenos*, the unconscious dimensions will create the space that places the child in relation to the other, with him or herself and with their own body. According to Hillman (2009), lasting personality changes can only occur when the body is also affected. In this sense, Ramos (2006) clarifies that, from the psychosomatic perspective, the body-mind phenomenon cannot be considered separately; consequently, psychological processes will always be accompanied by a corporeal representation, either at the somatic level or the anatomical level. Clinical evidences also demonstrate that through Sandplay therapy the individual is able to re-trace the drama of his or her life and to elaborate possible traumas at a level which enables him or her to resume the course of their development (Matta, 2015; Bradway & Feldman, 2002; Herrmann, 2008).

For all these reasons, the Sandplay experience offers a secure environment to express, experiment, re-experiment, activate the vital forces of the Self, and ultimately to re-signify one's inner universe. By constellating and activating the Self, new psychic energies (archetypal forces) are mobilised, both intra-psychically and consequently in life and in other personal relationships. This occurs because 'the symbols act as transformers, their function being to convert libido from "lower" into a "higher" form' (Jung, 1911–1912/1952, para. 344).

Finally, Sandplay therapy involves the following processes: the relativisation of the ego, the progression and regression of the libido, the activation of the healing forces of the Self (manifestation of totality), the partial elaboration of the complexes, shadow integration, the emergence of the counter-sexual element (anima/animus), and the development of the symbolic experience. These processes result in revitalised ego, thus enabling integration of symbolic experiences and interaction with outer reality (Ammann, 2004; Weinrib, 1993).

Case presentation

We present below the case of Pedro (fictitious name) to illustrate how gender identity issues arising during childhood were elaborated using Sandplay therapy. In this discussion we want to show how Sandplay therapy helped Pedro to unlock his gender potential as well as the strength necessary to face challenges. It is in the creative *temenos* of Sandplay that we explored the archetypal forces intrinsic to the symbolic experience; it is in the intermediate, sacred, free, and protected space of Sandplay's analytical setting that the unconscious and conscious unite, that psyche and matter merge through the body (Ammann, 2004).

Pedro's mother and father were present at the initial interview. The mother reported experiencing much sadness and anxiety during her pregnancy because it coincided with her mother's illness. According to his parents, Pedro was breastfed for 11 months and his neuromotor development was normal. Pedro is an only child and although he has a good relationship with both parents, he has a stronger identification with his mother. At the age of two he went to school, an environment in which he adapted relatively well. The mother also said that Pedro was a curious, affectionate child who liked to read and who was also very reserved, and explosive when annoyed.

Pedro was six years old when he came to therapy. The parents stated that he had many fears, feelings of anxiety, and that he had difficulty facing typical development challenges. The parents also reported his tendency towards isolation and his difficulty with interpersonal relationships. According to them, Pedro was always interested in things belonging to the feminine universe, and was often 'corrected' by family members. Pedro was in therapy for 18 months (06/2013 to 09/2014), and had to be interrupted because the family moved abroad. He had a total of 56 (fifty-six) sessions.

Pedro was receptive to the resources available in the setting, engaging enthusiastically with the proposed activities. He introduced himself as a cheerful, interested, and at the same time timid child, but who opened up as he built a relationship of trust with the therapist. During the initial evaluation, it was possible to infer the presence of conflicts, mainly related to self-esteem, sensitivity to criticism, and issues related to body image and gender identity. He complained of feeling different compared to his friends, and stated how much he enjoyed toys and activities normally played by girls. Although deeply identified with his mother and the female universe, he had not yet spoken out about his gender conflict. Despite his cognitive ability, Pedro presented some dysfunctional social abilities as reported by his parents. Aspects of this difficulty could be observed in his emotionally immature behaviours, in aggressiveness, in the lack of resilience, in the difficulty of socialisation, in the feeling of inferiority, and in the tendency to live more in fantasy than in reality.

Pedro's ability to symbolise and his immediate engagement with Sandplay pointed towards a positive prognosis in the initial evaluation. The involvement of Pedro with the miniatures and with the process of creating the scenarios also revealed his positive transference with Sandplay. Thus, after the initial five sessions, it was possible to conclude that Sandplay work and the positive transference with the therapist represented a promising possibility of a truer encounter with himself, with the people around him, and with his life. The therapeutic process aimed at working with his gender issues and also with strengthening his ego functions.

The therapeutic process can be divided between three main phases: the first one related to the separation of the dependent relationship with mother, the second was allied to the strengthening of internal father principles, and the third to the activation of the hero archetype, which was when Pedro started to bring up his gender issues. During the first phase, most of Pedro's scenes involved the symbolism of the house, the hourglass, and the rainbow. The first Sandplay scene he created contained a father figure and two children, a boy and a baby girl. The mother lived in another house according to his description. In this first scene we have already an important aspect to observe: the need to separate from the mother, the need to strengthen the relationship with his father, and the need to create a space to integrate the inner feminine qualities represented by the baby girl.

The dependent relationship with his mother had also generated a difficult relationship with his own instinctual sphere, with his sense of identity, and his adaptation in the world. Lima Filho (2002, p. 289) explains this impasse in the archetypal developmental: 'this is likely to happen in an environment where the male figure lacked patriarchal interventions and is therefore not able to imprint the meaning of limit on the child's psyche'. The consequence is a precarious or non-existent training to adapt to the rules and customs of the greater world, especially to instances of masculine principles irrespective of whether the child is a boy or a girl, cisgender or transgender.

Various scenes that included a house and its interior were constructed repeatedly for approximately five months. The rainbow, a symbol of union, was also often present in the scenes, representing a search to integrate the mother and father principles and to integrate the archetype and the experience. According to Lexikon (2009) the rainbow represents the union between heaven and earth, symbolising the search for reconciliation between conscious and unconscious. We could also extend this interpretation to explain his need to integrate his masculine reality and his feminine potential. The presence of the hourglass in the scenes, on the other hand, also reaffirmed the notion of two realities, continuity, and fluency. The complexity of the scenes, observed over the months, and the inclusion of elements of nature, animals, and people, reflected his increasing maturity and his ability to deal with the paradoxes of his life with more enthusiasm and resilience.

During this stage Pedro became more receptive to the therapist's holding and to the therapy, a fact that brought us closer to Kalf's (1980) understanding of the concept of *temenos*: a space that is not limited to the therapy room or to the Sandplay tray, but a space which is created with the presence of the therapist since he or she is deeply attuned to the patient's personal and symbolic sphere. During these five months of therapy, positive and constructive aspects of his creative process had already unfolded. Thus, we could infer, from the evolution of the scenes, that his feelings and emotions could manifest and be welcomed, appreciated and understood. Although gender issues had not yet been dealt with directly during this period, the sense of ego-strengthening was clearly expanding out of the analytic setting, as if he were literally beginning to incarnate in his body, life, and relationships.

The second phase of the therapy activated themes of patriarchal symbolism, not as a confrontation to his identification with the feminine principles, but as part of the archetypal stage of development that he was going through. There were several scenes suggesting themes of construction, destruction, and reconstruction. He seemed also to understand that darker and deeper aspects of him-self could be revealed. He used excavators which now began to move the earth and mobilise stagnant energies. At the same time, the positioning of the various miniatures that have phallic representations (castle, post, and tower) tells us that the masculine function was also active. As we had hoped, contrary to fixation of the libido in the primal relationship and matriarchy, he was able to direct the flow of psychic energy towards the solar stages of the ego, 'in which the ego has connected with the masculine self and the archetype of the father, which symbolically manifests itself as the daytime sky and its center, the sun' (Lima Filho, 2002, pp. 111–112, our translation).

We could infer, therefore, that Pedro was overcoming his resistance to making the transition from matriarchal dynamism to patriarchal dynamism since he was realising that activating the figure of the 'inner father' would not mean giving up his feminine qualities, but instead, would help him feel more autonomous, courageous, and able to be himself and socialise better with others. During this phase of the therapy, which lasted approximately seven months, Pedro was able to experience all his interests in activities belonging to the feminine universe, such as playing with dolls, and the doll's house, creating stories of princesses, but also other less stereotyped activities, such as dancing and singing, more spontaneously. It was also an important period in terms of orientating his parents and the school regarding gender identity issues. We could then witness how the masculine principle was more integrated in his life as he improved in terms of autonomy, achieved a greater balance between fantasy and reality, as well as a greater capacity to deal with fears and to socialise with his colleagues. We hoped that he would continue to develop his potential, towards the construction of what Neumann

(1991) called positive-integral ego, that is, an ego more capable of assimilating and integrating qualities, even when they are negative or unpleasant.

In counter-transferential terms, the therapist experienced feelings of trust and the need for Pedro to tell and retell his story many times, perhaps as attempts to resignify the facts. Hence the importance of the non-verbal/non-interpretive holding offered to him to enable symbolic evolution, healing of the injured ego and psychological renewal (Kalf, 1980).

The fact that Pedro had a strong connection with his mother and with feminine qualities, but a fragile connection with male references, made it difficult for him to abandon the matriarchal dynamism. Neumann (1991) called this difficulty detaching from maternal ties 'self-perpetuating inertia'. It was the projection of a positive father figure who did not threaten Pedro´s feminine inner references that enabled him to activate the patriarchal dynamism in his life and in his relationships. Through an improved dialogue between these two instances, conscious and unconscious, Self and ego, shadow and persona, facilitated by the analytic process, he was able to experience more naturally the gradual process of 'spiritual development', that is, the enlargement of consciousness, made possible by the entry of the vertical axis – Logos – in the process of structuring his personality (Neumann, 1991).

The third and last phase of the therapy related more to the hero's journey. The challenge was to expand the protected therapy experience to the world. The themes were now mostly about superhero leagues and their super powers. Pedro reproduced the situations of his daily life, conflicts with friends and family members, parties, etc. Here the Sandplay experience was vital to Pedro since it enabled him to experience a secure environment to express, experience, re-experience, activate the vital forces of the Self, and ultimately re-signify his inner universe. The experience of therapy showed, in Ammann's words (2004, p. 64), 'that every child has in their unconscious knowledge about their psychic potential and their possibilities of cure'. We just need to offer a physical and emotional space for this potential to constellate.

Pedro used the dragon extensively in his Sandplay scenarios during this last phase. Amplifying the meaning of the symbolism of the dragon, we realised it had a positive meaning for his process. It is a mythical animal venerated for bringing luck and averting adversity in the Far East: 'It grants fertility because it is closely related to the forces of water and therefore to the yin principle; but it represents at the same time the masculine and active forces of Heaven and, thus, the yang principle' (Lexikon, 2009, p. 77).

It is important to point out how Pedro came to act more spontaneously and felt safer in terms of being and expressing his uniqueness, despite the challenges he faced. He was more lucid about his identification with the feminine universe, and feeling stronger to follow through his desire to live as a girl, a choice now supported by his parents.

Pedro´s positive attitude toward his development process, his desire for growth, as well as the cognitive and emotional resources he presented were indicative of the potential for psychological maturity. The supportive environment Pedro experienced in the Sandplay setting and the positive relationship with the therapist also helped him sediment the seed of transformation he planted in his life. However, the therapy had to be interrupted because the family had to move abroad, but they all understood the importance of continuing the therapeutic process in their new home.

Conclusion

We may conclude that the analytical setting of Sandplay seems to favour the meeting of inner and outer reality, through the tangible three-dimensional expression of the unconscious contents that are represented in the images. As Weinrib (1993) makes clear, we ultimately seek to establish harmony between 'conscious' and 'unconscious'.

Children can find in Sandplay therapy a creative space to actualise potentials, work with inner conflicts and strengthen the ability to face their developmental challenges. Pedro was able to integrate his female gender potential and at the same time move through the archetypal phases, bringing more integrity and alterity to his life.

In these times of great changes in the values that guide the way we think and act, we feel deeply insecure about the results of this dramatic moment in our history. Something is dying and something is being born. According to Tarnas (2007), we are on a threshold of transformation, as we can witness through the emerging paradigms. Much is focused on deconstruction and little is dedicated to contemplation of the new. We do not know where and we do not know how. We are no longer talking about what is right or wrong, but how to prepare ourselves to withstand the anguish of emptiness and uncertainty. We can only contemplate, identify, and recognise these changes in the direction of the alterity that we seek. Since children are the living representation of the preconscious aspect of the collective soul, they have much to teach us about changes of that order, toward alterity and singular expression for every human being.

References

Ammann, R. (2004). *A Terapia do Jogo de Areia: imagens que curam a alma e desenvolvem a personalidade*. 2nd ed. São Paulo: Paulus.
Arán, M. (2012). 'Do diagnóstico de transtorno de identidade de gênero às redescrições da experiência da transexualidade: os desafios do atendimento psicológico na rede pública de saúde'. In E. A. da Silva(ed.), *Transexualidade: Princípios de atenção Integral à Saúde*. São Paulo: Santos, 57–72.
Benedetti, M. (2005). *Toda Feita: o corpo e o gênero das travestis*. Rio de Janeiro: Garamond.
Bradway, K., and Feldman, B. (2002). 'Child analysis using Kalff and Fordham'. *Journal of Sandplay Therapy*, 11 (1), 43–49.
Byington, C. A. B. (2013). *A viagem do ser em busca da eternidade e do infinito:as sete etapas arquetípicas da vida pela psicologia simbólica junguiana*. São Paulo: Edição do autor.

Ceccarelli, P. R. (2014). 'Inquilinos no próprio corpo: reflexões sobre as transexualidades'. In M. T. A. D. Coelho and L. L. P. Sampaio (org) (eds.), *Transexualidades: um olhar multidisciplinar*. Salvador: EDUFBA, 53–63.
Chevalier, J., and Gheerbrant, A. (2006). *Dicionário de símbolos*. 20th ed. Rio de Janeiro: Editora José Olympio.
Coelho, M. T. A. D., and Sampaio, L. L. P. (2014). 'As transexualidades na atualidade: aspectos conceituais e contexto'. In M. T. A. Coelho and L. L. P. Sampaio (org) (eds.), *Transexualidades: um olhar multidisciplinar*. Salvador: EDUFBA, 13–23.
Colling, L., and Sant´ana, T. (2014). 'Um breve olhar sobre a transexualidade na mídia'. In M. T. A. Coelho and L. L. P. Sampaio (org), *Transexualidades: um olhar multidisciplinar*. Salvador: EDUFBA, 255–256.
Hillman, J. (2009). *Suicídio e alma*. Rio de Janeiro: Vozes.
Herrmann, S. B. (2008). 'Treatment of an abandonment trauma'. *Journal of Sandplay Therapy*, 17 (2), 5172.
Hopcke, R. (1991). *Jung, Jungians and homosexuality*. Eugene, Oregon: Shambhala Publications.
Horschutz, R. W. (2008). *O sofrimento infantil e a demanda de análise psicoterápica*. Trabalho apresentado no X Simpósio Regional do Instituto de Psicologia de Campinas (IPAC) – Campinas.
Johnson, D. (2015). 'Models of the "self": gendered, non-gendered and trans-gendered'. *Self and Sociey. An International Journal for Humanistic Psychology*, 43 (3), 219–225.
Jung, C. G. (1911–12/1952). 'Symbols of the mother and of rebirth'. In *Collected works*, Vol 5, *Symbols of transformation* (2nd ed.) London: Routledge & KeganPaul, 1995.
Jung, C. G. (1926). 'Spirit and life'. In *Collective works*, Vol. 8, *The structure and dynamics of the psyche* (2nd ed.) London: Routledge & Kegan Paul, 1991.
Kalf, D. M. (1980). *Sandplay: a psychotherapeutic approach to the psych*. Santa Monica: Sigo Press.
Kaylo, J. (2009). 'Anima and animus embodied: Junguian gender and Laban movement analysis'. *Body, Movement and Dance in Psychotherapy: International Journal for Theory, Research and Practice*, 4 (3), P.185.
King, A. (2012). 'The daw of a new identity: aspects of a relational approach to psychotherapy with a transsexual client'. *British Journal of Psychotherapy*, 28 (1), 35–49.
Lexikon, H. (2009). *Dicionário de símbolos*. São Paulo: Pensamento-Cultrix.
Lima Filho, A. P. (2002). *O pai e a psique*. São Paulo: Paulus.
Matta, R. M. (2015). *Trauma em crianças e acolhimento institucional: Avaliação e transformação por meio do processo psicoterapêutico da Terapia do Sandplay*. PhD. PUC-São Paulo.
Mackenzie, S. (2006). 'Queering gender: anima/animus and the paradigm of emergence'. *The Journal of Analytical Psychology*, 5 (3), 401–421.
Marsman, M. A. (2017). 'Transgenderism and transformation: an attempt at a Jungian understanding'. *The Journal of Analytical Psychology*, 62 (5), 678–687.
Moleiro, C., and Pinto, N. (2015). 'Sexual orientation and gender identity: review of concepts, controversies and their relation to psychopathology classificatives systems'. *Frontiers in Psychology/Psychopathology*. V(6), 1–6.
Neumann, E. (1991). *A criança*. 10th ed. São Paulo: Cultrix.
Neumann, E. (2008). *A História da Origem da consciência*. 13th ed. São Paulo: Cultrix.

Ramos, D. G. (2006). *A psique do corpo: a dimensão simbólica da doença*. São Paulo: Summus.
Samuels, A. (1984). 'Gender and psyche: developments in analytical psychology'. *British Journal of Psychotherapy*, 1 (1), 31–49.
Singer, J. (1995). *Androginia: rumo a uma nova teoria da sexualidade*. São Paulo: Cultrix.
Stieglitz, K. A. (2010). 'Development, risk, and resilience of transgender youth'. *The Journal of the Association of Nurses in AIDS Care*, 21 (3), 192–206.
Tarnas, R. (2007). *Cosmos and Psyche: intimations of a new world view*. Pacific Graduate Institute.
Vancer, S. R., Ehrensaft, D., and Rosenthal, S. M. (2014). 'Psychological and medical care of gender nonconforming youth'. *Pediatrics*, 134 (6), 1184–92.
Weinrib, E. L. (1993). *Imagens do self: O processo terapêutico na caixa-de-areia*. São Paulo: Summus.010234930Information Classification: General00Information Classification: General

Chapter 7

Bernini and the Pont Sant'Angelo
The transcendent hermaphrodite as symbol of individuation

William T. Farrar, IV

Introduction: The discovery of the hermaphroditos

Around 1620, Gian Lorenzo Bernini was given an unusual commission by his patron, Scipione Borghese (Haskell & Penny, 1981). Bernini had already established his talent at sculpting the human form in works like *The Martyrdom of Saint Lawrence* and *Aeneas, Anchises, and Ascanius*. But now, Bernini was asked to create a pedestal for *The Sleeping Hermaphroditos*, a copy of a Hellenistic statue attributed to Polycles (Pliny the Elder, trans. 1850, XXXIV.19), which had recently been excavated during the renovation of a church in Rome.

There are many such copies of the *Sleeping Hermaphroditos*. It is usually assumed to have functioned as a whimsical *au naturel* decoration reclining in a semi-public outdoor setting (Ajootian, 1995, 1997; Szepessey, 2014). When looked at from behind, it appears to be a woman in repose. However, when one walks around to the front of the statue, there's a surprise: the 'woman' has a penis!

Bernini made this particular copy extraordinary by sculpting the extravagant *matarrazo* [mattress], which creates a paradoxically intimate space that is now considered an integral part of the sculpture. Like Duchamp's last masterpiece, *Étant donnés*, it is an artistic ensemble that involves the viewer in its exhibitionism (Høy, 2000). Those who choose to assert their gaze upon the work's full form become ensnared by their own psyches as voyeurs caught in *flagrante delicto*.

This transformation of art into psychological theatre foregrounds the *Sleeping Hermaphroditos* as more than just a 'frivolous' sculpture. It has a deeper significance: 'myth, religion, cult, gender, sexuality, sex, love and marriage rites are all inextricably interwoven themes in the … hermaphrodite body in art' (Szepressy, 2014, p. 5). And in Bernini's time, the hermaphrodite also symbolised:

> liminal beings who dwell in the border between genders, between the human and the monstrous, between science and mythology, hermaphrodites represented for the early modern mentality the daunting mystery of mediation. It should not surprise anyone that love philosophers evoked them to better understand the complex relation between the spiritual and the sensual after all, for the Greeks, Eros himself was a mediator.
>
> (Maurette, 2015, p. 896)

Thus, the sculpture's 'effect of contrast and ambiguity, indeed this taste for the strange that plays with the viewer's emotions' (Bénédicte, 2011, para. 4) becomes a subtle *tour de force* that may astonish viewers into the awareness that the hard oppositions that define human existence (e.g., male versus female, the sacred versus the secular) may actually be more fluid than they seem.

The psychology of two and one: Jung, the *rebis*, and hermaphroditos

Jung (1940) also shares a liminal interpretation of the hermaphrodite, which he views as a psychological '*symbol of the creative union of opposites*, a "uniting symbol" in the literal sense' (para. 293). According to Jung, the hermaphrodite denotes both the first stage of the psyche's development process, in which the psyche is sexually undifferentiated, and the last stage of the process, the *coniunctio oppositorum*, in which the fully developed psyche successfully integrates both its male and female aspects. This perspective is similar to Aristophanes' allegory on eros in Plato's *Symposium* (trans. 1891, 189c–193e). Here, the original humans were wholes of various gender combinations – female/female, male/male, and female/male. They were then split by the gods and now spend the remainder of their lives seeking their lost half to regain their unity. Jung makes it clear, however, that the *coniunctio* of the hermaphrodite addresses only a heterosexual union: 'it is readily understandable that the primordial image of the hermaphrodite should reappear in modern psychology in the guise of the male-female antithesis' (para. 296). As if to emphasise this point, Jung (1937) notes that this *coniunctio* is often represented by the image of a *rebis*, a creature with two heads, usually one of each sex, and a single body that is split into engendered halves (cf., figures 125 & 199).

However, the *rebis* may be a problematic symbol of the *coniunctio* because its engendered halves rely on an oppositional complementary approach. The principles of this approach are described by Samuels (2015): one creates a list of properties or statements about a construct (e.g., the 'male' animus) and then builds a complementary list of its opposite (e.g., the 'female' anima). Though these lists are often used to demonstrate the equality and wholeness of their unification, they are fundamentally hierarchical. The first list usually illustrates what the second lacks (e.g., 'the animus is rational'; 'the anima is emotional'); and, 'If the socially dominant list is presented first, as in Jung's analysis, then it is not at all hard to predict the contents of the second list' (p. 232), which are implicitly subordinate.

Enns (1994) points out such an approach reinforces inherently dualistic thinking: 'the very labeling of certain qualities as masculine or feminine encourages individuals to see certain traits as opposites, which may lead to selective perception and distortions of the actual behaviors of men and women' (p. 131). Jung may have realised this as well. Though he once stated that 'As civilization develops, the bisexual primordial being turns into a symbol of the unity of personality, a symbol of the self, where the war of opposites finds peace' (Jung, 1940, para.

294), he later realised this peace is only apparent, as the symbolism of the *rebis* manifests 'a visible seam or suture' (Jung, 1951, para. 390).

The suture in the *rebis* may make a true *coniunctio* difficult, if not impossible. For example, Singer (1976/1989) presented an androgyne model that addresses how aspects of the self, which are traditionally labelled masculine and feminine, make up everyone's psyche. She also discussed how people could bring these aspects into a unified whole. But this model remains limited because its foundation is in the *rebis*, whose oppositional complementaries are not truly integrated but merely stitched together in an illusion of *coniunctio*. For example, Singer states that 'the new androgyne is not in confusion about his or her sexual identity. Androgynous men express a natural, unforced and uninhibited male sexuality, while androgynous women can be totally female and have their own sexuality' (p. 14); in other words, the androgyny is founded in expressing oneself through one engendered side or the other of the *rebis'* suture. The presence of this seam can also be seen in some of the diagrams Singer provides, which summarise the relation of 'feminine' and 'masculine' as complementary lists of generalised properties (e.g., women/dark/diffuse; men/light/focal) (p. 158, p. 174). The attempted *coniunctio* creates an illusion of integration but leaves the separating power of oppositional complementarities intact: 'put them together, and there is a perfect wholeness. Divide them ... and one can see how one list constructs the other' (Samuels, 2015, p. 232).

The problem of the *rebis* is that its manifests the image of its own failure. Wholeness remains sutured because it is expressed through the division of oppositional complementaries that maintain their unique identities. The two heads of the *rebis* show the split remains, and it is unclear which head will have the final say. As Doniger and Eliade (2005) put it: 'androgynes are popularly supposed to stand for a kind of equality and balance between the sexes, ... they more often represent a desirable or undesirable distortion of the male-female relationship or a tension based on an unequal distribution of power' (p. 337).

Weil (1992) proposes an alternative to the androgyne model based on Ovid's version of the Hermaphroditos myth in the *Metamorphosis* (trans. 1899, Book IV). Hermaphroditos is a single, one-headed being that embodies opposites as unities. According to Kerényi (1951), Hermaphroditos is the child of Hermes and Aphrodite, who are sometimes said to beget Eros as well. In fact, Kerényi playfully suggests that the names Hermaphroditos and Eros may denote the same offspring. As Kerényi tells the story, Hermaphroditos was born male, but was transformed when the nymph Salamakis fell in love and embraced him while swimming. Answering Salamakis' prayer, the gods transformed both into a single being that transcends classification into either gender.

Weil (1992) argues that Hermaphroditos embodies a singular unity that fuses and confuses traditional gender distinctions in an 'endless play of (sexual) "difference"' (p. 141). This idea of hermaphroditic play, which suggests was partly inspired by James Hillman's archetypal theory (McKenzie, 2006), aims to break down complimentary oppositions and transform them into a multiplicity of unique qualities that allows one 'to imagine a multidimensional dance of gender traits' (Weil, 1992, p. 408). As with the 'half-playful, half-erotic' (Bénédicte, 2011, para. 4) *Sleeping Hermaphroditos*, the presence of such a psychic or physical being implicitly destabilises and unmoors engendered dichotomies and serves as reminder that each individual is potentially unique and surprising.

Hermaphroditos is not necessarily superior to the *rebis*. Hermaphroditos may avoid sutured complementarities; but it too may create a false *coniunctio* where the multivalent, unengendered oppositions do not really come together. As Jung (1958a) stated about a shadow aspect of the hermaphroditic Mercurius symbol, it can represent 'two worlds which interpenetrate yet do not touch' (para. 726). Part of the reason for this is that the suture of oppositional complementaries is culturally ubiquitous. Language's historic semantic accretions have infused its concepts with engendered categorisations that daily impact human beliefs and actions through its power to support sex stereotyping (e.g., see Brannon, 2016 for a review). Discarding these categorisations can distort words' meanings and can result in a potential loss of communion and communication. Direct language can be lost, and Hermaphroditos can start sliding 'into irony in order to express a fragmentation of consciousness that both responds to and playfully aids in the creation of a world unmoored, tending anxiously if not wholly into chaos' (Feldman, 1995, p. 91). The lack of connection may even risk destruction (cf., Jung, 1958a, paras. 725–729).

The hermaphrodite and the transcendent function

Interestingly, Jung (1942) also hints at a Hermaphroditos model in his discussion of Mercurius, which he describes as a fluid, unstable multiplicity whose constantly shifting traits transcend not only the dichotomies of male and female, but other oppositional complementaries (e.g., *puer* and *senex*) (Jung, 1942, paras. 267–269). In addition, an unpublished, hand-written diagram that Jung sent to Victor White (Lammers & Cunningham, 2007) provides clues on how this Hermaphroditos multiplexity can be expressed amidst the social realities of oppositional complementaries. A schematic of the lower half of this diagram, which linked together a number of *quaternios* [fourfold aspects of the psyche] is presented in Figure 7.1 (cf., Jung, 1951, paras. 347–390). As can be seen in the figure, Jung labelled the point that linked the higher and lower (i.e., *paradise and physical matter*) *quaternios* together, the *Hermaphrodite*.

Unlike the *rebis*, whose two engendered heads separately look toward the left and right, the gesture of this hermaphrodite translated into the vertical, in which the multivalent aspects of heaven (i.e., the four rivers of paradise) interact with the multivalent aspects of the material world (i.e., the four elements). This vertical movement illustrates the *transcendent function*, which brings 'onscious and unconscious together and so arrive at a new attitude' (Jung, 1958b, para. 146). The hermaphrodite is no longer a 'seamed' engendered *rebis*, as the sexual oppositions become merely the transverse, or background.

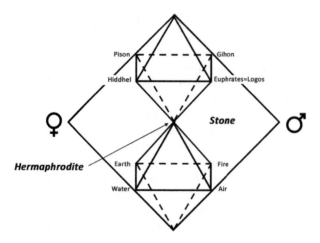

Figure 7.1 Jung's diagram of the hermaphrodite (adapted from Lammers, 2007)

This unified *transcendent hermaphrodite* (henceforth called the *trans*) becomes the bridge that rises above the undercurrents of engendered oppositions to enable the multiplex elements of the psyche to interpenetrate and touch. The contrast between *rebis* and *trans* is analogous to the underlying difference of the *coniunctio oppositorum* and *the coincidentia oppositorum*. Henderson (2010) points out that Jung often used the two terms interchangeably. However, their semantics imply a subtle, but important difference. The *coniunctio* implies a union of opposites, where two are joined as one. As previously mentioned, this process entails imbalance: joined oppositional complementaries often result in one side dominating the other (e.g., masculine dominating feminine). *Coincidentia* implies no explicit joint or 'seam' between opposites, but a shared presence in a single location: 'Two phenomena coincide when they occupy the same space, be it logical, imaginative or material space' (Henderson, 2010, p.103). In Figure 7.1, the point at which the paradise and the material world interpenetrate and touch can be understood as *coincidentia*, symbolised by the *trans*.

The *Sleeping Hermaphroditos* provides a striking example of the *trans*' ability to overcome the limits of language. When the sculpture's illustration of the *coincidentia* is surprisingly discovered – both breasts and penis existing in an unsutured unity – the revelation can evoke a variety of non-discursive responses (e.g., laughter, repulsion, desire, an intellectual insight, or a mix of all of these). Even after the initial surprise wears off, there may remain a sense of mystery not fully fathomed. For example, Maurette (2015) points out that the discovery of the *Sleeping Hermaphroditos*:

> prefigures some of the main characteristics of an intellectual sensibility that would dominate the following two centuries and beyond: a renewed interest

in corporeality, a more nuanced and self-aware approach to issues of gender, a revaluation of the role of the senses, a reaction against long-established dualisms, an exaltation of curiosity, and a fascination with the eccentric, the paradoxical, and the ambiguous. Across disciplines, languages, and time the hermaphrodite would bespeak all of these characteristics like few other figures did

(pp. 894–895)

Bernini the trickster: Bringing forth the transcendental hermaphrodite

In what follows, I suggest that Bernini's life and art can be read as an example of the process of individuation – the integration of the conscious and unconscious (Jung, 1939) expressed through the symbol of the *trans*. Specifically, many of his artistic works from the early *matarrazo* to his final sculpture, *Salvator Mundi*, can be understood as signifiers of psychic development in which the *rebis* of the *coniunctio* gradually transforms into the *trans* of the *coincidentia*. I also suggest that Bernini's role in seventeenth-century Rome led him to take on the role of a Hermetic trickster. This role allowed him to apply his mercurial talents toward dissolving the boundaries between matter and imagination to create new spaces of artistic and emotional expression (cf., Stein, 1999). What makes Bernini so powerful an example of the individuation process is that it was not done in solitude, but through a series of successful public masterpieces that continue to evoke awe and wonder to this day.

One of the keys to understanding Bernini's sense of creative imagination is the concept of *bel composto*, which aims to bring together the arts of architecture, sculpture, and painting into a beautiful whole (Baldinucci, 1682/2007; Lavin, 1980). In addition, Bernini was a master of *tenerreza* [tenderness], a Baroque technical term that describes how an artwork can create a powerful emotional experience by transforming sculptural material into a surface that recalls the feel of flesh (see Mormando's introduction in D. Bernini, 1713/2011). Through *tenerreza*, vision creates an anticipation of a touch that reveals the softness, warmth, and life that is absent from the actual marble itself. Bernini's skills can give viewers the illusion that his works also have 'what lies beneath the surface of living things – the invisible *anima* or *spiritus* that distinguishes a living, breathing being from mere inert matter' (Bolland, 2000, p. 391).

Bernini's *bel composto* also included theatrical skill. Bernini wrote and designed the scenography for as many as 20 plays (see Beecher, 1984, Lavin, 1964/2007, Mormando, 2011), for which he created special effects such as thunder, lightning, rain, and the movement of the sun (Witt, 2013). He also crafted meta-theatrical deceptions that break down the distinction between audience and stage, fooling the audience that a backdrop has caught fire; staging a flood to look like it would swamp the entire theatre, and creating a mock audience of actors who mirrored and parodied the real audience. Most of his plays were comedies that poked fun at Roman society to get laughs, and many were self-referential distortions of issues Bernini faced as an artist. In one such play, a main character, who served as Bernini's alter ego, states, 'Ingenuity and design constitute the Magic Art [sic] by whose means you deceive the eye and make your audience gaze in wonder' (Mormando, 2011, p. 117).

Bernini's knowledge of illusion makes him the master of the liminal. His works dissolve the distinction between appearance and reality so that they evoke a sense of cognitive vertigo in viewers. In *Apollo and Daphne* for example, the suggestion of human action – the gestures and poses that have not yet reached their point of repose – illustrates his mastery of *tenerezza*, in which inanimate stone implies a passionate touch. The work of art appears to reach toward the viewer, invoking a sensuous emotion where the distinctions between what is alive and what is not dissolve into insignificance.

Bernini's artistry creates a space of immediacy that transforms the fantastic into a sense of the possible. Lavin (2008) describes Bernini as 'always quick, facile, impulsive, and elegant in everything he did' (p. 292), and elsewhere states, 'The virtuoso technique, the dramatic, even provocative emotions, the lavish color, the tumultuous design, the illusionistic devices, including the intermingling of two- and three-dimension formal – all this seems 'sham-ful' (Lavin, 1980, p. 4). Similarly, Warwick (2012) calls Bernini's ability to suffuse marble with life a 'marvelous deceit' (p. 14), and further suggests that as his art evolved, he increasingly entwined theatrical devices into his sculpture, turning them into a 'porous proscenium', 'spaces of art and of audience ... interwoven' (Warwick, 2012, p. 39). In other words, Bernini's mastery of weaving illusions fulfilled the characteristics of a trickster.

Basil-Morozow (2017) argues that the trickster role emerges in cultural milieus in which previously rigid social structures are in the process of destabilizing. The trickster injects a chaotic element that breaks up the milieus' stagnation and lack of perspective. This chaos can facilitate social collapse (i.e., the 'apocalyptic' trickster; Basil-Morozow, 2017) or bring cultural renewal (i.e., the 'Hermes' trickster) by allowing an adaptive restructuring (cf., Burkert, 1977/1996; Fertel, 2015; Kerényi, 1976/1992).

Rome needed a trickster. In Bernini's time, it was a hotbed of scandal where many cardinals and nobles were using the Church to perpetuate self-indulgent livelihoods (Mormando, 2011). Further, the Protestant reformation had undermined the religious hegemony of Catholicism over Europe. Although the Council of Trent (1545-1563) provided a direction for confronting these challenges, the renewal called for a disruptive creativity to give its counter-reformation artistic expression.

As Mormando's (2011) biography attests, Bernini's personality also fulfilled the trickster role. Tricksters move across social boundaries, break moral taboos, express sexual instability, and often avoid punishment; they also maintain a constant wittiness and a fluid sense of spontaneity (Doty, 2005). Bernini's life exemplified all of these. He crossed class boundaries and changed his social form to suit the circumstances. On one hand, he was the knighted '*Cavaliere*' who was gracefully intimate with popes and royalty. On the other, he could easily stoop to cutting backdoor deals with working-class suppliers, taking credit for other people's work, and falsely buttressing his reputation by telling 'self-mythologizing exaggerations and untruths about his personal development and professional career' (pp. 8–9). He also expressed taboo-breaking sexual impulsivity. For example, Bernini had an affair with Costanza Bonarelli, the wife of one of his co-workers. This affair lasted until he found out she was also 'cheating' on him by also sleeping with his brother, Luigi. Bernini then had his lover's face slashed and attempted to maim his brother (McPhee, 2006). And yet, because of his talent, the sole repercussion for this act was the requirement by the Pope that he get married.

Bernini's life illustrates the eternal enigma of the 'Hermes' trickster. Though his own life reflects the social chaos of the time, the artifacts he leaves behind can create a new order. In the case of Bernini, these artifacts have led him to be described as a person 'so at peace with society that he could express ... the pleasure of the collective, the sensuality of the pious, the ecstasy of obedience. The individual's desires are not subsumed, but are at one with those of the social order' (Jones, 2003).

One of the works that illustrates this Hermes nature of creating order out of simple stone is *The Four Rivers Fountain* in Rome's Piazza Navona. This fountain epitomises the *coincidentia oppositorum* by appearing to fuse earth into an inseparable whole that uplifts a 59-ton obelisk into the heavens. When Pope Alexander questioned Bernini about the stone, Bernini answered that all the structural elements so enjoined one to the other, their interconnections harmonise marvelously to sustain the whole (D. Bernini, 1713). It is in such creative acts that Bernini renewed the visual vocabulary of the Catholic Church to give its chaos form. He allowed it to express its counterreformation message with 'directness, intelligibility, theatricality, flamboyance, emotionality and sensationalism. It wore its heart on its sleeve' (Preston, 2013, p. 51) and it still touches the world today.

In the role of Hermes, Bernini becomes the lover, pursuing his eros for the spirit of beauty. He called the Hellenistic sculptures in the Vatican his 'girlfriends', he said that 'going to work ... was like entering a garden of delights'; and when people tried to pull him away from his work, he would say 'Let me be, for I am in love'(Mormando, 2011, pp. 29–30). According to Paris (1986) the object of such an eros can be symbolised by Aphrodite, whose beauty 'springs from the deep sexual encounter and ... has the power of transmuting the physical experience into ecstasy' (p. 17). Aphrodite represents the power of beauty as a civilising force, which Paris illustrates with a quote from the poet Claire Lejeune: 'Beauty alone brings us to our knees without abasement, washes away all humiliation, heals us of all rancor, and reconciles us with the universe' (Paris, 1986, p. 17). In this manner, Bernini's artistic development can be seen as a constant attempt to achieve a *hieros gamos* [holy espousal] in which his Hermes nature can fuse with the beauty of Aphrodite, giving birth to the *trans*.

Bernini's life and art: Individuation and the transcendental hermaphrodite

Bernini's struggle to achieve the *hieros gamos* can be seen in two pieces he created soon after completing the *Sleeping Hermaphroditos*. The first piece was *Rape of Proserpina*. This work, although praised for its handling of the marble to simulate flesh (Hibbard, 1965/1991), illustrates the attempted use of violence to bring together engendered oppositional complementaries: 'Pluto [i.e., the "masculine"] storming forward at the instant of his violent snatch at Proserpina [i.e., the "feminine"] ... interpreted ... as a conflict of brutal lust and desperate anguish' (Wittkower, 1955, p. 5). It is a failed *coniunctio* that promises only a damaged future in a hell of lifeless damnation.

The second piece, *Apollo and Daphne*, can be seen as an alternative illustration on failed *coniunctio*. In this case, union of opposites is not grasped through direct conquest, but through the violence of unreciprocated desire. Bolland (2000) sees *Apollo and Daphne* as a complex meditation on the relationship between the nature of love, touch and art itself. The sculpture is an intricate and beautiful work, evoking the Renaissance ideal of the touch, which implies both intimate knowledge and the 'erotic gratification-the caress, the kiss, the sexual embrace' (p. 319). But the work subverts itself by testifying to its own non-consummation: 'Apollo sees soft flesh and is shocked to feel hard bark, just as a viewer who might attempt to caress the transformed marble of Bernini's statue, which looks as soft as modeled wax, would be surprised to touch cold, hard stone' (p. 322). The work appears to critique the violence in a lack of reciprocity, which destroys the attempted *coniunctio*, as the active, desiring subject reduces the other half into an inert inaccessible subject. Such pseudo-integration recalls the seamed *rebis*, with its illusion of unequal identity. As Bolland summarises the message *of Apollo and Daphne*: 'What you see is not what you get' (Bolland, 2000, p. 322).

When the *Saint Teresa in Ecstasy* was commissioned for the Church of Santa Maria della Vittoria, it was like a summons for Bernini to once more reconsider the question of the *coniunctio*. Though it had been 30 years since he carved *matarazzo*, the *Sleeping Hermaphroditos* had recalled him, for it was underneath this very church that it had been originally excavated (Haskell & Penny, 1981). In the interim, Bernini had become the premier artist of the Catholic Church. But at the time of this commission, he had temporarily fallen from the papal grace due to an architectural fiasco at St. Peter's Basilica. The smaller, more intimate scale of the *Ecstasy* allowed Bernini the latitude to more fully return to the question of how to represent the union of heaven and earth.

In this work, Bernini uses his Hermes' skill to navigate an 'ideological tightrope' (Call, 1997, p. 36). A statement from the Council of Trent (1563/2011) commanded that 'in the invocation of saints, ... all lasciviousness be avoided; in such wise that figures shall not be painted or adorned with a beauty exciting to lust' (Session 25). Yet the *Ecstasy* foregrounds sensual beauty. Bernini uses sexual allusion, the shifting beauty of light, the movement of draped clothing, all of which are attributes of erotic Aphrodite (Paris, 1986) to invent a moment of sacred realisation (Bolland, 2014; Lavin, 1980). This ambiguity allows the work to be seen as either a high expression of mystical devotion within the Church or as a low manifestation of sexual lasciviousness (Landre, 2015). It has been variously described as the expression of a visionary experience of God (Warma, 1984), a taste of the moment of death (Bolland, 2014), or a blatant orgasm (Nobus, 2015). And an anonymous tract written in Bernini's lifetime stated that the work had 'dragged that most pure Virgin [Teresa] down to the ground' while 'transforming her into a Venus who was not only prostrate, but prostituted as well' (Mormando, 2011, p. 65). Both the mystical and erotic interpretations are apt if the work is seen as expressing the spirit of Aphrodite, who also links the spiritual to the sensual (Paris, 1986). In the words of Hillman (1998), Aphrodite represents 'the desire to suffuse imagination with an erotic tinge, to give it wings, a *frissonne*, that reminds and calls: "to more, to farther, to other", a wondrous lifting not of this world ... or, filling this world with the light of another' (62:16).

The *Ecstasy* captures the moment after Teresa's *transverbation* – the spiritual piercing of the heart – when the lance has just been withdrawn. Bernini used Teresa's own words to guide his vision (Mormando, 2011): when the angel 'drew it out. ... The pain was so sharp that it made me utter several moans; and so excessive was the sweetness caused me by this intense pain that one can never wish to lose it' (Teresa of Avila, 1565/1995, p. 164). This *coniunctio* is one of mutuality. The touch that penetrates to the heart was given only because it was desired and the response to its withdrawal is an emotionally complex one that transcends simple emotional categorisation.

The *Ecstasy* expresses the transcendent as well. The lance of the transverberation 'becomes the point of contact between earth and heaven, between matter and spirit' (Lavin, 1980, p. 113), through which all becomes liminal. Teresa appears to be rising on a cloud, and the angel seems to be pulling Teresa's drapery gently upward. This angelic gesture is similar to that in another Bernini sculpture, *Habakkuk and the Angel*, in which an angel gently lifts a tuft of Habakkuk's head to raise him from his ordinary world and into one of higher purpose (Daniel, 14:33–39, Vulgate version). In the *Ecstasy*, Bernini seems to imply that Teresa's experience is not merely a physical sensation, but a singular moment of immediacy that will transform her life's *telos* (cf., Olive, 2009).

In the *coniunctio* of the *Ecstasy*, the signifiers of engendered complementaries begin to dissolve. Though the angel is the 'male' and Teresa is the 'female', this difference is diminished. The angel's gender seems polymorphously fluid; Teresa's gender disappears beneath the drama of her drapery, in which the 'accumulation of folds hides, and even obliterates, the vast majority of the saint's body ... allowing her to achieve ... a union with God in which the body is absent' (Farmer, 2013, p. 397–398).

The *Ecstasy* takes the idea of the *coniunctio* to its limit: though it represents the touching of opposites, the residuum of the *rebis*' suture remains. This can be seen in the controversies regarding the sculpture's treatment of gender, which still reflects oppositional complementaries (see Call, 1997; Farmer, 2013): it is still debated whether the *Ecstasy* depicts a woman's freedom to achieve the heights of spiritual expression or whether it illustrates the oppression of the women in a context of masculine interpretation. Further, the suture is exacerbated by the work's intentional division of the subjective and objective. The *Ecstasy* was designed to be viewed from one ideal location (Lavin, 1980) which places the viewer as member of a jury of sculpted male spectators who are debating Teresa's experience, which remains an internal psychic event subject to an external social interpretation.

The Pont Sant'Angelo and beauty: The transcendental hermaphrodite as embodied presence

It was 20 years later that Bernini created a work that went beyond the limits of the *Ecstasy*'s *coniunctio*. In the Pont Sant'Angelo, Bernini applied his skill in *bel composto* to express the *coincidentia oppositorum*, in which the residuum of complementaries (e.g., male and female, objective and subjective, inside and outside) is dissolved as oppositions enfolded in the singular moment of immediate experience.

The Pont was ideal as an image of the *coincidentia*; for centuries, it had served as the primary source of commerce and communication over the Tiber River between Rome and the Vatican (Weil, 1974). More importantly, it served symbolically to span the boundary between the sacred and profane. Papal processions entered secular Rome via the Pont. For pilgrims, the bridge was the last station for reflection and recollection before entering into the holy space of St. Peter's Basilica.

Like the *Ecstasy*, the Pont relies on angels to represent the connection between heaven and earth. These angels were commissioned by the church to recall a sixth-century CE appearance of Archangel Michael above the Castel Sant'Angelo, which is on the Vatican side of the bridge (Weil, 1974). The angels, who display the instruments of Christ's passion (e.g., the lance, the crown of thorns, the whip, and the nails), were also intended as reminders of Christ's sacrifice. In addition, they were meant to assure believers that their prayers will be heard in heaven through God's messengers. The fact that the Pont has remained unchanged for hundreds of years testified that Bernini fulfilled the Church's objectives for propagating the faith.

Once more, however, Bernini created a work that works on multiple levels. Bernini used his skill at scenography to create an emotion-evoking work of psychological theatre that enfolds the pilgrim within its space. For instance, Bernini uses the Tiber River as a design element. Mather (1952) details how Bernini integrated water as 'living and moving element' (p. 119) into many of his works (e.g. *The Fountain of the Four Rivers*) to express a sense of psychic integration. Lavin (2005) also points out how Bernini created open balustrades on the Pont, which made the flowing water visible as an element that adds a dynamic contrast to the bridge's sculptures. Lavin also suggest that the flowing adds to the bridge's symbolic significance as a liminal centre. Not only does the horizontal axis of the bridge bring together the secular and the sacred, but the vertical axis also unites the obscure depths of the waters with the brilliant openness of the sky.

Only two of the Pont's sculptures are directly based on Bernini's work, but he determined every element of the bridge, including the modelling and design of the other angels (Lavin, 2005; Weil, 1974). The end result illustrates what the seventeenth-century architect Furttenbach (cited in Warwick, 2012) says about Bernini's scenography skill: it leaves the 'spectator … "so overcome with wonders that he scarcely knows if he is in the world or out of it" (p. 33)'.

The act of semblance on the Pont uses Hermetic trickery to bring us into an experience of the transcendence. Unlike the *Ecstasy*, we are no longer restricted to a gaze at a fixed location at a safe distance. Instead, as we enter an increasingly intimate space, we advance toward the centre of the bridge. It is a space where we find ourselves enclosed in an existential immediacy where multiplicities of phenomenological modalities – the imaginal and the perceptual, the constructed and the natural – become merged.

We are no longer viewers judging Teresa with our distant gaze. Rather, we become like Teresa: participants in our own personal relationship with the Pont's angels. These sensuous forms with their obscure gender and instruments of Christ's suffering express the *trans* as *coincidentia* of eros and passion.

The Pont's poetics of the *coincidentia* evokes the subjective logic of the included middle, where two apparently contradictory concepts are bridged in the unity of an experiential event. 'It is an affective logic, an uncanny logic … irreducible to verbal propositions but encompassing involuntary memories, images, and non-discursive formations … making sense via its very embodiment' (Semetsky, 2013, p. 230). The resulting *coincidentia* in this theatre of water, sky, stone, and personal presence can be analogous to the *I–Thou* relationship described by Buber (1923/1999), in which the '*Thou* meets me. But I step into direct relation with it. Hence the relation means being chosen and choosing. … Concentration and fusion into the whole being can never take place through my agency, nor can it ever take place without me' (p. 17).

This acute moment of fused recognition is similar to that described by Barthes (1980/2010): 'It is not I that seek it out … this element that arises from the scene, shoots out of it like an arrow, and pierces me. A Latin word exists to designate this wound, this prick, this mark made by a pointed instrument: … *punctum*' (p. 26). In both the *Ecstasy* and the Pont, it is an angel that enacts the transcendent *punctum*. The *Ecstasy* displays the effect of this *punctum* after the transverberation pierces Teresa's heart. But on the Pont, the *punctum* is not meant to be seen but felt within our heart. Rather lance and the instruments of the passion are meant to create an individual immediacy that has the power to pierce us as the incarnate fuses with the transcendent.

The immediacy of the angel's *punctum* can be overwhelming, as the author Charles Dickens (1847) attested when his own emotional response led him to call these inanimate stone sculptures 'breezy maniacs' (p. 199).

Yet, the experience can also be life changing, in a manner reminiscent of Rilke's (1912) 'First Diuno Elegy':

> Who, when I cry aloud, would hear me from among the angelic
> hosts? And even if one of them was to take
> me suddenly to heart: I would dissolve
> within its greater being. For beauty really is nothing
> but the inception of a terror that we can only just bear,
> and we hold it in awe because it serenely disdains
> to destroy us. Every angel is terrifying.
>
> (p. 7, paraphrased from the German)

As Rilke attests, the arousal derived from the juxtaposition of eros and passion have the potential to be experienced as an emotion that ranges from ecstasy to terror. Such emotional possibilities hearken back to the *Ecstasy*. Just as the angel's withdrawn lance symbolises Teresa's liminal experience as bridge between heaven and earth, so do the angel's instruments of passion symbolise potential transverberation for each of us who are open to the message of the Pont. These instruments do not promise an unambiguously positive experience but an affectively complex one, like Teresa's. These experiences even risk being accompanied by painful insights that defy simple emotional categorisations: the punctum of a lanced heart, the lacerating knowledge of a thorn-crowned forehead, and the piercing pain of immobilised will.

The arousal of eros and passion also serves as a transcendent call, such as the one described in Diotima's speech in Plato's *Symposium* (trans 1891, 210a–212c) in which desire toward a singularly beautiful physical form draws us into the contemplation of a more subtle, unseen beauty (see Nussbaum, 1986/2001). This distinction is clarified by Konstan (2015), who argues that the ancient Greeks had two words for beauty, *kállos*, which is a 'physical beauty, above all the beauty associated with erotic attraction (p. 368)'; and *kalós*, a more abstract beauty of virtuous behaviour.

The Pont brings both *kállos* and *kalós* within the unity of the existential present. This is accomplished through Bernini's *bel composto* of dynamic sculpture and immersive scenography, which create the powerful sense of immediacy presence that also implies transcendent purpose. Such a sense of immediacy has been described by Gadamer (1960/1990) in his discussion of beauty: '"Being present" belongs in a convincing way to the being of beauty itself. However much beauty might be experienced as something supraterrestial, it is still there in the visible world' (pp. 481–482).

Gadamer (1960/1990) calls this experience of beauty *radiance*, in which the apparently unbridgeable gap between the senses and the transcendent is both manifest and overcome. This radiance has two paradoxical aspects. It reveals itself as kind of singularity: 'harmonious whole proportioned within itself' (p. 482). For example, on the Pont, this harmonious radiance is called forth from the disparate, disjunctive elements that compose the setting of the bridge. It is also dynamic, as Spuybroek (2014) describes: 'Parts that merge into a whole spill out of that whole. Parts that converge into a whole diverge from that whole. ... What at first seems a double movement – parts gathering, parts spilling – is turned into a single movement by beauty' (p. 120).

This experience of overflowing radiance can even transform the meaning of transcendence, which no longer signifies something beyond this life but an awareness of what it means to be a living human in the present moment. This immanent mode of transcendence is described by Brooke (2016) as human beings consciously exercising their freedom to interpret and interact with the events in their life and reflecting on them in a self-dialogue. It is a realisation that 'we live in the present and toward the future while still in relation to memory and the past (p. 27).

Spuybroek (2014) argues that the experience of overflowing radiance can also open us to a feeling expressed by the Greek concept of *charis* [grace], a sense of superabundance demanding to be reciprocated with others. An act of *charis* can include the physical giving of gifts, but more so, it also includes the giving of oneself as a gift to the community or world the participant is embedded in: 'beauty is circulating among the public and considered beneficial to that public, a public good' (p. 127).

This is the significance of Bernini's theatre on the *Pont*. It is a space in which once-polarised oppositions liminally coincide in relationships that do not assume oppositional complementaries. It symbolises and attempts to enact a radiant *coincidentia* which has the emotional potential to open each individual to an existential transcendent that not only reconstellates the present but can overflow through time, redefining the oppositions and relations in one's past and transmuting the intentionality of one's future. (cf., Brooke, 2016). The experience of *coincidentia* can even initiate the transformation of the psyche into a gift of the self to the self which can also overflow back into the world in *charis*.

Of course, the Pont itself does not demand such a transformation. For many who visit the Pont, a simple recognition of its artistry is testimony enough to Bernini's Hermetic talents. But the experience of the *coincidentia*, wherever it is experienced, may be life-changing. For each of us, it would be existentially unique. In the case of Teresa, her mystical experiences led her to continue her purpose in strengthening others' faith in God. For us, it may lead to a deeper understanding of our own nature, a resolution to change the nature of our deepest relationships, an awakening of a commitment to one's social truth, or perhaps just a fleeting experience of simple beauty.

Conclusion: The transcendental hermaphrodite as *Salvator Mundi*

The power of the *coincidentia* to deepen the human experience and dissolve oppositional complementaries can be seen in Bernini's last sculpture, *Salvator Mundi*, which he created when he was 80 years old. It is a work in which Bernini expresses atonement. However, even here, he remains a trickster who transforms the original sense of atonement as 'at-one-ment'. The unity expressed in the sculpture is an ideal illustration of a saying attributed to Jesus in the Nag Hammadi writings:

> When you make the two into one, and when you make the inner like the outer and the outer like the inner, and the upper like the lower, and when you make male and female into a single one, so that the male will not be male nor the female be female ... then you will enter [the kingdom] (Gospel of Thomas, trans. 1994, p. 22).

Christ the Redeemer becomes the *trans* as his features meld both masculine (e.g., the beard) and feminine (e.g., the hair), embodying the *coincidentia oppositorum* in a singular personality. This image of Christ, with his subtle eros, captures the *punctum* of the present in an act of *charis*. His benediction to the left blesses the passion he has already undergone; looking to the right, he looks with confidence at the promise of what is to come. The work can be interpreted as Bernini's last word on the *coincidentia*, in which the apparent oppositions of human existence come together in the unity of individuation.

References

Ajootian, A. (1995). 'Monstrum or daimon: hermaphrodites in ancient art and culture'. In B. Berggreen and N. Marinatos (eds.), *Greece and gender*. Bergen, Norway: The Norwegian Institute at Athens, pp. 93–108.

Ajootian, A. (1997). 'The only happy couple: hermaphrodites and gender'. In A. O. Koloski-Ostrow and C. L. Lyons (eds.), *Naked truths: women, sexuality and gender in classical art and archaeology*. New York, NY: Routledge, pp. 220–242.

Baldinucci, F. (2007). *The life of Bernini*. C. Enggass (trans.). University Park: Pennsylvania State University. (Original work published in 1682).

Barthes, R. (2010). *Camera lucida: reflections on photography*. R. Howard (trans.). New York, NY: Hill and Wang. (Original work published in 1980).

Basil-Morozow, H. (2017). 'Loki then and now: the trickster against civilization'. *The International Journal of Jungian Studies*, 9, 84–96. doi:10.1080/19409052.2017.1309780.

Beecher, D. A. (1984). 'Gianlorenzo Bernini's *The Impresario*: the artist as the supreme trickster'. *University of Toronto Quarterly*, 53, 236–247. doi: 10.3138/utq.53.3.236.

Bénédicte, A. M. (2011). *Sleeping hermaphrodite*. Retrieved May 24, 2018 from Louvre website https://www.louvre.fr/en/oeuvre-notices/sleeping-hermaphroditos.

Bernini, D. (2011). *The life of Gian Lorenzo Bernini by Domenico Bernini: a translation and critical edition, with introduction and commentary*. F. Mormando (ed. and trans.). University Park: Pennsylvania State. (Original work published in 1713).

Bolland, A. (2000). 'Desiderio and diletto: vision, touch, and the poetics of Bernini's Apollo and Daphne'. *The Art Bulletin*, 82, 309–330.

Bolland, A. (2014). *Alienata da'sensi*: reframing Bernini's St. Teresa. *Open Art Journal*, 4, 134–157. doi: 10.5456/issn.2050-3679/2015w08.

Brannon, L. (2016). *Gender: psychological perspectives* (7th edn.). New York, NY: Routledge.

Brooke, R. (2016). 'Some common themes of psychology as a human science'. In C. Fischer, L. Laubscher, and R. Brooke (eds.), *The qualitative vision for psychology: an invitation to a human science approach.* Pittsburgh, PA: Duquesne University Press, pp. 17–30.

Buber, M. (2004). *I and thou.* R. G. Smith (Trans.). London, England: Continuum. (Original work published 1923).

Burkert, W. (1996). *Greek religion: archaic and classical.* J. Raffan (trans.). Oxford, England: Blackwell. (Originally published in 1977).

Call, M. T. (1997). Boxing Teresa: the counter-reformation and Brenini's Cornaro Chapel. *Woman's Art Journal*, 18, 34–39. doi: 0.2307/1358678.

Dickens, C. (1847). *Pictures from Italy* [Electronic copy]. Paris, France: Baudry's European Library. Retrieved June 10, 2018 from https://play.google.com/store/books/details/Charles_Dickens_Pictures_from_Italy?id=EW89AAAAcAAJ

Doniger, W., and Eliade, M. (2005). 'Androgynes'. In L. Jones (ed.), *Encyclopedia of religion* (2nd edn., Vol. 1). Detroit: Macmillan Reference USA, pp. 337–342. Retrieved May 16, 2018 from http://link.galegroup.com.libproxy.estrellamountain.edu/apps/doc/CX3424500152/GVRL?u=mcc_estm&sid=GVRL&xid=aad24a70.

Doty, W. G. (2005). 'A lifetime of trouble-making: Hermes as Trickster'. In W. J. Hynes and W. G. Doty (eds.), *Mythical trickster figures: contours, contexts, and criticisms.* Tuscaloosa, AL: University of Alabama, pp. 46–65.

Enns, C. Z. (1994). 'Archetypes and gender: goddesses, warriors and psychological health'. *Journal of Counseling and Development*, 73, 127–133. doi: 10.1002/j.1556-6676.1994.tb01724.x.

Farmer, J. (2013). ''You need but go to Rome': Teresa of Avila and the text/image power play'. *Women's Studies*, 42, 390–407.

Fertel, R. (2015). *A taste for chaos: the art of literary improvisation.* New Orleans, LA: Spring Journal.

Feldman, J. R. (1995). '[Book review of *Androgyny and the denial of difference* by K. Weil]'. *Modern Philology*, 93, 89–92. doi: 10.1086/392287.

Gadamer, H.-G. (1990). *Truth and method.* New York, NY: Crossroads Publishing. (Original published in 1960).

Gospel of Thomas. (1994). S. Patterson and M. Meyer (trans.). Retrieved May 16, 2018 from http://gnosis.org/naghamm/gosthom.html (Original dated ca. 140CE).

Haskell, F., and Penny, N. (1981). *Taste and the antique: the lure of classical sculpture, 1500–1900.* New Hartford, CT: Yale University.

Henderson, D. (2010). 'The coincidence of opposites: C. G. Jung's reception of Nicholas of Cusa'. *Studies in Spirituality*, 20, 101–113. doi: 10.2143/SIS.20.0.2061145.

Hibbard, H. (1991). *Bernini.* New York, NY: Penguin Books. (Original work published in 1965).

Hillman, J. (1998). *Pink madness: why does Aphrodite drive us crazy with pornography?* [Audio Recording] New York, NY: Continuum. Retrieved May 26, 2018 from https://www.youtube.com/watch?v=bt8R9f4O-Lw.

Høy, P. (2000). 'Marcel Duchamp – *Étant donnés*: the deconstructed painting'. *tout-fait: The Marcel Duchamp Studies Online Journal*, 1. Retrieved May 15, 2018 from http://www.toutfait.com/issues/issue_3/Articles/Hoy/etantdon_en.html.

Jones, J. (2003, August 8). 'Costanza Bonarelli, Gianlorenzo Bernini (c1636–1637)'. *The Guardian.* Retrieved May 17, 2018 from https://www.theguardian.com/culture/2003/aug/09/art.

Jung, C. G. (1937). 'Religious ideas in alchemy'. In *Collected works*, vol. 12, *Psychology and alchemy* (2nd ed.). Princeton, NJ: Princeton University Press.

Jung, C. G. (1939). 'Conscious, unconscious and individuation'. In *Collected works*, vol. 9i, *The archetypes and the collective unconscious* (2nd ed.). Princeton, NJ: Princeton University Press.

Jung, C. G. (1940). 'The psychology of the child archetype'. In *Collected works*, vol. 9i, *The archetypes and the collective unconscious* (2nd ed.). Princeton, NJ: Princeton University Press.

Jung, C. G. (1942). 'The spirit Mercurius'. In *Collected works*, vol. 13, *Alchemical studies* (2nd ed.). Princeton, NJ: Princeton University Press.

Jung, C. G. (1951). 'The structure and dynamics of the self'. In *Collected works*, vol. 9ii, *Aion: researches into the phenomenology of the self* (2nd edn.). Princeton, NJ: Princeton University Press.

Jung, C. G. (1958a). 'Flying saucers: a modern myth'. In *Collected works*, vol. 10, *Civilization in transition* (2nd ed.). Princeton, NJ: Princeton University Press.

Jung, C. G. (1958b). 'The transcendent function'. In *Collected works*, vol. 8, *The structure and dynamics of the psyche* (2nd edn.). Princeton, NJ: Princeton University Press.

Konstan, D. (2015). 'Beauty'. In P. Destrée and P. Murray (eds.), *A companion to ancient aesthetics*. New York, NY: Wiley, pp. 366–380.

Kerényi, K. (1951). *Gods of the Greeks*. N. Cameron (trans.). London, England: Thames and Hudson.

Kerényi, K. (1992). *Hermes: guide of souls*. M. Stein (trans.). Dallas, TX: Spring Publications. (Original work published 1976).

Lammers, A. C. (2007). 'Jung and White and the God of terrible aspect'. *Journal of Analytical Psychology*, 52, 253–274. doi:10.1111/j.1468-5922.2007.00662.x.

Lammers, A. C., and Cunningham, A. (eds.) (2007). *The Jung-White letters*. New York, NY: Routledge.

Landre, S. (2015). The *bel composto* in Gian Lorenzo Bernini's Cornaro Chapel (Masters thesis). Retrieved May 21, 2018 from https://dc.uwm.edu/cgi/viewcontent.cgi?article=2013&context=etd.

Lavin, I. (1980). *Bernini and the unity of the visual arts*. New York, NY: Pierpont Morgan Library/Oxford University Press.

Lavin, I. (2005). 'Bernini at St. Peter's: *singularis in singulus, in omnibus unicus*'. In W. Tronzo (ed.), *St. Peter's in the vatican*. Cambridge, England: Cambridge University, pp. 111–243.

Lavin, I. (2007). 'Bernini and the theatre'. In *Visible spirit: the art of Gianlorenzo Bernini* (vol. 1). London, England: Pindar, pp 15–32. Retrieved May 17, 2018 from https://publications.ias.edu/sites/default/files/Lavin_BerniniTheater_2007.pdf (Original work published in 1964).

Lavin, I. (2008). 'The baldacchino. Borromini vs Bernini: did Borromini forget himself?'. In G. Satzinger and S. Schütze (eds.), *Sankt Peter in Rom 1506–2006, Akten der internationalen Tagung 22.–25.02.2006 in Bonn*. Munich, Germany: Hirmer Verlag, pp. 275–300. Retrieved from https://publications.ias.edu/sites/default/files/Lavin_BaldacchinoBorrominiBernini_2008.pdf.

Mather, J. M. (1952). 'Bernini's fountains: an illustration of how this art-form can be said to symbolize the emotional stability of its creator – the seventeenth century genius'. [Master's Thesis]. Retrieved from https://open.library.ubc.ca/media/download/pdf/831/1.0104561/2.

Maurette, P. (2015). 'Plato's hermaphrodite and a vindication of the sense of touch in the sixteenth century'. *Renaissance Quarterly*, 67, 872–896.
McKenzie, S. (2006). 'Queering gender: anima/animus and the paradigm of emergence'. *Journal of Analytical Psychology*, 51, 401–421. doi: 10.1111/j.0021-8774.2006.00599.x.
McPhee, S. (2006). 'Costanza Bonarelli: biography versus archive'. In M. Delbecke, E. Levy, and S. F. Ostrow (eds.), *Bernini's biographies: critical essays*. University Park, PA: Pennsylvania State University, pp. 315–376.
Mormando, F. (2011). *Bernini: his life and his Rome* [Kindle version]. Chicago, IL: University of Chicago. Retrieved from www.amazon.com.
Nobus, D. (2015). 'The sculptural iconography of feminie jouissance. Lacan's reading of Bernini's *Saint Teresa in Ecstasy*'. *Comparatist*, 39, 22–46. doi: 10.1353/com.2015.0019.
Nussbaum, M. C. (2001). *The fragility of goodness: luck and ethics in Greek tragedy and ethics*. New York, NY: Cambridge University Press. (Original work published in 1986).
Olive, C. J. E. (2009). 'Self-actualization in the lives of medieval female mystics: an ethnohistorical approach'. (Doctoral dissertation). Retrieved May 27, 2018 from https://digitalscholarship.unlv.edu/thesesdissertations/1113/
Ovid. (1899). *The metamorphosis of Ovid*. H. T. Riley (Trans.), Vol. 1, pp. 151–155. Philadelphia, PA: David McKay. Retrieved from https://archive.org/details/metamorphosisov00jrgoog/page/n155 (*Metamorphosis* originally dates from ca. 8 CE).
Paris, G. (1986). *Pagan meditations: Aphrodite, Hestia, Artemis*. Dallas, TX: Spring Publications.
Plato. (1891). 'Symposium'. In B. Jowett (ed. & trans.), *The dialogues of Plato* (vol. 1). London, England: Humphrey Milford. Retrieved from https://archive.org/details/in.ernet.dli.2015.8098/page/n551 (Original work dates ca. 370 BCE).
Pliny the Elder. (1857). *The natural history of Pliny*. J. Bostock and H. T. Riley (trans.), vol. 6). London, England: Henry G. Bohn. Retrieved from https://archive.org/details/naturalhistoryof06plin/page/182 (Original work dates from ca. 77 CE).
Preston. (2013). 'Counter-reformation and baroque'. *Journal of Baroque Studies*, 1, 33–51.
Rilke, R. M. (1923). 'Die Ersten Elegie'. In Duineser Elegien.[Duino Elegies]. Leipzig, Germany: Insel-Verlag. Retrieved May 17, 2018 from https://de.wikisource.org/wiki/Die_erste_Elegie.
Samuels, A. (2015). 'Global politics, American hegemony and vulnerability, and Jungian psychosocial studies: why there are no winners in the battle between Trickster, Pedro Urdemales, and the Gringos'. *International Journal of Jungian Studies*, 7, 227–241. doi: 10.1080/19409052.2015.1016882.
Semetsky, I. (2013). 'Deleuze, *edusemiotics*, and the logic of affects'. In I. Semetsky and D. Masny. (eds.), *Deleuze and education* .pp. 215–234. Edinburgh, Scotland: Edinburgh University Press.
Singer, J. (1989). *Androgyny: the opposites within*. Boston, MA: Sigo. (Original work published 1976).
Spuybroek, L. (2014). '*Charis* and radiance: the ontological dimensions of beauty'. In S. Van Tuinen (ed.), *Giving and taking: antidotes to a culture of greed* . pp. 119–150.Rotterdam, Netherlands: nai010 Publishers.
Stein, M. (1999). 'Hermes and the creation of space'. *Quadrant: The Journal of the C.G. Jung Foundation*, 29, 21–36. Retrieved from http://www.jungatlanta.com/articles/Hermes-and-the-Creation-of-Space.pdf.

Szepressy, V. L. (2014). 'The marriage maker. The Pergamum hermaphrodite as the god hermaphroditos, divine ideal and erotic object'. (Master's Thesis). Retrieved May 17, 2018 from http://www.academia.edu/7393694/The_Marriage_Maker._The_Pergamon_Hermaphrodite_as_the_God_Hermaphroditos_Divine_Ideal_and_Erotic_Object.

Teresa of Avila. (1995). *The life of Teresa of Jesus: the autobiography of Teresa of Ávila*. E. A. Peers (trans. & ed.) (Electronic book) (Original published around 1565). Retrieved June 10, 2018 from http://www.carmelitemonks.org/Vocation/teresa_life.pdf.

Vulgate: (n.d.). 'The holy bible in Latin language with the Douay-Reims English translation'. Retrieved July 7 2019 from http://vulgate.org/ot/daniel_14.htm.

Warma, S. (1984). 'Ecstasy and vision: two concepts associated with Bernini's *Teresa*. *Art Bulletin*, 66, 508–511.

Warwick, G. (2012). *Bernini: art as theatre*. New Haven, CT: Yale University.

Weil, K. (1992). *Androgyny and the denial of difference*. Charlottesville, VA: University of Virgina.

Weil, M. S. (1974). *The history and decoration of the Ponte S. Angelo*. University Park, PA: Pennsylvania State University.

Witt, M. A. F. (2013). *Metatheater and modernity: baroque and neobaroque*. Madison, NJ: Fairleigh Dickinson University Press.

Wittkower, R. (1955). *Gian Lorenzo Bernini: the sculptor of the Roman Baroque*. London: Phaidon Press.

Chapter 8

Problems of symbolisation and archetypal processes

The case of male same-sex desire

Giorgio Giaccardi

Introduction

When a symbolic space is not found, when no representations are available for a given human experience, a gap remains open which keeps one closer to a more archaic and less humanised level of existence. The ensuing quality of thoughts and feelings appears more compulsive, haunting, totalising, extreme, and intensely cathected. Pasolini (1992, p. 201) expressed the importance of imagination: 'Probably I owe my salvation (not becoming mad, not consuming myself) to my imagination which is able to find a concrete image for every feeling and – it seems to me – imprisons it, prevents it from working away frantically in my brain'.

The psychoanalytic reflection is well acquainted with developmental experiences whose failure of symbolisation leaves the experiencing subject exposed to the raw power of archaic objects. For instance, the unthinkability of parents' badness or of the responsibility of the perpetrator of an abuse leaves room for non-humanised representations of archetypal proportions (Kalsched 1996). In this psychic state, one is more liable to feelings of utter isolation, banishment from the human community, panic attacks, suicidal thoughts, guilt, shame, and overwhelming affective intensification in general.

This paper can be read as an illustration, based on the particular psychic occurrence given by a type of sexual orientation and its clash with a symbolic order to which it feels alien, of the broader situation in which a path of individuation is activated by a missed encounter between an archetype and symbolic representations. The archetype remains in such case an instinct without a portrait, a magnet without its metal, so that its primary force will attract the individual close to its turbulent and compelling depths in an unmediated way.

Representation of same-sex desire

Same-sex desire within a heteronormative symbolic order, like other experiences against which anti-representation forces of various nature are active, may indeed prove to be one of such precipitating entry points into an archetypal level of psychic functioning. Heteronormativity has been defined as

> the institutions, structures of understanding, and practical orientations that make heterosexuality not only coherent – that is, organised as a sexuality – but also privileged. ... It consists less of norms that could be summarised as a body of doctrine than of a sense of rightness produced in contradictory manifestations – often unconscious, immanent to practices or to institutions.
> (Berlant and Warner, 1998, p. 548)

The consequences of the lack of adequate symbolisation are likely to take deep roots, monopolise psychic resources, and generate enduring internal tension, as Pasolini (1992, p. 324) lucidly described in relation to his 'difficulty in loving' men in a heteronormative symbolic world:

> In me the difficulty in loving has made the need for love obsessive: the function made the organ hypertrophic when, as an adolescent, love seemed to me an unattainable chimera: then when with experience the function had resumed its proper proportions and the chimera had been deconsecrated to the point of being the most miserable daily matter, the evil was already inoculated, chronic and incurable. I find myself with an enormous mental organ for a function which by now is negligible.

Facilitating the creation of a space for psychological reflection on same-sex desire in a cultural environment from which it is banned or misconstrued is the essence of a process that I call 'mending the symbolic' (Giaccardi, 2019). Without this mending, affective states, instead of feeding the symbolic mind, remain in an ever intense, floating and confusing state, as a young Pasolini (1992, p. 179) describes:

> A continual disturbance without images and even words beats at my temples and blinds me (p. 192). ... Life here would be nice if a continual bitter agitation [orgasmo] – which sometimes turns into a sort of panic fear or depression [spleen] – did not constantly undermine me.

These words were written in a letter to a friend, and bear witness to the need to articulate and convey this unnamed state of mind to a receiver, who is enlisted in the pursuit of the formation of some meaning, quite the opposite attitude of the psychologically detrimental 'don't ask, don't tell'.

I will try and render what may it feel like to be in this space and what the psychological process of survival and adjustment to the perceived gap is like, beyond theoretical psychoanalytic assumptions, by considering the pangs of birth of self-representations of such a state from within and ways in which it develops an awareness of itself.

Because the experience of same-sex desire in a heteronormative symbolic order undermines the possibility of considering oneself as a fully fledged man according to the dominant canons, an elusive but corrosive sense of diminished worth and radical disorientation are likely consequences. For gay boys, ordinary Oedipal identification doesn't usually work to the effect of establishing a firm enough male identity. Inasmuch as father's desire is perceived as non-relatable, the paternal ideal cannot lend itself to identifying processes in the realm of desire. This leaves the problem of construction of subjectivity for the gay boy open to various types or responses, whether defensive and paranoid or productive and creative.

There are two main reasons for which I think this kind of analysis is still relevant, in spite of the fact that same-sex desire is nowadays more present and accepted in the collective consciousness of the Western world – although by no means uniformly, as repressive forces against non-binary sexualities are still present and in some parts of the world or sections of society even on the increase.

First, social and political recognition and acceptance of same-sex desire does not necessarily mean that its process of symbolisation has reached a stage where reflection is less needed. The taboo may have been lifted, but the assimilation of a psychic experience in the symbolic is a different process, one of which liberal views and an accepting attitude are enabling but not sufficient components. As Bartlett concisely puts it, after the time of 'coming out' it is more a case of 'going in' and developing a knowledge of SSD from within its own psychological language (Bartlett, 1988, p. 206).

Second, many adult men, from their 30s onwards, are still likely to have grown up in a world where available representations around same-sex attraction to men have often felt at the very least inadequate to express their desire, which, as I will argue later, leaves traces on a man's relationship to desire and life in general, even as and when more adequate symbolic containers are found. We know much about the repression of same-sex desire, but less has been written about how the repression of the space for spontaneous psychological representation might have contributed to shape some men's psychic make-up, beyond the most visible traits connected to internalised homophobia.

I will explore some effects on the individual of a mismatch between same-sex desire and symbolic order in the next section, where I broadly refer to this situation as numinous exclusion. In the second extended section, I will consider archetypal processes activated by this tension and their function in repairing the symbolic gaps. This is a process which, as I have argued in detail elsewhere (Giaccardi op. cit.), is also embedded in a transformative interplay with collective consciousness and is both affected by and productive of cultural practices.

As I have already mentioned in this introduction, I will frequently refer to the writings (letters and poetry) of Pier Paolo Pasolini, the Italian intellectual, writer, poet, novelist, and film director. His same-sex desire crystallised in his adult life in the shape of exclusive attraction to young underclass heterosexual men. This position of Pasolini buttresses the heteronormative edifice inasmuch as it implies the maintenance of its supremacy, while cutting for himself a defiantly transgressive (and guilt-ridden) stance. For these reasons, Pasolini's way to homosexuality has largely been seen as unhelpful to the gay cause, both on a cultural and a political level. However, his sensitivity and lucidity have translated into verses and reflections of great perceptivity and insight on the themes of being outside the symbolic order on account of one's desire, both in its more romantic and melancholic form as a youth and in its highly sexualised state as an adult. Some poems' translations (as indicated) are original, for which I wish to thank my friend and expert translator Valentina Ajello.

Numinous exclusion

Perhaps, the most fundamental trait of the psychological life of men whose desire for men has not found a representation in the symbolic is exclusion. The melancholic shadow cast by the exclusion from the heteronormative symbolic can have a stultifying effect, the spontaneous movement ahead of desire being saddled by a sense of impossibility. The rejecting heteronormative gaze on the gay boy, often evoking a repressive and punitive parent, can also be likened to that of a depressed mother looking at her baby, whom she cannot really see.

During formative years, such blank spots can engender a sense of radical divide from the rest of humanity. Puberty always confronts a boy with an acute tension between sexual arousal and the capacity to process it, but for gay men there is an additional issue of lack or unsuitability of containers for the representation of sexual fantasies. In my work with gay men, I have generally noticed that when this lack has been very severe (and/or the internal psychological resources of the boy are limited), sexuality as a whole may have been deeply repressed and desire switched off, leaving these boys flat and deprived of the animation that connection with desire would have brought. Even as and when they come out later, their desire has no history, as it seems to emerge out of an ice age straight into a suddenly torrid summer, where it can be so easily channelled into extreme practices – such as chemsex – and burn to dissipation.

If instead the tension in puberty is held and some representations of aspects of same-sex desire are found that allow desire to maintain an awareness of itself, albeit externally hidden and unlived, adolescence – at whatever age that might happen – will probably be marked by a feast of fantasies into which desire and a capacity for emotional involvement overflows, even though it may remain fused with a melancholic sense of difference and incommunicability. Excitement and sadness may develop coterminously, one implying the other, as deep furrows along the unfolding path of one's desire, and this emotional coalescence may endure even in subsequent circumstances more favourable to one's inclinations. In other words, because melancholy gets fused with desire, it ends up being pursued for the sake of psychic intensification. The Japanese writer Mishima captured this state when he wrote: 'some instinct within me demanded that I seek solitude, that I remain apart as something different'. This compulsion was manifested as a mysterious and strange malaise. In Millot's reading of Mishima, his relation with desire was marked by the 'eroticization of the exclusion' (2001, pp. 210–215). And similarly Pasolini (1992, p. 201) in an early letter: 'My existence is a continual shudder, a fit of remorse or sense of nostalgia'. Brogan (2018, p. 370) recalls

'Freud's statement that "people never willingly abandon a libidinal position", i.e., that of the first relationship'. In a sense, what is pursued here is the libidinal position of the first relationship between same-sex desire and the rejecting gaze of the heteronormative symbolic order. The immersion in this space often assumes numinous qualities, whether as an inexhaustible question that keeps interrogating, a source of unrepresented intensity, or as an intimation of paradise or hell.

The lack of available representations for desire is a potent catalyst for introversion, a process often mistaken and pathologised as individualistic, whereas it primarily represents the only connection that is felt possible with aspects of oneself not adequately recognised by the collective. What gets activated is a process of withdrawal, resulting from the impossibility to cathect objects, which in Jungian terms could be described as a state of introversion where libido (psychic energy) is turned inwardly, often assuming mournful and dreamy qualities. As Jung's biographer Homans argues (1979/1995, p. 60), introversion neurosis was indeed Jung's non-pathologising take on narcissism, which he contrasted to hysteria and transference.

The frequentation of this inner world, often protected by secrecy and a degree of dissociation from ordinary life, is a practice that provides reassurance about the survival of a potential of desire, however shapeless, embryonic, or even doomed it might feel. It is like having a secret greenhouse where bare roots are preserved, not knowing whether and in what shape they may eventually grow. Psychic life intensifies between an internal desire of consuming intensity and projections of its fulfilment into a fantasised reality out of reach. In his poem *La Realtà*, Pasolini conveys this feeling poignantly: 'I have never crossed the border between love of life and life' (in Gordon 1996, p. 172). Mishima further articulates this position as follows:

> During my childhood I was weighed down by a sense of uneasiness at the thought of becoming an adult, and my feeling of growing up continued to be accompanied by a strange, piercing unrest. ... My indefinable feeling of unrest increased my capacity for dreams divorced from all reality.

The propensity to lingering in an internal space, coupled with the lack of templates to imagine one's future life, may often lead to procrastination of engagement with reality. This presents emotional costs, such as feelings of wasting time and opportunities, guilt and self-reproach, regrets, as well as practical ones, given that internal cultivation of same-sex desire can indeed monopolise psychic resources and make them unavailable for other pursuits.

Even if procrastination is eventually overcome by turning desire from an object of internal contemplation to some form of integration in one's life (which is what is referred to in shorthand with the expression 'coming out'), the relation to psychic time has been altered and what remains is a sense of finding oneself in a warped temporal trajectory, with different ages coexisting in the same person, which Neil Bartlett (1988, p. 221) epitomises when he writes 'We are born late'. The emotional corollary of this position ranges from an empowering sense of newly found youthfulness to anxiety around inadequacy, immaturity, or age inappropriateness. Whatever the consequences are, the emergence from the closet is a radical event, because, as the writer Paul Monette describes (2000, p. 2), 'there's a pain that stops, and you know it will never hurt like that again, no matter how much you lose or how bad you die'.

What often remains, even after 'coming out', is a sense of precarious existence of one's desire. It might feel as though desire might as well be sucked back into the holes of the heteronormative symbolic if it stops being kept in mind. A desire that lacks representation requires ongoing maintenance lest it dissolves into the state of non-existence in the symbolic from where it originated. Constant attention is given not only to desire per se, but also to one's relation to it, the wedges it creates with others, the losses it entails, the impact on life possibilities it brings with it, and in general the contours of one's existence as a desiring subject that have to be drawn over and over again as they often seem too flimsy and faint.

Such a precarious state in the symbolic order, where dependency on a given meaning is not an available option, calls for a heroical attitude, a capacity of being self-reliant and independent. In a way, the heroic attitude formed in a condition of non-belonging and psychological self-begetting could be seen as precursor of the hero of contemporary times, when meaning is increasingly shifty and blurred and the individual is called upon to navigate through a sea of symbolic uncertainty and create a path as he treads on it. Unsurprisingly, such contemporary heroic figures may present depressive traits in the shadow, as Pereira describes in relation to heroes of post-modernity: 'Depression in contemporary times can be seen as the other side of autonomous individuals, who are, supposedly, free and sovereign in themselves' (2018, p. 430).

Besides that, a sense of exclusion may continue to colour the way in which desire is pursued in life, which seems to be oriented by a deep-seated mistrust of what may be found in one's proximity, as though the symbolic alienation experienced in the realm of desire casts a shadow of an ever-present divide from one's immediate surroundings. One response to this difficulty may lead to project onto distant shores the possibility of fulfilment of desire – not only as a distant point in time but also as an object of desire somewhat exotic, whether in terms of culture, geography, status, class, race, or age. Another type of response to the dread of exclusion, more defensive and regressive, consists of seeking fusional experiences in the realm of Mother, where the other is needed to establish a pre-symbolic state of merger.

The process by which same-sex desire responds to a heteronormative symbolic order, both in an adaptive/defensive and in a dynamic/creative way, can also be understood by considering the particular archetypal declinations that such an encounter produces. According to Lopez-Pedraza (2010, p. 135), a broad archetypal exploration is important for clinical work with men, as it 'could encourage psychic movement by following the dominant archetype in which erotica among men appears, and it would accept this dominant as the very vehicle for psychotherapeutic movement'.

Understanding what archetypal dynamics are at play in same-sex desire and what dynamics ignite the psyche according to their gradient are key aspects of the process of mending the symbolic, which allows psychological life to become richer and less subjected to alienating and superimposed meanings. Symbolisation, from this perspective, happens through reflection on one's specific archetypal configurations underpinning the way in which same-sex desire is experienced and the development of awareness of other archetypal possibilities available – as well as of different declinations and developments of the same archetype – to mobilise desire in one's life.

I will describe these processes with particular reference to the Senex/Puer background to same-sex desire, as it represents the quintessential archetype for male *coniunctio*. Its split state, as argued by Hillman (2005, p. 38), causes 'frustration of homosexual Eros'. Other archetypal perspectives which I will consider are Persona, Anima, Father, Trickster, Pan, Shadow, as well as what may be seen as an archetypal tendency of the male psyche, not explored by Jung, towards forms of 'communality'.

Facing the gaps: Archetypes at work

i. Persona

When the response to the anxiety around same-sex desire is sought on a Persona level, the difficulties around symbolising it are transposed onto a question of gender role. Instead of allowing same-sex desire to find in time its own representations, a solution to anxiety is found by adopting a presentation to the world based on a given type of identification with gender styles. Indeed, identification processes, which are typical of early or regressive developmental phases, appear as dominant in one's psychic organisation ruled by Persona, allowing one to avoid relating to an internal world and offering a mask that hides it or simplifies it.

Instances of such identifications, often the result of a need for dissimulation, can be seen in figures such as macho men, muscled armours, overachievers, Don Juans and aggressive bullies. However, a response on the level of Persona to same-sex desire is also given by figures that adopt the opposite-gendered Persona, characterised by stereotypical feminine traits, which is a form of caving in the (male patriarchal) aggressor by declaring one's inability to compete with men for the possession of masculinity. From this archetypal perspective, a passport saying 'I am much less manly than all other men' is psychologically akin to one that says 'I am a very manly man' – just a different positioning along the same gender axis and in relation to the same need of settling the uncertainty around how one is perceived by others in terms of gender roles. Clearly, I am not referring to spontaneous inclinations of character that may be read as more feminine from a binary perspective, rather to the confusion easily engendered within a heteronormative order whereby attraction to men must mean that there is something faulty in one's make-up as a man – an imputed fault which is then construed as an effeminate Persona.

These two types of Persona often adopted by gay men, albeit in seemingly opposite ways, help eliminate the process of decodification of the complexities of same-sex desire and its tension with the heteronormative order. While the macho Persona is meant to hide the existence of same-sex desire – or to avert the risk of attracting projections of femininity – and is inherently paranoid, the effeminate one represents a surrender to the charge of diminished masculinity and can easily blend with martyrdom traits and repressed rage, as I will explore in the section on Shadow.

Because these types of identification usually appear rather fixed by the time one reaches adolescence, they might easily continue working as alienating containers throughout one's lifetime, partly because renegotiating one's position within society (others' expectations) is not an easy task, unless one is carried by an internal necessity due to the activation of other archetypal processes. However, in the initial phase of acute anxiety about what same-sex desire means and the dread of its impact on one's life, a defined Persona might represent the only face that one feels able to show to society. It represents a tightly sealed facade behind which conscious or unconscious works may be carried out.

ii. Father

Archetypal processes around same-sex desire in the area of Father offer a different way of relating to the symbolic order – via the paternal function rather than via socially constructed roles on the level of the Persona.

Same-sex desire creates a hiatus between the world of fathers and the world the son can imagine for himself. This is a portentous symbolic and emotional rupture, particularly in the moment when one realises that, on account of his desire, he is cast out of the world in which he has lived until then. The world of fathers and their similarly oriented sons who will be fathers, from then onward, will be looked at one remove.

Pasolini (1970, p. 128, our translation) lyrically conveys what the unbroken continuity of fathers and sons looks like from a position of alienation to the dominant symbolic order:

> gentle rebels,
> and, together, content with father's future:
> this is what makes them so beautiful …
> orderly teams of flowers in the chaos of existence.

The apparent easiness of living granted by the symbolic intergenerational continuity is turned by Pasolini into an object of contemplation, between lucid idealisation, empathic tenderness and moral indictment of vileness (1970, pp. 127–128, 130, our translation):

> the life he was destined with
> is the right one … Humble, for sure. And what will be

their coward way to accomplish
themselves (their lot is cowardice)
is still almost as dawn
on unknown trees, in which
nature has only gems in a standstill
of extreme pureness ....
in whom no deed is dishonest as their desire is without tragedy ...
Ah which God guides them so self-assured!

By articulating this perception, Pasolini gains awareness of an ethical task that has befallen him, which is to learn to withstand the break from the order of Father, to accept that desire will be tainted with guilt and a sense of betrayal, and in the process to establish a relation with desire that cannot be immediate and granted, rather constantly accompanied by self-monitoring. The experience of same-sex desire is concomitant with the activation of a part of the mind that observes it.

While registering a problematic difference between Father's object of desire and his own, a connection may still be developed by the gay son by relating to symbolic aspects of this archetype. For instance, psychological functions like a capacity for sublimation, ethical concern for the world, and responsibility for the normative structures in which it is embedded, as traits of Father, can assume a particular importance in providing building blocks for the construction of meaning for gay men – all the more so as the vast majority of them do not have children and therefore have less opportunities for the Father archetype to incarnate in the dimension of family. Perhaps this is what Freud (in Wortis, 1954, pp. 99–100) had in mind when he wrote that 'the homosexual component is one of the most valuable human assets, and should be put to social uses' in a sublimated form, although he didn't see how this social use could coexist with an unsublimated use of the homosexual component – to put it in his terms.

Father's concern for the world represents a symbolic inheritance that provides opportunities for and recognition of the ethical involvement with others. For the gay son, remaining receptive to these aspects of Father in the face of a gap between the latter's desire and his own requires a capacity to tolerate ambivalence and to build whole objects representations, in which aspects experienced as radically other from oneself do not thwart the possibility of developing a bond. In fact, I find that among my young gay patients the sublimating/ethical Father is very often an object of unconscious yearning but also of conscious avoidance. This causes a rift that needs repairing, one which the ethical stance of the analyst, on account of the capacity for responsibility and sublimation it objectively conveys, can crucially contribute to work with in the transference.

The rift with Father is likely to be more acute when the Senex/Puer archetype is split and when the relation to Anima is thwarted, so these are archetypal processes that need comprehending, activating, and integrating.

iii. Senex/Puer

If representations for desire are missing, the software of meaning appears incomplete and needs constant rewriting. For gay men, it is true in a specific sense that life is written and made up as it unfolds.

One way of reflecting on these difficulties in meaning formation is through the Senex-Puer archetype. The giver of fixed meaning, which is the Senex (for Hillman [2005, p. 45], the archetypal background to 'the hardness of our ego certainty') may be torn from the Puer, if the latter's formless and turbulent energy cannot be helped into shape by the former on account of some incommensurability of their relation to desire. On the one hand, we have the fuel for meaning, and on the other, structures to bring it to life. As identification with the Senex qualities of Father is necessary to consolidate a sufficient degree of stable meaning, the missed encounter with it leaves the subject exposed to corrosive forces attacking the consolidation of meaning. Senex structures may then be constantly exposed in their arbitrariness and rejected wholesale, well beyond the binary codification of desire, so that entry into the world of the Senex will prove difficult. This is the point of rupture in this quintessentially male-to-male archetype which the work of mending the symbolic has to address in order to build a space where the relation between these split polarities may be restored.

In terms of cultural practices, one form of corrosive attack has found expression, for instance, in queer theory (that recodes sexuality from a binary phenomenon to a logically infinite series of signs: LGBTQIA+), or in drag (queens or kings) performances, that – as Susan Sontag put it in her definition of 'camp' – 'see everything in quotation marks'. The shadow of this position is in the fact that – very much like with the hyper-modernist discourse in general – it may leave the subject who identifies with this vertex deprived of anchoring points to a shared symbolic, albeit provisional, and more liable to self-attacks on the very possibility of defining meaning, as the process of meaning-making is countered by a deep-seated force that delegitimises such operation.

On the other hand, because nobody can ever be outside the symbolic order, the process of the formation of gay subjectivity will still present attempts – whether conscious or not – to relate to some stable representations of the Senex. In my clinical work with gay men I have witnessed a range of such attempts.

For instance, a stable meaning might be sought in the fantasy of fully belonging with the ordinary, as is the case with patients overly worried about not being normal and average enough. This might lead to the formation of a normotic illness (a notion introduced by Bollas [1987] albeit in a different context) in which the yearning for conformity and *homo*-logation leads to the fusional identification with a dry Senex blended with the empty, objective, and reassuring order of things – or, in Bollas' words, where the person aspires to become an 'it'.

Another attempt to generate a Senex resorts to identification with an idealised one, through which a given order of meaning is assigned a superior status, while the devalued and ego-dystonic parts of himself are projected onto others.

For instance, one patient proved very attached to his superiority in terms of ethical choices in opposition to a world of people perceived as unprincipled, whereas another one found gratification in his ascetic aspiration and rejection of the mundane, or yet another one identified with a sanitised world of rules and regulations leading to the adoption of obsessive rituals, occasionally punctured by panic attacks that signalled fear of unruliness and impurity. The same patient developed hypochondriac obsessions around the purity of his body, constantly fearing germs and contamination.

An outcome of such a situation might result in the submission to a fascist Senex who strictly dictates and restricts the rules of enjoyment. This is the case for instance with some 'communities of jouissance', i.e., communities that define themselves on the basis of shared pursuits of sexual satisfaction (Laurent 2009, p. 83), such as dating apps, in which sexual practices often happen to be defined very strictly and people are 'blocked' (in a repetition of the experience of exclusion from the collective) if they are perceived as divergent from the prescribed profile. Also, an interesting analysis of the fusional longing for an omnipotent Father, which I would see as an extreme instance of this particular attempt at solving the Puer-Senex split, is conducted by Ruth Stein with reference to the homoerotic qualities of religious fanaticism, which she understands as a case of 'abject submissiveness and ecstatic glow. I call it vertical mystical homoeros' (2010, p. 51).

A particular dynamic with a gay patient of mine in his early 30s may illustrate the ambivalence around the Senex order. When he started seeing me, his relation with the Senex was compromised, as he was fraught with anxiety about the possibility of rejection from the world, while at the same time feeling quite ambitious in terms of worldly goals. I was cast from the outset in the place of the secretly yearned for Senex – namely a representative and functionary of the adult world – and outwardly credited with some trust, but periodically sabotaged, something he found difficult to recognise. This half-hearted connection allowed him to make important headway in the professional and social areas of his life, as if he could at least borrow a sense of potency and belonging, but attempts at sabotaging the connection continued, for instance by tampering with time-keeping, frequency, and payments. These two parallel binaries – overt cooperation and covert antagonism – remained unaware of each other for a long time, resisting interpretations around the conflicting motives and making it difficult for him to gain a stable sense of his relation to me. I was made aware of this unresolved tension also through my countertransference response to his achievements, far muter than I know I would normally experience and resonate with, as though my empathic resonance with them were withheld by some scepticism around their lack of groundedness.

Without getting into the details of this work, I would just add that an important shift took place after sabotage intensified, in the shape of a series of missed sessions with scant and delayed communication on his part. At some point, it became clear enough that he needed me to take the initiative and offer him a definitive date and time to meet again and discuss what was going on, which I did. He had probably felt anxiously unseen when he was not coming and communicating properly, and left alone with his feelings of hopelessness about our disconnected relationship, and his guilt for his own contributing elements of destructiveness, waiting for me to rescue him.

Being unseen, uninvited, and not rescued by the collective of insiders are some of the most excruciating aspects of growing up as a gay boy in a heteronormative environment, as in this void he can easily be prey to primitive states of mind, including radical abandonment and total irrelevance. To help him start to articulate all this, the Senex had to suspend the formal Law and make a gesture signalling his desire for involvement with the proud but lost Puer. By doing so, the analyst/Senex initiates the Puer to the experience of a non-narcissistic desire to relate, compatible with but no longer thwarted by his antagonistic feelings and reservations about the adequacy of the symbolic world presided over by the Senex.

iv. Anima

In general, overcoming this split relies upon the connecting power of Anima, which rescues the Puer-Senex relationship from the dynamics of subjugation or fusion and allows mutual engagement with the 'fascinating' sides of each other that may set in motion hitherto unconscious resources. The word fascinating has a specific meaning here as it comes from 'fascinum', a term used by the Romans to indicate the embodiment of the divine phallus (Monick, 1987). From this perspective, the Anima archetype is the spark for a living sense of maleness, as generated by the involvement of the Senex with the 'queer' potential of the Puer and of the latter with the worldly bounty over which the Senex rules.

If this marriage succeeds, the sense of isolation recedes as one finds orientation even in the unknown maps of an alien symbolic order by being able to rely on this internal *coniunctio* that leaves both polarities sufficiently transformed. Each polarity, in itself, can be cold and callous. Hillman (2005, p. 38) describes their similarities in terms of egocentricity, absence of the feminine, coldness of feelings, and resistance to change. However, their coming together opens up a psychological space for relatedness and warmth. Conversely, in the homoerotic fusional solution previously mentioned with regards to religious fanaticism, what is lacking is precisely Anima, so that the coldness of the two polarities is mutually strengthened to psychopathic proportions.

This is a different notion of Anima from the way it was classically thought of as projected onto female figures. Rather than as a psychic content, it consists of a psychological function, which offers infinite possibilities for the psychologisation of desire, in line with Beebe's argument (1993, p. 155) that 'the job of the Anima is ... opening up the man's inner depths to himself, and if these depths are homosexual, the Anima engagement will make him more homosexual, not less'.

As is well known, Jung claimed that 'homosexuals' were identified with Anima on a Persona level and projected a masculine Persona on their erotic objects. Jung had the important intuition that for a significant number of gay men Anima is not a contra-sexual internal other but an archetypal modality integrated in their ordinary way of functioning. However he couldn't make full use of this insight because, being steeped in an unrecognised heteronormative frame, he identified Anima with the feminine and conflated sexual orientation with gender identity, therefore drawing a range of arbitrary considerations on supposedly typical attributes of the latter for gay men. Also, following a rather abstract argument, he argued that if Anima is identified with at the level of the Persona, it cannot be available as an internal function connecting to the unconscious – an argument that recalls his misconceptions about women and soul.

In my opinion, Jung's thesis should be reviewed by clarifying that the relationship of gay men with Anima is key to finding a space in which their desire can be kept alive and validated when such space is not found in the symbolic order, lest, as Mishima (1948/2007, p. 81) wrote in relation to his childhood, such desire 'is tossed onto the rubbish heap of neglected riddles'. Anima is the guide to the fascinating and unseating aspect of life, and when desire strikes, Anima is activated. For Hillman (1985, p. 21), Anima is the target of Eros, 'that which love works upon'.

The ground offered by Anima to desire is a special one, as it reflects its inherent butterfly-like flimsiness, which therefore may keep the relation to desire in a rather fluid state, vividly coloured by fantasies but often difficult to marry with reality, being perceived as more attractive than the reality of emotional involvement. Anima's attraction can be pretty stubborn and little inclined to be tied down to the mundane world, and this may lead to the risk of forever confining same-sex desire into a private or volatile Anima experience. Again Pasolini (1970, p. 169, our translation) was quite perceptive on this very aspect of Anima:

> In the shade of a life
> which unfolds too tied
> to the radical sloth of my soul [anima].

v. Pan, the Trickster, and 'communality'

Many socio-cultural productions of gay men are about the creation of social spaces – the institutions of a world where men are allowed to be attracted to men – in which horizontal erotic bonds can be experienced and facilitate the development of an embodied sense of belonging to the community of men.

These spaces represent spontaneous products of the strength of a desire that, although not yet fully born, has survived the suicidal threat caused by living in an alien world. Unsurprisingly, the spontaneous birth of these places is strongly centred around sex, which provides a basic foundation for the preservation of a sense of an embodied self when possibilities for symbolisation are thwarted.

Archetypally, this is the Pan-like territory of impersonal sexuality. Pan, as Lopez-Pedraza (1989) reminds us, is the offspring of Hermes' love for the nymph of mortal King Dryops (whose flock he was tending). This is an indirect kind of relationship, a 'falling in love with another man's fantasy [nymph]' (p. 136), similarly to the experience of masturbation, in which the fantasy takes centre stage and overshadows the personal relationship that is instrumental to the experience of the arousing fantasy. Pedraza opposes this 'hermetic relationship between two men' (ibid) to the kind of more personal relationship exemplified by Apollo-Admetus, a pastoral couple that initiates the adolescent to manhood. Pan's presence in the 'communities' of same-sex desire points to an impersonal way of relating because its meaning is not around a personal encounter, but about the enjoyment of communality of desire, or, in Leo Bersani's expression, about 'intimacies devoid of intimacy' (1995, p. 128). Pasolini (1970, p. 128, our translation) captures the archetypal nature of this desire, where individuals are seen primarily as representatives of a universal and impersonal image, when he writes:

> They are thousands. I cannot love one.

Shared spaces for proximity with other male bodies have long been one of the most exciting fantasies and practices of gay men. Some of them, such as gyms' locker rooms or other male-only environments like military barracks, entail the coexistence of men who nevertheless are not supposed to desire each other. This fantasy appears to be a trickstery one as it 'steals' a situation and turns it into the object of gratification that it was not supposed to be. In such a case, Hermes comes to the rescue of same-sex desire, appropriating a space that is not supposed to be available for it but that, in fact, lends itself well to represent secret homoerotic fantasies. Adopting and adapting heteronormative practices to the representation of same-sex desire – which Halperin (2012) defines as 'appropriative identifications' – is a basic tool of a survival kit in a world experienced as alien.

Other spaces working as institutions for the gay community – from cruising arenas to gay saunas to virtual spaces like dating apps – are social products, resulting initially out of spontaneous and clandestine practices, then planned, created, and often turned into businesses (thereby reaching an integration with the collective consciousness via the economy of money rather than that of desire). Particularly in the clandestine phase, these spaces work well as external projections of that internal chamber where desire is kept alive. Similar to the need for constant revisiting of one's desire, that I mentioned earlier, these spaces are revisited over and over again not necessarily to find sex or actually meet anyone but, primarily, to ritually make a space for desire to exist every time anew.

As for the strong sexual intensification that occurs within them, the closeness of this desire to archetypal, pre-humanised seriality – Pan chasing indiscriminately any nymphs – can be a source of numinosity, having an initiatory ritual quality that gets repeatedly sought and performed. However, if the tension between this sexual impersonal activation and the individual incarnation of the archetype in a personal encounter is not pursued, and Pan comes to dominate the whole internal archetypal balance, the energetic gradient will be lost over time and desire might ossify, as Pasolini (1970, pp. 170–171, our translation) came to acknowledge:

Slowly the thousands of sacred gestures,
the hand on the warm bulge,
The kisses, each time, on a different mouth,
each time more virgin,
each time closer to the charm of the species,
to the rule that makes the sons tender fathers,
Slowly
they have become stone monuments,
which in their thousands crowd my solitude.

vi. Shadow

The emergence of same-sex desire entails a confrontation with the shadow, as it lends itself to be construed as the receptacle of negative and residual projections by the heteronormative symbolic order. A sense of awfulness is hardly avoidable in the process. Same-sex desire may be experienced as the shadow of parents' expectations, the receptacle of peer groups' toxic insecurities around gender, a marker of perversion and sexual addiction, an affront to decorum when shown in public, a sad signifier of lack of generativity, a guilty attitude of greed and egoism for putting one's desire before the demands of the collective and so forth.

As these experiences of wrongness are to some degree inescapable, the constellation of shadow is an ever present companion of same-sex desire in a heteronormative order, and much of gay men's psychological balance is predicated on their relation to shadow and their capacity to absorb its poison, detoxify it, and contain it. Detoxifying the shadow is indeed an important contribution that many gay men, through their endurance, have offered to younger generations whose homoerotic experiences will probably constellate a shadow with a paler shade of black.

Some solutions of gay men to the problem of shadow, however, have been marked by an identification with it, at times exciting and exhilarating. In this case, a sort of intoxication prevails over attempts at detoxifying it. Pasolini's position, for instance, was to identify with guilt and embrace it (in Sartarelli, 2014, p. 103):

I love my guilt,
which in the adults' museum
was the fold in my trousers and
the throbbing of my timid heart.

This is an incarnation of the Sebastian complex that sacralises the position of the martyr, associated to a range of pleasures bordering on the ecstasy of transgression and punishment – another frequent fantasy in gay men's sexual imagery and practices. This attitude presupposes the desire to uphold the patriarchal symbolic within which guilt, evil, and the exciting attribution of power are inscribed. Pasolini said he could not have sex with any of his 'idols' (young heterosexual men) more than once. It seems that, while on the first sexual encounter the other is still excitingly perceived as a representative of the heteronormative order (a symbolic virgin), the second time the feeling of wrongness would have to be shared by both partners, which would nullify the opposition upon which the attraction to this complex, in which there are no equals, resides.

A typical variation of the Sebastian complex is obtained when it is conjugated with an iconoclastic attack on patriarchy, an attitude of self-debasement and corrosive irony. This is the drag queen position. Both the Sebastian complex and the drag queen position are forms of identification with the victim, as they share the need for self-exposure and attack by the dominant symbolic order, but with important differences. Sebastian is not capable of irony, being monolithically defined by its victim position, while the drag queen makes a massive recourse to it, bordering on sarcasm, hence the corrosive nature of its attack on patriarchal projections. Sebastian leaves the aggression completely in the hands of the perpetrator, while the drag queen is a phallic figure that takes control of the attack and throws it back in the face of the attacker. Sebastian finds greatness by self-aggrandisement as a sinner and enjoyment by embracing guilt, whereas the drag queen identifies with the abject projections of the heteronormative order by taking them to such an extreme degree that is bound to scare even the aggressor, gaining excitement in harnessing this potency and reversing the power balance.

Although shadow is not detoxified in the drag queen position, its tragic qualities, which are prominent in the victim Sebastian tied to death, are fused with irreverent lightness and irony, thereby still altering the nature of the shadow experience and somehow making it more bearable. A complex position formed by tragedy, embracing stigma and irony has also characterised a typical attitude of the gay community struck by AIDS in the 80s that developed this type of defence in response to the degree of suffering and the projections of abjectness that the onset of AIDS epidemic caused.

In general, what may appear in many aspects of gay men's lives as a contrived effort to happiness, pleasure, and 'gayness', is in fact, at least on a symbolic level, a defiant rejection of the curse of a grim and doomed destiny that the emotionally petrifying, heteronormative Medusa's gaze has long irradiated on them.

Conclusion

If individuation means embracing one's trajectory in life, the capacity to face and repair the gaps in the symbolic for same-sex desire is the key to such a process.

My aim has been to show the relevance of defensive and creative responses that gay men have developed facing these gaps. Such responses may be seen as an instance of the broader process of psychic adjustment to the lack or inadequacy of symbolic containers for a given human experience, one that is bound to crucially affect the shape of individuation.

Once the sense of alienation from the world is traversed and the archetypal landscape around same-sex desire is reconfigured, allowing gay men to be rescued from the risk of chronic melancholic stultification, a newly found sense of potency within one's diverse trajectory in life could be experienced, one which I would express by borrowing another verse by Pasolini (1975, our translation):

> That difference that made me magnificent.

There is indeed a possibility, and perhaps a necessity, for narcissistic inflation and 'pride' when facing the task of creating a space, hitherto unavailable, for symbolising one's desire. Pasolini (1970, p. 129, our translation) expressed this state of mind in a highly intensified way, albeit mixed with a 'funerary' intimation of demise:

> sometimes I feel that nothing has the extraordinary
> pureness of this sentiment. Better to die
> than to go without it. I must defend
> this immense desperate tenderness
> that, as everyone in the world, I received when being born.
> Perhaps nobody has lived up
> to such desire – funerary anxiety,
> which fills me like the sea its breeze.

By referring to specific configurations that archetypal dynamics may assume along this process, I have indicated how a symbolic language more suitable to comprehend same-sex desire comes into existence, one in which such desire has the possibility to speak for itself.

Even when this process is facilitated by an accepting psychological, social, and legal environment, this task remains arduous and demanding because feelings, fantasies, and practices associated with same-sex desire cannot rely on the degree of automatic acceptance that centuries of binary thinking have granted heterosexual desire. It is a chaotic, tentative, and experiential process that can only work by monopolising psychic resources over a sustained period, while remaining precarious and exposed to regressive falls. As Foucault (1981) put it succinctly, 'we have to work at becoming homosexuals'.

References

Bartlett, N. (1988). *Who was that man? A present for Mr Oscar Wilde*. London: Serpent's Tail.
Beebe, J. (1993). 'Toward an image of male partnership'. In R. H. Hopcke, K. L. Carrington, and S. Wirth (eds.), *Same-sex love and the path to wholeness*. Boston, MA/London: Shambhala.
Berlant, L., and Warner, M. (1998). 'Sex in public'. *Critical Enquiry*, 24 (2), 547–66.
Bersani, L. (1995). *Homos*. Cambridge, MA: Harvard University Press.
Bollas, C. (1987). *The shadow of the object: psychoanalysis of the unthought known*. London: Free Association Book.

Brogan, C. (2018). 'Donald Winnicott's unique view of depression with particular reference to his 1963 paper on the value of depression'. *British Journal of Psychotherapy*, 34 (3), 358–375.
Foucault, M. (1981). 'Friendship as a way of life'. *Gai Pied*, April. Available at https://caringlabor.wordpress.com/2010/11/18/michel-foucault-friendship-as-a-way-of-life., 7 May 2019.
Giaccardi, G. (2019). 'Mending the symbolic when a space for same-sex desire is not found'. In L. Hertzmann and J. Newbigin (eds.), *Sexuality and gender now. Looking beyond heteronormativity*, Tavistock Clinic Series. London: Karnac.
Gordon, R. S. C. (1996). *Pasolini. Forms of subjectivity*. Oxford: Clarendon Press Oxford.
Halperin, D. (2012). *How to be gay*. Harvard: University Press.
Hillman, J. (1985). *Anima. Anatomy of a personified notion*. Putnam, CT: Spring Publications.
Hillman, J. (2005). *Senex et Puer*. Putnam, CT: Spring Publications.
Homans, P. (1979/1995). *Jung in context*. Chicago, IL: The University of Chicago Press.
Kalsched, D. (1996). *The inner world of trauma. Archetypal defenses of the personal spirit*. London: Routledge.
Laurent, E. (2009). 'A new love for the father'. In L. J. Kalinich and S. W. Taylor (eds.), *The dead father. A psychoanalytic inquiry*. New York, NY/London: Routledge.
Lopez-Pedraza, E. (1989). *Hermes and his children*. Einsiedeln: Daimon. 2010.
Millot, C. (2001). 'The eroticism of desolation'. In T. Dean and C. Lane (eds.), *Homosexuality and psychoanalysis*. Chicago, IL/London: University of Chicago Press, pp. 210–249.
Mishima, Y. (1948/2007). *Confessions of a Mask*. London: Peter Owen.
Monette, P. (2000). *Becoming a man*. New York, NY: Quality Paperback Book Club.
Monick, E. (1987). *Phallos. Sacred image of the masculine*. Toronto: Inner City Books.
Pasolini, P. P. (1970). *Poesie*. Milano: Garzanti.
Pasolini, P. P. (1975). *Le Poesie*. Milano: Garzanti.
Pasolini, P. P. (1992). *The letters of Pier Paolo Pasolini*. London: Quartet Books.
Pereira, H. C. (2018). 'The weariness of the hero: depression and the self in a civilization in transition'. *The Journal of Analytical Psychology*, 63 (4), 420–439.
Sartarelli, S. (2014). *The selected poetry of Pier Paolo Pasolini*. Chicago, IL/London: The University of Chicago Press.
Stein, R. (2010). *For the love of the father. A psychoanalytic study of religious terrorism*. Stanford, CA: Stanford University Press.
Wortis, J. (1954). *Fragments of an analysis with Freud*. New York, NY: Charter Books.

Part 3

Liminality between borders and symbol formation

Chapter 9

An invisible magic circle
A Jungian commentary on *When Marnie Was There*

Mathew Mather

Introduction

Japanese film director Hiromasa Yonebayashi's critically acclaimed film *When Marnie Was There* (2014) is a coming of age story of a young girl called Anna. Suffering from asthma, social awkwardness, and a general malaise (loss of soul) she is advised by her doctor to have a holiday away from the congested city, to get some fresh sea air. Subsequently, at her relative's house by the sea, she encounters a mysterious blonde girl, Marnie, the same age as herself. Their ensuing friendship ushers in a newfound vitality, revelations about their problematic past, and hopes for a worthwhile future. In this article I explore the symbol of the magic circle (mandala) as it appears in a number of contexts throughout the film, as well as the indeterminate state of the mysterious Marnie, who can be interpreted as either imaginary friend or ancestral spirit, or both, relative to Anna.

When Marnie Was There is a young adult novel written by English writer Joan G. Robinson (1910–1988), published in 1967. Robinson (p. 10) so adroitly describes:

> things like parties and best friends and going to tea with people were fine for everyone else, because everyone else was "inside" – inside some sort of invisible magic circle. But Anna herself was outside. And so these things had nothing to do with her. It was as simple as that.

As a bestseller it has been translated into several languages, including Japanese. Robinson would apparently frequently comment on this specific novel of hers saying, 'You can write books, but there's only ever one book that's really you' (Robinson, 2014). In a postscript of the latest Harper Collins publication, Joan's daughter Deborah wrote that, 'Of all her books this is the one she loved the most' (cited in Robinson, 2014, p. 286).

The book also inspired a BBC production as part of a children's show made in 1971, filmed on location at the seaside village Little Overton in North Norfolk. Over the years the book and the BBC production have inspired tourists to visit the seaside village, and explore the setting of this most enchanting of tales. One of these tourists, 30 years after the book's publication, was a Japanese man Hiromasa Yonebayashi, who had read the novel as a teenager.

A few years later, the renowned Japanese Studio Ghibli announced it had chosen *When Marnie Was There* for a film production, with Yonebayashi selected as the director. The film was released in July 2014, and has received mostly favourable critical acclaim. Amongst its many accolades and awards are an Oscar nomination, and winner of the best animated feature film award at the Chicago International Film Festival.

True to much of Studio Ghibli's legacy, the film creates an enchanting otherworldly atmosphere and storyline with emphasis on a traditional watercolour-style 2D aesthetic. The film's theme song 'Fine on the Outside' was written and performed by American singer and songwriter Priscilla Ahn (the first English language theme song for a Studio Ghibli film).

Film background and storyline

The film follows the basic story of the book, though diverges in places, and also adds elements. A notable difference is the transposition of location from North Norfolk to a seaside village in Hokkaido, Japan. Apart from Anna and Marnie, character names are changed into Japanese. Distinctly Japanese elements, such as the inclusion of the yearly Tanabata festival, only appear in the film. Much of the mise-en-scène portrays an English–Japanese synthesis. Anna's room at the seaside village, for instance, includes British paraphernalia. A broader East–West synthesis is evident also in the characterisation – most notably as Marnie's Caucasian, Western looks that include blue eyes and luxurious blonde hair. Anna has dark hair typical of Japanese, though her exquisite blue eyes belie mixed race.

In terms of style and genre, the film has been described variously as a coming of age film, as girlhood romance, fantasy, and also as a Gothic mystery. It could also be construed as a story of girlhood same-sex love, though this interpretation is problematic.

Concerning this last point, the film's poster and DVD covers portray our two main protagonists, Anna and Marnie, standing at the seawater's edge back-to-back holding hands. An impressionist-like palette of blues, greens, and rays of sunlight help to convey a beautiful romantic backdrop. Anna appears boyish, wearing shorts, a shirt, and with short dark hair. In contrast Marnie is very femme with long curled and wavy blonde hair and wears a soft, flowing white nightgown. At first appearances, the film cover looks like a boy–girl love story. It can therefore come as a surprise to discover they are both actually girls. Such overtly same-sex connotations would have been highly risqué for a feature film aimed at family viewing a decade or two back, especially for an older generation and a heteronormative Western audience. In Ireland, for instance, gay marriage was only legalised in 2015, a year after *When Marnie Was There* was released. Indeed the film might have, surreptitiously, been a timeous nudge toward naturalising same-sex love.[1]

A playful nuance of girlhood same-sex love is corroborated by much of the dialogue between Anna and Marnie. To illustrate, there is a boat scene in which Marnie is instructing Anna on how to row, amidst a backdrop of a deeply emotive 'pearl sky' sunset – a sunset touted as one of the most stunning in the animated form. Freudian psychoanalysis could have much to say about their intimate body-on-body rhythmic rowing, as a thinly veiled symbol of coitus. During this scene, Marnie whispers to Anna, 'Remember I said last night that you're my precious secret.' In the same scene, a few moments later, Marnie then steps onto the helm of the boat with her arms spread out in rapture amidst the spectacular pearl sky sunset. An obvious intertextual reference is of Rose's similar gesture in the blockbuster film *Titanic* (1997) (perhaps one of the most romantic scenes in modern cinema, establishing itself as an icon of romantic love and freedom). Further, in their intimate sharing of personal secrets in a number of deeply sensitive scenes there is a build-up of what could be construed as 'forbidden love'. Ideologically, the narrative arc as a whole mirrors and perhaps even helped to shape a significant cultural moment, as a pivotal time in history in which many cultures were transitioning toward greater tolerance and acceptance of sexual differences.

However, this same-sex theme, although developed, is problematic for at least two reasons. The first is that Marnie is clearly in love with a young man, Kazuhiko, and later ends up marrying him. Secondly, in the film's resolution, it turns out that Marnie is actually the spirit of Anna's deceased grandmother. Thus, if we are to read it as a same-sex romance then we would also need to consider an incest theme. Much of the appeal of the film, from a same-sex point of view, is no doubt weakened by this final resolution. This also illustrates a significant difference between the film and the book. The book is clearly a girlhood friendship story with little, if any, same-sex connotation.

The story, in its Japanese appropriation, infuses a barely hidden sexualised theme. This is interesting in that Japanese culture, historically, has been more accommodating of sexual themes, including lesbianism and homosexuality, to a young adult audience in media such as film and comics (manga), compared to the Christian West. In my opinion, the same-sex theme was intentionally developed by Yonebayashi and creators of the film, yet also 'paradoxically' deconstructed to ensure acceptance with a more conservative family viewing genre. Such a strategy surely secured a healthier financial profit for Studio Ghibli.

From a Jungian perspective one could explore the two protagonists Anna and Marnie as suggestive of a split-anima/shadow animus. Apparently Maro (a nickname for director Hiromasa Yonebayashi) 'draws only beautiful girls, and blond hair'.[2] It has also been suggested that such blonde girls are part of a Japanese complex related to the West (just as many Caucasian, Western men find Asian girls attractive). If so, then Marnie with all her otherworldly mystique could function as an anima figure for many Japanese men; as well as women.[3] In the book Anna's real name is revealed toward the end as Marianna, which got shortened to Anna. This signifies the close bond between Anna and her grandmother, Marnie.

In the film's resolution this close bond is restored, which could be interpreted as a healed anima.

In what follows is not the above theme. Rather, I touch on the motif of 'an invisible magic circle' from a number of perspectives. This includes love across earthly and spiritual realms, Merlinesque cycles of time, squaring the circle, and the circular structure of the Heroine's journey.

When Marnie Was There – film synopsis

The story is of Anna Sasaki, an artistic, introverted 12-year-old girl living with her foster parents Yoriko and her husband in the Japanese city of Sapporo. After collapsing from an asthma attack her foster parents, having consulted a doctor, decide to send her for a summer holiday with Yoriko's relatives, Setsu and Kiyomasa Oiwa, at a seaside village, to get some fresh sea air. Anna is isolated, suffers from depression, abandonment issues, and a lack of self-confidence and believes her adopted parents don't love her. Having blue eyes proves she is of mixed ethnicity, and this adds to her feeling of isolation.

Anna is welcomed by her kindly relatives, Setsu and Kiyomasa, who give her free reign to explore the seaside, forest, and village. During one of her lonely wanderings, Anna comes across an abandoned and mysterious mansion across the salt marsh which she finds strangely familiar. Distracted, she gets trapped by the rising tide but ends up getting rescued by a taciturn, old fishermen, Toichi, who brings her back in his boat. Safely back home, Setsu mentions the house was used for foreigners as a vacation home, but has been empty for years. That night she dreams of a mysterious blonde girl in the house. The dream recurs.

During the yearly Tanabata festival, Anna gets into a fight with one of the girls at the festival, calling her 'a fat pig'. After this frisson, she ends up leaving the festival and following her dream, by running to the marsh shore-side and taking Toichi's boat. After awkwardly rowing across the lake, she arrives at the marsh house where the mysterious girl in her dream meets her. They are immediately enamoured with each other and strike up a strong and secret friendship, and agree to meet the following evening. Thus begins a friendship like no other.

They begin to meet regularly and divulge personal secrets to each other. Anna reveals that her real parents died in a tragic car crash and that her foster parents are paid by the government to take care of her. She assumes they only adopted her for the money. Marnie reveals her wealthy and respected parents are always travelling abroad and are rarely at home, and are always too busy to attend to her. She is overly protected, isolated, and looked after by a nanny and two maids. She discloses being physically and psychologically abused by them – such as brushing her hair far too hard, and threatening to lock her inside an old grain silo down the road. Both Anna and Marnie suffer from an intense sense of abandonment.

During one of their meetings, Marnie disguises Anna as a flower girl, and introduces her to her parents and parents' friends at a lavish party. Amidst the merriment, Marnie dances with a boy, Kazuhiko, which provokes Anna's jealousy.

An invisible magic circle 151

Marnie later soothes Anna by dancing with her by the lakeside away from the party, amidst the flickering stars and a full moon.

During one of their secret meetings, whilst in the forest, Anna decides to help Marnie confront her fear about the silo. After leading her there, Marnie experiences a trauma having climbed up its spiral staircase. The weather also turns stormy with thunder, lightning, rain and a dramatic howling wind. Marnie falls into an unconscious stupor. Anna desperately tries to wake her, but also ends up collapsing into unconsciousness. Kazuhiko eventually arrives to save Marnie and takes her away with him. Anna feels betrayed and abandoned by Marnie. The following morning, she is found asleep outside the post office. Back at home, she dreams of Marnie and confronts her about leaving her.

During her daytime beach wanderings, Anna also befriends an older woman artist, Hisako, who spends her time painting the marsh house. On seeing Anna's beautiful sketches of Marnie, she recounts how the image reminds her of childhood memories of the marsh house, and her friendship with a girl called Marnie. Hisako also mentions to Anna the house is to be renovated for new owners.

Anna is curious and visits the house during the day while the new owners are moving in. She befriends the family's young daughter, Sayaka, who reveals to Anna that she found an old diary in her room, written by a girl named Marnie. Sayaka at first mistakenly thinks Anna is Marnie. Intriguingly, many events described in the diary correlate to Anna and Marnie's friendship, such as the party at the house, her dressing up as a flower child and Kazuhiko. Some pages are missing though. Later Sayaka finds these, on the same day as Anna is leading Marnie to the Silo. After the event, the missing pages reveal to Anna what happened at the Silo, and of Marnie being rescued by Kazuhiko. This information all reinforces Anna's sense of abandonment by Marnie.

Yoriko then comes to fetch Anna to take her back home after the summer holiday. Yoriko and Anna have a heart-to-heart conversation, Anna forgives Yoriko, and accepts her care and love. A bit later, Anna introduces her to Hisako as her *mother* (instead of the usual title of *auntie*). Hisako proceeds to tell them the story of the marsh house, Marnie, and the fond memories of their childhood friendship. She further explains that Marnie ended up marrying Kazuhiko and they had a daughter, Emily. Kazuhiko then died of an illness shortly after and Marnie, bereft, was committed to a sanatorium. Emily, abandoned and with no one to look after her, was sent to a boarding school. Marnie was only discharged from the sanatorium years later, when Emily was 13. Emily never forgave Marnie for abandoning her, and so ended up running away from home to marry her sweetheart, having become pregnant. Emily gave birth to a daughter. Tragically though, both Emily and her husband were killed in a car accident when their daughter was only a year old. Marnie then took her baby granddaughter in and looked after her. However, when Marnie died some years later, her four-year-old granddaughter was put into foster care.

However, it is only later, when Yoriko gives Anna an old photograph of the marsh house that Anna was very attached to as a young child, that the pieces of the puzzle finally fall into place. When Anna sees Marnie's name on the back of the photograph, she suddenly realises that she is Emily's daughter (and hence Marnie was her grandmother). This revelation brings an enigmatic yet satisfying closure to her search for identity. At the end of the film, as they are driving home, Anna looks back and sees Marnie in the marsh house window frantically waving goodbye and shouting promises to never forget her. During this final scene the films touching theme song *Fine on the Outside* plays, and the credits begin to roll.

Marnie: Imaginary friend or ancestral spirit?

As a touching scene from the book:

> Marnie flung her arms around Anna's waist. "You don't know how much I wanted someone like you to play with! Will you be my friend for ever and ever?" And she would not be satisfied until she had drawn a circle round them in the sand, and, holding hands, vowed eternal friendship. Anna had never been so happy in her life.
>
> (Robinson, 2014, p. 128)

There are two predominant Jungian style interpretations of Marnie, relative to Anna. The first is as Anna's imaginary friend; the second is as an ancestral spirit of Anna's grandmother. Considering the imaginary friend possibility, we should remember that Anna was brought up by her grandmother for the first three or four years of her life, and told Anna stories of her childhood and of the marsh house, and even gave her a photograph of the house which Anna became very attached to in her early childhood. Thus, upon seeing the marsh house on holiday would explain Anna's déjà-vu-like fascination. Further, Marnie and the events in the diary could have been a case of cryptomnesia – Anna could have unwittingly constructed these from the stories relayed by her grandmother, and from the old photograph.

Psychologically, Marnie could be viewed as compensatory to Anna, as a case of a positive shadow figure. Anna is a tomboy, wears boyish clothes, has short, dark hair, and is quiet and introverted. In contrast, Marnie is femme, wears girly dresses, has long, curly blonde hair, and is extroverted, mischievous, and adventurous. They share major psychological wounds of abandonment and isolation. Marnie's parents were almost always away travelling; Anna's parents were killed in a car crash. Marnie, as the daughter of high society parents, is overly protected from the everyday world, and appears very much as a 'damsel in distress' in her upper-story bedroom, behind windows portrayed like prison bars. Anna's isolation is more psychological, in that being introverted and wounded she finds it difficult relating to people.

The alternative interpretation of Marnie as the ancestral spirit of Anna's grandmother is an equally credible explanation. Upon their first meeting at the house we have the following dialogue, from the book (Robinson, 2014, p. 65):

> This is a dream, thought Anna. I'm imagining her, so it doesn't matter if I don't say anything. And she went on staring and staring as if she were looking at a ghost. But the strange girl was looking at her in the same way.
> 'Are you real?' Anna whispered at last.
> 'Yes, are you?'
> They laughed and touched each other to make sure. Yes, the girl was real, her dress was made of a light, silky stuff, and her arm, where Anna touched it, was warm and firm.
> Apparently the girl, too, had accepted Anna's reality.
> 'Your hand's sticky,' she said, rubbing her own down the side of her dress.
> 'It doesn't matter, but it is.'

In the film, the old artist woman, Hisako, also mentioned that Marnie cared for her granddaughter, Anna, so much that she promised she'd never be alone, even when she died.[4] Their common wounds of abandonment and isolation and a deep love for each other formed a core raison d'etre of their friendship, even beyond the grave. The intensity of this bond even thinned the veil of the ancestral realm to 'rupture' and 'bend' time.

Returning to the passage where Marnie draws a circle in the sand, embraces Anna, and offers eternal friendship: we see here a moment of fullness. It occurs on the beach, symbolic of the liminal zone between consciousness and the unconscious. The vastness of sea, sand, and sky establish the background as a spacious infinity. Here Marnie, as a personification of Anna's unconscious, as her *anima*, inscribes the two of them in a mandala. For Jung, mandalas are not only emergent ordering expressions from the unconscious during times of distress, but can also 'possess a "magical" significance, like icons' (Jung, 1959, para. 645). With this gesture Marnie can be interpreted as a healing agency of the unconscious, functioning to restore Anna's 'loss of soul'. Marnie as anima thus also embodies the centralising archetype of the self.

As mentioned above, we can deploy an alternative perspective that rather interprets Marnie as Anna's ancestral spirit, as ontic reality, and thus as her deceased grandmother. Apparently Jung sometimes preferred such a perspective, when analysing dreams that involved the dead. In Marie-Louise von Franz's *On Dreams and Death: A Jungian Perspective* we read:

> A similar situation arises in the interpretation of those dreams wherein the dead appear to a still-living person ... [*and where we*] ... interpret them as if they referred, on the objective level, to the postmortal life of the dead person (not to the life of the dreamer). I have had myself certain dreams which Jung interpreted in this way, which at the time was rather astonishing to me (italics mine). (von Franz, 1986, p. xv)

The *indeterminate space* of understanding Marnie as either imaginary friend or ancestral spirit can thus be fruitfully considered from these two perspectives.

Viewed as an imaginary friend lends itself to analysis using standard Jungian concepts such as typology, complex, archetype, shadow, anima, self, and individuation. We might categorise this approach as a #1 style of interpretation. Alternatively, viewing Marnie as an ontologically valid ancestral spirit takes us into the elusive waters of a #2 style of interpretation, with a sensibility commensurate with Jung's more outré 'secret knowledge' and the possibility of a re-imagining of our understanding of the 'Jungian unconscious'.[5]

Marnie and Merlin

In *Memories, Dreams, Reflections* (MDR) we read: 'It might be said that the secret of Merlin was carried on by alchemy, primarily in the figure of Mercurius. Then Merlin was taken up again in my psychology of the unconscious and – remains uncomprehended to this day!' (Jung, 1995, p. 255)

In MDR we read of Jung's childhood 'imaginary/ancestral friend' initially catalysed whilst on holiday at Lake Lucerne with family friends when he was 12 years old. We read that

> to his delight' the house was right on the lake, and had a boathouse and a rowing boat. A reprimand from the master of the house about his wrong approach whilst taking the boat sparked an intense yet unexpressed emotional response. It awoke in him a different inner personality that he subsequently recognised as an older, important man with buckled shoes and a white wig from the eighteenth century.
>
> (ibid. p. 51)

Over his lifetime this unusual companion would evolve and change into figures such as Elijah and Philemon, so richly evident in *Liber Novus*. In a more known example, in MDR we even read of Jung going on illuminating garden walks with his psychagogue Philemon – a spirit guru (ibid. pp. 207–209).

Later, this figure would also become conflated with Merlin. For instance, in advanced old age, he expressed an impulse to chisel the words *Le cri de Merlin* on the reverse face of his Bollingen stone: 'For what the stone expressed reminded me of Merlin's life in the forest, after he had vanished from the world. Men still hear his cries, so the legend runs, but they cannot understand or interpret them' (ibid. p. 255). It is no understatement that Jung's 'imaginary/ancestral friend' was integral not only to his healing, but to the making of his psychology. In this seminal memory of a boat, house, and lake we thus witness an almost literal resonance point between Jung and the story of Anna and Marnie.

The letter M

The *M* sound in Merlin can be linked etymologically to our earliest experiences as a baby – to mmmm, ma, mama, and has been linked to our primal instinct of desiring and suckling breastmilk – an experience that connects us, before the appropriation of language, with mother and matter. The sound associations can be extended: moon, magic, mystery. More arcane names such as mermaid, Melusina, Mercurius, and Mercuria all conjure a certain otherworldly and medial quality.

Apparently Jung's alchemical collaborator, Marie-Louise von Franz, allowed a small inner circle of friends to call her by the nickname Marlus. There is a certain ring of enchantment to this name, in its connotations to figures such as Merlin, Mercurius, and Melusina. Similarly, we might ponder upon director Hiromasa Yonebayashi's nickname of *Maro*, not to mention the name *Marnie*. One of the promotional posters of the film has the word Marnie written in a spiral-like 'faery script' reminiscent of her flowing hair, flamboyant personality, and a mysterious anagogic sense of time.

Another feature of Merlin is a profound affinity with the natural world with its rhythms and cycles. For instance, in one version of his death he is buried alive underground in a tomb. This has been interpreted animistically: 'to signify Merlin's totemic quality as a being immanent in nature, yet, at the same time, consubstantial with human life' (Watanabe in Spivack Ed., 1992, p. xx).

Robinson's descriptions of Marnie intimate such an immanence with nature as well as her otherworldliness: 'Marnie in her long white dress, with the reeds standing up all round her, and the moonlight shining on her pale hair, she looked more than ever like someone out of a fairy story,' and further ' her eyes were the same colour as the sea, and her hair, blowing across her face, was pale yellow, like the dry grasses on the dyke, only lighter the prettiest girl she had ever seen' (Robinson, 2014, p. 83, p. 121).

Marnie, like Merlin, is often depicted against a backdrop of the moon, the stars, and amidst breath-taking natural scenery – the 'pearl sky sunset' – as well as dramatic, stormy weather such as the scene at the silo. They also share an affinity for the forest, and are both associated to a 'tower' existence (Marnie's upstairs room that looks out onto the lake, the stars, and the Moon). Her golden-blonde hair, with each lock having three twirls, gives a sense of zodiacal 'cycles of time'. In one scene in the film we see the back of her head, whilst she is rowing, with her hair shown as four locks, each with three swirls. One could read into this the zodiacal circle, associated to Merlin, with its division into four sets of three to make twelve (four elements – fire, earth, air, and water with three qualities as cardinal, fixed, and mutable). In other scenes we count five or six such golden-blonde locks, perhaps symbolic of alternative time cycle patterns.

If Merlin is a specific cultural expression of the self, as Emma Jung and von Franz have cogently elaborated (Jung E. & von Franz, 1970/1998, p. 372) then Marnie, to an extent, can be considered a contemporary feminine symbol that expands such an archetypal expression, as a stronger eros and feeling-orientation, reminiscent of Merlin's love interest as Nimue or Viviane.[6]

The Tanabata festival[7]

The first time Anna actually meets Marnie, having already dreamed of her, occurs on the night of the Japanese Tanabata festival, celebrated yearly on the seventh of July (though the date varies according to locale and year).⁸ The origin myth of the festival is derived from a Chinese love story between the stars Vega and Altair (visible as part of the 'summer triangle' with the other star being Deneb). The star-deity lovers, Orihime and Hikoboshi, are separated by the Milky Way and have the opportunity of meeting only once a year, usually on the seventh day of the seventh month. However, if it rains on that day, they have to wait another year. Traditionally, boys and girls are encouraged to make a wish, with emphasis on improving their skilfulness in crafts such as sewing (girls) and handwriting (boys). In modern Japan, it has been extended to any personal wish, and not only for children. It is considered the most romantic day of the year.

Elements of the festival that appear in the film include dressing in traditional gowns, writing a personal wish on a piece of paper to be attached to a tree, and carrying colourful lanterns to a common meeting place.⁹ Setsu lends Anna her old gown, which has lavender- and lilac-coloured star couples on a lighter lilac gown. Each five-pointed star has a couple of green leaves, with three petals on each leaf (ivy!). As such the image is of a star-flower that combines an earthly and ephemeral flower with the distant and 'eternal' star.

This is the only time in the film we see Anna in a 'dress'. Its colouring as light-lilac is also more traditionally feminine. She has changed from her everyday persona to a ritualistic persona, in that her gown captures the symbolic essence of the love story between the two stars. In Taoist fashion, and probably unknowingly, she has enrobed herself in the mythos of the star story. In taking on this more feminine persona she has integrated some of her shadow, and thus expanded her consciousness. There is a moment of *coniunctio* between her inner masculine and feminine. It prospectively intimates the possibility of a 'completed individuation' as having become one with her inner stars, as symbols of the self. However, five-pointed stars, especially when combined with plant growth, suggest a *unio naturalis*, meaning an unconscious unity and wholeness and a *participation mystique* with nature. A 'squaring of the circle' as an opus of a creatively lived life grappling to become more conscious.

As the gown was originally Setsu's, we can surmise, considering the simplicity of a children's tale, that Setsu once had an adolescent wish consonant with the symbolism of the gown – of the coming together of two star-struck lovers. Perhaps her sweetheart wish was to win the love of Kiyomasa, her life-long partner. Their humble and simple lives, their seemingly 'good enough' relationship, and their journey of living together past mid-life would have required a level of maturity and consciousness, and hence a level of individuation in which the opposites have been united. Considered this way, Setsu's Tanabata gown is imbued with a talismanic potency that might be induced into Anna. It may have contributed toward giving her courage. For the first time in the film, at the start of the evening festival, she speaks her mind by lashing out at one of the other girls, calling her 'a fat pig'. This though sends her into an emotional crisis, and she ends up running away from the festival, launching Toichi's boat and following her impulse, to leave the crowd. In the twilight, she rows to the marsh house hoping to encounter the mysterious girl in her dreams. This reflects an 'as above, so below' moment of the mythic star lovers crossing the river of the Milky Way to meet. Anna has entered sacred time, the *Ilud Tempus*, and crosses to another world.

Marnie, functioning in many ways as Anna's psychopomp, wears a centrally placed ruby-coloured hairclip, in the shape of a squared circle. This is clearly seen in the boat scene where we see Marnie's hair from behind, while she is rowing. As a symbol, it could be understood as the alchemical rubedo, as goal of the opus, in the centre of the 'everyday wheel of time'. The circle is symbolic of the eternal, and the square can symbolise one's earthly incarnation within space and time. Squaring the circle, a well-known alchemical procedure, can thus mean a materialisation of the spirit, by means of an individuation. In front of Anna, as her future, is the guiding muse as her soul friend. Marnie inspires her toward her life's fulfilment and completion, of slowly realising the eternal through the finite. She is a symbol of the self.

A heroine's journey

Anna's adventure follows an archetypal pattern that has resonances with Joseph Campbell's Hero's Journey monomyth. This is represented as a circular journey in three acts. In the first act something is typically amiss with the protagonist which leads to a separation from the everyday habituated world. The second act is characterised by initiatic trials and ordeals in a 'special' or supernatural world which catalyses psychological and spiritual insight. The third and final act involves a return to everyday life, with various boons for both self and society.

The film follows this basic structure. At the beginning there is something amiss with Anna. She suffers loneliness and a lack of self-confidence, feels unloved, and is insecure about her artistic talents. Everyday life for her is wan, as mirrored in her skilful yet colourless grayscale sketches. The inciting event as a chronic asthma attack results in a decision by her parents to send her to a seaside village to stay with relatives. She separates from home and city life and leaves by train to the seaside village. Living at the seaside with Setsu and Kiyomasa is a 'special world' in a sense of physically healing her asthma, and forming a closer bond with nature.

Within this special world is an 'inner chamber' supernatural world as the marsh house where the heart of the story takes place.[10] Marnie functions as a psychopomp for Anna, allowing the gradual sharing of painful emotions and awakening Anna to feelings of being deeply loved, and of mystery and enchantment. They also help each other to face their fears. These are complex emotions, such as jealousy and abandonment fears, but, in the end, loyalty and love prevail.

Act three sees Anna returning to her everyday life, having undergone a profound transformation. She returns home to her foster mother, a newly found mutual love for each other having blossomed. She is also more able to make friends and harmonise with her peers, is inspired with her art, and no doubt cherishes the otherworldly mystery. Using Campbell's nomenclature, she has achieved a *freedom to live*, and is *master of two worlds* as the ordinary and the supernatural (the unconscious). Viewed another way, she has undergone a shamanic initiation, contacted the ancestors, undergone renewal, and returned to her community with the potential of a healing elixir, as connection with the ancestral realm.

The story differs, however, from much of Campbell's monomyth. Most noticeably, there is no violence. We do not see abductions, brother or dragon battles, dismemberments or crucifixions. There is also no explicit boy–girl union as a 'sacred marriage' (though the Tanabata star festival allows a context for Anna's 'repressed femininity' to be projected onto Marnie, and some integration between her inner masculine and feminine is achieved). There is no father atonement, as the father in the narrative is conspicuously absent. There is no apotheosis, although Anna is opened to the numinous through her encounter with Marnie. We also do not see elixir thefts, threshold struggles, rescues, or resurrections.

In overview, it is not a dramatic phallocentric epic, but rather a nuanced eros-oriented wonder-journey. Exquisite moments are established through a convergence of stunning aesthetics, narrative charm, animatic cinematography, and depth of emotion. As such, it registers more closely with Maureen Murdock's feminist revision of the monomyth than with Campbell's original structure.[11]

Conclusion

In today's Japan, a phenomenon has arisen known as *hikikomori* (meaning 'pulling inwards'). Flavio Rizzo, assistant professor of comparative literature, elaborates that they are 'a lost generation of young recluses who never leave their homes and rely on their parents to survive an obscure alternative to mainstream society'. He gives a typical image as 'likely a school dropout, may or may not have specific skills, most likely unemployed unless he has an online gig of sorts spends the day daydreaming, roaming the internet, flipping TV channels, floating in his room' and as exhibiting 'an involuntary form of counter-culture born within a desperate and genuine desire to fade and yet be alive and, most of all, connected while being disconnected a grand ball of contradictions.' Citing a Dr Akhtar, he enumerates six basic traits of the *hikikomori* as: '1) contradictory character traits, 2) temporal discontinuity in the self, 3) lack of authenticity, 4) feelings of emptiness, 5) gender dysphoria, and 6) an inordinate ethnic and moral relativism.' In expanding his account to include a sociological dimension, Rizzo describes them as 'a materialization of our societal unconscious' (Rizzo, 2016).[12]

Returning to the film, and in conclusion, an argument could be made that Anna personifies an ailing anima of much of contemporary Japanese society suffering a loss of soul (*hikikomori*). Marnie could then be a personification of Studio Ghibli functioning as anima-muse to re-enchant and heal with its soulful artistry, authenticity, and exquisite creativity.

Notes

1 In Ireland, though the film only screened in a few mainstream cinemas in June 2016, after the referendum.
2 See comment on http://www.ghibli.jp/marnie/poster/

3 If we include a post-Jungian reformulation of the anima, that also acknowledges the anima as a feature of the female psyche. See Susan Rowland's *Jung: A Feminist Revision* (2002).
4 Hisako embodies a Wise Old Woman archetype by revealing the bigger picture of the marsh house, Marnie, and toward Anna's identity. As a skilled artist working on similar themes as Anna, she also awakens Anna to the use of colour and the rewards of a life-long dedication to art. This is symbolic of Anna's own life moving from black and white to colour. As such, Hisako functions as a symbol of the self for Anna by prefiguring future growth potentials.
5 Film scholar and Jungian analyst Christopher Hauke, citing Arthur Miller, writes about Jung's #1 and #2 psychologies, as related to his #1 and #2 personalities. He notes: 'there has been, until recently, a great fear of endorsing and thinking in terms of this, most important, side of Jung' (Hauke, 2000, p. 208).
6 Here we can also reflect on the Elijah-Salome duo in *Liber Novus*.
7 Also known as the Star festival. Tokyo Disney Sea celebrates the festival with Mickey and Minnie Mouse as the 'star lovers'.
8 For example, the Tanabata festival in the city of Anjo in Japan took place over the 3rd, 4th, and 5th of August 2018 (my conference presentation related to this article took place on the 4th of August, 2018, at the joint IAAP/IAJS conference in Frankfurt). More precisely, in the Japanese lunisolar calendar, the seventh day of the seventh lunar month is on the 17th of August, 2018.
9 A paper strip for making a wish signifies a thank you and good wishes for the earth. The 2008 G8 summit, held in Hokkaido, was during Tanabata. As a symbolic gesture the Japanese Prime Minister invited leaders of the G8 to write a wish on a piece of paper and hang it on a bamboo tree, as a gesture to make the world a better place.
10 See Christopher Vogler's *Writer's Journey* for a modification of Campbell's monomyth, to include an inner sanctum within the special world.
11 From Marnie's point of view the 'special world' could be our ordinary world, wherein she is called to resolve unfinished 'earthly business' before being released back to the ancestral realm. Viewed this way, she requires Anna's help to re-experience a traumatic memory at the silo, after which she is saved by Kazuhiko and guided through a doorway to a realm of light.
12 According to a recent documentary on *hikikomori* by Euronews (2018) the number of *hikikomori* in Japan, under 40 years old, has been estimated as 540,000. If older people are included, the estimate expands to around 1.5 million (1 in every 100 people).

References

Campbell, J. (1949). *The hero with a thousand faces*. London: Paladin Grafton Books.
Euronews. (2018). *Cut off from Society: Japan's Hikikomori*. https://www.youtube.com/watch?v=KMkZjsDVKks.
Hauke, C. (2000). *Jung and the postmodern: the interpretation of realities*. Hove/New York, NY: Brunner-Routledge, Taylor and Francis Group.
Jung, C. G. (1959). *Collected works*, Vol. 9i, *The archetypes and the collective unconscious* (2nd ed.). London: Routledge & Kegan Paul.
Jung, C. G. (1995). *Memories, dreams, reflections*. London: HarperCollins.
Jung, C. G. (2009). *The red book: Liber Novus*. S. Shamdasani (ed.); M. Kyburz, J. Peck, and S. Shamdasani (Trans.). New York, NY/London: W. W. Norton.
Jung, E., and von Franz, M.-L. (1970/1998). *The grail legend*. Chichester, West Sussex: Princeton University Press.

Rizzo, F. (2016). *Hikikomori: the postmodern hermits of Japan*. Retrieved from http://www.warscapes.com/opinion/hikikomori-postmodern-hermits-japan. [accessed 26 July 2018]

Robinson, J. G. (2014). *When Marnie was there*. London: HarperCollins.

Rowland, S. (2002). *Jung: a feminist revision*. Cambridge: Polity/Malden, MA: Blackwell.

Spivack, C. (ed.) (1992). *Merlin versus Faust: contending archetypes in western culture*. Lewiston: E. Mellen Press.

Vogler, C. (1992). *The writer's journey: mythic structure for storytellers and screenwriters*. Sydney: Image Books.

Von Franz, M. (1986). *On dreams and death: a Jungian perspective*. Boston, MA: Shambhala Publications, Inc.

Chapter 10

Duality of the Japanese 'fish' symbol
Standing at the edge of life and death

Yuka Ogiso

Introduction

At all times and places, the motif of the 'fish' has occupied an especially important position among numerous familiar, animal images as a symbol representing fertility and life from the association with prolificacy or the sea. Psychologically, the 'fish', connected with 'water = unconscious', is an object swimming freely between depth/height, sacred/secular, life/death, and singular/multiple; hence it always has a character of duality.

From an astrological point of view, about 2,000 years before the birth of Christ, the fish corresponds to the time when the vernal equinox had been located in Pisces. As is well known, the 'fish' is also a traditional icon representing Christ. Jung (1948, para. 255) argues the dynamic ambivalence expressed in 'twin fish', likening it to Mercurius, which leads to the image of swimming freely in the unconscious waters of life.

The rich development of the symbolic expression of the 'fish' is seen obviously not only in Christian communities, but also around the world, including the legend of Osiris and Isis in the Egyptian myth, Jonas and the Whale, and the fish god Oánes in Babylonia. In Japan, as an island country surrounded by the sea, fishing has been highly developed since ancient times, and it can be argued that the strength of their interest in fish is unparalleled in the world. As an indispensable food comparable to rice, fish in Japanese culture is also deeply associated with Shintoism in rituals.

In this paper, I will focus on 'duality' related to the 'fish' symbol, above all in Japan, and explore it from the viewpoint of 'Mercurius', which dynamically integrates the opposites. As a key to this exploration, I will first narrate a certain Japanese short story.

A synopsis of the short story, 'Dream Carp'

> A Buddhist priest named Kôgi of Mii-dera temple, on the bank of Lake Biwa, was always drawing pictures of fish swimming. Immersed in the painting, he often entered into a dream and swam with various fishes both large and small. On waking up, he drew them in a picture and put it on the wall.

One year, Kôgi became sick and died after lying in bed for seven days. Nevertheless, he was still somewhat warm and three days later, he opened his eyes again.

He explained what had happened during that time as follows: He took off his clothes and plunged into the lake to cool him down. Then he received clothes of a gold carp from a messenger of the sea god, and swam about freely, becoming a carp. However, unable to endure sudden hunger, he was caught by the temptation of a fishing bait. His desperate resistance proved in vain; he was put on a cutting board, and came within an inch of being chopped up with a kitchen knife … then he awakened.

Kôgi regained his health and lived to a ripe old age. When death finally approached, he scattered his drawings of carps into the lake. Detaching themselves from the paper, the fishes came to life and swam about in the lake.

This tale is entitled 'Muô-no-Rigyo' ('Dream Carp', contained in *Ugetsu-Monogatari* (*Tales of Moonlight and Rain*), written by the famous writer in the Edo period, Ueda Akinari. *Ugetsu-Monogatari* (1776) has five volumes, comprising nine short tales of the supernatural.[1] 'Dream Carp', converted from two old Chinese novels, has less colour of a 'ghost story' compared to the other tales, and it has been controversial in its interpretation. Here, it is described vividly as a lively fish's swimming leap, and a view of the world where the relationship between subject and object are repeatedly reversed. Within the clues of the images induced by this story, I would like to advance a discussion of this thesis. Although the fish of this work is a 'carp', I will first of all consider the meaning of the 'fish' symbol in general.

Two fish or duality of fish

It can be said that there is a specificity to fish as a symbol, because it is a symbol that can be eaten. Fish have a very familiar and especially physical relationship to humankind in the sense that it becomes our blood and meat. There are many other primitive animal symbols, such as lion, snake, eagle, and cow, etc. but the fish seems to be the only one edible in its entirety. Through the act of eating it, from its head to tail, the fish suggests wholeness, and a moment of fusion or union. Fish meat is strictly distinguished from animal flesh and it is difficult to regard as mere meat (see that pesco-vegetarian exists and that there is a case where only fish is allowed during fasting). We often hear stories of being swallowed whole by a big fish, which has the moment of subject and object reversing. For example, Jung (1911–1912/1952, paras. 509–510) takes the example of Jonah being swallowed by a whale in discussing the night voyage in heroic mythology. Regarding such a motif as 'fishes that swallow' some detailed and meaningful analyses have been carried out from the perspective of analytical psychology, for example, Jungian analyst Edinger's (1995) analysis of Herman Melville's *Moby Dick* (1851), and Schenk (2002) on sunken treasure in the unconscious and the symbol of the fish.

Since the fish is related with prolificacy or the sea, on the one hand it is a symbol representing fertility and life, but, on the other hand, 'fishy', the adjective form has a negative connotation. According to *Longman Dictionary of Contemporary English 6th Edition*, 'fishy' has the following two main meanings: '(informal) seeming bad or dishonest', and second, 'tasting or smelling of fish'. In short, fish includes the exact opposite meaning: life, freedom, wisdom, on the one hand, but hatred, mess, and distrust, on the other.

Jung describes this duality of the fish as follows:

> The ambivalent attitude towards the fish is an indication of *its double nature*. It is unclean and an emblem of hatred on the one hand, but on the other it is an object of veneration. It even seems to have been regarded as a symbol for the soul.
>
> (Jung, 1950a, para. 187, italics by the author).

In this quotation from *Aion, Researches into the Phenomenology of the Self*, co-authored with von Franz and written in the middle of Jung's research on alchemy, Jung deals with this problem in a straightforward way, 'Aion' means an era, a certain characteristic time where Jung attempts to clarify the transition of the mental situation of the 'Christian era (Aion)' with the clues of symbolisms in Christianity, Gnosticism, and alchemy.[2]

Jung states in the Foreword: 'It is therefore only natural that my reflections should gravitate mainly round the symbol of the Fishes, for the Pisces aeon is synchronistic concomitant of two thousand years of Christian development'.

Because the Earth's axis inclines from the centre axis of the sun, the vernal equinox shifts through each sign of the zodiac about every 2,160 years. Around the birth of Christ, the vernal equinox moved to *Pisces*. So, about 2,000 years since then is the era of Pisces.

The constellation of Pisces is derived from Greek mythology as follows: when the gods were holding a feast at the banks of the Euphrates River, the Great Monster Typhon appeared. As the gods were running away, Aphrodite, the goddess of beauty and her son, Eros, jumped into the river and changed into fishes. Not to be separated, they tied each other firmly on their tails with a string. In this way, the upward vertical fish and the right-facing horizontal fish tied together became Pisces.

In the former quotation, Jung explains that the Pisces aeon has a strong connection with Christianity. It is well-known that 'fish' in Greek is 'ichthus', written as ΙΧΘΥΣ. The spelling of this Greek word is also regarded as the symbol representing Christ as being the first letter of five words 'ΙΗΣΟΥΣ (Jesus)', 'ΧΡΙΣΤΟΣ (Christ)', 'ΘΕΟΥ (God's)', 'ΥΙΟΣ (Son)', 'ΣΩΤΗΡ (Savior)', which, it is said, was used by Christians in Rome when Christianity was still persecuted as a symbol to confirm mutual faith. In addition, there are many fish examples in the Bible: four of 12 apostles were fishermen: Peter, Andrew, Jacob, and John. In such a description, 'from now on you will fish for people' (Luke, 5:10), believers are likened to fish; the miracle of bread and fish is the origin of Holy Communion. Through the ceremony, Christians incorporate the body of Christ into the body.

In *Aion*, Jung pays attention to the motif of 'two fish swimming in the opposite direction', came to be seen frequently as the Christian era. Let us follow the discussion that Jung develops in *Aion*. According to Jung, literature describing the conflict of fishes emerged during the 11th century. At that time, heretical religious movements occurred one after another, such as the growth of mendicant monasticism, the Gnostic Renaissance, the apocalypse of John, alchemical texts, all which heralded the latter thousand years of the Christian era (1950b, paras. 137–139: 1950c, paras. 233–235). In the 12th–13th century, Albertus Magnus (c. 1193–1280), Roger Bacon (c. 1214–1294), and Meister Eckhart (c. 1260–1327) were influential as philosophers interested in alchemy (1950b, para 143); in the 15th–16th century, the Renaissance, church splitting, and religious reform led to the Enlightenment, which is characterised by rationalism or materialism (1950d, para. 78; 1950b, 149–150).

Jung interprets the first vertical fish as Christ. This is the 'Gothic' effort oriented upward. And then, the movement of Enantiodromia occurred. The second horizontal fish is Antichrist. This is the horizontal motion oriented toward control of nature (1950b, para. 149). Jung argues that the important issue in our modern time is 'the problem of the union of opposites', and it can be 'solved only by the individual human being' (ibid, para. 142). This is the main point illustrated by *Aion*; moreover, Jung proposes three important aspects of the fish symbol, as follows:

First, the two fishes often correspond to mother and son. Jung states that this idea 'has a quite special significance because this relationship suggests that the two fishes were originally one' (1950e, para. 173). Second and related to this, the mother archetype as such is often associated with the fish. For example, Goddess to the Phoenicians Atargatis (her son's name is Ichthus), Goddess of Love Ishtar, Aphrodite (as the planet Venus is noticable at Pisces), the heroic night voyage and overcoming death of the Prophet Jonah are connected with greediness, swallowing, desire, vanity, and pleasure on the one hand, and at the same time, dominating the sea, Deity, Holiness on the other. These opposing characteristics of the mother archetype are given to the fish symbol.

Third, Jung discusses the fish appearing in alchemy, as the jellyfish and the remora (sucking fish), which are also symbols of the Lapis, called *magnes nostra* (our magnet). With the regard to the jellyfish, because of the form of Hydromedusa (in which tentacles extend radially from the centre), it is related to the four main compass points. Especially 'in the [North] Pole is found the heart of Mercurius' (1950c, para. 206). Here, this fish is equivalent to Mercurius, with its double nature, and symbolises the dynamic nature of the unconscious. With regard to Remora, it has a sucker on the back fin and moves by attaching itself to other fish or to a ship's bottom larger than itself. It is a very small creature in the centre of the ocean, but has enough power to stop a large ship, so it is the smallest but also

Figure 10.1 Symbol of the Fish, divided into two as the Sign of Pisces

the strongest. As Jung states, 'highest and lowest both come from the depths of the soul, and either bring the frail vessel of consciousness to shipwreck or carry it safely to port' (ibid., para. 209).

To summarise this section, I would like to mention the sign of Pisces again. The fish is originally one, but it is divided into two, and then the two are bound back to back by a horizontal line, which means union of separation and union (Figure 10.1). The symbol reminds us of the image of alchemy that Jung uses (1946, paras. 453–456) (Figure 10.2)[3] for the immersion in the bath. The central motif of the king and queen seem to be the symbol of Pisces rotated 90 degrees. They enter the fountain of transformation and these opposite elements will be combined into one.

Fish and boundary: The case of Japan

Japanese people and fish have a long and close relationship. It is said that one-sixth of the world's catch of fish is eaten by Japanese. Before rice cultivation, more than 5,000 years ago, Japanese people ate fish. For example, in the Torihama ruins, there are remains of fish fossils of the early Jomon period plus about 70 kinds of fish bones, including deep sea fishes, found in shell mounds.

Japanese people have a very strong interest in fish, as such. The oldest historical books *Kojiki* (*The Records of Ancient Matters*) and *Nihon Shoki* (*Chronicles of Japan*) contain many fish names, and there are over 1,600 Kanji for fish (together with characters imported from China and native, original characters). There are also many legends about fish, sometimes appearing as vehicles of sea gods and sometimes appearing as 'talking fish' predicting earthquakes and tsunamis.

Fish for the Japanese also have an aspect of giving an offering to the gods. In *Kojiki*, (see Chamberlain, 1982) such an episode is found:

> Then, after accompanying Saruta-biko-no-kami[4] on his return, Ame-no-uzume-no-mikoto[5] returned; and, chasing together all the wide-finned and the narrow-finned fish, she inquired: 'Are you willing to serve the offspring of the heavenly deities [as offerings]?' Then all of the fish said as one: 'We will serve'. (*Kojiki* 40: 5–7)

Figure 10.2 Rosarium philosophorum: King and Queen holding the symbol of unity. Frankfurt, 1550

Only the Sea cucumber does not reply; Ame-no-uzume becomes angry and a sword erupts from its mouth. It is said that this is why the mouth of the sea cucumber still erupts to this day.

As a custom of Japanese Shintoism, there is a ceremony called 'Naorai'. After the end of the God Festival, those who are principals of the priest and the parishioners clear the dishes of the divine and eat them together. It is based on the faith that 'through God and people eating the same things, people can assimilate with God and are given the divine power'(Yano, 2016, p. 34). Traditional offerings include rice, rice wine, rice cakes, *sea fish, river fish*, wild birds, water birds, seaweed, vegetables, confectioneries, salt, and water. Here again, fish is an essential element. Although, at first glance similar to holy communion, it differs in that fish is not equivalent to the divine, but only the object.

After Buddhism was introduced to Japan in 538 AD, fish eating was prohibited, in addition to other animal meat, because of the commandment against killing. However, as with many prohibitions, there were always exceptions. People managed to rationalise eating fish anyway. 'Fish without a foot was treated as having little sin and Kegare (impurity)'(Harada, 2005). Eventually, fish was still widely eaten, and fishing increasingly developed.

In the Middle Ages, the idea of 'shojin' came to Japan. Shojin means a purification, by monks mainly, in pursuing their training by refraining from eating animals. Buddhist priests took vegetarian meals (very strictly, with the exception of some pungent vegetables), but such a way of thinking spread to the general public as well. At the popular level, the period of shojin time has become established in cases such as mourning the dead and before a festival. Alongside this, the border between entering shojin time and leaving it was made and the latter was splendidly celebrated.

Kunio Yanagita, a famous Japanese folklorist, discusses this in detail in his work, *Food and Heart* (1940). He states that a Japanese word 'iwai' (celebration) is derived from 'imoi' (mourning). In order to emphasise the contrast of rigid prohibition in imoi and the delight of liberation in iwai, it must be clearly distinguished from the state of imoi in the ceremony of iwai. In that scene, 'namagusa' plays an essential role. Namagusa means something fishy and smelling is alive. A sea fish was selected as the material for this aspect. It was used as a boundary signature between this world and the other world. Many celebrations for coming out of shojin related to fish are still present in modern times: the feast at the end of mourning often offers a sushi (fish on rice) dish to people attending funerals; a pair of herrings at the gate of a house as an ornament to celebrate the end of the obon festival (returning ancestral spirits); special dishes for New Years, almost always containing fish; noshi (a paper ornament attached to a gift at an ordinary time), in order to distinguish it from gifts for shojin, originally used a pressed abalone, but nowadays are simplified with a paper ornament attached; children's birthdays; New Years decorations; and prayer for safe travel are also included. Furthermore, I would like to mention the ceremony of okuizome as one clear example (Figure 10.3).[6] It means a weaning ceremony, in many cases on the 100th day after birth. Parents encourage babies to eat food for the first time hoping that they will not suffer from food shortage throughout their lifetime. The menu of the ceremony generally contains one sea bream served whole, red rice (rice cooked with azuki beans, as an amulet), soup (so that the ability to suck becomes strong), simmered dishes (carrots and radishes, red and white vegetables as festive colours or pumpkin and shiitake mushrooms cut into the shape of a turtle shell, a symbol of something congratulatory), pickles of seasonal vegetables, accompanied by a stone for hardening the teeth, praying for durable teeth to come later.

The sea bream is a fish that is indispensable for many celebrations because of its festive red colour. It is also popular as a fish caught by Ebisu, the god of wealth, which has been eaten at celebrations for a long time in Japan. Furthermore, it is important to serve it complete with head and tail. As a contribution to God, it is said to be auspicious when it is not impaired and it has a wish of longevity to be served 'from head to tail', meaning to be complete from beginning to end. By putting this whole fish to its mouth, the baby steps figuratively into this world for the first time.

Yanagita explains about the symbolic meaning of the sea fish to the Japanese:

'The fact that things in the ocean have been all happy, all free, and regarded as food with the power to release the restraint of shojin, is supposed to be a

Figure 10.3 The Ceremony of Okuizome

relic that the ancestors of this nation flourished around the ocean and lived their lives more closely with it than in the present age'.

(Yanagita, 1940, p. 207)

Iwashi (sardine)

In order to know more about the symbolic character of fish in Japan, I select a certain kind of fish, iwashi (sardine). It is the most familiar fish for the Japanese which is eaten salt-grilled, fried, simmered with salted plum, raw, or (the young) simply scalded. In Chinese characters, sardine is written as 'weak' (the right side) to fish (the left), symbolising the weakness and humility, something fishy. But on the other hand, it has another name, 'murasaki' (the color of purple), called by women serving at the court. It is because sardines taste better than the luxury fish, sweet fish, called 'ai' (the colour of indigo). In addition to the original valuable meaning of the colour of purple, murasaki is reminiscent of nobility in Japan, because the name of the author of the Japanese most famous court literature *The Tale of Genji* is Shikibu Murasaki. Thus, the sardine has totally opposing meanings in itself, which is equivalent to the duality of fish in general.

The sardine, even today, is often used as an effective amulet on the day of Setsubun, which is the day before the beginning of spring on around February 4, New Year's Eve on the lunar calendar. On the day of Setsubun, oni (demons) are supposed to invade the human world, because on the day of such seasonal change, the boundary between this world and the other world loosens.[7] In western Japan, there is a custom to eat sardines on that day, to exorcise evil spirits by the strong smell and smoke incurred when sardines are cooked. In addition, there are customs to decorate the ornament of hiiragi-iwashi (holly and sardine), in various parts of Japan. It is made by piercing the head of a sardine with a twig of holly and attaching it to the gate of each house, so that no demon can enter the house because the thorns would stab their eyes, and the odour and smoke of cooking salt-sardines would drive them away. For example, this practice is drawn also in picture scrolls at the beginning of the 14th century (Figure 10.4).[8] This work is part of a picture scroll titled *Kasuga Gongen Kenki Emaki* (Miraculous Stories of Kasuga Deity Picture Scroll) (1309), which depicts the spirit of the Kasuga deity who prayed for the prosperity of the Fujiwara clan, by a famous Japanese aristocrat, and is regarded as valuable historical material for showing the Medieval period in Japan, because the customs of the time are so finely drawn.

In a private house, a sick person lies on the floor. Can you see the red oni sticking upside down on the roof and looking at the inside? The oni is trying to steal the life of the sick man but since the entrance door is decorated with hiiragi-iwashi, it remains unable to enter. There are signs of a bonfire in front of the house, where sardines would have been the burning within the rising black smoke.

Another example is a painting by Kyôsai Kawanabe, an eccentric talented painter who was active in the late Edo period and the Meiji era. This picture,

Figure 10.4 The Oni and Hiiragi-Iwashi in *Kasuga Gongen Kenki Emaki* (1309)

Bakebake-gakkô (1874), was drawn as a caricature when the school system was introduced to Japan. This is a school of monsters, and the oni plays the role of a teacher on the upper-side teaching the students about things related to monsters in the human world, in which hiiragi-iwashi is included.

So far, we have seen some cases of the relationship between fish and the Japanese people. In summary, it can be said that in Japan fish stand at the edge of life and death, betwixt and between this world and the next. Fish bring meaning as a signature indicating that there is a world of the living on the near side from the fish (the other side is the world of the dead).

Conclusion: Around the 'Dream Carp'

I would like to reconsider the story I mentioned at the beginning of this chapter, 'Dream Carp.' For that purpose, I will give an overview of the symbolic meaning of the carp in Japan. The fish has five major meanings:

First, there is the 'Climbing up Ryûmon [Dragon gate] Legend' in China, familiar to Japanese people. Ryûmon is a rapid in the middle of the Yellow River in China, and it is said that the carp which has swum upstream here has ascended to Heaven and become a dragon. This, in turn, is used as a representation of the first step to a successful career, as a narrow opening to highly prized membership: 'A carp is a river fish, but the nature that turns it into a dragon is qualified as a residence of the Sea God's Palace' (Tsuda, 2012).

Second, the carp is a symbol of the sennin (hermit). The famous legend of Kinko-Sennin tells how he disappeared when trying to catch a dragon's child, and reappeared on the red carp on the promised day. Thus, the relationship between the carp and the dragon is stressed as representing the power of the heavens.

Third, the carp is regarded as a noble fish in Japan. During the early 14th century in a famous collection of essays *Tsurezuregusa* (*Essays in Idleness*), it is written that: 'Carp is a noble fish because only a carp is cut even in front of the Emperor' (Yoshida, 1330, p. 231).

Fourth, carps tend to be associated with femininity and motherhood. There are several reasons for this, but mainly for two reasons. firstly, carp is called 'koi' in Japanese, reminiscent of love or of women because it is pronounced the same as the word 'koi', expressing love, and secondly, it is said that eating koi-koku, a stewed carp with miso soup, improves breast milk after birth.

Finally, because the carp is very nourishing, it has been a medical fish taken not only by the above-mentioned postpartum female but also as a symbol of longevity.

Let us now examine the story of the priest who became a carp.

The development of the story is divided into four moments as follows: 1) separation from the worldly; 2) swimming in the lake; 3) fished up and lying on a chopping board; and 4) back to life, or, afterwards. I would like to consider these in order.

Separation from the worldly

At this stage, Kôgi lives apart from secular life. Day after day, he buys fish caught by fishermen in Lake Biwa, and releases them back into the lake. Then, he sketches them as they swim about. Immersed in his own pictures too much, he often dreams of swimming with fish. He even states, 'I will not give away pictures of fish to sacrilegious laymen who kill living things and eat their flesh'. From such an attitude, it suggests that he is not living as a person of this world. In the meantime, he suddenly suffers from illness and dies.

Swimming in the lake

In the next scene, Kôgi transforms into a golden carp, thanks to the sea god. He is swallowed by the carp and becomes fully integrated with it, wrapped tightly in the suit of the carp received from the god.

Having become a carp, Kôgi swims around the lake freely. This scene is drawn extremely vividly by using a special, traditional Japanese rhetoric method, michiyukibun,[9] which attracts many authors of later generations and is highly appreciated:

> I found myself covered with glittering golden scales, as if I had been transformed in a twinkling into a carp ... I wagged my tail, waved my fins, and swam about freely in the lake ... I dived back to the bottoms of the lake and swam about desperately in search of a dark hideaway. Then, at night, the lights of Katada were reflected on the water's surface ... The midnight moon turned the lake into a vast, silvery mirror, flooding the nearby peaks with light and illuminating every nook and corner of the numerous inlets on the opposite shore ... Surprising, too, were the crimson walls surrounding the shrines on Okitsushima and Chikubushima, the islands in the lake.

From the west to the east, from the water surface to the depth, from the morning to the night, there is a dynamic movement in the water, which suggests a charmed fusion experienced by Kôgi[10]. And then, he gets struck by a strong sense of hunger.

Fished up and lying on a chopping board

Kôgi bites into fishing bait to quell his hunger, which means he has become a living creature with an appetite for the first time. He is raised to land by a fishing line. The motion of rising and landing is a *vertical* movement. He has been raised as a fish, but psychologically, he himself may have been the fisherman because there is a human commitment to raise the essentials to consciousness.

In spite of his desperate resistance, Kôgi is finally laid on a chopping board as meat of the feast, exposed to death. This motion in would be a *horizontal* movement. The feast reminds us of the sacrament, in other words, as the integration with the sacred. In his *Confessions*, Augustine wrote: 'it [the earth] feeds upon that fish which was taken out of the deep, upon that table which thou hast prepared in the sight of the faithful. For therefore was he taken out of the deep, that he might feed the dry land' (13:21). And here, a cutting knife is swung downward.

Back to life, or, afterwards

Here the death of Kôgi has happened, but he awakes from his dream and comes back to life (Figure 10.5).[11] The fact that a namasu (pickled) salad of fish remains in the house where the feast is being held means that Kôgi has separated from the fish and returns to human form, but he might not be the same as he was. In Kôgi's last moments, the drawn carps detach themselves from the paper, come to life, and swim about in the lake, which may mean his union with fish is therefore essential. He swims in the unconscious with the appearance of a fish and becomes a human being paradoxically only through becoming a fish completely.

Figure 10.5 Kôgi escaping from the month of the Carp in Ugetsu Monogatari

As above, I have considered the fish symbol from the viewpoint of its duality. It has a Mercurius character that dynamically combines consciousness and unconsciousness, and in Japan it plays a role of the boundary 'betwixt and between' life and death. In this paper, I have deepened the fish symbol through the case of Japan, but I would like to develop this discussion further at a future date with a cultural comparison of the symbolic meaning of the fish throughout the world.

Notes

1 'Dream Carp' is included as the second tale of Volume 2.
2 Liz Greene (2018) studies Jung's involvement with astrology in detail, examining how he applied the findings to theories of psychology and treatment of patients. She shows that we cannot grasp the essence of Jung's psychology without his astrological research.
3 *Rosarium Philosophorum*, Frankfurt, 1550. This picture is the fourth of ten pictures drawn by Jung (1946) from here.
4 One of the Japanese indigenous gods who was supposed to rule the land from long ago.
5 A famous goddess who administers entertainment. In the legend of Ama-no-Iwato (Cave of Heaven), amaterasu-Omikami, the goddess of the sun, hiding herself in the cave, was brought out by Ame-no-uzume's half-naked humorous erotic dance.
6 Photography by the author.
7 In the Western tradition, this may be equivalent to Halloween at the boundary between autumn and winter. I would like to continue considering whether or not something like a fish plays a similar role there.
8 Takakane Takashina et al, *Kasuga Gongen Kenki Emaki*, National Diet Library (Japan) Digital Collections, 1309.
9 Michiyukibun means a rhymed description of scenes reflected in the eyes of a traveler, written almost in seven-and-five syllable meter. This part of 'Dream Carp' sings in praise of Ômi-hakkei, eight representative scenic spots around Lake Biwa. The writers who highly appreciate this include Osamu Dazai and Yukio Mishima, both of whom are very famous Japanese novelists in modern times. Above all, Mishima expresses this as 'the ultimate poetry that Akinari attempted' and states that 'the Sabbath of the Soul is breathed into the lake seen by this carp' (Mishima, 1949).
10 It is also pointed out that 'it goes north on the west coast and goes around the east coast and goes around Ômi-hakkei' (Takada, 1980). It is very interesting that this is drawn as 'north turn', so far as considering the relationship between the fish in alchemy and the north pole as discussed in the second section.
11 An illustration from *Ugetsu Monogatari*.

References

Augustine. (397–398/2014–2016). *Confessions*. Carolyn J.-B. Hammond (ed. & trans.). Cambridge, MA: Harvard University Press.
Chamberlain, B. H. (1982). *The kojiki: records of ancient matters*. Tokyo: C.E. Tuttle.
Edinger, E. (1995). *Melville's Moby Dick: an American nekyia*. Toronto: Inner City Books.
Greene, L. (2018). *Jung's studies in astrology*. London/New York, NY: Routledge.
Harada, N. (2005). *Rice and meat in history: food, emperor, and discrimination*. Tokyo: Heibonsha.

Jung, C. G. (1911–12/1952). 'The dual mother'. In *Collected works*, Vol. 5, *Symbols of transformation* (2nd edn.). Princeton, NJ: Princeton University Press.
Jung, C. G. (1946). 'The psychology of the transference'. In *Collected works*, Vol. 16, *The practice of psychotherapy* (2nd edn.). Princeton, NJ: Princeton University Press.
Jung, C. G. (1948). 'Mercurius as quicksilver and/or water'. In *Collected works*, Vol. 13, *Alchemical studies* (2nd edn.). Princeton, NJ: Princeton University Press.
Jung, C. G. (1950a). 'The ambivalence of the fish symbol'. In *Collected works*, Vol. 9ii, *Aion, researches into the phenomenology of the self* (2nd edn.). Princeton, NJ: Princeton University Press.
Jung, C. G. (1950b). 'The sign of the fishes'. In *Collected works*, Vol. 9ii, *Aion, researches into the phenomenology of the self* (2nd edn.). Princeton, NJ: Princeton University Press.
Jung, C. G. (1950c). 'The fish in alchemy'. In *Collected works*, Vol. 9ii, *Aion, researches into the phenomenology of the self* (2nd edn.). Princeton, NJ: Princeton University Press.
Jung, C. G. (1950d). 'Christ, symbol of the self'. In *Collected works*, Vol. 9ii, *Aion, researches into the phenomenology of the self* (2nd edn.). Princeton, NJ: Princeton University Press.
Jung, C. G. (1950e). 'The historical significance of the fish'. In *Collected works*, Vol. 9ii, *Aion, researches into the phenomenology of the self* (2nd edn.) Princeton, NJ: Princeton University Press.
Luke 5:10. Holy Bible. *The revised English bible*. Oxford/Cambridge: Oxford University Press.
Melville, H. (1851). *Moby Dick or the whale*. London/New York, NY: Penguin Classics, 1995.
Mishima, U. (1949). *About tales of moonlight and rain, Bungei-Ôrai 3,8*. Tokyo: Waseda University Press, pp. 48–51.
Schenk, R. (2002). *The sunken quest, the wasted fisher, the pregnant fish: postmodern reflections on depth psychology*. Ashville, NC: Chiron Publications.
Takada, M. (1980). *Interpretation of tales of moonlight and rain*. Tokyo: Yuseido.
Tsuda, M. (2012). *Carp swimming edo light literature, history of literature: nature view of Japanese classics, Volume 4: fish*. Tokyo: Miyayai Bookstore.
Ueda, A. (1776/2007). *Dream Carp, tales of moonlight and rain*. New York, NY: Columbia University Press.
Yanagita, K. (1940/1990). *Food and heart, the collection of Kunio Yanagita*, Vol. 17. Tokyo: Chikuma Gakugei Bunko.
Yano, K. (2016). *Cultural history of fish*. Tokyo: Kodansha.
Yoshida, K. (1330/1998). *Essays in idleness: the Tsurezuregusa of Kenkō*. Donald Keene (trans.). New York, NY: Columbia University Press.

Chapter 11

Heart of Darkness
An archetypal journey to the other side

Mirella Giglio

Introduction

This chapter is inspired by the conference held in Frankfurt 2018 on Indeterminate States and explores several themes, including immigration. It intends to explore the symbols in the novel *Heart of Darkness*, 1899/1995 (Joseph Conrad), in search of evidence of archetypical journeys to the other side. Conrad, himself, so vividly expressed it:

> But the wilderness had found him [Kurtz] out early, and had taken on him a terrible vengeance for the fantastic invasion. I think it had whispered to him things about himself which he did not know, things of which he had no conception till he took counsel with this great solitude – and the whisper had proved irresistibly fascinating.
> (Conrad, *Heart of Darkness,* p.93).

This chapter will approach the theme of the heart of darkness through symbols as an attempt to comprehend the immigration phenomenon as an archetypical journey. The hypothesis of this investigation is that the novel may be seen as an archetypal journey to the other side; therefore, it can help us deal with and understand the immigration issues of the present. The novel is a memorable piece of cultural manifestation, and, as such, may be seen as an expression of the collective unconsciousness. The symbols help in the understanding of such expression and that is why this research will focus on them (Penna, 2014, p. 71; 180). Personal shadow may be accessed by dreams, fantasies or symptoms; however, the collective unconsciousness is equally encountered in mythology, dreams, artistic expression, or historical events (Jung, 1934a, para. 205; 1934b, para. 235). The method applied in this research is the amplification of symbols in the novel *Heart of Darkness*. This means it will go beyond the limited comprehension of associations (Young-Eisendrath and Dawson, 1997, p. 80).

Nekyia

It is common to find writings that describe the difficulty of crossing from one side to the other. *Nekyia* is a term used to indicate the passage from one world to the other. This movement is illustrated in Homer's *Odyssey* (8th century BCE) in which Ulysses crosses boundaries (Jung, 1943a, para. 61). Jung uses *nekyia* to explain the descent to the underworld, which is seen in the few passages depicted in Greek Mythology (Hercules, Ulysses, Dionysus, Orpheus) with the journeys into Hades' world, or in classic literature such as Dante's experience in Hell, and as the pact of Faust with the devil (Edinger, 2006, p. 186; Jung, 1943b, para. 42; Marlan, 2011, p. 24). The *nekyia* is a path that diminishes the light of the ego, and sometimes leads to death. The construction of the ego is an individual and painful process, but it can lead to transformation. It is a dangerous path; however, it does not represent a fall off the cliff, but instead implies a significant entrance (Jung, 1940, para. 213; Marlan, 2011, p. 23). In analytical psychology we also analyse it as crossing the boundaries of consciousness and opening up the world of the unconscious.

Hillman (2013, p. 80, 90) makes a distinction between the *night sea journey* of the hero and the descent into the underworld. He states that the hero returns from the *night sea journey* in a better condition to deal with life, but if the process is *nekyia*, the soul is taken into the deepness of the underworld and may not return. Jung does not use the same connotation when he talks about the night sea journey. For Jung, the night sea journey represents liminality, the crossing from one margin (consciousness) to the other (unconscious), a theme frequently discussed in heroic journeys (Jung, 1943a, para. 61; 1943c, para. 436).

Joseph Conrad's *nekyia*

Joseph Conrad did not have information of a *nekyia* consciously in mind when he wrote *Heart of Darkness*. He was not overtly interested in psychology. Conrad was born in 1857 in Bierdchiev, Poland (then ruled by and part of Russia). His father's family fought for Poland's independence and criticised those who were not nationalists. Conrad's father was involved in nationalist movements and his family moved to different locations during Conrad's childhood. Besides political events, Conrad's father was also interested in literature, which influenced Conrad throughout his adult life. His father invested the little money they had in a publisher who only wrote political pieces. This political activity led to the family being exiled to northern Russia. They were sent to a very cold town, and Conrad's mother did not survive the weather. With Eva's death, Conrad's father became depressed and was unable to take care of a seven-year-old child. Conrad was sent to live with his uncle for a period of time, until his father recovered. However, Conrad's father's health deteriorated over time until he died two years later (Meyers, 1991, p. 25; Stape, 2009, p. 15). Conrad was sent to live with his grandmother, who sent him to a full-time boarding school. Although he was not a clever student, he loved maps and literature; in his diary he recorded an occasion in his childhood when he pointed his finger to a map; the finger was in the middle of Africa (by that time quite unknown), and he said: 'I shall go there one day' (Conrad, 1899/1995, p. 33).

As a teenager, Conrad lived with his uncle, Tadeuz, who became the only real father figure he knew. Conrad always expressed his desire to sail and explore the world. His uncle sent him on a sea journey with a tutor with the motive to discourage Conrad from sailing. The plan had the opposite effect and by the time Conrad was 16, he was travelling to Marseille on his own. Conrad learned French as a child during visits to his family in France. He recalled his journeys as inspiring and liberating, calling himself 'Young Ulysses'. He sailed with French companies because he knew the language well, but by the time he was 20, he had also learned English. At that time, because Conrad needed to avoid Russian military service, he became a British citizen.

Moving from place to place, by the age of 30, Conrad was unable to form any stable relationships. It was then he decided to visit the Congo, a place that was in the news (Meyer, 1967, p. 92). In 1889, Conrad was made the captain of a ship sailing to the Congo. A prominent reporter of that period, Henry Morton Stanley, had been responsible for 'rescuing' Emin Pasha, the German governor of Sudan. Conrad was motivated by the information Stanley offered about Africa, and his intentions were to 'take the light of civilization into the dark continent' (Meyers, 1991, p. 96). Conrad, as depicted in his central character Marlow in *Heart of Darkness*, soon found out that the violence was not perpetrated by the locals but by employees of European companies. Beside the psychological toll of the journey, Conrad was not in good physical health. He became very ill and had to return to England three months after arriving in the Congo, where he was supposed to stay for three years. The trip was a turning point in Conrad's life, not only because his physical health did not improve enough for him to take responsibility as captain of another ship, but his emotional health was weakened by the atrocities he saw that brought on the first symptoms of depression. Conrad kept a journal of his journeys, and a few years later he showed his first manuscript to a colleague who motivated him to continue writing (Meyer, 1967, p. 59; Meyers, 1991, p. 110; Stape, 2009, p. 65).

Conrad was an outsider most of his life. When he was a child as an exile in northern Russia, his family never forgot they were Polish. After losing his parents, he had no place of his own or a family he could identify with. His desire to go to sea and see new places made him an eternal immigrant as he was the only Polish sailor at that time, the only one who spoke three languages and read classical novels. His unusual ways were also witnessed in his relationships, when at the age of 37 he became involved with a woman, Jessie, 21 years younger. After their honeymoon in France, they chose to live in England, a place Conrad identified with most. As his health was poor, he decided to make his living by writing. The couple had two boys and although Conrad struggled to survive financially with his writing, he did not become famous until after his death. The biggest influence on his work was the sea, and it is easy to find the psychological aspects in the novels. The depression that followed him increased depending on the success of his novels that were published at the time. Above all, Conrad feared rejection. He died in 1924 without knowing the great impact his novel *Heart of Darkness* has had upon modern readership (Meyer, 1967; Meyers, 1991 p. 355; Stape, 2009, p. 271).

Heart of Darkness: A synopsis

Heart of Darkness was published in 1899 and its theme bears some similarity to the author's own life. Marlow, the main character, is a sailor, as Conrad was, and uses his personal contacts to journey to the Congo. He finds work in a Belgian company that imports ivory from Africa to Europe. Marlow is fascinated by the mysteries of Africa, such as its geographical and anthropological aspects, so the novel begins with Marlow on a ship with other men when he decides to tell them of his experiences of the Congo. He is employed as the sailor of a steamboat to journey down the Congo River to find a commander of a station that the Belgian company believes is going insane. The novel is divided in three parts: The first part consists of Marlow beginning the journey and fixing the steamboat to cross the river. The second part depicts Marlow journeying inside the jungle and meeting the Indigenous people. The European crew calls the African natives 'savages'. The name-calling comes as a shock to Marlow, not only because of the new individuals he would find in Africa, but also due to the way Europeans view the African people around them. They are seen as dirty, with no knowledge, and a threat, but at the same time less than human. The third part narrates how Marlow meets Kurtz. This is when Marlow begins to feel empathy and curiosity about another person. He finds that the Africans treat Kurtz as a god: they respect him, protect him and are devoted to him. The Europeans are afraid of him, because in their view Kurtz has become one of the 'savages'. 'Savage' means someone who is led only by his/her instincts, who would kill, protecting his/her nation or tribe. For Marlow, however, killing, following instincts, and lawlessness are also part of the European personality. Marlow's insight gained in his journey is to find that everyone has instinct, aggressiveness, violence, greed, and other negative aspects that we usually project onto others.

An archetypal journey

This is the first paper on the *Heart of Darkness* that seeks evidence of an archetypal journey to the 'other side' and attempts to connect it to immigration. Sociologists use the novel to learn about colonialism and to question what is called progress at that time. Some see Conrad as a racist in the way he describes the African natives (Alencastro, 2008). Racism is not the only criticism; some scholars see him as misogynist because of the few female roles in the novel (Dhain, 2015; Viola, 2006). The reason why he has so few female roles in the novel possibly was because he had few females in his life, and little space for anima in his consciousness. Jung defines anima as the inner attitude of men, usually associated with characteristics that are not predominant in the consciousness, such as emotions (Jung, 1923a, para. 804). Some interpretations of the novel involve a journey to the inner world to find the alter-ego or 'other' repressed by the forces of civilisation (Nassab, 2006, p. 14). Characterisations of Kurtz and Marlow are usually the main themes of any research about the novel. Some psychologists have concluded that Kurtz turns 'savage' because he is hollow inside and that leaves room for the 'savage' nature to enter him. Most researchers think that Kurtz has not become evil because of Africa, but because of the brutality he sees in the way the Europeans are colonising Africa. And what is the relationship between Marlow and Kurtz? Some conclude Kurtz is Marlow's alter-ego. The term alter-ego used by these authors is related to opposite characteristics of a person (Koohestaniana and Omarb, 2014, p. 235; Pfiffer, 2011, p. 161).

This research takes a different perspective. As mentioned earlier, the method of this research is to amplify the symbols in the novel. This is a qualitative investigation, since it is based on subjective interpretations and comprehensions of the phenomenon (Penna, 2014, p. 44). The analysed words chosen are those that frequently appear in the text or the ones the author spent a long time describing.

Darkness

Darkness is a word frequently used in the novel, including the title. Even though it is highlighted in the text there is no definition in the novel. As we search for meanings for this symbol we may find darkness related to the primordial chaos of the universe because humans believe that before the universe came into existence there was only darkness. This may lead us to think that darkness has great potential, since there is no shape, no defined theme, no right or wrong. If darkness is not defined it may be a projection of what is unknown to us, about ourselves. Maybe darkness embodies those 'negative' characteristics we do not want to possess (Hillman, 2013, p. 135). Monsters live in the darkness along with all the most horrifying creatures in our imagination (Hillman, 2013). According to analytical psychology, there is a healthy way of dealing with dark, unknown monsters (Cirlot, 1971, p. 76; Aras, 2012; Ferreira, 2013, p. 158): the more we open our minds to our positive and negative features, the less we will project them onto the others. Bearing this in mind, 'darkness' in the title and throughout the text suggests primordial Chaos, and a space for projection. Projection is experienced in the novel, especially in the relationship between the Europeans and the Indigenous Africans. These groups will be discussed towards the end of the article.

Journey to Hades

Conrad uses *contrasting words* such as light and dark, wilderness and civilisation. When the author journeyed to the Congo, little was known about Africa; the map did not have the names and details we have today; it was a dark space on the globe (Conrad, 1899/1995 p. 35). In the novel, Marlow travels from Europe to Africa, which we could describe as a descent by its geographical position on the map from north to south. Would it be possible to associate Marlow's journey with a mythological descent to the world of Hades and call it a descent from consciousness into the unconscious, even though we know the unconscious is not a place – it is called the unknown aspect of the psyche? Contact with the unconscious aspect may happen voluntarily or involuntarily (Hillman, 2013, p. 86). The first contact may happen through analysis, therapy, or in another environment that promotes self-knowledge. The second path is not optional, because life situations sometimes lead to depression. We can see immigration as an opportunity to amplify knowledge about ourselves; if the descent is applied to immigration, then we can interpret *Heart of Darkness* as an archetypal journey to other side.

The snake

Before Marlow begins his journey, he sees the shape of a *snake* on the map. He imagines that the snake depicts the shape of the Congo River (Conrad, 1995). Even though there are not many animals mentioned in the novel, the few we find are essential to our search of archetypes. The snake is used several times in the history of mankind, and it carries a plethora of meanings. Transformation is seen in the symbols of snakes since they change their skins from time to time; they also symbolize the endless cycle of life, creation and destruction, and life and death (Bachmann, 2016, p. 177, p. 183). This animal is present in different myths from several cultures guarding hidden treasure. Therefore, we may say the journey to Congo foresees the encounter with something precious. In Greek Mythology, the snake is found in Asclepius' rod (the God of medicine) representing healing (Cirlot, 1971, p. 246) as opposed to the symbol of the serpent in the Bible that has been interpreted as a 'sinful' thirst for knowledge. Bearing this in mind, we can say that the main character is getting close to the hidden treasure that contains a self-knowledge that might lead to a cure.

Marlow fears going into the snake-like river, as a reference to the universal fear of crossing the boundary into the unknown, into a new country, into a new experience, of shedding an old skin and becoming a new person. According to the analytical psychology, when this fear of the unknown is confronted, the individual opens him/herself to the possibility of transformation, of rebirth (Rosen, 2009). Why is it important as psychologists reflecting about immigration to detail the several meanings of the snake? The snake in the novel involves Marlow in boundary issues, of crossing borders and journeying into creative, unfixed, liminal spaces. Is it possible for us to say that the snake as a symbol opens us up to contact with different people that may also generate a healing process?

Ivory as the treasure

Opening ourselves to people who are different is possible for everyone, and this point is illustrated well in *Heart of Darkness*. Even though the Europeans in the novel do not value the Indigenous Africans, they want to obtain one object very precious to them: ivory. The value of ivory for the Europeans in the novel contrasts with the undervaluing of the Indigenous Africans. As ivory is a part of Africa, the continent is only valued by that material value and not by its people. The first time ivory appears in the novel is as the material in the dominoes being played before Marlow begins his story (Conrad, 1899/1995, p. 5). If the reader unaware that ivory is the material that led Kurtz to the Congo, the reader will not appreciate the connection. Why is it important to notice the ivory in the domino pieces? Dominoes is a game built by logical rules, which requires using mathematical concepts to dominate the opponent. Ivory is only obtained when the elephants are dead; therefore ivory is also a product of slaughter. This may also be seen as an analogy of what is happening in the Congo with the Europeans trying to use their so-called logic to dominate and win from the Africans. Even though the ivory is important to the Europeans, they did not see value in the population from where the ivory is extracted. This leads us to question: Who is valuable to us? Do we see valuable qualities in those who were not born amongst our kind? For Hillman (2013, p. 95), the ego has difficulty in recognising any valuable content found in darkness. With this in mind, we may see a connection between the ego and its reaction towards its shadow by the Europeans in the novel. This will be discussed later in the paper when we analyse the character of the pilgrims. Ivory appears in Greek Mythology as Hades' gate, which links Marlow's Congo to the underworld, and is shown in the relationship between Kurtz and Hades.

Light and darkness

Throughout the novel, it is possible to highlight the words light and darkness. Light appears in the novel in two ways: from lamps or candles and from the African sun. As the first category of light is usually very low, it might represent European consciousness because these lights are where the Europeans are found in the novel (Conrad, 1899/1995). On the other hand, the light from the sun is very strong and intense. The sun could represent the idea that Africans have about themselves and their instinctual nature. Once we know that light symbolises consciousness, we also remember that being in contact with the light is not a comfortable position, since there is a reason why we keep some aspects in the shadow; it is unbearable for the ego (Stein, 1998, p. 22). When we discuss the sun as well as darkness, we arrive at *Sol Niger*, the black sun as a composite image. This is a term used in alchemy to depict the initial stage, the point of the beginning of something. Its meaning is close to what we know as the Self, since both contain light and darkness, life and death, spirit and matter (Marlan, 2011, p. 219). For analytical psychologists, dealing with the Sol Niger, is like watching the Self moving from one stage to another in a liminal state following an unknown, dark path towards transformation (Marlan, 2011, p. 219).

As Marlow gets in touch with the jungle and the Indigenous people, he notices that the light and dark are not as separate as the Europeans thought. Sol Niger may be represented in the novel because it is a black sun with a light inside it. If this is true, we may say that as the character enters in contact with what is dark, he will also find light and knowledge of something hitherto unknown. Once the character opens his consciousness to aspects that are hidden in the darkness, the result is definitely transformative. Symbolic death needs to happen for transformation to occur. In this case, the transformation happens in the ego, which means that some characteristics of the ego must die (Rosen, 2009, p. 61).

Symbols and mythology

As we approach the symbols in the novel with depth, we may find several associations with concepts of analytical psychology and mythology. The Europeans in the novel could represent the ego, an ego with Apollo's features of seeking to organise, structure, categorise, number, and limit (Jung, 1923a, para. 210). These are important characteristics, but they need to be balanced by Dionysus' features: instinct and pleasure, among others. The Europeans in the novel can be associated with the ego trying to avoid contact with the Africans, the shadow. If the Europeans behave as how the ego relates to the shadow, then we see an ego that tries to maintain order, repress instincts, and dominate. They think the Africans are destructive, savage, and brutal. According to analytical psychology, they project shadow elements of themselves onto the Africans, and at the same time, force their own point of view about what is acceptable and what is not. Too much ego consciousness may result in a patriarchal repression and denial of the shadow aspects (Marlan, 2011, p. 14).

The main character, Marlow, changes his opinion about Africa and Europe throughout the novel. Even though he is himself European, his experience of Africa is different from the Europeans employed by the Belgian company. He notices that those who see destructiveness in others are destructive themselves. Marlow realises that what we call negative aspects are found within our own hearts, and not only in the heart of others.

From a psychological perspective, Marlow is the only character who can cross borders in a healthy way. The passage to the other side is not an easy task. After dealing with the descent and with the symbols constellated during that phase, we now approach the passage to the other side in the novel. When Marlow arrives in Africa, he finds the company's chief accountant a very peculiar man (Conrad, 1899/1995, p. 21). He is another example of the European mindset portrayed in the novel. He is one of the few Europeans able to stay in the Congo for a long time and keep his clothes clean and white:

> I saw a high starched collar, white cuffs, a light alpaca jacket, snowy trousers, a clean necktie, and varnished boots. No hat. Hair parted, brushed, oiled, under a green-lined parasol held in a big white hand.
> (Conrad, 1899/1995, p. 31)

Why is this relevant? Several Indigenous African work for the accountant, but they are the ones 'in the dirt'. 'In the dirt' means not only being in the mud, but also dying from diseases contracted from the Europeans (Conrad, 1899/1995, p. 31). The Indigenous Africans are getting sick and dying, but this does not concern the accountant, as if the Africans did not matter to him. Keeping his clothes clean also means he does not let the Congo penetrate him. We could say this character is the defensive aspect of the persona because he is so connected to his social position that he did not even have a name, only a professional label (Young-Eisendrath &

Dawson, 1997, p. 223). Sometimes the persona is so distant from the individual's shadow that he/she is only conscious of him/herself through his/her persona. The persona is the link between the individual and others; a healthy persona is flexible and open to connections from the inside to the outside (Jung, 1923b, paras. 754–757). The accountant is not a healthy version of a persona; he is a typical case of someone who distances himself from the unknown, despite being surrounded and shrouded in darkness.

Gates and doors 'betwixt and between' borders

All sorts of polarity are seen in this novel: light and dark, Europe and Africa, inside and outside, among others. When we think about two sides, we also need to consider crossing borders. *Gates* and *doors* populate *Heart of Darkness*. According to the concepts of analytical psychology, they symbolise the separation between consciousness and the unconscious. Marlow is the character who opens and crosses gates as he approaches Kurtz. We call this a rite of passage and the possibility of transcendence (Hillman, 2013, p. 254).

Marlow physically crosses borders using the steamboat to reach Kurtz. Steamboats have different symbolic interpretations, but in this paper I shall approach it through mythology. Charon is the ferryman in Greek mythology who takes the souls to Hades' underworld (Roman and Roman, 2010, p. 116). The Egyptians believe the boat is a means of transportation for the sun at night; the sun is taken on a boat to the other side where it would rise again the next day. The symbol of boat in Egyptian and Greek mythology is thus associated with death and rebirth.

These associations help us approach the hypothesis that *Heart of Darkness* is an archetypal journey to 'the other side'. With this interpretation, we find resources that help us deal with the unknown. The more we avoid crossing borders in order to expand knowledge about ourselves, those aspects from the other side cross the borders themselves to diminish the distance we think we have from them. The approach from the other side might represent death, but may also come with a rebirth:

> [Y]ou lost your way on that river as you would in desert, and butted all day long against shores, trying to find the channel, till you thought yourself bewitched and cut off forever from everything you had known once – somewhere – far away – in another existence perhaps.
>
> (Conrad, 1899/1995, p. 59)

Pilgrims

Hope for rebirth is not always joyful, once we know that the process also involves death. The characters who express reaction to death are the pilgrims. They are a group of Europeans looking for Kurtz, but equally interested in the ivory he has collected (Conrad, 1995, p. 61). Even though they are on the steamboat with Marlow, it seems they have a different experience. They are very scared; they would shoot at nothing, aiming at something they cannot see: 'They wandered here and there with their absurd long staves in their hands, like a lot of faithless pilgrims bewitched inside a rotten fence' (Conrad, 1995, p. 44). Through the lens of analytical psychology, the fear of the pilgrims may relate to the fear of the ego when faced with something unknown. The ego may be aggressive, resisting the chance to survive because it actually fears death. Death in this case is the symbolic death of the ego and not the concrete death of person (Rosen, 2009, pp. 70–74).

What are the pilgrims really afraid of? In the novel, the pilgrims fear what aspects the 'savages' represent to them. 'Savage' is the term used by Marlow in the novel to describe the Indigenous Africans who do not interact with Europeans. In the beginning, the 'savages' are also among the group, but lacking identity. They are violent in defending themselves and in protecting Kurtz from those who are entering the jungle (Conrad, 1899/1995, p. 79). One African character who makes an impact in the novel is the helmsman who takes Marlow and his crew on the steamboat down the Congo River to find Kurtz. Normally, Marlow does not show any feeling of friendship during his journey; that is how his personality functions. He makes no distinction between the Europeans and the Africans, but he does show feelings, perhaps of sadness, when the African helmsman dies. The helmsman dies when Kurtz's 'tribe' attacks the steamboat, when they notice that the boat approaches to take Kurtz away. The helmsman falls down after he is shot and Marlow feels his blood trickling to his feet (Conrad, 1899/1995, p. 81).

This passage would pass unnoticed except that Marlow himself stops to look down, takes off his shoes as if to distance himself from the blood. Blood is pumped by the heart so we remain alive; the heart is also the place in the body associated with emotions. Does this mean that Marlow feels something about the death of the helmsman? And what about the fact that he takes off his shoes? As already discussed, we associate clothes with the concept of persona. Shoes are objects used by the Europeans in the novel; if we follow this train of thought we can say that throwing away his shoes filled with blood may means that Marlow is distancing himself from the colonialism that is killing life in the jungle.

This is a turning point in the novel. Some studies suggest that being barefoot represents a change of point of view (Aras, 2012). This makes sense in the novel, because at this stage of the journey, Marlow begins to feel disappointed with the actions of the Europeans in Africa which he can no longer condone. From this turning point, Marlow approaches the encounter with Kurtz

Marlow and Kurtz, ego and shadow

Arriving at Kurtz's station, Marlow meets the Russian harlequin. He is the connection between Marlow and Kurtz. Before meeting the person responsible for the station, Marlow receives several facts about Kurtz through the Russian harlequin (Conrad, 1995). He is also the one who takes Marlow to meet Kurtz, and has some resemblance to Hermes from Greek mythology. Hermes is the messenger of the gods and the conductor of the dead souls in the underworld (Hillman, 2013, p. 161).

Before we meet Kurtz, we need to discuss the concept of 'shadow' (see Jung, 1950a, paras. 13–19; 1946, paras. 455–457) and its use in the novel. The word shadow is mentioned several times by Conrad in *Heart of Darkness*, including when Marlow describes Kurtz (Conrad, 1899/1995). Although they meet in the novel, Kurtz's appearance is difficult to define. The word shadow is also associated with the *nigredo* state in alchemical study, as the initial stage of the opus. It is after the *nigredo* that the sun arises, and a person embraces his/her characteristics that are denied until then. In analytical psychology, the *nigredo* is the *prima materia* before consciousness is enlarged (Harding, 1970). It is associated with darkness and death, but, again, we are considering the symbolic death of the ego, resulting in transformation (Edinger, 2006, p. 186). Kurtz is related to the shadow, not only in the physical aspect, but also as a character we do not have enough information about. We could say that Kurtz is an alter-ego, considering alter-ego to be the shadow of ego (Cirlot, 1971, p. 49). What does Conrad reveal about Kurtz? To repeat the quotation mentioned at the beginning of this chapter, Conrad intuits the following about Kurtz:

> But the wilderness had found him out early, and had taken on him a terrible vengeance for the fantastic invasion. I think it had whispered to him things about himself, which he did not know, things of which he had no conception till he took counsel with this great solitude—and the whisper had proved irresistibly fascinating. It echoed loudly within him because he was hollow at the core.
>
> (Conrad, 1899/1995, p. 93)

This passage in the novel reveals that Kurtz has many problems but his biggest is that he tries to control chaos and his shadow overcomes him. Kurtz, like many of us, try to overcome the unconscious as our unknown aspects. The result of this effort is that the shadow, without differentiation, can swallow the ego, and this is what happens to Kurtz. The attempt of Kurtz to become God the Creator and obtain control fails. Even though he fails, Kurtz is also associated with the god of the underworld, Hades, because he reigns in a land full of disease, conflicts, fear, and death. Remember the gates of ivory? In Greek Mythology, the dead souls were taken to the underworld by boat (Roman and Roman, 2010, p. 414).

The work we do in psychoanalysis is to attend to the underworld (Hillman, 2013, p. 84). This underworld is also reached by situations that force us to deal with shadow projection, such as the ones we project onto immigrants, because they may represent characteristics that we are neglecting to differentiate in ourselves. We need to dive into our own shadows to evolve as part of the individuation process. It is when we do not look at and differentiate these aspects that these issues kidnap us. This is what happened to Kurtz; he was taken by his own shadow, because he wanted to control it. And this led him to his concrete death.

The return

There are several ways to deal with the jungle, the shadow, or with what is unknown. In *Heart of Darkness* Kurtz is overtaken by it; on the other hand, the Europeans do not get involved at all. Different from both Kurtz and the Europeans, Marlow is able to deal with the shadow in a healthy form. This leads us to discuss the *return* in the story. When Marlow returns to Europe after his trip to the Congo, he is a different person (Conrad, 1899/1995, p. 115). If we look at this factor through the lens of analytical psychology we may say this is healthy, because some aspects of the ego have remained the same (Rosen, 2009, p. 70–74). Marlow and Kurtz have a relationship similar to that of ego and shadow. When the ego faces the shadow, it is important for a part of the ego to maintain its integrity, otherwise the encounter might lead to a split personality, or be dominated by the shadow, just as Kurtz was. Marlow, however, is able to cross to the other side, change his mind, and return. When Marlow returns to Europe, something inside him is different from those around him, revealing how much his experience in the Congo has influenced him.

Conclusion

Considering the story as a whole and its symbolic description, we may associate the novel with the term *nekyia*. Remember this term also represents the journey to Hades' underworld and the encounter with the shadow (Jung, 1950b, para. 311). From his night sea journey, Marlow is able to see in himself, and in the Europeans, characteristics that are projected onto the Indigenous Africans. Marlow recognises in himself and in the Europeans features such as barbarianism, a desire to be accepted in society, and the willingness to act freely without having to adapt. These may be found in all human beings. The less we are willing to know about ourselves, the less we are willing to know about others. We tend to project onto others and projection distances us from meaningful relationships. When we are not engaged in learning about who the next person really is, the less we are open to ourselves.

With all that has been said, can we consider *Heart of Darkness* an archetypal journey to the other side? Such a journey may be an opportunity for us to know ourselves better as we dive into our own darkness (Macdonald, 2013, p. 17). If Kurtz is a modern version of Hades, then we may see evidence that the novel is an archetypal journey into the underworld. The term underworld is not related to north and south, but to the unknown. As I have already said, the journey to the underworld may be part of the individuation process, since it is a way of recognising in ourselves what we have denied. When we are not willing voluntarily to make this journey, the Self leads us to other occasions for the ego to expand. Receiving and welcoming immigrants is a way to amplify what we know about ourselves, once we begin to see others with an open, humane mind. When in immigrants we see an opportunity to grow, we can learn from them. As with any contact with the unknown, opening ourselves to the immigrant 'other' may involve a symbolic death, a death of the ego before transformation happens. Discovering another 'me' is not an easy task; it may actually feel monstrous. However, it may lead to awakening a curiosity of understanding the 'other' (Marlan, 2011, p. 41). Once we are willing to look deeper into ourselves, the relationship we establish with those around us may be life-changing for both sides.

References

Alencastro, L. F. (2008). 'Postfix: persistency the darkness'. In J. Conrad (ed.), *Heart of darkness*. São Paulo: Companhia das Letras .

Archive for research in archetypal symbolism (ARAS). (2012). *The book of symbols: reflections on archetypal images*. Cologne, Germany: Taschen Verlag, pp. 808.

Bachmann, H. I. (2016). *Animal as symbolism in drams, myths and fairy tales*. Rio De Janeiro, Brazil: Editora Vozes, pp. 264.

Cirlot, J. E. (1971). *A dictionary of symbols*. 2nd edn. London: Routledge & Kegan Paul Ltd.

Conrad, J. (1899/1995). *Heart of darkness*. London and New York: Penguin books.

Dhain, A. Y. (2015). 'Symbolism in heart of darkness'. *International Journal of Social Science and Humanities Research*, 3 (2), 486–490.

Edinger, E. F. (2006). *Anatomy of the psyche: alchemical symbolism in psychotherapy*. Chicago: Open Court Publishing.

Ferreira, A. E. A. (2013). *Dicionário de imagens, símbolos, mitos, termos e conceitos Bachelardianos*. [ebook] Londrina: Eduel. Available at http://www.uel.br/editora/port al/pages/arquivos/dicionario%20de%20imagem_digital.pdf (accessed 20 April 2017).

Harding, E. (1970). *The value and meaning of depression*. London and Los Angeles: Analytical Psychology Club.

Hillman, J. (2013). *The dream and the underworld*. Petrópolis: Editora Vozes .

Jung, C. G. (1923a). 'Schiller's ideas on the type problem'. In *Collected works*, col. 6, *Psychological types* (2nd edn.). London: Routledge and Kegan Paul, 1989.

Jung, C. G. (1923b). 'Definitions'. In *Collected works*, Vol. 6, *Psychological types* (2nd edn.). London: Routledge and Kegan Paul, 1989.

Jung, C. G. (1934a). 'The personal and the collective unconscious'. In *Collected works*, col. 7, *Two essays in analytical psychology* (2nd edn.). London: Routledge and Kegan Paul, 1990.

Jung, C. G. (1934b). 'The assimilation of the unconscious'. In *Collected works*, vol. 7, *Two essays in analytical psychology* (2nd edn.). London: Routledge and Kegan Paul, 1990.

Jung, C. G. (1940). 'Picasso'. In *Collected works*, vol. 15, *The spirit in man, art, and literature* (2nd edn.). London: Routledge and Kegan Paul, 1990.

Jung, C. G. (1943a). 'Individual dream symbolism in relation to alchemy'. In *Collected works*, vol. 12, *Psychology and alchemy* (2nd edn.). London: Routledge and Kegan Paul, 1992.

Jung, C. G. (1943b). 'The psychological problems of alchemy'. In *Collected works*, vol. 12, *Psychology and alchemy* (2nd edn.). London: Routledge and Kegan Paul, 1992.

Jung, C. G. (1943c). 'The prima materia'. In *Collected works*, vol. 12, *Psychology and alchemy* (2nd edn.). London: Routledge and Kegan Paul, 1992.

Jung, C. G. (1946). 'The fight with the shadow'. In *Collected works*, vol. 10, *Civilization in transition* (2nd edn.). London: Routledge and Kegan Paul, 1991.

Jung, C. G. (1950a). 'The shadow'. In *Collected works*, vol. 9ii, *Aion; Researches into the Phenomenology of the Self* (2nd edn.). London: Routledge and Kegan Paul, 1989.

Jung, C. G. (1950b). 'Gnostic symbols of the self'. In *Collected works*, vol. 9ii, *Aion; Researches into the Phenomenology of the Self* (2nd edm.). London: Routledge and Kegan Paul, 1989.

Koohestaniana, F., and Omarb, N. (2014). 'Captains of the unconscious: Joseph Conrad's portrayal of a true modern self'. *Procedia - Social and Behavioral Sciences*, 118, 235–241. Available at http://ac.els-cdn.com/S1877042814015626/1-s2.0-S1877042814015626-main.pdf?_tid=6d96b7a6-00dc-11e7-b952-00000aab0f6c&acdnat=1488633419_b01b47cf8b31003d74ee13b6b08c5a27 [accessed June 29, 2016].

Macdonald, Y. H. R. (2013). *Divagar, devagar: depressão e criatividade*. Curitiba: Appris.

Marlan, S. (2011). *The black sun: the alchemy and art of darkness*. 3rd edn. College Station, Texas: A&M University Press.

Meyer, B. (1967). *Joseph Conrad: a psychoanalytic biography*. Princeton, New Jersey: Princeton University Press, 1967.

Meyers, J. (1991). *Joseph Conrad, a biography*. New York, NY : Cooper Square Press

Penna, E. M. D. (2014). *Processamento Simbólico-Arquetípico: pesquisa em Psicologia Analítica*. São Paulo: EDUC/FAPESP.

Pfiffer, G. A. (2011). *No Coração das Trevas: O paraíso e o inferno do outro em Bernardo Carvalho e Joseph Conrad*. Rio de Janeiro, Brazil: Universidade do Estado do Rio de Janeiro.

Roman, L., and Roman, M. (2010). *Encyclopedia of Greek and Roman mythology*. New York, NY: Facts on File, Inc .

Rosen, D. (2009). *Transforming depression: healing the soul through creativity*. 7th edn. Lake Worth, Florida: Nicolas-Hays, Inc.

Stape, J. (2009). *The several lives of Joseph Conrad*. New York and London: Vintage Book, p. 369.

Stein, M. (1998). *Jung's map of the soul*. 12th edn. São Paulo: Editora Pensamento-Cutrix LTDA.

Viola, A. (2006). 'A black athena in the *Heart of Darkness*, or Conrad's baffling oxymorons'. *Conradiana*, 38 (2), 165–173.

Young-Eisendrath, P., and Dawson, T. (eds.) (1997). *Cambridge companion to Jung*. Cambridge: Cambridge University Press.

Part 4

Border crossing and individuation

Chapter 12

Re-visioning individuation
Opening to a witness consciousness

Eileen Susan Nemeth

Introduction

The venue where I gave a seminar in Zürich during the fall of 2017 was once the home of Katharina von Zimmern, the last Abbess at Fraumünster Convent between 1496 and 1524. During the Reformation, she gave up her position as Abbess. From 1540 until her death in 1547 she lived in this house where I now have my practice. I feel as though I am being held in a space that is filled with religious, political, and cultural upheaval. As I work in this room, I am constantly reminded that we are all actors in ongoing stories, both personal and collective, and that we must continue to create and change with the demands of our time.

The seminar I gave was entitled: 'Jung and the Body: An Authentic Movement Experience'. The participants were students of analytical psychology and newly graduated analysts. We gathered together after our fourth session and reflected on the experience of moving and witnessing. The realisation of our basic need to be witnessed was again revealed. As the Sufi mystic poet, Mansural-Hallaj expressed it: 'I saw my Lord with the eye of the Heart, I said "Who are you?" He answered "You"'.

To be witnessed, to be seen, is as essential as the intake of nourishing food, dreaming in sleep, the touch of another, and underscores any therapeutic work, or any relationship we encounter. Within our understanding of individuation, to witness would be the ability 'to see' the 'other' with a clear vision, with eyes that make what is invisible, visible, and with this 'seen' truth we are able to envision new possibilities out of places of tension, change, and transition for the individual and the collective. Without this experience of witnessing as part of an individuation process, we limit our relational life and endlessly circle around the personal complexes, not letting that circle grow to a larger sphere that embraces all of sentient life.

Where does a witness consciousness fit into our understanding of individuation? Is there a witness as archetype that needs to be explored, not only as analytical psychologists, but as individuals living in a shifting world, with changing borders and boundaries we once thought were fixed? We are now learning through the complexities of an ever-metamorphosing, indeterminate world that nothing is fixed. We need to incorporate a depth of vision that supports a flexibility and relatedness needed in changing times.

What is the 'eye of the Heart' spoken centuries ago by al-Hallaj (ca. 900 AD). Is it from this place that we can begin to espy 'us' instead of 'me', or is it from this place that we begin to sense our shared humanity and where we feel the depth of soul in all of life? Through the writing of this article, presented at the joint IAAP–IAJS Conference in Frankfurt, my personal story begins to take on new meaning. I turn from personal fears, as I face the changing world around me, that threaten 'my' existence. Only by including an 'us' could my roots begin to connect, interweaving with the deep roots of others and knowing our survival depends on that intertwining. At the time of questioning the significance and value of my presentation at the Frankfurt conference, I read an article about Hannah Arendt, called 'The Illuminations of Hannah Arendt', by Richard J. Bernstein. I quote her, because it speaks directly to my thoughts in this paper and the 'illumination' I/we need at this particular time in history.

> Even in the darkest times we have the right to expect some illumination.
> (Arendt, 1968, p. ix)

I hope this small personal light will illuminate you as we move forward ...

I have divided this paper into five main sections: firstly, I present an intergenerational perspective; secondly, a dream analysis; thirdly, I analyse the tree symbol as a transcendent function; fourthly, I propose authentic movement as a ritual for balancing between the borders of the physical and the psyche, particularly in times of life threatening political repression, that creates existential uncertainty, and loss of roots; finally, I take the symbol of the eye as a witness consciousness in the individuation process which includes 'us' as well as 'I'.

A granddaughter of immigrants: An intergenerational perspective

When I began my research for this paper, I realised that I must start with some autobiography as a granddaughter of immigrants, for it is this aspect that prompts me to approach this intriguing and complex topic of opening to a witness consciousness. It is a concept spanning studies in theology, philosophy, and psychology, particularly with the effects of inter-generational trauma caused by migration and crossing borders into, as yet, unchartered territory. Therefore, I approach this concept with great circumspection.

The story I know begins with this piece of paper (see Figure 12.1). It is the manifest from the passenger ship *President Lincoln* that landed at Ellis Island in February 1911.

There, in the list of passengers is my grandfather, Aaron Felner, 20 years old, shown in Figure 12.2.

Russian, because Poland was then part of Russia; listed are his age, languages, religion, and how much money he possessed (30 dollars), where he was going, and his

Figure 12.1 National Archives, New York City

Figure 12.2 Aaron Felner

profession as shoemaker. He travelled with his sister Esther, 18, who had 20 dollars. My grandmother, Gussie Felner (see Figure 12.3), didn't travel with him because she had one small child who would accompany her a year later. She had to wait until there was a place to live and money to support their small, but growing, family.

My grandfather arrived in the United States in 1911, leaving a life he knew behind him. As I grew older, I was told by many family members that he never talked about his family or of the life he had left behind. Therefore, because of his silence, I will never know if he left Poland because of the persecution that he experienced as a Jew, or because he wanted to have a better life-style, financially and socially, for himself and his family in the United States.

This grandfather once came to me in a dream, whispering mischievously in my ear: 'You know I am a Buddhist'. I clearly saw my Grandfather as a wise man, who understood the interconnectedness between things, and that deep soulful need one has for relationship with another, not only to become aware of oneself, but mindful of the humanity one shares.

Then in 2016, I saw this picture of people walking across a field in Macedonia, Syrian refugees, escaping war, devastation, and persecution in their own country (see Figure 12.4).

Figure 12.3 Gussie Felner

Figure 12.4 Bild von Flüchtlingen in online Focus vom 14.3.2016 dpa/Nake Batev, 'Verzweifelte Lagerbewohner aus Idomeni marschieren zu Fuß in Richtung Mazedonien'. Translated it reads 'Desperate migrants from Idomeni march on foot in the direction of Macedonia'.

Since that first image of hundreds of men, women, and children walking through fields, carrying very little, we have seen other desperate pictures of people from Africa, some also escaping war, but many wanting simply to survive and have a better life for themselves and their children. Is that so different from my grandparents? I feel caught between empathy and fear, anger and compassion; sadness wells up along with the fear of not knowing what the future brings. Yet, I know that I am a part of this drama, evolving at a speed that leaves me often helpless and anxious and, faced with questions I have no direct answers to and yet, trying to understand how to survive in a changing world, consciously and creatively.

A dream vision: Personal and collective

After this first visual confrontation of the masses of refugees walking across fields in Macedonia, I had this dream:

> I was walking in a large open field, more like a savannah in Africa. Suddenly all the wildlife, lions, tigers, antelopes, giraffes, and others, began to run towards me. Something had made the animals scared and they were running for their lives. I also began to run, afraid of being stampeded. I ran toward

the only tree I saw standing. On the way I had picked up my dear and loving cat. When I reached the tree, I held Artie, the cat and my husband wrapped us both in his arms and held on to two hinges on the tree. On the other side of the tree, also holding on, was an Asian man. We knew there was a storm coming and we had to hold on very tightly until it passed. I hoped the tree with its deep roots would hold. I had to trust that it would.

This dream, for me, undeniably states that as fear and anxiety overwhelm us, we must hold on to the tree, the Tree of Life, with its roots reaching down into the soul of the earth, the Great Earth Mother to us all, protecting and nourishing all of life (Jung, 1937, para. 499). The powerful verticality of the tree, connecting heaven and earth, and the horizontality of the two sets of arms circling and holding on, express a relational life with the 'stranger', the Asian man. As our arms encircled the tree, I am reminded of the Tree of Life symbolism found in so many cultures. The image is often with roots defining a circle and the tree growing out of its 'centre', wherein all creation begins. It is an archetypal image containing much mystery and power (Cook, 1974, p. 9).

As I researched the African savannah mentioned in the dream, I was stunned to find that the savannah itself is a transitional space, between forest and grassland or desert. Due to climate change, the African savannah is now under threat. That same threat of extinction is felt by the sentient life in my dream as they face the oncoming storm. The savannah is also an important ecosystem that sustains a high plant and animal life, which some ecologists believe plays a large role in regulating the global climate.

Therefore, as the environment of the dream, the African savannah, itself, has a regulating ecological function, the same function that we give to the Jungian concept of the Self, a self-regulating function in the psyche. Even before my research on the African savannah, I sensed that the dream has a strong Self-regulating function, preserving, protecting, and fostering life.

Native to the African savannah, where the climate is extremely dry and arid, the tree, often the Baobab three, is a symbol of life and positivity in a landscape where little else can thrive. The Baobab tree can provide shelter, food, and water for animals and humans. The tree, as the symbolic Tree of Life caught my attention, but I kept feeling the balance between the Asian man, my association being that he was a Japanese animus figure, and the anima and soul animal at the opposite side of the tree. The image clearly presents an inner protective animus energy, not only with the strength to hold on to the hinges (I, as dream ego, was afraid that I would not have the physical strength to hold on through the storm), but also resembling a protective shell around the less protected life of the soul. Since the dream is personal and collective, my personal association to the Asian man comes from my many years of sitting in Zen meditation. Perhaps that is the balance I felt, through the body–soul image on one side of the tree, connecting to the spirit image on the other: the opposites connecting and forming a circle, one circle, reinforcing a feeling of wholeness and integration. As I step back and try to understand this powerful image, I sense that the energy of each is needed as we are challenged, personally and collectively, in turbulent times of migration across borders.

A quote from a friend and colleague, Jody Schlatter, helped me understand this dream: 'It looks like a major challenge which evokes instinctual panic but which can be overcome by clinging to the Self and its ability to pull us through things, in spite of the odds'.

Or put in another way:

> For there is hope for a tree,
> If it be cut down that it will sprout again,
> And that its shoots will not cease
>
> (Job 14:7)

I think that both directions – the horizontal and vertical – and the 'eye of the Heart', or that place of union between opposites, the 'still-point' that contains all, are essential for our and all of humanity's survival. The Tree of Life believed by many cultures to take care of life on earth, symbolises that which connects all forms of creation. It will, to quote Schlatter, 'pull us through things, in spite of the odd' or as T. S. Elliot (1941) expresses it as Axis Mundi, '*still-point-of-the-turning-world*'.

The powerful symbolism of the Tree of Life, has one of its central tenets that all of life on earth is interconnected (Jung, 1945, paras. 354–482). The powerful animal instinct in the dream, knowing there is a storm coming and running to safety, propels the dream ego to its place or source of life, to sustain life in its moment of peril, to safety and providing protection for both, body and soul. In the Celtic culture, the oak tree was worshipped in Druidic theology and ritual not only because it enshrines the spirits of the ancestors but because it provides nourishment (nuts and fruit) as vital elements (Spence, 1996, pp. 326–327). Trees represent how the forces of nature combine to create balance and harmony as that place in which all tensions are contained, truly the 'still-point-of-the-turning-world'. In Genesis, the Tree of Knowledge contains both good and evil. The Tree of Life, also known as the Cosmic Tree, reflects renewal and regeneration through its undying centre, the Axis Mundi, an umbilical cord providing for all of life (Cook, 1974, p. 16).

Jung was fascinated by the image of the tree, finding it in dreams and fantasies, in the myths and art of diverse cultures and in the unconscious images of people he worked with. After his studies in alchemical symbolism he was confirmed in his view that the tree image's purpose was to strengthen the individual's conscious realisation of the Self (Jung, 1945, paras. 304–305). The tree image appears at an important time of one's life, with a supportive function leading towards growth and integration (Cook, 1974, p. 27; Jung, 1943, paras. 241–245). The tree in many cultures is also a symbol of death and rebirth, losing its leaves in winter leaving it in a skeletal form and replenishing itself in a bountiful growth of leaves during spring.

Such archetypal images always connect one to the collective unconscious, and therefore, express the same goal of transformation needed in the collective psyche as it faces conflict and turmoil, a desperate need of growth, integration, and renewal (Jung, 1934a, para. 80).

Jung felt that the objective psyche produced the tree image because it is the all-embracing image of the Cosmic Tree, standing at the centre, its roots and bough uniting heaven and earth: the roots symbolising the unconscious source, the trunk as the conscious realisation, and the crown of the tree as the transpersonal Self. All of these aspects represented the ultimate goal of individuation, the wholeness of psyche, or the realisation of the Self (Cook, 1974, p. 12; Jung, 1938, para. 198).

Another beautiful image of death and rebirth through the union of opposites is found in the Scandinavian *Eddas*, a collection of Medieval Icelandic literary prose and poetry, based on historical and mythological themes, written between the 10th and 13th century (perhaps even earlier). It states that at the end of the world:

> the great tree is said to shake, bringing about the destructions of the gods and the world. However, concealed within its trunk are the seeds of the world's renewal in the form of a man and woman from whose union a new race will appear to repopulate the world.
>
> (Cook, 1974, p. 12)

I conclude my associations of the tree image by quoting Hippolytus, Bishop of Rome, in the 3rd century (Cook, 1974, p, 21) as part of the Easter ceremony he gave:

> The tree, wide as the heavens itself, has grown up into heaven from the earth. It is an immortal growth and towers between heaven and earth. It is the fulcrum of all things and the place where they are all at rest. It is the foundation of the round world, the centre of the cosmos. In it all the diversities in our human nature are formed into a unity. It is held together by the invisible nails of the spirit so that it may not break loose from the divine. It touches the highest summits of heaven and makes the earth firm beneath its foot, and it grasps the middle regions between them with immeasurable arms.

The dream of the stampeding wildlife gives me a sense that the very ground I stand on is shaken by the instinctual fear of the animals as they feel the storm approaching. What can hold me as I fear that a storm is drawing near? How do I feel the deep roots of the tree, and the human potential to live between the horizontal and vertical axis, as I know so well in the symbol of the cross and the Jungian Self-concept (Jung, 1945, par. 446)? What gives me the balance and strength to hold on, and trust that the tree will not be uprooted?

Authentic Movement or Movement-in-Depth

I turn to the practice I know best that connects me to those deep roots needed when all is shifting and changing, a practice that fosters an openness of heart and embraces a kind of realism, eliminating judgement of myself or the other. The discipline I refer to, Authentic Movement, supports an acceptance of human nature in all its sinuosity and struggles, and strengthens a more rooted relationship to a witness consciousness which allows a presence of being that is fully awake, and not caught in an ego disconnected from the tree, or self. Witnessing means a seeing through the eye as a mirror of the soul, not with the eye as a distant observer, and finding truth at that place of union between the horizontal and vertical, mind and body, spirit and matter, that allows for a deep and resilient holding for those 'seeing and being seen'.

Authentic Movement, as I mentioned earlier, is a Jungian-based dance-therapy discipline. Here is a very brief history for those who have never heard of it. For the reader who would like a more in-depth history please refer to 'Dance Therapy and Depth Psychology' by Joan Chodorow, published in 1991. Authentic Movement or Movement-in-Depth was explored and developed by Mary Starks Whitehouse, beginning her work in the 1950s and continuing until her death. She was an American and a teacher of Modern Dance in California. She turned to Jungian psychology when she needed support in her life, travelled to Zürich and studied at the Jung Institute. She did not become a Jungian analyst but returned to her work in Modern Dance. What she took back with her to the United States was a new way of working with the Jungian concept of active imagination. Instead of a dialogue between the analysand and figures of the unconscious, supported and enhanced by the analyst, she took the concept and evolved it through movement. The mover, with closed eyes, or inwardly focused, would allow a direct connection to unconscious material and let the body express and dialogue with the images and bodily sensations that emerged. The witness, with eyes open, was there to contain the images and emotions that arose; to bring consciousness to the experience of the mover, to let the other, the mover, appear, in their uniqueness and wholeness and seen without judgement in a place of acceptance.

Mary Starks Whitehouse realised very quickly that this was not dance improvisation, but an access to an inner world filled with images, emotions, desires, and bodily sensations. She began to use it as a form of personal growth, or self-realisation. The mover and witness became the defining elements in this discipline, along with the intimate and intricate relationship that unfolds between the two, that delicate exchange of 'seeing and being seen'.

Authentic movement invites us to move into the imaginative, symbolic and sensate world of both mover and witness. As the boundaries shift and blend in space and time, we are able to enter a liminal, transitory space which could be seen as ritual enactment, a 'symbolic, self-reflective performance that makes a transition as a time and space out of the ordinary', having cognitive, as well as, bodily experience (Alexander, 1991, pp. 24–25). This ritualised and transformative space allows for a confrontation between the ego and the unconscious. The mover, held and reflected by the witness' gaze gains in conscious awareness, self-realisation, and taps into the deep well of creative potential as the ego–Self axis is strengthened.

'Eye of God' and the transcendent function

Psychotherapist Grace Ann Montgomery profoundly describes in *Grief Needs a Witness*, witnessing as that place of meeting between mover and witness that we meet the Eye of God, as an all seeing, knowing and loving presence. It is a presence that allows the existence of the other, taking what is invisible and making it visible through the eyes of the witness. It is the eye witnessing us in dreams and the eye peering out from other human beings, or animals we encounter, either in sleep or everyday life. It is the eye connecting us to the source of our being and the world we share together. (Montgomery, 2015, p. 88)

Jung writes about the symbol of the eye in a lecture to the psychological club in 1932.

> [T]he eye, as you know, is the place where things begin, the place of rebirth ... And that the eye is the place of rebirth is the meaning of the eye of Horus which plays such a mystical role in Egyptian mythology. So here we have an example of something dark, locked, inaccessible, suddenly becoming alive through contemplation.
>
> (Jung, 1932, p. 675)

I would like to add here 'becoming alive' and visible, through contemplation.

In *Zarathustra*, Jung (1934b, p. 64) recounts this story about why god made another, which touches on the universality of the witness consciousness as follows:

> They say in the East that God was all alone in the beginning, and he didn't feel well at all because he didn't know who he was; so, he created the universe in order to see who he was. He created distinct beings in which he could mirror himself. For you never know who you are unless you can look at yourself from without: you need a mirror to see what your face is like, how you look. ... The old philosophers always supposed of God that he was without an opposite, without the second one; but he needs that in order to become aware of himself.

As we open to a witness consciousness, the soul's mirror, we expand our field of vision, moving beyond ego to the larger circumference containing the Self, in its personal and transpersonal aspects. This expansive vision allows for an open heart and mind, moving out of duality, or the subject–object dichotomy, unlocking doors that see kinship mutuality, and not separation. Perhaps, we could say that we symbolically perceive ourselves as microcosms mirroring the great cosmos – a life embedded in something larger – otherwise we see with such limited sight – a sight caught within our own psyche – our own ego, our own complexes, which narrows our vision, removing any possibility of a peripheral vision.

In Jungian psychology we could parallel witnessing to the transcendent function, which Jung called the heart of individuation (Jung, 1921, paras. 823–828). It is the psychic possibility of holding the tension of opposites, and therefore moving away from the need to judge, to condemn, and distinguish and fixate between love and hate, right and wrong, good and bad. It is a moment of freeing Self from ego and encircling one's arms around the vastness of possibilities in relating to others, and to the world. It is clearly the place, or function of the psyche, that is open to new possibilities, or as Jung so cogently states, the place of 'rebirth', or 'where things begin' anew (Jung, 1932, p. 675). In Jungian psychology the transcendent function takes place within an individual psyche and leads one on the path to self-realisation; hopefully, continuing a development that allows and acknowledges the other 'Selves'.

Cultural complexes and a need to belong

My grandfather belonged to an Orthodox Jewish synagogue, but said to me he was not religious, that he belonged to a synagogue because humans need to feel part of a group, a place, a community. In order to feel satisfaction with one's life one needs a social life, as well as a private life. That is why he took part in his religious community. The need to belong is a universal desire. Hannah Arendt stressed that the loss of community has the consequence of expelling a people from humanity itself (Bernstein, 2018; Arendt, 1968, pp. 11–17). Cultural anthropologist, Victor Turner (1969, pp. 94–97) interprets ritualised, liminal activity as sacred, forming communitas between people in order to experience their shared humanity and participate together as a 'moment in and out of time' that evokes courage and cohesion (Alexander, 1991, p. 36).

The Jewish people, amongst other minority groups, carry the shadow projection of the 'other' (Pichot, 2001). I realise that I not only identify with the 'other', the exiled people fleeing war and persecution, but also with the Jewish collective cultural complex threatened with annihilation, or the loss of a European culture identity, being caught between compassion and fear (Singer, 2004, pp. 17–22). Singer (ibid, pp. 4–5) states that 'cultural complexes can be thought of as arising out of the cultural unconscious as it interacts with both the archetypal and personal realm of the psyche ... as filtered through the psyches of generations of ancestors'. He further clarifies: 'At any ripe time, these slumbering cultural complexes can be activated ... can seize the imagination, the behavior and the emotions of the collective psyche and can unleash tremendously irrational forces in the name of their "logic"' (p. 7).

Brain Feldman (2004, p. 51) defines the 'other' as 'those individuals who are perceived as being outside the predominant social group and are often excluded or marginalized'. Jung saw individuation as a process within the psyche, as an awareness of the 'other' within as shadow aspects needing further differentiation (Jung, 1948, paras. 13–19; 1947, paras. 444–458). Since Jung's writings, various Jungian analysts have developed this concept further (Henderson 1990; Singer, 2004; Kimbles 2004; 2014), developing cultural complexes as a way of understanding and healing prejudices, and understanding how shadow projections work within society.

By working through these unconscious cultural complexes, we are better able to re-vision individuation and move into the space of the witness, not only seeing ourselves with compassion and recognition, but also looking out and seeing the 'other' with the same possibility, in a democratic space whereby 'both subjects are equally dignified and ethically obligated to respect the other' (Benjamin, 2016, p. 71).

A mirror of the soul: Seeing and being seen

> Jung states (1946, para. 454) that 'The unrelated human being lacks wholeness, for he can achieve wholeness only through the soul, and the soul cannot exist without its other side, which is always found in a "You". Wholeness is a combination of I and You, and these show themselves to be parts of a transcendent unity whose nature can only be grasped symbolically.

As therapists and analysts, one is often a mirror for patients, in some phases of the work more so than others. Therefore, an integration of the witness consciousness is essential for a deep soul mirroring. But how does one make that leap of faith and move the witness out of the therapy room into a world that desperately needs a presence of being with new 'vision' and 'sight' and of allowing a flexibility and mutability in consciousness, to truly 'see' the other? This would then allow the togetherness needed in moving towards the yet unknown, indeterminate possibilities, stepping forward into the challenges that face everyone.

As Henry David Thoreau, in his journal from 1840, said, 'I begin to see such objects only when I leave off understanding them' (2001, p. 67). For Thoreau that meant that there is a greater possibility of seeing the developments in our culture and societies today, when they are not reduced to conformity, to our own social patterns of thought and social habit of perception and expectation. (Niebuhr, 1996, p. 6). When therapists and world citizens are not caught in their personal and collective complexes, they give space for the unknown, and are able to respond with an open heart and mind as they feel the 'other' person, culture, and religion move into their world as they know it. With this as yet an unknown and indeterminate factor, one can still move in accepting, compassionate, and conscious ways. Falling into fear and rage is destructive to oneself, as well as to the other. To remain in touch with our witness consciousness, Mark Saban (2008a, p. 94) has addressed the gulf that exists between the inner and outer circumstances that needs to be bridged to avoid serious socio-political consequences.

Re-visioning individuation within a relational field

A re-visioned individuation, not only as analysts, but as citizens of the world, would assimilate a witness consciousness, a consciousness that is relational to oneself, to others, and to the world, as we journey through time metamorphosing at a rapid pace. A witness consciousness is essentially psychoid in nature, spanning the spectrum that moves between spirit and matter, archetype and instinct. It eliminates those artificial boundaries that are perhaps needed for the development of the ego, but as one individuates the boundaries or borders, one needs to become porous and extended so that the 'other' is not seen as an enemy, and thus threatening, but as humans struggling in their own battle to be, to exist, to feel a part of a whole, or perhaps to feel their own wholeness, and move out of their own fear, anger and hate. When seen through the eyes of the witness, the loneliness of displacement is replaced by hope, the hope of belonging and becoming a part of what is new, and still yet unrevealed.

In this liminal space, between the past and the future, we find great creative potential. It is the place of transition, waiting without knowing. It is here, in this place of transition, that we can refigure old patterns of exclusivity into new structures of inclusiveness. It is essential that we re-vision individuation as a development within a relational field broadening the 'me' to include and 'us'. The Sufi mystic, Al-Hallaj, says it so clearly in these simple worlds: 'I saw my Lord with the eye of the Heart. I said "Who are you?" He answered "You"' (Stoddart, 1976, p. 83). Jung (1936, p. 795) expresses the relatedness between the 'me' and the 'us' as follows:

> [T]here really could be no self if it were not in relation, the self and individualism exclude each other. The self is relatedness. Only when the self mirrors itself in so many mirrors does it really exist-then it has roots. ... Not that you are, but that you do is the self. The self appears in your deeds, and deeds always mean relationship; a deed is something that you produce which is practically outside of you, between yourself and your surroundings, between subject and object-there the self is visible.

Moving beyond the 'me' to include an 'us'

Steven C. Hayes (2016, p. 217) extends 'us' as a basis of human consciousness and calls it our ability to move beyond the 'me' to an 'us' by stressing the social need in all human perception and knowing. We are always both speaker and listener and that allows an understandable communication. Indeed, there is never a singular me but always an extended us. Only through this 'us-ness' can we express, in a verbal and categorical sense, what we feel, think, sense, and remember. Through this 'us-ness' we begin to understand individuation not only as a development of the individual, but as individuals connected to other individuals, not seeing the ultimate goal as personal individuality or interiority. As Mark Saban (2008b, p. 99) correctly surmises: 'the ultimate cost of this emphasis on individuality and interiority will be disengagement from concrete human embodied life in community'. Saban sees humans as relational beings in that our embodied seeing and being seen is reciprocal (Saban, ibid, p.123)

Jung (1921, para. 758) earlier recognises the individual not as a separate being, but always as a part of a collective relationship. He underlines the importance of the relational field in the development of any psychological growth and differentiation: 'As the individual is not just a single, separate being, but by his very existence presupposes a collective relationship, it follows that the process of individuation must lead to more intense and broader collective relationships and not to isolation'.

Temenos: The empty circle containing all

As therapists and analysts, awareness is modelled in that relational space as a ritualised temenos, seeing the world of the patient through their eyes. Therapeutic compassion and empathy when felt by the patient allows the possibility of self-compassion. Within this field of empathy, integrating a witness consciousness, it is then safe to see and be seen by others. Hayes (2016, p. 221) furthers clarifies this mutual and holding relationship: 'When both parties to a therapeutic relationship can step back and be aware of what is in the room between them, the relationship itself becomes a model for the mindful and symbolically extended "us" that is inside a first-person perspective'.

If it is possible to move away from, and not be attached to, one's own reactions, feelings, and thoughts, therapists, analysts, and social selves can be more open and compassionate towards the other as a space of 'us' and not trapped in the 'me'. In that way, they are not imprisoned in their socially learned and conditioned responses to the world or stuck within the emotional core of a complex. The complex stays, but one is freely able to 'see' through eyes that can reveal, reflect, and incarnate the values by which one wants to live by. Already formed sight is not brought to a situation, knowing that sometimes limits do not expand our vision.

If we see the psychotherapy or the analytical space as a space of transition and transformation, or an indeterminate liminal space between status values, then we open ourselves to the witness as archetype, revealing, reflecting, and incarnating the potentialities for individuation.

The analyst: Observer, witness, or both

I would like to clarify the similarities and differences between observing and witnessing. This question comes up constantly with Authentic Movement. If I change the word witnessing to 'observing' I have a different immediate emotional response. I become an object or 'thing' to the other. One concise definition of observing is 'to watch carefully especially with attention to details or behaviour for the purpose of arriving at a judgement'. The need to be 'seen' is so clearly calling for not only the human eye, but the 'eye of god'. Jung would call the 'eye of god' the objective psyche, with its loving, caring, and deep acceptance of another, without judgement and expectation, moving out of the personal into the transpersonal realm.

As an analyst, I sometimes observe and sometimes I witness. Joan Chodorow's description of moving from observer, logos, or directed consciousness and to witnessing, the imaginative or Eros consciousness, is very helpful and supports Jung's observation of two kinds of thinking (direct and indirect) that intertwine with each other (Jung, 1911–1912/1952, paras. 4–46). Within this insight I must not make observing seem wrong or witnessing as mystical. It becomes a natural process of moving between Eros and Logos, Sol and Luna. The solar consciousness separates parts and I see in more detail, more objectively, and with more differentiation. With a lunar consciousness I find that place of merging, that is more subjective, reflective, and imaginative (Chodorow, 1991, p. 150). Lunar consciousness can also be seen as a waxing and waning of the moon as the Great Mother archetype constantly in a state of flux (cf. Baring & Cashworth, 1991, pp. 162–163). It is a 'liminal space', described by Victor Turner (1969, pp. 94–95) as a place of transformation, outside of chronological time. Liminal entities are 'neither here nor there'; they lay 'betwixt and between' designated social values and, as such, their ambiguous and indeterminate transit nature is expressed by symbols frequently associated with death, to being in the womb, to invisibility, and darkness. Liminality stretches boundaries and, therefore, exposes that place of vulnerability (death) and the openness we need to re-create ourselves (Wirtz, 2014, p. 62) as a death–rebirth process.

As an analyst, the ability to move from this type of thinking to the other, that is, holding the clear eye of the observer, and, at the same time, maintaining an empathic relatedness and emotional attunement to the analysand is essential for an effective democratic relationship between the ego and the unconscious for both the analyst and the analysand. In this way, the analyst is in and out at the same time; the objective and subjective stance is always shifting, holding and offering safety to the analysand through difficult, emotional life transitions. The ability to witness is hopefully carried over the threshold into everyday life outside the therapy room.

A witness consciousness

Alice Miller, a well-known advocate of the witness in the therapy relationship discusses in her article, 'The Essential Role of an Enlightened Witness in Society' (1997) the therapy needed for abused children, and states clearly that if there is just one person, not necessarily a parent, but through his or her presence, this person gives them a notion of trust, and of love. She calls such persons helping witnesses. This presence of the helping or enlightened witness allows one to survive and flourish against all odds (Miller, 1997). This type of witness consciousness is needed in analysts, therapists, and others as they move through a landscape filled with conflict, tension, torture, homelessness, loss of identity, and worse.

If one is seen and sees through the eyes of the witness that contain the deep roots of the tree in my dream, all are given that precious thing, the right to exist. Does not everyone fight for recognition of the right to live? Are not all prejudices a fear of losing identity, space, and the right to exist? A witness consciousness is able to contain the opposites, the tension of division, the barrier between 'me' and 'us'. It is that place of relational, ritualised empathy.

Conclusion

The possibility of 'seeing' and 'being seen' through the witness' gaze is needed in any individuation process, not just as therapist, but as a person living in turbulent times. From that inclusive field contained within a witness consciousness, one can navigate new possibilities, not by splitting and projecting our shadow onto others and the world but by recognising between all tensions of opposites, within one's psyche or within the collective psyche, there is a desperate need for relatedness. Perhaps, individuation, which is often seen as personal growth and development, also experiences that place 'between yourself and your surroundings' (Jung, 1936, p. 795), as a moving, ritual embodiment towards/with other and world.

I would like to conclude with a quote from Merleau-Ponty in his work *The Primacy of Perception* (1964, p. 10): 'All human acts and all human creations constitute a single drama, and in this sense we are all saved or lost together. Our life is essentially universal'.

Acknowledgement

I greatly thank Elizabeth Brodersen for her substantial contribution, along with her careful and skilful editing of this paper.

References

Alexander, B. C. (1991). *Victor turner revisited, ritual as social change.* Atlanta, GA: Scholars Press.
Arendt, H. (1968). *Man in Dark Times.* San Diego, New York, London: Harcourt Brace.
Baring, A., and Cashford, J. (1991). *The myth of the goddess, evolution of an image.* London/New York, NY: Penguin Books.
Benjamin, J. (2016). 'Moving beyond violence, what we learn from two former combatants about the transition from aggression to recognition'. In Pla Gobodo-Madikizela (ed.), *Breaking intergenerational cycles of repetition, a global dialogue on historical trauma and memory.* Opladen, Berlin & Toronto Barbara Budrich Publishers
Bernstein, R. J. (June 20, 2018). 'The illuminations of Hannah Arendt'. *New York Times.*
Bible (1989 ed.). *The revised English Bible.* Oxford/Cambridge: Oxford University Press.
Chodorow, J. (1991). *Dance therapy and depth psychology, the moving imagination.* London/New York, NY: Routledge.
Cook, R. (1974). *The tree of life: image for the cosmos.* New York City, NY: Avon Publishers of Bard, Camelot, Discus, Equinox and Flare Books.
Elliot, T. S. (1941). *The four quartets.* Burnt Norton: Harcourt.
Feldman, B. (2004). 'Towards a theory of organizational culture, integrating the 'other' from a post-Jungian perspective'. In T. Singer and S. L. Kimbles (eds.), *The cultural complex, contemporary Jungian perspectives on psyche and society.* Hove/New York, NY: Brunner-Routledge.
Hayes, S. C. (2016). 'Human language and subjective experience: the symbolically extended 'us' as a basis of human consciousness'. In *Thinking thinking, Practicing Radical Reflection*, D. Schoeller/V. Saller (eds.). Freiburg and Munich: Verlag Karl Alber.

Henderson, J. L. (1990). 'The cultural unconscious'. In *Shadow and Self*. Wilmette, IL: Chiron.
Jung, C. G. (1911–12/1952). 'Two kinds of thinking'. In *Collected works*, vol. 5, *Symbols of transformation* (2nd ed.), Bollingen Series XX. Princeton, NJ: Princeton University Press.
Jung, C. G. (1921). 'Definitions'. In *Collected works*, vol. 6, *Psychological types* (2nd ed.), Bollingen Series XX. Princeton, NJ: Princeton University Press, 1977.
Jung, C. G. (1932). Lecture II, 11 May 1932- In *Visions, notes of the seminar given in 1930–1934 by C.G. Jung*. Claire Douglas (ed.). The first version, transcribed by shorthand notes taken at the seminar meeting. London: Routledge, 1998.
Jung, C. G. (1934a). 'Archetypes of the collective unconscious'. In *Collected works*, vol. 9i, *Archetypes and the collective unconscious* (2nd ed.), Bollingen Series XX. Princeton, NJ: Princeton University Press, 1980.
Jung, C. G. (1934b). *Nietzsche's Zarathustra*, vol. 1, Bollingen Series XX. Princeton, NJ: Princeton University Press.
Jung, C. G. (1936). *Nietzsche's Zarathustra*, vol. 2, Bollingen Series XX. Princeton, NJ: Princeton University Press, 1988.
Jung, C. G. (1937). 'The lapis-Christ parallel'. In *Collected works*, vol. 12, *Psychology and alchemy* (2nd ed.), Bollingen Series XX. Princeton, NJ: Princeton University Press, 1977.
Jung, C. G. (1938). 'Psychological aspects of the mother archetype'. In *Collected works*, vol. 9(i), *Archetypes and the collective unconscious* (2nd ed.), Bollingen Series XX. Princeton, NJ: Princeton University Press, 1980.
Jung, C. G. (1943). 'The spirit mercurius'. In *Collected works*, vol. 13, *Alchemical studies* (2nd ed.), Bollingen Series XX. Princeton, NJ: Princeton University Press, 1983.
Jung, C. G. (1945). 'The philosophical tree'. In *Collected works*, vol. 13, *Alchemical studies* (2nd ed.), Bollingen Series XX. Princeton, NJ: Princeton University Press, 1983.
Jung, C. G. (1946). 'The psychology of the transference'. In *Collected works*, vol. 16, *The practice of psychotherapy* (2nd ed.), Bollingen Series XX. Princeton, NJ: Princeton University Press, 1975.
Jung, C. G. (1947). 'The fight with the shadow'. In *Collected works*, vol. 10, *Civilization in transition* (2nd ed.), Bollingen Series XX, Princeton, NJ: Princeton University Press.
Jung, C. G. (1948). 'The shadow'. In *Collected works*, vol. 9ii, *Aion, researches into the phenomenology of the self* (2nd ed.), Bollingen Series XX. Princeton, NJ: Princeton University Press.
Kimbles, S. L. (2004). 'A cultural complex operating in overlap of clinical and cultural space'. In T. Singer and S. L. Kimbles (eds.), *The cultural complex, contemporary Jungian perspectives on psyche and society*. Hove/New York: Brunner-Routledge.
Kimbles, S. L. (2014). *Phantom narratives. The unseen contribution of culture to psyche*. Lanham/New York, NY/London: Bowman & Littlefield.
Merleau-Ponty, M. (1964). *The primacy of perception*. Evanston, Illinois: Northwestern University Press.
Miller, A. (1997). 'The essential role of an enlightened witness in society'. Available at https://www.alice-miller.com/en/the-essential-role-of-an-enlightened-witness-in-society-2/. Accessed August 20, 2019.
Montgomery, G. A. (2015). *Grief needs a witness*. Doctoral Dissertation, Pacifica: Pacifica Graduate Institute.
National Archives, New York City. Aron Felner, *SS President Lincoln* Passenger Manifest, February 17, 1911; stamped frame 619, line 25; Passenger and Crew Lists of Vessels

Arriving at New York, 1897–1957 (National Archives Microfilm Publication); Records of the Immigration and Naturalization Service. 1934 archived and accessible.

Niebuhr, R. R. (1996). 'Looking through the wall: a meditation on vision'. *Parabola: The Witness*, X1 (1), 6–18.

Pichot, A. (2001). *The pure society, from Darwin to Hitler*. D. Fernbach (trans.). London/ New York, NY: Verso, 2009.

Saban, M. (2008a). 'Fleshing out the psyche: Jung, psychology and the body'. In R. Jones, (ed.), *Body, mind, and healing after jung: a space of questions*. London: Routledge, 2010.

Saban, M. (2008b). 'Staging the Self: performance, individuation and embodiment'. In R. Jones (ed.), *Body, mind and healing after Jung: a space of questions*. London: Routledge, 2010.

Singer, T. (2004). 'Introduction'. In T. Singer and S. L. Kimbles (eds.), *The cultural complex, contemporary Jungian perspectives on psyche and society*. Hove/New York, NY: Brunner-Routledge.

Singer, T. (2004). 'The cultural complex and archetypal defenses of the collective spirit: Baby Zeus, Elian Gonzales, Constantine's Sword, and other Holy Wars, with special attention to 'the axis of evil'. In T. Singer and S. L. Kimbles (eds.), *The cultural complex, contemporary Jungian perspectives on psyche and society*. Hove/New York, NY: Brunner-Routledge.

Spence, L. (1996). 'Druidic theology and ritual'. In J. Mathews (ed.), *The druid source book*. London: Blandford Press.

Stoddart, W. (1976). As quoted in *Sufism: the mystical doctrines and methods of Islam*. New York City, NY: Harper Collins Distribution.

Thoreau, H. D. (2001). *Reflecting heaven*. Robert Lawrence France (ed.). Boston, MA/ New York, NY: A Mariner Original/Houghton Mifflin Company.

Turner, V. (1969). *The ritual process, structure and anti-structure*. New Brunswick/ London: Aldine Publishers.

Wirtz, U. (2014). *Trauma and beyond: the mystery of transformation*. New Orleans, LA: Spring Journal, Inc.

Chapter 13

The tension and paradox between determinate and indeterminate state

Clinical, social, and cultural aspects

Toshio Kawai

Introduction

Psychotherapy and the dialectics of indeterminate and determinate state

In this paper, I would like to explore the basic attitude and technique of psychotherapy as a tension between the determinate and indeterminate. However, in the course of this exploration the necessity would become clear to revisit the dialectic of the determinate and indeterminate because of the change of the state of psyche.

Holding the indeterminate state is regarded as the basic attitude of psychotherapy. This is not only the case in the therapy of analytical psychology, but in general in psychotherapy. The non-directive or client-centred approach of Carl Rogers is a typical example. It has the strategy of listening to and approving of what the client is saying. Even when the psychotherapist is asked directly which opinion he or she has, he or she would reply, 'Why would you like to know my opinion'? or 'But what is your opinion'? In this way the therapist tries to keep the indeterminate state in the session. The same can apply to the psychoanalysis. It uses the method of free association in which the client tries to express whatever comes to his or her mind while the therapist keeps a free-floating attention and avoids any criticism or giving advice as to what the client is saying. In this method of free association, one tries to keep the indeterminate state in therapy, as well.

While a determinate action or judgement is usually required in daily life, the basic attitude in psychotherapy is creating an indeterminate state without rushing into a quick solution which can end up in a so-called acting out. For example, if the therapist tries to intervene in a school situation or change the school of the client's child because the child is being bullied at the school, the psychological problem is often not solved and can cause another problem. That is why the therapist tries to help the client to endure and confront the actual situation first.

It is both interesting and remarkable that psychotherapy tries to keep the indeterminate state, despite an urgent situation that needs an immediate solution and intervention. This is the paradox of the basic attitude of psychotherapy. The patient has an expectation that a determinate action or response will be given immediately. But a concrete, determinate solution is not given in most cases and the answer is kept open till the next session. As result, a strong tension between the indeterminate and the determinate continues to exist.

However, I ought to mention that even in psychotherapy there is a growing tendency and expectation to use a determinate method and to take a determinate and immediate action. Cognitive Behaviour Therapy (CBT) as a psychotherapeutic method and Evidence Based Medicine (EBM) as prevailing resources are typical examples of this tendency. It is increasingly difficult to keep an indeterminate state during the process of psychotherapy. The attitude of keeping the indeterminate state can be regarded as slow, ineffective, and useless. In schools and hospitals, the therapist has to cooperate with teachers and medical staff to offer quick and concrete solutions. Even in the field of psychotherapy where the basic attitude is to keep the indeterminate condition, there is a growing control by the system of manipulative operations based on science and technology.

Psychotherapy consists not only in the basic, indeterminate state and attitude. Out of this indeterminate state a determinate action or image can emerge unexpectedly in the course of psychotherapy. This can be in the form of a dream or a constellation in reality. Sometimes an action on the side of therapist is needed. In this sense, there is a kind of dialectic between the indeterminate and determinate attitude. Holding the indeterminate state can eventually lead to a determinate action.

There are various aspects of dialectics between the indeterminate and the determinate states in psychotherapy. It is important to offer a free and protected space for the client, which is the basis of psychotherapy. But to give this free and indeterminate state, psychotherapy needs a limitation, a determinate setting. The time of therapy is fixed; it uses always the same place. To create a free and indeterminate state, psychotherapy needs, paradoxically, a limitation. Therefore, the dialectic between the indeterminate and the determinate is the essence of psychotherapy and can be seen in many aspects.

Theoretical background: Neuroscience and the indeterminate

To the background of the prevalence of goal-oriented and manipulative action, even in psychotherapy there is the dominance of the scientific model and economic considerations. A clear relationship between cause and effect must be shown in psychotherapy. An effective therapy is welcomed by economic principles. The establishment of a national status of psychotherapists and the use of insurance in many countries has accelerated this tendency. But the question arises about which direction contemporary and future science is heading. Quantum theory, chaos theory, complex system theory, and so forth do not seem to follow determinism. The deep learning of the artificial intelligence which is attracting much attention recently does not correspond to a one-to-one solution.

Neuroscience seems to promote determinism: psychological functions and pathologies can be reduced to certain parts and points of the brain. One typical example is the autistic spectrum disorder (ASD), which is now regarded as dysfunction of the brain and the central nervous system. Psychological factors are almost excluded in this view. Sonu Shamdasani (2003) and Ellenberger (1970) showed that the 'unconscious' was the key concept for understanding science by the end of 19th century. Not only psychology and psychiatry, but even biology and physiology used this term. At present, the brain and the central nervous system, instead of working with unconscious processes, has become the key concept in contemporary psychology and science.

Recent research on the default mode network (DMN), however, supports the indeterminate function of brain concerning creativity. The default mode network (DMN) was first identified as a baseline state of the normal adult human brain in terms of the brain oxygen extraction fraction (Raichle, et al., 2001). The DMN is a large-scale brain network of interacting brain regions known to have activity highly correlated with each other and distinct from other networks in the brain. The default mode network is most commonly shown as active when a person is not focused on the outside world and the brain is in a wakeful rest, such as when daydreaming and mind-wandering. Shinya Yamanaka who was awarded the Nobel Prize for Physiology or Medicine in 2012 for his discovery that mature cells can be converted to stem cells (discovery of the iPS cells) stated that he hit on this idea while he was taking a bath and feeling relaxed (NHK, 2018). This indicates that the discovery was not a product of goal-oriented thinking.

There is much research concerning DMN during meditation, so DMN must be connected to the basic attitude of psychotherapy in which the mind is left in an indeterminate state. For creative thinking and action, not thinking derived from outer stimuli, the internal thinking process is important. The internal and autonomous thinking is exactly the function of DMN. This idea can support the basic attitude of psychotherapy which avoids the therapist giving advice, i.e., outer advice.

Recent research shows that creativity needs to converge with free-floating thinking at certain points. In this sense, the activity of prefrontal cortex should be combined with the DMN (Beaty, et al., 2014, p. 96). Again, we notice the necessity of the relationship between indeterminate and determinate states. Recent neuroscientific results tend to support the basic therapeutic attitude which is difficult to understand in the contemporary world. I would like to explain the methodology of analytical psychology compared with that of CBT based on the research of DMN. To put it in a simplified way, the CBT tries to change from one determinate state (A), a wrong or distorted cognition or behaviour, to another determinate state (A').

$$A \rightarrow A'$$

Analytical psychology, however, starts from the determinate state (A) and moves first to the indeterminate state (X), then it tries to restart from there to reach a new, determinate state (B) as a kind of creative product or, as Jung expresses it, as a 'natural product of psyche' (Jung 1928, para. 210), which often constitutes a dream. In this case, the new determinate state is unpredictable.

The relation between DMN and creativity seems to support the methodology of analytical psychology.

I ought to mention that this comparison between analytical psychology and CBT is made only on the basis of one model. Therefore, other research may have to be devised to show if there are real differences in brain functioning during therapy or within the brain functioning of the therapist and between analytical psychology and CBT.

Change of pathology and the indeterminate state

The theory and praxis of psychoanalysis and analytical psychology were based on the personality functioning at a neurotic level which presupposes the structure of well-established ego-consciousness. The determinate ego can have its counterpart as an unconscious impulse or a complex (complex as personality), which can lead to a conflict or opposition. This is why Jung emphasises the importance of holding tension between the opposites as the title of one of his main books *The Relations between the Ego and the Unconscious* demonstrates (Jung, 1928, part 11). The shadow can only appear because the ego is established and holds its position. In the same way, an unconscious desire can emerge only when the ego tries to control everything.

Holding the tension between the opposites means that one ceases to have determinate actions and remains in an indeterminate state of liminality. This attitude can be described as a process of regression, or as a creation of the initial *massa confusa*, chaos in the alchemy. This implies that the change from the determinate position to the indeterminate state is crucial for the concept of analytical psychotherapy. The indeterminate state can eventually lead to an image as the third out of conflict or as result of transcendent function as defined by Jung (1923, paras. 823–828).

As I already mentioned, this shift from the determinate to the indeterminate state at the beginning of therapy presupposes the structure of well-established ego. Unfortunately, we have fewer clients with well-established ego. Concerning clinical phenomena, we had an increasing number of borderline patients in the 1970s and 1980s, and during the 1990s, more patients with dissociative personality disorders. Since 2000, the frequency of ASD (autistic spectrum disorder) patients or patients who have similar features of the ASD has increased world-wide.

There is much epidemiological research which proves the increase of ASD patients world-wide (Croen, et al., 2002, Rutter, 2004, Kim, et al., 2011). Autism was discovered independently by Leo Kanner (1943) and Hans Asperger (1944). It is important to notice that this symptom was recognised relatively late in the history of modern psychiatry, in comparison with other psychotic symptoms such as schizophrenia and manic-depressive states. This late discovery could indicate that ASD is linked to historical developments and the contemporary state of psyche.

Since Lorna Wing (1996/2002) proposed a comprehensive concept of 'autistic spectrum syndrome', there has been a prevailing idea to include various kinds of autistic presentation as a spectrum. Three main features of the autistic spectrum syndrome are: impairments of social interaction, communication, and imagination (Wing 1996). Our meta-research of successful psychotherapy with ASD patients suggested that the key problem of ASD can be regarded as a 'lack of subject' (Kawai, 2009) and weakness of agency.

I will not delve into the whole problem of the weakness of the subject and agency in ASD here but would like to focus on the indeterminate aspect of ASD patients. ASD patients have a weak agency and show difficulty in choosing or making a decision. One of my patients said that she could talk to someone well when there were only two persons present, but she had difficulty when there were more than three people: she could not choose which person to focus on, person A or person B. As result, she could not find anything to talk about. Several patients of mine have said to me they had difficulty discerning the voice of a lecturer from the whispering of a person in a neighbouring seat or even from the noise in the lecture room. The agency to focus on and select something important seems to be lacking. They cannot select something concrete and tend to remain in an indeterminate state.

Chihiro Hatanaka compared the result of Rorschach tests between a group of ASD patients and a group of students (Hatanaka, 2013). She found that the ASD group showed statistically more 'undefined responses' in the Rorschach test than the student group. An example of undefined responses is: 'a kind of animal' instead of saying a specific animal, for example 'a lion'. Another type of undefined response is: 'this is a tiger, no, it can be a cat, no, probably a dog, Oh, I am not sure …'. The response shifts from one to another. They have difficulty in defining the response. This shows that the ASD patients have a greater tendency to remain in an indeterminate state.

While an indeterminate state is required for the usually determinate ego conscious in a classical psychotherapy setting, the emphasis on the indeterminate state can be problematic and contra-productive in therapy for the ASD patients. If we ask an ASD patient to make free associations, he or she would have difficulty: the patient can remain in a totally indeterminate state without coming to a concrete content in talking. If the therapist does not answer the question of what to do, the patient may remain continuously in an indeterminate state. It surely belongs to the fundamental attitude of psychotherapist not to give an answer to personal questions, but then the patient may not find a concrete point of reference to his or her therapist.

Because an ASD patient is in an indeterminate state from the beginning, the therapist has to be ready to go into that indeterminate state, too. But out of this indeterminate state, a definite response or an action from the side of therapist is sometimes needed to reach the determinate state. The therapist usually does not answer such a personal question as 'Where do you live'? But in some cases of therapy with an ASD patient, to give a direct response such as 'I live in Kyoto' is necessary to offer a clear and concrete image of therapist. Sometimes a concrete confrontation and suggestion from the side of therapist such as 'Why don't you go to work'? can be therapeutic.

This should not be confused with and misunderstood as instruction and/or a lesson given by the therapist. The response and action of therapist should be a spontaneous one born out of the indeterminate state. I would like to illustrate the difference between an instruction and a spontaneous reaction. While an instruction or advice is a horizontal transition from a determinate condition A to another determinate condition B, a spontaneous action comes from the indeterminate.

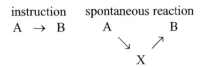

The action in B can come either from the patient or therapist. The movement from the indeterminate state X to B makes the breakthrough possible. The freedom in the session has the dialectics of limitation of time and space in usual psychotherapy. However, the total freedom in the therapeutic session may be too indeterminate for the ASD patient. More limitation than the usual setting is needed to facilitate the freedom and movement. It is better to give more limitation and a specific task to do, for example, by asking the patient to draw a picture or to sand-play. Both actions can facilitate the emergence of a determinant subject. The picture or sand-play can be a smaller framework than the usual therapeutic framework of time and space.

In this sense, analytical psychology has a better chance to dialogue with ASD patients. As Wing pointed out, the lack of imagination is one of the main features of ASD patients, so asking and using images with an ASD patient in therapy seems to be difficult and useless. Very often an ASD patient reports dreams which are exact repetitions of what actually happened. He or she draws a picture which is only a reproduction of reality, seemingly without symbolic meaning. But we can still come to the conclusion that the use of images with ASD patients is productive because we can offer a smaller framework in this way. It depends furthermore on how to work with images. For example, in case of ASD patients, it is not productive to keep a free-floating attention to all parts of images, but to try to focus on certain points.

Cultural and contemporary background of the indeterminate

The prevalence of ASD patients in Japan can be related to cultural characteristics that also feature in contemporary times. Culturally, Japanese have had difficulty with an agentic and determinate action. For example, when they go for lunch or dinner in a group, they prefer to wait to hear the preference of others rather than to give their own clear choice first. Lack of agentic action often leads to a long process of decision making at a meeting. Instead of asserting one's own position from the beginning, one tends to wait to hear what others think first. The conclusion comes not as result of personal leadership or confrontation among different positions, but as a kind of natural consensus in the group.

In a traditional Japanese society, however, social roles and manners were well determined so that there was no need to select and decide something personally. For example, marriages and jobs were prescribed by the community and there were clear rules how to behave oneself in the relationship and ritual. With the loosening social structure, people, however, are faced with many possibilities and compelled to select and decide individually; this has brought into focus the lack of determinate decision making. For example, while a child in the past had to go to school, there are many kinds of different schooling now for those who don't want to attend school at all. While the arranged marriage was normal 100 years ago, now one can not only select one's partner of the opposite sex, but also the sexual preference of one's own and one's partner.

Related to this point, it is worth mentioning that Jung's psychology was based on a fixed perspective of gender identity (see Jung, 1950, paras. 20–42). This is why anima and the animus as the contra-sexual other gender was central in analytical psychology: in the case of a man, anima as an unconscious 'female' figure, in the case of a woman, animus as unconscious 'masculine' figure. But it is rather important to cope with the psychic 'other' who appears in the unconscious, whatever his or her gender is. The other can sometimes appear as 'shadow', same-sex aspects. I have already observed in my therapeutic work in Lugano in Switzerland during the late 1980s and in Japan during the 1990s that the contra-sexual psychic 'other' as an image was not always the other gender even when patients were not in a gender minority.

While it is desirable when a possibility of choice exists, this can cause confusion and keep people in an indeterminate state from making choices. Because of such options, they don't go to school, don't go to work, and don't select a partner, etc. The indeterminate state of not attending school, not finding a job, and remaining at home looks similar to the symptoms of ASD, which is characterised by the lack of agency. In this sense, the prevalence of ASD is partly culturally and historically determined.

The tendency towards an indeterminate state is not only limited to Japan but seems to be a global tendency. Even in the USA, an increasing number of young people remain in their parents' home (Krieg, 2001). I would like to explain this situation in reference to Herman Melville's (1853) novel *Bartleby, the Scrivener* and its interpretation by Giorgio Agamben. Here I owe my discussion partly to the explanation of Japanese sociologist Masachi Osawa.

Bartleby is a type of clerk, a copyist, who obstinately refuses to do the sort of writing demanded of him. Whenever he is requested to check his own work or do a different task apart from copywriting for his employer, he says politely he would prefer not to. Bartleby is homeless, lives illegally at the office of his employer, and eats very little, mainly ginger biscuits. His hard work, modesty, and stubbornness in staying strictly within the parameters of what he knows makes this short story an interesting study of the fear behind crossing borders into freedom and into the uncertainty of the 'unknown'.

One can interpret indeterminacy as liminality, as defined by anthropologist Victor Turner (1964), as entering the rites of passage between one status value to the next in a state of 'betwixt and between'. Perhaps, Bartleby is halted before he has entered the rites of passage because he is unable to separate from the safety and status value of his work and develop new skills that are needed to be more open-ended and self-critical.

This attitude of non-doing and non-commitment seems to be characteristic for the contemporary, postmodern world. Agamben (1999) classifies four categories following *Elements of natural right* by Leibniz. His summarisation of the figures of the modality are shown in Table 13.1.

I will not go into the complicated theological questions here. The pre-modern world seemed to be dominated by the logic of force and necessity: you have your life and your fate which cannot be avoided. A profession belonged to this category of necessity.

The modern age has been dominated by the axis of the possible and the impossible. One has a desire to obtain and realise something that is, however, very often impossible. The psychology of Jacque Lacan can be situated here. One has a desire for an object which is paradoxically impossible to achieve (cf. Lacan, 1992, pp. 5–6; pp. 285–286).

The dominating logic of the contemporary, postmodern world seems to be the logic of contingency, which is shown in the way of Bartleby's behaviour: I would prefer not to. With the possibility of not doing and not choosing, it keeps many things indeterminate.

Chihiro Hatanaka (2016) compared the responses given by students to the Rorschach test in 2013 and 2003. The group of 2013 showed significantly more 'undefined response' than the group of 2003. Her previous paper showed that ASD patients made more undefined responses than the normal group, which

Table 13.1 The Figures of Modality (Leibniz)

Possible	can	do (or be true)
Impossible	cannot	do
Necessary	cannot	not do
Contingent	can	not do (able not to do)

indicated a weak agency and tendency to remain in the indeterminate state among ASD patients. But this second paper suggests that there is growing tendency to keep the indeterminate state even among non-ASD persons. The logic of contingency seems to dominate the postmodern age.

Because the dominant logic of keeping things open and the indeterminate state are seen as too threatening, the prevailing logic tends to be counter-balanced by the need to have a determinate one. Freedom and open, democratic possibilities seem to lead to a return to a reactive authoritarian conservatism and fundamentalism world-wide, as for example, shown by the dogmatic cultural tenets of Islamic fundamentalism and the conservative and populist movement of the Tea Party in the United States. People tend to adhere to the old, logically obsolete, determinate ethics, religion, and way of life, perhaps out of fear of exploring new avenues inherent in the democratic process that includes opposition.

The Internet has made possible to connect at any point, with any person worldwide. This infinite possibility and openness can cause fear and a strong need to belong to one definite entity as is practiced, for example, in a small circle of SNS. Young people, at least in Japan, tend to form a small intimate group of SNS and keep it as intense as possible. Each member of the group feels obliged to reply as soon as possible to messages, so that one is even afraid of taking a bath and responding to a message too late. This reminds me of the village life of some hundred years ago in Japan where people in a community scrutinised each other very carefully. Here again, we notice the dialectics of the determinate and indeterminate states. While the contemporary logic is moving towards the indeterminate, there are strong reactions pulling against it. People try to adhere to the old and obsolete determinate rules, perhaps because they offer safe structures.

Some hints of how to cope with the indeterminate state

While it was necessary for analytical psychology to loosen the determinate ego and open up or descend into the indeterminate state of the unconscious first, it is important for contemporary therapy to emerge from the indeterminate state to reach a determinate point. Although the contemporary logic seems to be contingent and indeterminate, there are some reactionary tendencies to stay with the old determinate rules. It is important to recognise that we cannot start from and stick to a determinate point. Given this situation, it seems to be necessary to find a way of dealing with indeterminacy. The logic and practice of Buddhism may give a hint of how to cope with it. According to the understanding of Hua-Yen School of Buddhism (Kawai, 2018; Izutsu, 1981), there is a differentiation in daily consciousness based on the differentiation of language. Everything seems to have its own essence, i.e., its determinate contour and content. Zen Buddhism expresses this condition as 'mountain is mountain, river is river'. With a deepened consciousness, however, objects lose their differentiation; they are merged together as one, to reach the state of nothingness. It is expressed as 'mountain is not mountain, river is not river'. One reaches the indeterminate state.

This state of nothingness can be compared with the state of union in Jungian terms (cf. Jung 1954, paras. 1–35). It is important to analytical psychology that the isolated ego is united with the psychic other who appears as anima or animus. But in the case of Buddhism, the reverse movement is more central. One does not remain in the state of nothingness, but out of nothingness, things appear again and come to a new differentiation. The phrase 'Mountain is mountain, river is river' returns. While the way to nothingness is crucial in the Buddhistic practice, the movement from the nothingness, from the indeterminate to the determinate, seems to be important for contemporary therapy and the world. The movement from the nothingness to the determinate seems to be similar to what the emergence theory illustrates (cf. Knox, 2003; Hogensen, 2005; Merchant, 2012, pp.165–169). The meaning of Buddhistic logic should be further explored for the contemporary world and science.

Conclusion

In conclusion, I would like to show another example of coping with the indeterminate by referring to the works of Haruki Murakami, probably the most famous Japanese contemporary novelist. Most of his works are translated into English. In many novels of Haruki Murakami, the protagonist is in an indeterminate state: he has a provisional job, and a provisional relationship. The time of the novel *Norwegian Woods* (1987), his first bestseller, is set in 1968 when the radical student movement was popular in Japan as it was world-wide. Young people tried to change society and politics by various kinds of activity including sit-ins, demonstrations, and violence. It was a time of anti-authoritarian movements and generational protest.

The protagonist, Toru Watanabe, is, however, socially inactive and indifferent. This attitude, especially in Murakami's early works, is called 'detachment'. In reference to Agamben we can call it contingency. In his novels after *The Wind-up Bird Chronicle* (1995) however, the protagonist shows much more activity and commitment. The protagonist in *The Wind-up Bird Chronicle* lives without a job, and his wife leaves him. Unlike the protagonist in Murakami's earlier works, the protagonist in this novel tries to find his wife by all means possible and to fight against his wife's brother, a dubious politician, who is involved in his wife's disappearance. The change from an indeterminate state to one of a sudden rise in the subject's agency is impressive. As Haruki Murakami is popular not only in Japan, but world-wide, his novels show the prevailing indeterminate state in the contemporary world and in the dialectics between the indeterminate and the determinate. The commitment and the abrupt emergence of the subject in his novels can be taken as a hint for coping with the indeterminate state in contemporary times.

References

Agamben, G. (1999). 'Bartleby, or on contingency'. In D. Heller-Roazen (ed). *Potentialities: collected essays in philosophy.*, Stanford, CA: Stanford University Press pp. 243–271.

Asperger, H. (1944). 'Die autistischen Psychopathen in Kindesalter'. *Archiv für Psychiatrie und Nervenkrankheiten*, 117, 76–136.

Beaty, R. E., Benedek, M., Wilkins, R. W., Jauk, E., Fink, A., Silvia, P. J., Hodges, D. A., Koschutnig, K., and Neubauer, A. C. (2014). 'Creativity and the default network: a functional connectivity analysis of the creative brain at rest'. *Neuropsychologia*, 64, 92–98.

Croen, L. A., Grether, J. K., Hoogstrate, J., and Selvin, S. (2002). 'The changing prevalence of autism in California'. *Journal of Autism and Developmental Disorder*, 32, 207–215.

Ellenberger, H. F. (1970). *The discovery of the unconscious*. New York, NY: Basic Books.

Hatanaka, C. (2013). 'Hattatsu shogai niokeru image no aimaisa: Rorschach Test niokeru 'Fukakutei hannou' kara [The ambiguity of images produced by autism spectrum disorder patients: 'Uncertain response' in the Rorschach Test]'. *Archives of Sandplay Therapy*, 26 (2), 29–40.

Hatanaka, C. (2016). 'The apparent lack of agency, empathy, and creativity among Japanese youth: interpretations from project test responses'. *Psychologia*, 58 (4), 176–188.

Hogenson, G. B. (2005). 'The self, the symbolic and synchronicity. Virtual realities and the emergence of the psyche'. *Journal of Analytical Psychology*, 50, 271–284.

Izutsu, T. (1981). 'The nexus of ontological events: a Buddhist view of reality'. *Eranos-Jahr Buch*, 1980, 357–392.

Jung, C. G. (1923). 'Definitions'. In *Collected works*, vol. 6, *Psychological types* (2nd edn.). Princeton, NJ: Princeton University Press.

Jung, C. G. (1928). 'The personal and the collective unconscious'. In *Collected works*, vol. 7, *Two essays in analytical psychology, Part 11* (2nd edn.). Princeton, NJ: Princeton University Press.

Jung, C. G. (1950). 'The syzygy: anima and animus'. In *Collected works*, vol. 9ii, *Aion, Researches into the Phenomenology of the Self* (2nd edn.). Princeton, NJ: Princeton University Press.

Jung, C. G. (1954). 'The components of the coniunctio'. In *Collected works*, vol. 14, *Mysterium coniunctionis. An enquiry into the separation and synthesis of psychic opposites in alchemy* (2nd edn.) Princeton, NJ: Princeton University Press.

Kanner, L. (1943). 'Autistic disturbances of affective contact'. *Nervous Child*, 2, 217–50.

Kawai, T. (2009). 'Union and separation in the therapy of pervasive developmental disorders and ADHD'. *Journal of Analytical Psychology*, 54, 659–675.

Kawai, T. (2018). 'The loss and recovery of transcendence* perspectives of Jungian psychology and the Hua-Yen School of Buddhism'. In J. Cambray and L. Sawin (eds.), *Research in analytical psychology: applications from scientific, historical, and cross-cultural research*. London/New York: Routledge.

Kim, S. J., Kim, Y. K., Lim, E. C., Cheon, K. A. (2011). 'Prevalence of autism spectrum disorders in a total population sample'. *American Journal of Psychiatry*, 168, 904–912.

Knox, J. (2003). *Archetype, attachment, analysis: Jungian psychology and the emergent mind*. London: Brunner-Routledge.

Krieg, A. (2001). 'Reclusive shut-ins: are Hikikomori predominantly a Japanese problem?'. In Marcus E. Raichle, Ann Mary MacLeod, Abraham Z. Snyder, William J. Powers, Debra A. Gusnard, and Gordon L. Shulman (eds.), A default mode of brain function. *PNAS*, 98, 676–682.

Lacan, J. (1992). *The ethics of psychoanalysis, 1959–1960. The seminar of Jacques Lacan*. Book VII, London/New York, NY: Routledge.

Melville, H. (1853). *Bartleby, the scrivener: story of Wall Street*. New York, NY: Start Publishing, 2012.

Merchant, J. (2012). *Shamans and analysts. New insights into the wounded healer*. London/New York, NY: Routledge.

Murakami, H. (1987). *Norwegian wood*. London/New York, NY: Penguin Books.
Murakami, H. (1995). *The wind-up bird chronicle*. London/New York: Penguin Books.
NHK. (2018). 'NHK special "Human body series" 5', accessed on February 4, 2018. Available at http://genjapan.com/en/blog/content/2187
Raichle, M.E.., MacLoed, A.M. , Snyder, A.Z. , (2001). A default of brain function: a brief history of an evolving idea. *PNAS journal*, 98 (2) 676–682.
Rutter, M. (2004). 'Incidence of autism spectrum disorders: changes over time and their meaning'. *Acta Paediatrica*, 93, 1–13.
Shamdasani, S. (2003). *Jung and the making of modern psychology: the dream of a science*. Cambridge: Cambridge University Press.
Turner, V. W. (1964). 'Betwixt and between: the liminal period in *Rites De Passage*'. In W. A. Lessa and E. Z. Vogt (eds.), *Reader in comparative religion, an anthropological approach* (4th edn.). Harvard: Harper Collins, pp. 234–243.
Wing, L. (1996/2002). *The autistic spectrum: a guide for parents and professionals*. London: Robinson.

Chapter 14

The consequences of freedom

Moving beyond the intermediate states of broken individualisation and liquidity

Stefano Carpani

Introduction

In this work, I attempt a comparative study of Swiss psychoanalyst C. G. Jung's individuation process, German sociologist Ulrich Beck's individualisation theory, and Polish sociologist Zygmunt Bauman's concept of liquidity, leading to the proposal that in the current second-modern, individualised and liquid societies,[1] there is a renewed need for individuation. In doing so, I will look into the sociological concept of anomie and explore its role as a possible 'indeterminate state' (betwixt and between). To look at the concept of individualisation and liquidity, freedom and its consequences is fundamental because of 'the betrayed promise of freedom and happiness for all',[2] which leads to a state of *broken individualisation* (anomie). The comparison will serve to introduce a new configuration of psychosocial studies, wherein Jung is used to consider the psychic and Beck and Bauman the social. As Rachel so poignantly expresses it, 'what use was it then, having my independence, if I have never really been happy'?

(Václav Havel, 1976, *Horský Hotel*)

To this end, I address the so-called 'missing unconscious in sociology', whereby traditional sociology has failed to take the unconscious into account. I also claim that it is insufficient merely to adopt a Freudian sociology (as in Classical drive theory) or a post-Freudian sociology (and psychosocial studies);[3] it is also necessary to consider Jung's immense contribution, without, however, claiming that a Jungian approach is sufficient on its own – as this too would be a mistake. Instead, I propose that Jung, the post-Jungians, and the contemporary-Jungians be studied alongside Freud, the post-Freudians, and the contemporary-Freudians (as well as alongside all the major contributors in this field), as is the case in relational psychoanalysis.

In attempting to demonstrate the validity of this approach, I will answer the following research question: What is the best tool to understand the nature of development of narratives of self-identity at the beginning of the 21st century? To better understand the current world (and in response to Beck's latest work *The Metamorphosis of the World* (2017)), I claim that there is an imminent necessity to build a bridge from sociology towards psychoanalysis, or from Beck's individualisation and Bauman's liquidity to Jung's individuation (and not vice versa), and in so doing, leave behind traditional sociology in order to open the door to the unconscious with a psychosocial approach. To illustrate my findings, I will use a clinical vignette, inspired by a patient who – during our first session – reported a 'sense of emptiness', of 'feeling stuck' and that 'sentimental relationships don't last'. While this patient is sociologically individualised and (apparently) well adapted in a liquid society, it remains to be seen whether she is individuated. I leave this question open while I first explore what individuation means for Jung, what individualisation means for Ulrich Beck, and what liquidity means for Zygmunt Bauman.[4]

C. G. Jung's individuation

While Jung was not the first to introduce the concept of individuation, he was the first psychiatrist to do so and he adopted the word individuation from Schopenhauer and von Hartman.[5] According to Jung, individuation is one's own 'identification with the totality of the personality, with the self' (Jung, 1990, p. 138) and a process 'of differentiation, having for its goal the development of the individual personality' (1921, para. 757). Thus, individuation is a time when the individual is at 'a point of intersection or a dividing line, neither conscious nor unconscious, but a bit of both' (1917, para. 507). Individuation can also be described as 'the process in which the patient becomes what he really is' (1935a, para. 11).

Verena Kast (1993, pp. 5–6) furthers this definition, stating that to individuate means to *become* (the person you have never been). This means that one must:

1. Become independent from parents and from parental complexes;
2. Become more competent in relationships;
3. Become more of who and what you are and become more 'whole' (spiritual).

James Hillman (1997a, p. 87–88), meanwhile, describes individuation as comprising the following steps:

1. Descend.
2. Make peace with your biological family.
3. Find a place you can call home.
4. Give something back to society.

Sonu Shamdasani (2013, p. 92) underlines that individuation 'enables someone to envisage new possibilities, to imagine new ways of consideration' and that individuation is a way out of solipsism. In this regard, Ann Casement (2001, p. 147) claims that in addition to becoming 'wholly and indivisibly oneself', individuation also means 'gathering the world to oneself in order to fulfil collective qualities more completely and satisfactorily'. Thus, individuation is intended to be intrinsically antithetical to any individualism that a given person may harbour.

Both Kast's and Hillman's concepts help to better understand Jung's individuation and what needs to be done to *become* in an individualised/liquid society. Both concepts will become helpful later in this chapter, when investigating the clinical vignette.

Ulrich Beck's individualisation

Like Jung, Beck also worked on his individualisation theory throughout his life and it became one of his *trademarks*. It was in *Risk Society*, published in Germany in 1986, that Beck first mentioned individualisation theory and the concept of second modernity. He subsequently worked with Elizabeth Beck-Gernsheim[6] on the collection of essays dedicated to the Anglo-Saxon countries titled *Individualization* (2002). According to Beck, the concepts of risk, individualisation, cosmopolitanism, and the transformation of intimacy are intrinsically related.

Beck and Beck-Gernsheim (2002, p. xxii) refer to individualisation as 'institutional individualism', that is 'the paradox of an individualizing structure as a non-linear, open ended, highly ambivalent, ongoing process ... related to the decline of narratives of given sociability'. They (1995) also note that individualisation is not a new concept but one that Weber, Simmel, Foucault, Burckhardt, and Elias have already investigated. However, they claim that the individualisation of second modernity differs from that previously discussed since 'one of the most important aspects is its "mass character"', which 'occurs in the wealthy western industrialized countries as a side effect of the modernisation process designed to be long term'. They continue: 'While earlier generations often knew nothing but the daily struggle for survival, a monotonous cycle of poverty and hunger, broad sections of the population have now reached a standard of living which enables them to plan and organize their own lives'. More importantly, they claim that we live 'in an age in which the social order of the nation state, class, ethnicity and the traditional family is in decline', in an age where 'the ethic of individual self-fulfilment and achievement is the most powerful current' (2002, p. 165).

From the outset of his research, Beck (1995, p. 6) claims that 'individualization means that men and women [are] released from the gender roles prescribed by industrial society for a life in the nuclear family'. Thus, Beck and Beck-Gernsheim (1995) claim that in a second modern society, people 'compulsively ... search for the right way to live, trying out cohabitation, divorce or contractual marriage, struggling to coordinate family and career, love and marriage, 'new' motherhood and fatherhood, friendship and acquaintances' and that individualisation corresponds to the Westerners need to create a so-called do-it-yourself biography; that is, the need to take control of their own lives. This, they (2002) argue, is an experimental life, condemned to activity, where everything is a matter of self-responsibility.

Therefore, individualisation, according to Beck and Beck-Gernsheim (2002, p. 3), is the process through which the normal biography becomes the 'elective biography', the 'reflexive biography', the 'do-it-yourself biography'. This does not necessarily happen by choice, nor does it necessarily succeed. The do-it-yourself biography is always a 'risk-biography', indeed a state of permanent (partly overt, partly concealed) endangerment. That being the case, they claim, following Ley (1984, cited in Beck, 1995) that 'standard biographies are transformed into "choice biography"' and that 'biographies are removed from the traditional perceptions and certainties, from external control and general moral laws, becoming open and dependent on decision-making, and are assigned as a task for each individual' (Beck and Beck-Gernsheim, 2002). They (2002, p. 5) also claim that the concepts of family, marriage, parenthood, sexuality, and love are no longer fixed, but vary. Thus, individuals must negotiate the meaning of these concepts, even if doing so 'might unleash the conflicts and devils that lie slumbering among the details'.

In sum, for Beck (2002, p. 5), individualisation means that:

> the human being becomes (in the radicalization of Sartre's meaning) a choice among possibilities, *homo optionis*. Life, death, gender, corporeality, identity, religion, marriage, parenthood, social ties – all are becoming decidable down to the small print; once fragmented into options, everything must be decided.

Moreover, in the individualised society, people 'think, calculate, plan, adjust, negotiate, define, revoke (with everything constantly starting again from the beginning): these are the imperatives of the "precarious freedoms" that are taking hold of life as modernity advances'. Responding to his critics, Beck (2002, p. 6) states:

> It is sometimes claimed that individualization means autonomy, emancipation, the freedom and self-liberation of humanity. This calls to mind the proud subject postulated by the philosophy of the Enlightenment, who will acknowledge nothing but reason and its laws. But sometimes anomie rather than autonomy seems to prevail – a state unregulated to the point of lawlessness. … Any generalization that seeks to understand individualized society only in terms of one extreme or the other – autonomy or anomie – abbreviates and distorts the questions that confront us here.

Having presented Beck's and Beck-Gernsheim's individualisation, I will now shift my focus to Bauman's liquidity, before assessing why Beck, while he notes that individuation is a term from depth psychology, does not investigate further. I will also examine his final work *Metamorphosis of the World* (2017, p. 3) in which he seeks to rescue himself from a major embarrassment when examining today's world, claiming that 'there was nothing – neither a concept nor a theory – capable of expressing the turmoil of this world in conceptual terms, as required by the German philosopher Hegel'.

Zygmunt Bauman's liquid society

Bauman's theory of liquidity (2000) overlaps with those of Beck and Beck-Gernsheim in claiming that, in second modernity, individuals become responsible for their own lives. However, while for Beck and Beck-Gernsheim individualisation is a matter of options, for Bauman, liquidity is an existentialist matter. Therefore, Bauman acknowledges that liquidity is linked to such values as free choice, inner strength, authenticity, personal responsibility, self-determination, and individualism. It remains to be seen, however, whether Bauman's liquidity comprises 21st-century existentialism in the line of Kierkegaard, Nietzsche, Camus, Sartre, or R. D. Laing.

In *Liquid Modernity* (2000, p. 82), Bauman notes that what unites all forms of modern life 'is precisely their fragility, temporariness, vulnerability and inclination to constant change'. Thus, 'to "be modern" means to modernize – compulsively, obsessively ... forever "becoming", avoiding completion, staying underdefined'. For Bauman, the modern person never reaches completion, but is, rather, embroiled in a never-ending series of new beginnings with 'each new structure' replacing the previous 'as soon as it is declared old-fashioned'. Thus, a *sine qua non* of modernity is being at all times 'post-something', while in liquid modernity, 'change is the only permanence, and uncertainty the only certainty'.

According to Bauman (2005, p. 2), this 'liquid life' is precarious; 'the conditions ... change faster than it takes the ways of acting to consolidate into habits and routines'. This forces its members 'to forget, erase, leave and to replace' their relationships and work (ibid., p. 11). Bauman also cites Italo Calvino's *Invisible Cities* 'whose inhabitants, the day they "feel the grip of weariness" and can no longer bear their job, relatives, house and life, simply move to the next city and take up a new life' (2005, p. 4). Thus, with its 'succession of new beginnings', liquid life is marked by 'swift and painless endings, without which, new beginnings would be unthinkable' (p. 2). It is these endings that comprise its most challenging moments, leading to acute anxiety 'of being left behind, of overlooking "use by" dates, of being saddled with possessions that are no longer desirable'. Moreover, with its rapid cycle of change, liquid life cannot retain 'its shape or stay on course for long' (2005, p. 1) and the burden of responsibility that fluid modernism places on the individual comprises the need to replace traditional patterns with self-elected ones (2000, p. 8).

Bauman (2005, p. 6) then asks how can the individual select, from the multiple patterns on offer, that which best suits his current situation, while remaining ever ready to dismantle the various parts of the patchwork of options he has sewn together? He responds that, in the face of 'erosive forces and disruptive pressures', the individual is in constant battle with the 'crumbling walls' of his identity. Thus, he must 'master and practice the art of "liquid life"' with its attendant 'disorientation', and 'absence of itinerary and direction' (2005, p. 4).

This begs the question: Can we really accept this state, or do we simply founder in a state of disorientation? Moreover, is it really possible to develop what Bauman terms 'immunity to vertigo', a tolerance for the absence of direction and for infinite travel without purpose? Finally, how far can consciousness take us on these quests, when the unconscious is excluded? I intentionally leave these questions unanswered.

In the next section, I critically examine Beck and Bauman and propose that, to contrast the hystericised and narcissistic 'succession of new beginnings', 'disorientation', and 'absence of itinerary and direction' where the individual is in constant battle with the 'crumbling walls' of his identity (Bauman, 2005, p. 4), there is a need to face one's own 'endings', to understand that there is no such a thing as 'painless endings' and that the systematic avoidance thereof is the very reason why people are unable to develop or liberate themselves. Finally, as an antidote to this never ending 'succession of new beginnings' (ibid, 2005, p. 2), I suggest meditation as effected in Jungian psychoanalysis.

Beck and Bauman contra Jung

Feminist and relational psychoanalyst Susie Orbach (2014, p. 17) underlines that 'being is constituted out of the enactment and living of both conscious behaviour and behaviour of which we are unaware' and that agents mutually influence each other while structure and agency are also mutually influential. Orbach (2014, p. 16) also claims that 'the individual is born into a set of social and psychological circumstances. The human infant is a set of possibilities – not id based, not instinctually driven – but in order to become recognized as a human, will need to attach' and later to separate. Following this, I propose that traditional sociology is not equipped to consider the unconscious, because it relies exclusively on classical drive theory, and has an ontological bias towards the rational and cognitive aspects of human behaviour. To this could also be added its loyalty to Durkheim's[7] view of psychology and the Frankfurt School's inability to go beyond Freud's dogma and examine the irrational side of the psyche. Finally, making of Jung a *persona non grata* in 20th-century sociology, the Frankfurters saw – following Walter Benjamin (cited in Samuels, 1993) – Jung's psychology as 'the devil's work' and an 'auxiliary service to National Socialism'. In contrast, I propose adopting Jung's psychosocial and relational viewpoint in line with the work of Erich Fromm (1941), Ian Craib (1989), Jessica Benjamin (1988 and 1995), Steven Frosh (2013), Susie Orbach (2014), Andrew Samuels (2014), and Mary Watkins (2003, 2008).

I also propose that Beck, Bauman, and traditional sociology lack the tools to examine the unconscious and emotions, since they look at these factors theoretically (sociologically) instead of clinically (symbolically). We must query why, at a time where people have gained freedoms that were unthinkable in earlier times, suicide rates have increased by 25% across the USA over nearly two decades (U.S. Center for Disease Control and Prevention, 2018). This fact alone is sufficient reason to look anew at the concepts of individualisation, liquidity, and individuation and to realise that to truly *become* liberated[8] in an individualised and liquid society, people need to individuate. Thus, Jung's individuation process comprises a valid theory for understanding the world as it is (thus opposing the idea that the world is out of joint). I propose that Jung's individuation comprises a theory of metamorphosis of the individual and therefore of the world. Moreover, metamorphosis is always linked to self-responsibility, in opposition to anomie.

What, then, is the link between precarious freedom, self-responsibility and leading a life made up of a succession of new beginnings, disorientation, and the absence of itinerary and direction? As discussed above, Beck and Beck-Gernsheim (2002) claim that when living an experimental life, everything is a matter of self-responsibility, and Bauman (2000) underlined that the burden of responsibility that fluid modernism places on the individual comprises the need to replace traditional patterns with self-elected ones. Self-responsibility and its burdens, I propose, are where individualisation and liquidity crack, because people have difficulty taking responsibility and instead engage in brooding, 'a sterile activity … not work but a weakness, even a vice' (Jung, 1943, para. 1810), before succumbing to depression and suicidal ideation, as per anomie.

In this regard, both sociologist Mauro Magatti, (2018) in his recent column 'There Is No Freedom without Responsibility' (*Corriere della Sera*), and Erich Fromm (1941) in *Escape from Freedom* underlined that 'Modern man still is anxious and tempted to surrender his freedom to dictators of all kinds'. Fromm (1941) also noted that 'If humanity cannot live with the dangers and responsibilities inherent in freedom, it will probably turn into authoritarianism'. However, in the words of Magatti and media sociologist and anthropologist Chiara Giaccardi (2014), if, in Western society, we have already liberated ourselves, 'what other liberation must we therefore seek'? Why are people not yet free if they have liberated themselves – again following Fromm (1941) – from the political, economic, and spiritual shackles that have bound them? Why are people not yet happy, as Václav Havel wrote already in 1976 in the play *Horský Hotel*? Why are anxiety, depression, and suicide rates increasing? This is, I propose, when the dichotomy between the wish for autonomy and anomie become apparent. Therefore, when there is a *broken individualisation* that equals 'the betrayed promise of freedom and happiness for all',[9] there can be no individuation. Thus:

- Individuation and individualisation/liquidity are antithetic.
- Individualisation/liquidity is a diagnosis while individuation is a prognosis.
- Individualisation means *homo optionis* and liquidity means *forever becoming* while individuation means *become who you are*.
- Individualisation/liquidity equates to the conscious mind and solipsism and leads to anomie (precarious freedom) while individuation equates to pluralism and creativity and leads to generativity (absolute freedom).
- Individualisation is linked to *will to power* while individuation is linked to *will to mutuality*.

Based on the above, Jung's individuation could provide an answer, perhaps even an antidote, to the current broken individualisation/liquidity and consequent anomie. This is because, following Watkins (2003), it is the capacity for dialogue, not reason, that distinguishes humankind from other living creatures. Furthermore, such dialogue takes place with oneself, with one's neighbour, and with God (Niebuhr, 1955, cited in Watkins, 2003), and this 'capacity for dialogue is a necessary precondition for human liberation' (2003, p. 87), particularly 'from rigid, stereotypic, and unidimensional narrowness'. In this view, development (which she calls liberation) is based 'on a paradigm of interdependence, where the liberation of one is intimately tied to the liberation of the other' (2003, p. 88). In this sense, 'the other' may comprise 'economic, political, sociocultural, spiritual, and psychological' entities. Additionally, Samuels (1989, p. 1) who introduced the concept of the plural psyche to 'hold unity and diversity in balance' and underlined that 'our inner worlds and our private lives reel from the impact of policy decisions and the existing political culture', suggested that within both the microcosm of an individual and the macrocosm of the global village, 'we are flooded by psychological themes'. If this is the case, however, why does mainstream sociology fail to investigate these themes? Why does Beck argue that individualisation might 'unleash the conflicts and devils that lie slumbering among the details' but does not say more? Why did Bauman underline that instead of facing their conflicts and devils, people prefer to look at new beginnings because they are unable to cope with painful endings? To all this – and as an antidote to broken individualisation and liquidity – I suggest examining Jung's concept of meditation.

In his essay 'Self-knowledge', Jung (1954, paras. 707–708) claimed that 'what I call coming to terms with the unconscious the alchemists called "meditation"' and added, citing Ruland, that meditation is 'an Internal talk of one person with another who is invisible, as in the invocation of the Deity, or communion with one's self, or with one's good angel'. In an individualised and liquid society, there is fresh need for renewed internal talk, and one way of engaging in such is through Jungian psychoanalysis. Jung (1954, para. 708) claimed that modern meditation methods are 'only for increasing concentration and consolidating consciousness, but have no significance as regards affecting a synthesis of the personality. On the contrary, their purpose is to shield consciousness from the unconscious and to suppress it'. That being the case, such methods are of no therapeutic value. Instead, Jung (1954, para. 708) proposes analysis as meditation, although 'there are relatively few people who have experienced the effects of an analysis of the unconscious on themselves, and almost nobody hits on the idea of using the objective hints given by dreams as a theme for meditation'.

More than 70 years since the publication of this essay, little has changed. While in Jung's day meditation had a bad reputation in the West, today, the *à la mode* forms of meditation and contemplation – yoga at lunchtime, daily morning meditation, weekend or holistic 'holiday' retreats, etc. – that have been adopted in the West do not facilitate internal talk. Instead, they facilitate a momentary calmness before returning (recharged) to the jungle of an affluent society. Thus, these techniques are akin to smartphone battery chargers: indispensable for recharging in our society, but never fully disconnecting.

Therefore, I agree with Jung's view that:

> No one has time for self-knowledge or believes that it could serve any sensible purpose. Also, one knows in advance that it is not worth the trouble to know oneself, for any fool can know what he is. We believe exclusively in doing and do not ask about the doer, who is judged only by achievements that have collective value. ... Western man confronts himself as a stranger and that self-knowledge is one of the most difficult and exacting of the arts.
> (1954, para. 709)

Giegerich's *realism* to contrast broken individualisation and liquidity

To further investigate the concept of inner talk (as a means to contrast the emptiness and meaninglessness of the affluent life) and the need people have in Western societies to find a momentary calm-ness before returning (recharged) to the jungle of an affluent society, I examine here the German psychotherapist Wolfgang Giegerich.

In *The End of Meaning and the Birth of Man*, Giegerich (2010) suggests making a person fully aware through confrontation with her/his unconscious ideas. However, he queries whether lack of meaning is sufficient cause to make one neurotic, or whether the quest for meaning is merely 'the expression of a neurotic pretentiousness, a claim to metaphysical grandiosity. It is the delusion that life is only life if there is, like in a dog race, that never-to-be reached one thing, the sausage 'to race after'. Giegerich (2010, p. 233) claims that Jung refused to see this, despite being aware of 'the danger of pointless seeking', which I compare to Beckett's (2010) 'waiting' for Godot: both actions are a sign of *légèresse*, indicating an impossible depth, substance, or purpose in life.

As Simone de Beauvoir noted, 'une femme libre est exactement le contraire d'une femme légère'. Going beyond sex and gender, depth (substance) may be the antidote to *légèresse* and a free individual is the opposite to a *légère* individual. Therefore, the concepts of emptiness, meaning, searching, and waiting are interwoven: all show traits of ambivalence, wanting, and rejecting, and meaninglessness is linked to a never-ending searching and waiting, until 'something' (perhaps the numinous) happens to the individual or a symbol appears. But what if this numinous event, this symbol, never arises, or we are so distracted by the daily noise of our affluent lives that we fail to recognise it when it does come? This is what I call broken individualisation and liquidity.

In this regard, Giegerich (2010, p. 233) recalls Jung's example of a woman who

> does not live the life that makes sense ... because she is nothing. But if she could say, 'I am the daughter of the Moon. Every night I must help the Moon,

my Mother, over the horizon' – ha, that is something else! Then she lives, then her life makes sense.

(1961, para. 630)

Giegerich claims that this is, in fact, not a cure, as Jung claimed, and that the 'Pueblo-Indian model' cannot be applied to the modern woman because it would involve 'an endless, futile search' (2010, p. 233); thus, 'Jung's suggestion feeds her neurotic craving, her "addiction"' (2010). Instead, Giegerich (2010, p. 234) proposes as a 'real cure' that she goes, I believe, towards what Thomas Bernhard (1976) calls *the opposite direction*; that is, that she be made fully aware that her unconscious idea that 'she ought to be the daughter of the moon ... is why she is desperately travelling'. Thus, she is confronted 'with the exaltedness, inflatedness of the unconscious demands and expectations' Giegerich (2010, p. 234). This is the very opposite attitude to that described by Bauman (and Calvino). Therefore, Giegerich (2010) claims: 'why should she not be able, like everybody else, to find satisfaction, contentedness, in ordinary life'? In this way, Giegerich's realism helps to understand the limitations of contemporary mainstream sociology, which does not examine unconscious motives. By realising that she is not 'a Queen in search for ... the recognition due but denied to her', it could permit her to accept, following Orbach (2020)[10], her ordinary unhappiness in contrast to the hystericised and narcissistic desire for accomplishment, and even allow new developments to arise.

In the next section, I examine how this can be achieved in practice by describing a clinical vignette from my own praxis.

A clinical vignette: Inner talk in action in Jungian psychoanalysis

Carla presented as a patient who was sociologically individualised and well adapted into liquid society. On the one hand, she had challenged the certainties of modern life, namely, the social order of the nation state, class, gender, ethnicity, and traditional family structure and had strived for self-fulfilment and achievement; simultaneously, however, albeit unconsciously, she felt trapped in the impasse described by Bauman. During our first session, she described a sense of emptiness, feeling stuck and that her sentimental relationships did not last. The first dream she presented in analysis was as follows (April 2017):

> We are at a rave party in Hatown in a huge space adjacent to Rebekka's parents (where we're staying). It's a weird rave party, in a huge cylindrical black container (like a water storing container), and somehow it seems like it's a Halloween party. But I'm not in fancy dress. Not everyone is. Rebekka, Clara, Penny and Cloe are there (we're about to start rehearsing tomorrow) and there are other friends from Berlin and London. Suddenly Mourice says 'careful', pointing at someone who's standing on some kind of a pulpit and I see the

'Joker' (from Batman) pointing at me with a water gun. I duck and cover my head, but I feel a gooey substance covering me and it's vomit. I stand up and I'm covered in vomit. I'm wearing a cream-white jumper and it's covered and I can even smell it. And I'm walking trying to figure out how to get out or clean myself, but I don't know where the exit or the toilets are.

In analysing the dream, the keywords that arose for Carla were humiliation and shame. I propose that these keywords are what the dream wants to bring: they are concrete feelings, not subjective. For example, the smell of vomit is an object-related feeling.

Carla commented that Hatown was where her theatre company had recently spent a week rehearsing, and that they had stayed at Rebekka's parents' country house. What, then, is the symbolic meaning of the weird rave party? It is somewhere where you lose yourself in. It is a powerful experience. Thus, it symbolises Carla's becoming unconscious (planning to get lost, taking drugs/drinking). Here, the contrast between work (rehearsal) and the rave is evident. The patient is supposed to be at Hatown for work, but she goes to a rave.

Mourice is Carla's ex-husband, a non-European gay man (her best friend at the time) whom she married so that he could renew his visa and avoid deportation. At first glance, Mourice seems to be a helper: he warns her of the impending danger. But is he really a helper? Given their history, he could symbolise how Carla has given up on relationships, since her 'sham' marriage occupied her libido space, thus preventing her from fully committing to a relationship based on mutuality.

The pulpit is linked to the theme of church, preacher, sin, and to a religious mother context that begs the question: is the sin that she has committed her participation in the rave, rather than working or living her own life, thereby, losing herself and unconsciously acting against her own dignity?

The Joker could express Carla's disgust with herself. He is the trickster that helps to break the rigid order. But why vomit? She feels and smells it and is disgusted by it. To return to the religious context, could we consider the vomit a type of baptism; perhaps reflecting the fact that the patient needs to become conscious of her own naïveté? Thus, the soul showers the dream ego in vomit to present it as disgusting, while the cream-white jumper symbolises her Ego's wish to be clean. However, Carla does not know where to clean herself or where the toilets are; hence she has no knowledge or consciousness and must bear the vomit sticking to her for a while.

This initial dream is a statement and a clear request for transformation, particularly if we examine the feelings of humiliation and shame, paralleled with the patient's sense of emptiness, feeling stuck, and that sentimental relationships do not last. But why the need for transformation, if she is already individualised (*homo optionis*)? In light of the theoretical discussion above, we may say that it is because she is not conscious of her emotions – and following Beck's view that in an individualised society individuals are driven by the wish of self-achievement – there is an emptiness to her achievement. This viewpoint is echoed in a recent conversation with Susie Orbach (Carpani, 2020),[11] which links to Beck's and Bauman's concepts:

> I've had the experience with some young women that they have ticked all the boxes, but they don't exist. I've got the boyfriend, I've got the body, I've got the job, but I don't – it's not even that I'm not happy. It's: I have achieved, but those things are not integrated, they are not part of me.

Orbach then added:

> I come across young women who feel it's very bad to have any dependency needs. … They needed to have been brought up to know that the world is full of struggle, and there are psychological struggles as well; to manifest themselves, to dare to express their longings, to dare to connect with others in a way that is both separate and connected.

Building on Orbach's comment, I will now examine Shamdasani and Hillman (2013, p. 92) who claimed, respectively, that individuation is to take 'someone out of solipsism' where solipsism is 'modern suffering. Being only an individual'. Is then Carla only an individual? It may be that the initial projection of freedom (her wish to leave her parents and live her own life as far as possible from them) stemmed from the desire for individualisation, which became solipsism and then led to anomie. What then if, following Giegerich, *substance* (vomit, therefore matter) and *purpose* were to replace *emptiness* and *meaninglessness* (the rave)? What if, in the sense used by Jung, Carla needs to learn the art of meditation? I propose that Carla, following Kast (see above), needs to separate from her parents and parental complexes, to become more competent in relationships, and particularly to become more 'whole' (spiritual). This will allow her, following Hillman, to find a place she can call home and to give something back to society.

The need to 'become independent from parents and the parental complex' was confirmed in the next dream, where the psychological content is 'coming home to her Self', to really be alone (to be adult means to be alone), to really separate.

> My mum tells me I have to look for my own flat because I am too old to keep living with her. I think, well … also my sister is too old. Then I realize that the flat where we live in is under my name. The contract is in my name and I tell my mum to look for a flat because I will not leave. It is my mum's idea that I have to leave. It is not my idea to separate from her.

In this dream, the good inner mother (as opposed to Carla's real mother with whom she has a difficult relationship) sends Carla on her own path. Looking for her own flat symbolises psychological independence from the parents and parental complexes. The good mother says: go! The patient also dreams, however, 'also my sister is old enough', and here we see a portrait of her inner defences.

The need to improve relationships is evident from the following dream (April 2018):

> I'm there with someone. In my room there's a woman who comes in. She's blonde. Short hair. Big. She looks like a serial killer. I know she didn't ring the bell. I know she used to live here before. She walks in as if it's her place and I tell her she can't just come in. I ask how she came in. She doesn't answer and pushes on. I stop her and I walk her out. I ask again how she got in. She says nothing. She has a ring full of keys in her hand. I take them off her and I close the door in her face. I find the key to my front door and I wake up.

'Being there with someone' means socialization and relationships, while 'to be in my room' means to be by herself. Carla calls the woman an intruder; thus, the attitude of the dream 'I' is defensive. Carla believes this woman is a serial killer, a projection related to fear. The dream 'I' does not want her there, although Carla knows this woman previously lived there. Carla asks her how she got in, but she does not answer and pushes on. Here, we see another defence from Carla. The woman ignores Carla's question, showing the impossibility of communication. Therefore, Carla walks her out (rejection) and then finds the key of her own door on the woman's key ring. There is an estrangement between the dream 'I' and the intrapsychic shadow 'other', and I suggested to Carla that it might be worth allowing the 'other' to enter (as suggested by alchemy) and not to reject her, because she is not threatening.

The need to 'become spiritual' is evident in the next few dreams (August 2017).

> *I was sleeping on my sofa when my neighbours invaded my house from the door and window.*

Carla is sleeping, therefore not conscious, active, or ready to respond. When asked who the neighbours are, she said they were the kids from the building and the very elderly woman living next door. Thus, both the kids (energy) and an elderly-woman (the experienced feminine) enter the flat. There is a tension between her young life (that is not integrated) and the old woman. However, these forces are seen as invading and she perceives them as ghosts, therefore as immaterial.

The need to 'become spiritual' is also portrayed in another dream (February 2018):

> I was asleep and then I woke up (in my dream) to see that the front door of my apartment had been broken in. The door was ajar, and the lock was still visible from the side of the door (as if it had been broken into but not broken). I get up and go out the door and I see my neighbour (the elderly woman who lives across the hall) and I tell her that I've been broken into and she just looks at me as if that's normal and carries on walking down the stairs.

Again, Carla is 'asleep', therefore unconscious, but the fact that she wakes up (in the dream) signifies a movement from an unconscious state to awareness. This is a development from the previous dream. 'To see' means to become really aware of the intrusion ('broken in'), another development since the previous dream. The fact that the door was ajar means change. The door has been broken-in but it is not broken, meaning that the patient can close the door again (a request for inner space). To go out of the door is a reasonable reaction and there she finds her neighbour (again the elderly woman), the experienced feminine. This woman looks at Carla as if what has happened is normal, as if she knows how it works and that the patient's shell has been broken into, but not the Self.

Both dreams beautifully portray the self-healing attitude of the soul, which knows it all. The patient needs to change her attitude and to gain substance and a sense of purpose to fight her sense of emptiness and fear of being stuck. This will allow her to find her own meaning for her life and possibly to develop, separated from her parents and parental complexes and more connected to her Self.

Conclusions

With this vignette, I sought to propose that *substance* and *purpose* are required to replace *emptiness* and *meaninglessness*. Otherwise, as suggested by Bauman (2005), people will continually move from one life/identity to another in a perpetual cycle of dissatisfaction (and search), of killing time and of being 'tired like the residents of Calvino's Eutropia of everything they have enjoyed thus far'.

Therefore, to return to the question asked in the introduction, whether Bauman's liquidity is a 21st-century existentialism in the line of Kierkegaard, Nietzsche, Camus, Sartre, and Laing, I propose that liquidity is the consequence of early existential theory (minus purpose and substance); the more we turn to existentialism, the more we turn to anomie (anxiety, depression, and suicide). This is because if, following Bauman, in the 21st century becoming never reaches completion, this is a symptom of our own lack of substance and purpose and the only certainty is impermanence. Meditation in the sense used by Jung, however, would allow individuals to look inward, to find substance and purpose in life, and by this means to compensate for emptiness and meaninglessness. As Jung suggested, to become 'one's own creator' is key (*The Red Book*, 2009, p. 188).

Finally, I propose that the anxiety and depression related to anomie, which are rife in our society, should not be viewed as pathological, but rather as attitudes towards life, as an opportunity for development and liberation, and as a key aspect of intermediate (pre-individuated) states. In sociological terms, anxiety and depression are linked to anomie, the state wherein individuals lose sight of the fact that they can actively shape their lives. Thus, when creativity and the contents of the unconscious are repressed, anxiety and depression result and this enables anomie. In this context, Jung's individuation is fundamental because the goal of psychotherapy, according to Jung (1935b, para. 99), is 'to bring about a psychic state in which my patient begins to experiment with his own nature – a state of fluidity, change and growth where nothing is eternally fixed and hopelessly petrified'. This, Jung claims, is always related to the opportunity to express oneself creatively, through dreams, painting, active imagination, or through the body. Moreover, Jung notes that the creative fantasy is an 'intrusion from the unconscious, a sort of lucky hunch, different in kind from the slow reasoning of the conscious mind' (1935a, para. 16).

Thus, one can equate individualisation and liquidity with the conscious mind, while fluidity can be equated with the unconscious mind. In this sense, authentic creativity (creative fantasy) is what is lacking in a liquid society, because, following George Berkeley (cited in Giegerich 2010), 'few men think, yet all will have opinions'. Therefore, creativity and creative fantasy help fluidity (and pluralism) and if fluidity, rather than liquidity, is fostered, there will be a chance to contrast anxiety, depression, suicidality, and, therefore, anomie. Anomie occurs when emotions are stuck, while, when one is able to 'translate the emotions into images – that is to say, to find the images which were concealed in the emotions' (Jung, *MDR*, 1963), one becomes inwardly calmed and reassured.

If we follow these lines, we could also say, with Hillman (2013, p. 94) that 'Individuation is a path of salvation' from the 'modern condition of cut-offness from the world, cut-offness from others, from the community, from nature and all the rest, the dead world of Descartes, where we are more and more individual and more and more alone, more and more isolated – anomie'. I therefore propose that – if individualisation and liquidity lead to solipsism and anomie – individuation is a way out through meditation.

The caveat remains, however, that individuation is not for everyone. Enantiodromia is useful to enhance the dichotomy between reason and those 'faculties and attitudes which are receptive rather than productive, which tend towards gratification rather than transcendence' (Marcuse, 1955, p. 111). As Marcuse emphasised, gratification links to the pleasure principle and this (the pleasure principle) links to a broken individualisation and liquid society, where people constantly seek gratification. Finally, transcendence and, as such, meditation is also not for everyone: it would be naïve to assume so.

Notes

1 According to British sociologist Anthony Giddens (1998, p. 94), modernity 'is associated with a certain set of attitudes towards the world, the idea of the world as open to transformation by human invention'. Modernity evolves into what Beck (2002) calls 'reflexive modernization' or 'second modernity', what Giddens (1991) calls 'high' or 'late' modernity and what sociologist Zygmunt Bauman (2000) calls 'liquid' modernity. In this work, amongst the wide range of possible definitions, I prefer to refer to the present epoch as a 'second modernity' in line with Beck´s definition.
2 As Giaccardi underlined at a conference titled 'Social Generativity. What it is and what it is good for' (Univeristá Cattolica del Sacro Cuore - Milano, 2018).
3 In the *Introductory Lectures on Psychoanalysis* (1991, p. 216), Freud claimed that 'sociology ..., dealing as it does with the nature of people in society, cannot be anything other than applied psychology'.

4   In the same years, Anthony Giddens was working on similar topics in *Modernity and Self-Identity* (1991, p. 185), referring to individualisation as the 'reflexive project of the self'.
5   I intentionally do not examine Jung's individuation in detail. For this purpose: Progoff (2013 (1955)), von Franz (1956 and 1978), Jacobi (1971), J. Campbell (1972), Samuels (1985), Stein (2005), etc.
6   His wife and co-author.
7   Following Lukes' (1982) introduction to Durkheim's *The Rules of Sociological Method*, we understand that Durkheim sought to demarcate sociology from psychology, claiming sociology to be a 'special psychology, having its own subject-matter and a distinctive method' (Durkheim, 1982, p. 253), while psychology is 'the science of the individual mind' whose object or domain is as follows (Durkheim, ibid,: p. 40): 1. states of individual consciousness; 2. explanation in terms of 'organico-psychic' factors, pre-social features of the individual organism, given at birth and independent of social influences; 3. explanation in terms of particular or 'individual' as opposed to general or 'social' conditions (focusing, say, on individuals' intentions or their particular circumstances); 4. explanation in terms of individual mental states or dispositions. However, if we look carefully into a psychosocial parallel between Durkheim and Jung, we might recognise that these four points can be linked respectively to Jung's concepts of (1) the personal unconscious, (2) archetypes and the collective unconscious, (3) the persona, and (4) Jung's theory of neurosis and psychodynamics (the Syzygy).
8   *Liberation* is a concept I borrow from Mary Watkins (2003 and 2008).
9   As Giaccardi underlined at a conference titled 'Social Generativity. What it is and what it is good for' (Univeristá Cattolica del Sacro Cuore, Milano, 2018).
10 'How Are Women Today? Feminism, Love & Revolution' Susie Orbach in conversation with Stefano Carpani (Chiron, 2020).
11 Ibid.

References

Adam, B., Beck, U., and Van Loon, J. (2000). *The risk society and beyond: critical issues for social theory*. London: Sage.
Aron, L., and Mitchell, S. A. (1999). *Relational psychoanalysis, Volume 14: the emergence of a tradition*. New York, NY/London: Routledge.
Bauman, Z. (2000). *Liquid modernity*. Cambridge: Polity Press.
Bauman, Z. (2001). *The individualized society*. Cambridge: Polity Press.
Bauman, Z. (2003). *Liquid love*. Cambridge: Polity Press.
Bauman, Z. (2005). *Liquid life*. Cambridge: Polity Press.
Beck, U. (1986). *Risikogesellschaft – Auf dem Weg in eine andere Moderne*. Berlin: Suhrkamp Verlag.
Beck, U. (1992). *Risk society: towards a new modernity*. London: Sage.
Beck, U. (2005 [2000]). 'Vivere la Propria Vita in un Mondo Frenetico: Individualizzazione, Globalizzazione e Politica'. In A. Giddens and W. Hutton (eds.), *Sull'Orlo di una Crisi* (Original title: *On the edge. Living with global capitalism*). 133–145, Trieste: Asterios Editore.
Beck, U. (2006). *Cosmopolitan vision*. Cambridge: Polity Press.
Beck, U. (2017). *The metamorphosis of the world*. Cambridge: Polity Press.
Beck, U., and Beck-Gernsheim, E. (1995). *The normal chaos of love*. Cambridge: Polity Press.

Beck, U., and Beck-Gernsheim, E. (2002). *Individualization: institutionalized individualism and its social and political consequences*. London: Sage.
Beck, U., and Beck-Gernsheim, E. (2013). *Distant love*. Cambridge: Polity Press.
Beck, U., Giddens, A., and Lash, S. (1994). *Reflexive modernization. politics, tradition and aesthetics in the modern social order*. Cambridge: Polity Press.
Beck-Gernsheim, E., and Beck, U. (1995). *The normal chaos of love*. Cambridge: Polity Press.
Beckett, S. (2010). *Waiting for Godot*. London: Faber and Faber.
Benjamin, J. (1988). *The bonds of love*. New York, NY: Pantheon Books.
Benjamin, J. (1995). *Like subjects, love objects: essays on recognition and sexual difference*. New Haven, CT: Yale University Press.
Bernhard, T. (1976). *Die keller*. Salzburg: Residenz Verlag.
Carpani, S. (2004). *The formation of narratives of self-identities. A study of the Turkish community in Berlin*. Unpublished M.Phil. thesis. Cambrdge, UK: University of Cambridge.
Carpani, S. (2020). *Breakfast at Küsnacht: Conversations on C. G. Jung and Beyond*. Hasheville, North Carolina: Chiron Publications.
Casement, A. (2001). *Carl Gustav Jung*. London: Sage.
Casement, A. (2007). *Who owns Jung?* London: Karnac.
Craib, I. (1989). *Psychoanalysis and social theory*. Hemel Hempstead: Harvester Wheatsheaf.
Durkheim, E. (1982). *The rules of sociological method*. New York, NY: The Free Press.
Eichenbaum, L., and Orbach, S. (1982). *Understanding women: a feminist psychoanalytic approach*. New York, NY: Basic Books
Eichenbaum, L., and Orbach, S. (1992). *Outside in. Inside out*. London: Penguin.
Freud, S. (1926). 'The question of lay analysis'. In J. Strachey (ed)*The standard edition of the complete psychological works of Sigmund Freud, Volume XIII* (1925–1926): *An autobiographical study, inhibitions, symptoms and anxiety, the question of lay analysis and other works*, pp. 177–258, New York: W. W. Norton & Company, The Standard edition (May 17, 1990).
Freud, S. (1991). *Introductory lectures on psychoanalysis*. London: Penguin Books
Fromm, E. (1941). *Escape from freedom*. New York, NY: Holt Paperbacks.
Frosh, S. (2013). 'Transdisciplinary tension and psychosocial studies'. *Enquire*, 6 (1), 1–15.
Giddens, A. (1982). *New rules for sociological method: a positive critique of interpretive sociologies*. London: Hutchinson.
Giddens, A. (1990). *The consequences of modernity*. Cambridge: Polity Press.
Giddens, A. (1991). *Modernity and self-identity. Self and society in the late modern age*. Cambridge: Polity.
Giddens, A. (1992). *The transformation of intimacy: sexuality, love and eroticism in modern societies*. Cambridge: Polity Press.
Giddens, A., and Pierson, C. (1998). *Conversations with Anthony Giddens: making sense of modernity*. Cambridge: Polity Press.
Giegerich, W. (2010). *The soul always thinks*. New Orleans, LA: Spring Journal.
Havel, V. (1976). *Horský Hotel*. Venezia: Marsilio
Hillman, J. (1997a). *Il Codice dell'Anima*. Milano: Adelphi.
Hillman, J. (1997b). *Archetypal psychology*. Woodstock: Spring Publications.

Hillman, J., and Shamdasani, S. (2013). *Lament of the dead: psychology after the red book*. New York, NY: Norton & Company.
Jung, C. G. (1917). 'The structure of the unconscious'. In *Collected works*, vol. 7, *Two essays in analytical psychology* (2nd edn.). London: Routledge and Kegan Paul, 1990.
Jung, C. G. (1921). 'Definitions'. In *Collected works*, vol. 6, *Psychological types* (2nd edn.). London: Routledge and Kegan Paul, 1989.
Jung, C. G. (1935a). 'Principles of practical psychotherapy'. In *Collected works*, vol. 16, *The practice of psychotherapy* (2nd edn.). London: Routledge and Kegan Paul, 1993.
Jung, C. G. (1935b). 'The aims of psychotherapy'. In *Collected works*, vol. 16, *The practice of psychotherapy* (2nd edn.). London: Routledge and Kegan Paul, 1993.
Jung, C. G. (1943). 'Depth psychology and self knowledge'. In *Collected works*, vol. 18, *The symbolic life* (2nd edn.). London: Routledge and Kegan Paul, 1993.
Jung, C. G. (1954). 'Self-knowledge'. In *Collected works*, vol. 14, *Mysterium coniunctionis* (2nd edn.). London: Routledge and Kegan Paul, 1992.
Jung, C. G. (1961). 'The symbolic life'. In *Collected works*, ol. 18, *The symbolic life* (2nd edn.). London: Routledge and Kegan Paul, 1993.
Jung, C. G. (1963). *Memories, dreams, reflections*. A. Jaffe (ed.). London: Collins; Routledge and Kegan Paul.
Jung, C. G. (1990). *Analytical psychology*. London: ARK Paperbacks.
Jung, C. G. (2003). *Psychology of the unconscious*. E. T. H. Lectures, Volume 5. New York, NY: Dover.
Jung, C. G. (2009). *The red book*. New York, NY: Norton & Company.
Jung, C. G. (2012). *The red book: a reader's edition*. New York, NY: Norton & Company.
Jung, C. G., and Jarrett, J. L. (1998). *Jung's seminar on Nietzsche's Zarathustra* (Abridged edn.). Princeton, NJ: Princeton University Press.
Jung, C. G., and von Franz, M.-L. (1964). *Man and his symbols*. Garden City, NY: Doubleday.
Kast, V. (1993). 'Animus and anima: spiritual growth and separation'. *Harvest*, 39, 5–15.
Lash, S., and Friedman, J. (eds.) (1992). *Modernity and identity*. Oxford: Blackwell.
Loewenthal, D., and Samuels, A. (2014). *Relational psychotherapy, psychoanalysis and counselling: appraisals and reappraisals*. New York, NY/London: Routledge.
Lorenz, H., and Watkins, M. (2003). 'Depth psychology and colonialism: individuation, seeing-through, and liberation'. *Quadrant*, 33, 11–32.
Lyotard, J.-F. (1984). *The postmodern condition: a report on knowledge*. Minneapolis, MN: University of Minnesota Press.
Lukes, S. (1982). 'Introduction'. In E. Durkheim (ed.), *The rules of sociological method*. New York, NY: The Free Press.
Magatti, M. (2018). 'Non può esserci libertà senza responsabilità'. In *Corriere della Sera*. Retrieved on 11 November 2018 from https://www.corriere.it/opinioni/18_settembre _10/non-puo-esserci-liberta-007b4212-b450-11e8-8b0b-dff47915528b.shtml.
Magatti, M. (2018). *Social generativity*. New York, NY/London: Routledge.
Magatti, M., and Giaccardi, C. (2014). *Generativi di tutto il mondo unitevi*. Milano: Feltrinelli.
Marcuse, H. (1955). *Eros and civilization*. Boston, MA: Beacon Press.
Orbach, S. (1996). *The impossibility of sex*. New York, NY: Simon and Schuster.
Orbach, S. (2014). 'Democratizing psychoanalysis'. In D. Loewenthal and A. Samuels (eds.), *Relational psychotherapy, psychoanalysis and counselling: appraisals and reappraisals*. New York, NY/London: Routledge.

Orbach, S. (2020). 'How Are Women Today? Feminism, Love and Revolution'. In S. Carpani (ed.), *Breakfast at Küsnacht: Conversation on C. G. Jung and Beyond*. Asheville, North Carolina: Chiron Publications.

Progoff, I. (1956). *The death and rebirth of psychology: an integrative evaluation of Freud, Adler, Jung, and Rank and the impact of their culminating insights on modern man*. London: Routledge.

Progoff, I. (2013 [1955]). *Jung's psychology and its social meaning*. London: Routledge.

Samuels, A. (1985). *Jung and the post-Jungians*. London: Routledge.

Samuels, A. (1989). *The plural psyche*. London: Routledge.

Samuels, A. (1993). *The political psyche*. London: Routledge.

Samuels, A. (2001). *Politics on the couch*. London: Profile Books.

Samuels, A. (2015). *A new therapy for politics*. London: Karnac.

Stein, M. (2005). 'Individuation: inner work'. *Journal of Jungian Theory and Practice*, 7 (2), 1–13.

Thompson, J. B. (1996). *The media and modernity: a social theory of the media*. Cambridge: Polity.

Thompson, J. B. (2006). *The media and modernity: a social theory of the media*. Cambridge: Polity.

Thompson, J. B. (2006). 'Sociology in the 21st century'. *Studi di sociologia* (interview by S. Carpani and M. Magatti), XLIV (2), 179–214.

von Franz, M.-L. (1956). *C. G. Jung: his myth in our time*. Toronto: Inner City Books.

von Franz, M.-L. (1978). 'The process of individuation'. In C. G. Jung (ed.), *Man and his symbols*. London: Picador.

Watkins, M. (2003). 'Dialogue, development, and liberation'. In I. Josephs (ed.), *Dialogicality in development*. Westport, CT: Greenwood.

Watkins, M. (2013). *Accompaniment: psychosocial, environmental, trans-species, earth*. Retrieved on 11 November 2018 from http://mary-watkins.net/library/Accompaniment-Psychosocial-Environmental-Trans-Species-Earth.pdf.

Watkins, M., and Shulman, H. (2008). *Towards psychologies of liberation*. New York, NY: Palgrave Macmillan.

Chapter 15

Vulnerability and incorruptibility
An aretaic model of the transcendent function

Niccolò Fiorentino Polipo

Introduction

In this chapter I present an attempt to translate the Jungian model of psychological development as expressed in the notion of transcendent function into a language of virtues. It has been noted that analytical psychology (AP) has long been under an anti-prescriptive 'spell' (Beebe, 2005, p. xii) or a reluctance to express itself in the language of normative ethics. Among other reasons, this has been traced back to Jung's own suspicion of moral speculation, and his stance as an empiricist, not a philosopher (Jung, 1949, para. 1408). However, in the past decades, an increasing number of contributions in AP has challenged this view of ethics and psychology as a 'kingdom within a kingdom' (Spinoza, 1677, p. 127) or two realms rigidly separated by the is-ought divide.

Considering the proliferation of these works, one may conclude that the spell has been broken. However, I believe that this is not so. There is still a tendency to address important questions (a–c), while simultaneously avoiding the most radical one (d).

(a) *In what sense is Jungian psychology 'ethical'?* – These are works that highlight the ethical dimension of AP (Aziz, 1999; Robinson, 2005; Barreto, 2018), which has now been extensively demonstrated.
(b) *What is Jung's (implicit) moral philosophy?* – These are scholarly reconstructions that rely on a philological approach to the *Collected Works* and rarely make reference to post-Jungian discussion. Here, Jung is treated as a moral philosopher, just as Kant or Nietzsche (Proulx, 1994), with any 'flaw' in his (reconstructed) system of ethics being taken out on him, despite his desire to be kept out of the discussion (Mills, 2018). The most relevant example is Merkur's (2017) monograph.
(c) *What are the ethical implications of Jungian concepts?* – These are articles that do not engage with the *corpus* of AP, but are only interested in the consequences of looking at specific situations or settings (e.g., occupational ethics) from a Jungian perspective: I am thinking, for instance, of the works of J. Fawkes (2010) and C. Rozuel (2016).

(d) *What is the best normative formulation of AP?* – These are theoretical efforts to derive ethical principles from AP and, if necessary, go beyond Jung. To the best of my knowledge, although not the only one available (Beebe, 1992; Madera, 2012), Erich Neumann's *neue Ethik* (1949a) is still the most systematic effort of this kind. Thus, I shall start from a critique of his proposal, before introducing my own.

Critical re-reading of Erich Neumann's *neue Ethik* (1949a)

In a revolutionary 100-page book that cost Neumann his exile from the Zurich circle (Jung and Neumann, 2015), Neumann first suggested that the Judeo-Christian ethics, based on the repression or suppression of evil, is responsible for its outwards projection and for a subsequent scapegoat psychology. Hence, it has to be replaced by a new ethic (NE), drawing upon the Jungian concept of Shadow integration, and encouraging individuals to take full responsibility for their 'dark side': if necessary, by doing evil in full consciousness, instead of living innocently at the expense of their neighbours.

I suggest three 'reforms' that extend NE's guidance into areas that had previously been neglected. In fact, Neumann's project appears to be constrained in an equation (process of individuation = integration of the Shadow = imperative of becoming conscious) that causes it to overlook three complementary aspects of the same removal, connected by a special nexus of consequence: (a) the first half of life, (b) the Anima/Animus projections, and (c) the imperative of confronting the unconscious.

The first half of life

In a footnote, NE is said to be concerned only with 'those people for whom the process of individuation is a necessity – that is to say, mainly with people *in the second half of life*' (Neumann, 1949a, p. 77, my italics). The term 'individuation', in fact, can mean 'generally the becoming of personality, and in particular the process of continuous transformation of an individual' (Pieri, 1998, p. 209), or a certain process of psychological development, occurring to few individuals in the second half of their lives. Neumann's NE is an ethic of individuation in the second sense of the term. A number of problems derive from this first limitation:

1. Neumann's decision to link NE with the individuation process in the second half of life looks like an orthodox application of Jung's theory of the stages of life (1930–1931). However, appearances can be deceptive. One of the most commonly reported reasons to keep young adults away from AP is that their egos are unready to deal with the deep contents of their psyche. But how *deep* exactly does NE require us to go? This question helps us realise how

the psychological work prescribed by NE (the integration of the Shadow), far from being beyond the capacities of young adults, is what Jung's theory actually assigns to them: the so-called 'apprentice piece' of psychological development. This paradox, which has passed unnoticed among Jungians, reminds us of the importance of making distinctions between the levels of confrontation with the unconscious. To gain some insight of one's 'inferiority' does not *uno actu* entail the risk of a psychotic enlargement of consciousness.

2. This leads us to the second question: what is the general relationship between NE and the Western sapiential tradition? Neumann would like to exclude young adults from NE by appealing to a matter of principle: the central position of their egos 'does not *allow*' them to acknowledge the regulative action of the Self (Neumann, 1949b, p. 410, my italics). This claim, however, is problematic because the introspective gesture prescribed by NE lies entirely *within the tradition*, as evidenced by the biblical passage on the brother's eye (Luke, 6:41–42) which Neumann never cites, but synchronistically recurs as a joke in his correspondence with Jung (Jung and Neumann, 2015, p. 296). Neumann's alleged impossibility contradicts the experience of all those who live according to a religious sentiment, whatever their age. As Steiner (1904) argued in his lecture on Goethe's Fairy Tale, it would be intellectually dishonest for modern movements to claim that they have found a substrate common to different pathways to wisdom and, at the same time, to present it as something radically new. The act of welcoming the influence of a transcendent principle into one's life is part of a millenary tradition of spiritual exercises (Madera, 2012). As long as AP does not hesitate to use the 'nearly obsolete word "wisdom"' and declare it the end of life (Ellenberger, 1970, p. 712), then it must also accept that wisdom needs to be prepared, and this is why Epicurus insisted that nobody is too young or too old to be concerned about the health of their souls. Ultimately Jung's distinction between the first and second half of life is a ramification of the classic debate between the active and the contemplative life. However, within this very tradition, one finds views more 'Jungian' than Jung's: for instance, Gregory the Great's understanding of the cyclicity between action and contemplation (Rocca, 2003).

3. If NE is restricted to a few adults midway through their life's journey, already well-adapted to societal expectations and willing to respond to a call out of their control, then one may wonder what happened to the universalistic tone of Neumann's *pamphlet* or its 'trumpet cry' (Jung and Neumann, 2015, p. 237). Ironically, the risk is to transform NE into an elitarian ethic for the 'Tzadikim Nistarim' (the 36 righteous ones in mystical Judaism). Then, its call would appeal to a humanity that has been excluded from the outset, being unworthy of its requirements, thus re-enacting the sadistic logic of the 'old ethic' (Neumann, 1949a).

4. The idea that the old ethic should remain valid as a function of societal conservation and ego strengthening in the first half of life, while the individual

quest for meaning should be postponed to the later stages of development, importantly neglects the *need* for meaning that people experience since their early adulthood, particularly in light of the so-called 'crisis of values'. Neumann himself notices how the modern subject is not characterized anymore by that 'naivety of the fighter' (Neumann, 1949a, p. 28) which would allow him to identify as the defender of the 'good'. Because of nowadays' accentuated acknowledgement of negativity, young people soon lose their trust in those values upon which they should base no less than half of their existence. The diagnosis of psychological unsustainability or ineffectiveness of the old ethic is either systematic, or wrong. Abandoning young people to themselves, or worse, encouraging the narcissistic expansion of their ego will only favour those who have an interest in this loss of balance. As Neumann once recognised, when dealing with 'the human soul's hunger for orientation', an excess of caution only leads 'human beings to go wherever they can to find bread, even if it is of the cheapest kind' (1952, p. 5). The same holds true for an ethic that, being afraid of burdening the youth, condemns them to the bread of nihilism or identification with collective dis-values.

On the other hand, plenty of theoretical supports are available for the *pars construens* of our first 'reform': extending NE to the first half of life.

1. Jacobi (1942, p. 79) beautifully defined the Jungian model of the mind as a 'contrapuntal structure'. This means that, according to AP, the sprout of a principle is always found in its opposite. This idea, famously represented in the Tao, is omnipresent in Jung's thought, except for the distinction between the first and second half of life: here, the relationship is purely sequential, 'a transformation of nature into culture, of instinct into spirit' (Jung, 1925, para. 335). The differences discovered by Jung should not be denied, but only conformed to the principle 'as above, so below'. A contrapuntal theory of the stages of life is warranted.
2. By reading the Jung–Neumann letters, one is surprised to discover that Neumann was the foremost critic of Jung's emphasis on the second half of life, which he considered an improper generalisation of his personal experience, an interference of the religious with the ethical and a curtailment of the possible reach of AP. Neumann was disturbed by the Jungian partiality for the 'third half of life' (Jung and Neumann, 2015, p. 212). For him, even *childhood* is a neglected area of moral development!
3. Several post-Jungians have already called for a revision of Jung's theory in support of a psychology of the *whole of life* (Samuels, 1985; Daniels, 1992). AP cannot confine all that is spiritual, inner, deep, or meaningful to the last stages of development. The experience of individual development speaks against this fragmentation. A continuity exists in the constitution of a moral character.

The Anima/Animus projections

My second criticism is that Neumann's NE neglects to consider any other psychological phenomenon, apart from Shadow projections, that can give rise to paradigmatic situations of practical disorientation along the journey of becoming-oneself. Jung made a similar point when he advised Neumann to clarify that his discussion was confined 'to the ethical aspect of the shadow problem' (Jung and Neumann, 2015, p. 369) and when, as a comment to his claim that 'That are thou' is the great and terrible motto of depth psychology, he added: 'The other leitmotiv of depth psychology is: "That is not thou", e.g. the anima or the Self' (p. 363).

On the other hand, the need to treat the Anima as a peril in its own right is all the more important considering that it is the projection-making factor *par excellence* (Jung, 1951, para. 20). If the Shadow is the apprentice-piece of psychological development, the Anima is its master-piece (Jung, 1934a, para. 61). Ironically, Jung believed that insight into Shadow projections is made easier by the fact that the *old ethic* provides us with some moral education (Jung, 1951, para. 35)!

It is not clear why Neumann based NE solely upon Shadow projections. I advance four hypotheses:

1. That Neumann, due to an ambiguity of the term, did not always make a thorough distinction between the Shadow as a specific instance of the psyche and as 'the other side' of the personality (the unconscious *tout court*). From this point of view, however, it remains unexplained why he would state that the confrontation with the unconscious should *start* with the Shadow (Neumann, 1949a, p. 77), without mentioning the other stages, or why he would use that circumlocution regarding 'Aphrodite's revenge' (p. 106), as if avoiding the term 'Anima projection'.
2. That Neumann conceived the Shadow as 'the personal component of the unconscious' (p. 93), meaning the only unconscious aspect that is subject to integration into consciousness. However, according to Jung (1951, para. 40), the personal contents of Anima and Animus can be made conscious, while their archetypal core cannot.
3. That Neumann, interpreting the moral problem as the problem of *evil*, identified the Shadow as its psychological representative and, consequently, the only morally relevant element in the psyche. This fallacy of circular reasoning is surprisingly common among Jungians. At the Jung–Neumann Letters Conference in Tel Aviv (2015), for instance, the lecture regarding NE was directly titled 'The Problem of Evil'. However, when ethics is equated with the problem of evil, NE ends up being compared only to Jung's 'Answer to Job' and the discussion becomes a theological dispute on the *privatio boni*. Yet ethics is more than that: it is the problem of orientation regarding what to do and what kind of person to be – it is the problem of *meaning*.
4. That Neumann, having neglected the first half of life, neglects the 'problem of the partner' as the 'main theme' of that developmental age (Neumann, 1949b, p. 407).

Unlike the resistance that ethical recognition for the first half of life may still encounter among Jungians, the claim that Anima/Animus projections have important practical consequences is almost a *cliché* (Sanford, 1980). It has also already been argued, in agreement with the moralists of all times, that specific obstacles along the path of character formation need *ad hoc* discussions, noting for instance that insight into one's Shadow or Anima/Animus demand different inner qualities (e.g., moral endurance, as opposed to self-reflection; Von Franz, 1980).

However, I would like to advance an additional hypothesis: that, from an ethical point of view, the difference between the Shadow and the Anima/Animus projections can be conceptualised in terms of the difference in the predominance of one of the two aspects of the numinous – the *tremendum* and the *fascinosum*, respectively. Thus, if I had to express my second 'reform' in a slogan, it would be that Neumann's NE helps us deal with those ego-dystonic cases when the recipient of the projection repels us (is an enemy), but tells us nothing about those ego-syntonic cases when it charms us with the promise of a wholeness that we have lost in our lives!

The 'Night Sea Journey'

My third criticism is that Neumann's NE does not take seriously enough the imperative of confronting the unconscious. The psychology of the Ego–Self axis has already been accused of 'keeping us from being moved by the unknown' (Giegerich, 1975, p. 129) by relying on the idealistic faith that the order of the Self must 'aprioristically end up with a fulfillment of meaning' (Vitolo, 2000, p. 18). However, I claim that the flaw in Neumann's view is not an excess of faith, but a lack of it. NE does not reflect that dialectical thinking (Solomon, 1994) which makes the transcendent function 'not a partial process running a conditioned course' (Jung, 1916a, para. 183), but one that requires 'giving the unconscious credit' (para. 184). The point of misalignment in the upward spiral of development can never be reached without a leap into the void; otherwise 'the unconscious counteraction ... loses its regulating influence' (para. 160).

In the re-evaluation of regression – that apparently involutive moment of development – lies all the difference between Jung and traditional morality (Jung, 1911–1912/1952a, para. 507); but in that lies also a procedural notion of becoming-oneself in general. That is why one does not find the description of stages leading to character formation in NE, but only the contraposition of two human types, with a Nietzschean flavour: the 'average man' (Neumann, 1949a, p. 40) and the enlightened one, who has grounded his roots in the unconscious and is now a 'focus of stillness amid the flux of phenomena' (p. 129). Neumann tries to present NE as the everlasting conquest of an individual who has become conscious of his Shadow. Yet, one does not enter into the unconscious with open eyes, to paraphrase Yourcenaur (1990, p. 295).

This mythologisation of the passage from one human type to the other is based on the same style of *intellectual* thinking (in the Hegelian sense) that afflicts the conceptualisation of the passage from the first to the second half of life: from completely acephalous to completely self-centred. This way of thinking fails to grasp the inter-penetration of opposites, and therefore pictures them as a diptych: here is A, there is ¬A. It is responsible for portraying the 'post-individuation' type as someone who is unable to fall in love again, because he now has 'himself and his emotions and affects in hand' (Jacobi, 1942, p. 140). In all of these cases, a blind eye is turned either to the early achievements or to late difficulties, and ultimately to fact that 'life has always to be tackled anew' (Jung, 1916a, para. 142).

Jung warns us that to have any 'moral force' (Jung, 1921a, para. 194) an ethic must not distance itself too much from the dynamics of the vital process. Since life 'flows from springs both clear and muddy' (Jung, 1921b, para. 415) and it is 'governed by law and yet not governed by law' (Jung, 1917, para. 72), an ethic cannot posit a value and then be uninterested in the process of its attainment. The process of acquiring it, in fact, will necessarily pass through its opposite, a non-value. This is why an ethic of consciousness is neither desirable nor possible, and why, instead of indicating the good, an ethic should delimit *the field of its pursuit*. Individuation not only approaches but also betrays the Self, in service of that 'melting together of sense and nonsense, which produces the supreme meaning' (Jung, 2009, p. 229).

The same lack of dialectical thinking is evident in Neumann's formulation of the ultimate principle of NE:

1. As the imperative of becoming conscious (Neumann, 1949a, p. 113).
2. Or stating that 'whatever leads to wholeness is "good"' (p. 126).

In the first occurrence, the problem is giving priority to the centripetal over the centrifugal moment; in the second, it is formulating a principle that is too abstract to be practically fathomable. In both cases, what is dubious is the quest for a 'Jungian categorical imperative', a single law containing all the duties of the subject of individuation (see also Zoja, 2007). In this way, it is taken for granted that, despite its attention to complexity, AP can hope for a monism of principles at the level of moral theory. On the contrary, Jung thought that no single rule can be 'absolutely valid, for on occasion the opposite may be equally true ... we have to learn *to think in antinomies*' (Jung, 1949, para. 1413, my italics).

Towards an ethic of centroversion

I have chosen to dwell on Neumann's NE because my model arises precisely as its critical re-reading. As each of the 'reforms' outlined suggests, the only way to bring NE closer to its original vocation of being an 'ethic of the whole' is to substitute the source of normativity: from individuation, as a process occurring to few individuals in a certain season of their lives, to the more comprehensive notion of centroversion (Neumann, 1949b). In this way, NE can be turned into a real map of meaning (Madera, 2012), substantiated by the tasks required for psychological development and available for the disoriented individual to consult.

Like Goethe, Jung holds human personality to be the 'the ultimate aim and strongest desire of all mankind' (1934b, para. 284). Therefore, an account of the ethical implications of AP should stem from its theory of psychological development. To this purpose, the notion of centroversion is appealing for two reasons:

1. It is relative to psychological development *as such*, from womb to tomb, thereby re-colonising the general meaning of 'individuation' as the field of the challenges awaiting the individual alongside:
   (a) both halves of life;
   (b) any paradigmatic situation of practical disorientation (e.g., Shadow, Anima/Animus, the Self);
   (c) the centrifugal as well as the centripetal movements of libido (in this sense, the term 'centro-version' is a synecdoche).
2. It is not simply a synonym of psychological development, but a theory-laden concept according to which psychological development occurs through the dynamic interaction of two sub-processes (Stein, 2006):
   (a) integration/*coniuctio* – the synthetic function by which the consciousness establishes a rapport with an unconscious counterpart;
   (b) differentiation/*separatio* – the analytic function by which consciousness frees itself from the rapport with an unconscious counterpart.

To become familiar with this theory of psychological development, which will later be translated into a language of virtues, let us look into one cycle of centroversion.

Everything starts with a certain conscious attitude (C1; Figure 15.1). Because of consciousness' unavoidable tendency to one-sidedness, over time C1 becomes increasingly inadequate to express the whole tendencies in one's psyche. At this

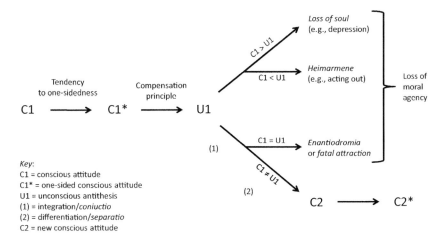

Figure 15.1 A cycle of centroversion

point, in virtue of the compensation principle, consciousness is faced with an unconscious antithesis or counterpart (U1). This happens because centroversion strives to ensure that the ego 'shall become more and more the representative of wholeness' (Neumann, 1949b, p. 298). Jung uses the metaphor of the 'spark' (1917, para. 78): on this golden flare at the end of the rainbow depends the possibility of any further development. However, due to its compensatory nature, U1 also brings out 'the most intimate things' (Jung, 1911–1912/1952b, para. 58). Hence, it is always *'the "wholly other", opposed to what one is'* that proves to be the *'numen from which development ... catches fire'* (Neumann, 1953, p. 63, my italics). This stage has a striking resemblance with Fichte's (1794–1795) notion of *productive imagination*: the ego is now opposed to a non-ego.

Following this event, there are two possibilities.

1. That consciousness resists U1 and starts 'arm-wrestling' with it. In this case, according to Jung's theory of psychodynamics, two scenarios open up.
   (a) C1 happens to be stronger than U1 and manages to keep it out of life. However, this occurs at the risk of a diminished energetic collaboration of the unconscious, which in turn may result in a 'loss of soul' (e.g., depressive symptomatology).
   (b) U1 happens to be stronger than C1 and imposes itself as a sheer psychodynamic force, which may result in unwanted, irruptive (e.g., acting out, parapraxis), or intrusive (e.g., obsessive-compulsive) symptoms. The Stoics called this *heimarmene*: either the dog follows the cart to which it is tied or it will be dragged.
2. The other possibility, following the epiphany of U1, is that consciousness embraces it. This is the moment of integration or *coniuctio*. Even in this case, two scenarios lie ahead.
   (a) C1 simply loses itself in U1. This is the case of *enantiodromia* (the conversion of a fanatism into its opposite) or other immediate, un-reflexive acceptances of U1. The likelihood of this option is increased by the fact that 'all unconscious contents', being charged with energy, have a tendency 'to assert themselves' as the centre (Neumann, 1949b, p. 298).
   (b) C1 actively recognises and welcomes U1, but only to find the right distance from it. This is the moment of differentiation or *separatio*, which operates a synthesis between U1 and its original plans, giving rise to a new attitude towards life (C2). Of course, C2 will eventually fall into one-sidedness and the cycle will repeat itself.

This theory of psychological development is valuable because, through the same 'narrow door' (Luke, 13:24), one attains the soul as both the end and the means to any end. In fact:

1. on the sub-processes of integration and differentiation, favouring the transcendent function, depends the development of one's personality, which is a value in itself (Jung, 1934b, para. 284).

2. but only by avoiding a series of 'bumps in the road' (loss of soul, heimarmene, etc.) does consciousness preserve that autonomy or *moral agency* which is needed to pursue any other moral good.

Finally, it is important to note how, in order to flow from C1 to C2, consciousness needs to adopt an overall *indeterminate* attitude. Let us imagine, in fact, that this cycle of centroversion is repeated an 'n' number of times, until the now ruling consciousness (Cn) has become so aware of its relativity that it has made a rule out of the need to be neither too anxious to be right, nor too ready to give away its own truth. In this asymptotic projection, consciousness will have acquired what psychoanalysts and poets interchangeably call 'negative capability' (Keats, 1817), 'evenly-suspended attention' (Freud, 1912), 'waiting without hope' (Eliot, 1943), 'being without memory or desire' (Bion, 1965) or 'building on sand as if it were stone' (Borges, 1974). The lesson is one and the same: a certain fluidity is necessary to cross the ever-moving boundaries of the soul (Heraclitus, B45 DK) because an indeterminate landscape requires an indeterminate subjectivity (Stein, 2006).

Analytical psychology as a virtue ethic

Having identified the ethical relevance of this theory of psychological development, the last step is to translate it into a language that is allusive to one of the three main approaches of contemporary normative ethics: consequentialism, deontologism, or virtue ethics (Slote, 1997).

Why Jung could never be a utilitarian is made clear in his defence of individuality against the 'statistical world-picture' (Jung, 1957, para. 499). The relationship between Jung and deontologism, on the other hand, is more complex (Zoja, 2007; Colacicchi, 2015). I see two reasons why Jung could never be a Kantian either: the first is my argument that a monism of principles is incompatible with his antinomical thinking; the second is that the categorical imperative is incompatible also with that part of 'recklessness' which is coessential to the leap into the void described above. At the price of trivialising Kant, undertaking only actions that can be universalised is the best way *not* to individuate oneself. Yet, risks cannot be taken on behalf of all humanity.

Instead, it seems that AP can be better understood as 'something like antique philosophy' (Barreto, 2007). Among the numerous analogies between AP and virtue ethics, the most important is certainly the idea that the moral life does not derive from some exoteric use of Reason, but from the difficult adjustment to the rules of human life itself (MacIntyre, 1999). As Jung states, there can be 'no higher moral principle than harmony with natural laws that guide the libido in the direction of life's *optimum*' (1921b, para. 356).

The integration between AP and virtue ethics could be a fulfilling occasion for both. On the one hand, AP could turn out to be that 'philosophy of psychology' which Anscombe (1958) was looking for: an account of what it takes for a human life to flourish. This is especially true if contemporary virtue ethicists are 'to do more than simply brush off and polish up ancient Aristotclianism' (Slote, 1997, p. 183). Let us take, for instance, Larmore's (1999) argument that, as modern subjects, we cannot accept anymore the idea that a well-lived life is the one carried forward according to a rational plan, and that we need instead a view that is able to account for 'the revelation that discloses new vistas of meaning ... which we least suspected' (p. 98). According to Larmore, neglected by classic moral philosophy is the fact that 'the good that we pursue ... is bound to *fall short* of the good that life has yet to reveal', and he goes as far as to say that one could '*welcome*' this 'unexpected good' that challenges 'our existing projects' (p. 111, my italics). Needless to say, what Larmore is describing in a philosophical language is the integration of the unconscious: making room for U1, intercepting the new direction of life.

On the other hand, AP may learn from virtue ethics by 'coming out of the closet' with regards to the normative that is at stake behind its use of a descriptive terminology that has been inherited from the natural sciences. In conclusion, I propose to adopt an aretaic language to refer to the two identified sub-processes that favour the transcendent function, in order to highlight their implicitly prescriptive use. The way they are commonly used by Jungians, integration and differentiation *already* respond to the classic definition of virtue as the disposition that, displayed by consciousness over time, can set the conditions for optimal development.

I thus introduce the virtues of vulnerability and incorruptibility as the normative equivalents of the naturalistic mechanisms of integration and differentiation, respectively.

1. Vulnerability translates the imperative of confronting the unconscious. It is the virtue needed by consciousness to open itself to the unknown coming from the unconscious in the form of a living symbol. *Vulnera* are the wounds of the psyche, from where the rejuvination begins. Jung (1911–1912/1952a, para. 553) uses the biblical image of new wine that needs to be poured into new wineskins. The concept of vulnerability bears a resemblance to the psychoanalytic concept of 'regression in the service of the ego' (Kris, 1952) and, with a Nietzschean terminology, it can be phrased also as a willingness to 'say yes' to U1. On the other hand, it should not be confused with today's ideological praise of vulnerability as fragility, unmanliness, and lack of shame for one's psychological 'inferiority'. In mythical terms, it corresponds to the principle of Eros, as opposed to Logos. The virtue is well represented by the story of Achilles: it does not matter how deep the subject is dipped in the waters of incorruptibility, there will always be a point from which he is held, and that will be his *vulnus*.
2. Incorruptibility translates the imperative of becoming conscious. It is the virtue needed by consciousness not to be seduced by the part, but to keep itself pointed to the whole. Incorruptibility means sacrificing any one-sidedness on the altar of the Self or waking up from the bridal bed of the *coniuctio*. It results in an equidistance from all the complexes that strive to centre the

psyche upon themselves. In alchemical terms, it is the virtue of gold and corresponds to the process of *coagulare*, as opposed to *solvere*. In mythical terms, it is exercised by refusing promises of immortality or omniscience. The concept refers to the fact that totality is not 'for sale', and has less to do with the survival of the flesh, although symbols of incorruptibility in this latter sense (e.g., the peacock) convey the otherworldliness that the concept implies. Incorruptibility can also be phrased as a 'loyalty to oneself' (Jung, 1916b, para. 498). It is a form of un-availability and it is well represented by the story of Saint Paraskevi of Rome, the virgin who refused to marry an emperor.

To adopt this *paradoxical* couple of virtues (Guggenbühl-Craig, 1995), instead of a monolithic 'Jungian categorical imperative', is a way of meeting Jung's invitation to think in antinomies. But it is also a way of finding a common ground between AP and those contemporary virtue ethicists who, with a not-so-distant mindset, claim that virtue is independence and 'acknowledged dependence' (MacIntyre, 1999). If there is no higher principle than following the *optimum* of life, and yet the *optimum* of life in turn follows 'the tidal laws of the libido, by which systole alternates with diastole', then it follows that the oscillations generating the whole become the actual 'individual life tasks' (Jung, 1921b, para. 356). At the level of moral theory, this is reflected in the fact that neither of our virtues is ever absolutely valid: not because 'on occasion' the opposite may become true (Jung, 1949, para. 1413), but because it does so *regularly*, in every cycle of centroversion.

In order to better understand these virtues, I will now use a method that is specific to virtue ethics and not new to Jungians (Hillman, 1996): not only defining things conceptually, but also pointing at concrete, virtuous, or vicious individuals.

Moral Cases

The Hobbit or the vice of in-vulnerability

I exemplify the need for vulnerability with the novel *The Hobbit* (Tolkien, 1937). Bilbo Baggins, a respected member of the Hill, lives a cosy life of simple pleasures. One morning, the wizard Gandalf comes to visit and invites him on an adventure. Bilbo politely refuses, but Gandalf leaves an invisible mark on his door, so that the following day a group of dwarves arrives and occupies Bilbo's house, eating and drinking at his expense. Later, Bilbo learns that this is the fellowship for Gandalf's expedition. At first, he refuses again; then, his pride is wounded and he decides to join.

Several aspects of this story can be interpreted according to our model:

1. The Bagginses are respected in the Hill because they never do 'anything unexpected' (Tolkien, 1937, p. 3). However, Bilbo's mother was a Took, and

it is said of the Tooks that there is 'something not entirely hobbitlike about them' (p. 4), since one of them would occasionally go off on an adventure. In Bilbo's split ancestry, one recognises the split nature of consciousness. On the one hand, all consciousness wants is to be in a safe and quiet hobbit-hole; yet, on the other, every 'consciousness ... perhaps without being aware of it, seeks its unconscious opposite' (Jung, 1917 para. 78).

2. This 'something a bit queer' (Tolkien, 1937, p. 5) that Bilbo inherited from the Took side does not emerge until he is 50 years old, living in the house built by his father. Of course, this passage could be read in support of Jung's theory of the stages of life, the house representing the place in society. However, from the perspective of the Ego–Self psychology, it is exactly when the ego has 'apparently settled down immovably' (p. 5) that a tendency towards centroversion arises to shake it from its comfortable position.

3. The title of the chapter is 'An Unexpected Party' and Bilbo is described as 'un-suspecting' (p. 5); however, thanks to the magical sign on the door, the dwarves arrive as if they 'had been expected' (p. 8). This interesting interplay can be explained by the fact that what is sudden for the ego is scheduled for the Self. From a wider perspective, Bilbo's very withdrawal from life (from anything unexpected) is a call for the Self to intervene; or, in Lacanian terms, it is his bourgeois hobbit-hole that sought to be filled up with fairy elements.

4. How does Bilbo react to the disturbing guests? He is awkwardly polite: he apologises, offers them food, and tries to look as if the occasion is perfectly ordinary. Here one finds the usual ego response to the visits of the unconscious: insistently reacting as one is accustomed is the definition of one-sidedness. C1* tries to deny the challenge or accommodate it in its living-room (the current attitude). It answers to the new in the old way, and, in this way, makes itself ridiculous.

5. Having eaten their fill, the dwarves start singing a song listing all the dreadful things that they plan to do to the house. Why? Because 'that's what Bilbo Baggins hates!' (p. 13). Now, in virtue of the compensation principle, we know that U1 overturns C1 in a mirrored way, doing exactly 'what the ego hates'. However, interestingly, while the visitors threaten to mess up Bilbo's home, they are actually putting things in order. The unconscious never simply turns the plans of the ego upside-down, rather it adjusts them with a view to a synthesis: it does not want us to betray our vision, but to become better rulers of the whole that we already are.

Damage or the vice of corruptibility

I exemplify the need for incorruptibility with the novel *Damage* (Hart, 1991), already a focus of ethical and psychoanalytic interest (Mellard, 1998). Stephen Fleming is a successful politician, completely absorbed by his social role and responsibilities: in Jung's view, the typical victim of Anima. All the capriciousness Fleming had banished from his life returns in the form of a violent projection in the moment he meets the perfect projective hook: Anna Barton, his son's new fiancée.

As the title suggests, the parabola of their affair shows the bitter consequences of this failed developmental opportunity, including the death of Stephen's own son and, more generally, the loss of his life as he knew it. Instead of reflecting upon and actively changing the premises of his existence, Stephen falls prey to U1; he performs the *coniuctio*, but is never able to emerge from it. For him, there is no difference between the object and the numinous quality with which it appears: being far from Anna feels like being far from himself. This lack of distance is well captured by the poster for the film adaptation (Damage, 1991), with the two lovers fused into one and in the act of blinding each other. As von Franz (1980, p. 142) so adroitly expresses, 'Whoever cannot surrender to this experience has never lived' (vulnerability), but 'whoever founders in it has understood nothing' (incorruptibility).

Odysseus or the subject of centroversion

The stories of Bilbo and Fleming seem to suggest that one is either too incorruptible or too vulnerable. Can an optimal balance between these virtues be found? The figure of Odysseus (Homer's *Odyssey*, ca. 8th century BCE) which has been repeatedly interpreted as a personification of the Western subjectivity (e.g., Horkheimer and Adorno, 1944) partly answers the question.

Never completely avoidant nor completely yielding with the figures that he encounters on his journey home, Odysseus' adventures strike the imagination as a series of successful cycles of centroversion. The hero stays no less than seven years with Calypso (vulnerability); yet, when the day comes, he moves on and refuses her offer of immortality (incorruptibility). This two-fold heroic attitude is most evident in the adventure with the Sirens. Unlike his companions, Odysseus is able to indulge in the experience, but also to remain mindful of his destination. The episode tells us two important things about the virtues of vulnerability and incorruptibility:

1. That incorruptibility actually consists of two aspects:
    (a) the ability, after *coniuctio*, to separate oneself from the object;
    (b) but also a 'prophylactic' aspect of incorruptibility, definable as a certain psychological mindedness or lack of naiveté, that the subject acquires from the previous figure of centroversion and applies to the next. Odysseus was able to outgrow the Sirens because he had received instructions from Circe; similarly, he was able to outgrow Circe because he had received an antidote from Hermes (if he hadn't, he would have been turned into a pig). This second aspect of incorruptibility makes the former (1a) more or less likely to happen depending on whether the subject has attached himself too much to the object in the first place or, conversely, has 'become conscious of the meaning of the situation' (Sanford, 1980, p. 32).

2. The second lesson is that the paradoxical nature of vulnerability and incorruptibility should never be underestimated. In fact, at first glance, the story of Odysseus seems to represent the optimal balance between giving in and staying safe; but here, too, appearances can be deceptive. The truth is that not even the myth could represent the coexistence of the two virtues *within the mind of the hero*. It is not the case that Odysseus is, simultaneously, inside and outside of the experience, confronting yet free from the unconscious. In that moment, he is only at the peak of vulnerability, begging his companions to be untied! By condensing into one image what typically is carried out in a dynamic, two-stage sequence, the myth had to use an external, 'non-psychological' expedient (the mast) to symbolise the second necessary virtue (incorruptibility). One can see here the same style of *intellectual* thinking that we have encountered before. The imagination struggles to convey in a sensible form the conceptual inter-dependence between recalcitrant opposites, and therefore resorts to picturing them as a diptych: here, the ravaged mind; there, the immovable mast.

In the end, the question remains: if vulnerability and incorruptibility are comparable to antagonist systems, the maximum of one virtue corresponding to the vice of the other, how should we imagine the subjectivity that manages to attain both? The answer comes from a 100-page book that was calling for a new ethic decades before Neumann:

> We do not plug up our ears with wax ... We do not bind ourselves ... to the mast ... nor by hearing and by embracing the Sirens do we abandon our ship, and perish. On the contrary, we seize the Sirens and pitch them into our boat so that even they may voyage with us; and we continue on our way.
> (Kazantzakis, 1927)

Conclusion

In the first section of this chapter, Neumann's NE (1949a) was 'reformed', extending its power of guidance to (a) the first half of life, (b) the Anima/Animus projections, and (c) the imperative of confronting the unconscious. This was achieved by putting the concept of centroversion at the source of normativity, moving NE away from its problematic definition as an ethic of individuation and closer to its original vocation of being an *ethic of the whole*.

To stay with the metaphor of the 'map of meaning' (Madera, 2012), it is important to understand that an ethic of centroversion is not only valuable for those who, like Goethe and Jung (1934b, para. 284), believe that the development of one's personality is an end in itself; it is valuable, more generally, for all those who recognise that morality and psychology are not a 'kingdom within a kingdom' (Spinoza, 1677, p. 127), and therefore admit that the pursuit of any moral good will be limited and determined by psychological laws and accidents. This is precisely what the notion of centroversion contains: a model of the 'vicissitudes' that mental contents are subject to, some of which include a dangerous loss of moral agency (Fig. 15.1).

The aim of the second section of the chapter was to illustrate that the only way to avoid this series of paradigmatic risks, associated with the trajectory of any conscious attitude, is to positively recognise the importance of the two sub-processes favouring the transcendent function: integration/*coniuctio* and differentiation/*separatio* (Stein, 2006). Since Jungians already make prescriptive usage of these two concepts, yet refrain from adopting an explicitly ethical terminology to refer to them (Beebe, 2005), the next step towards an ethic of centroversion was to translate this descriptive model of centroversion into a normative one.

Having questioned that AP's ethical reach could fit well into a utilitarian or a Kantian approach, the 'third method' of contemporary normative ethics was adopted – i.e., neo-Aristotelian virtue ethics. However, since I adopted Jung's invitation to 'think in antinomies' as the guiding principle of my formulation, not only the prospect of a 'Jungian categorical imperative' (Zoja, 2007) was abandoned, but also that of a monistic, overarching virtue (Beebe, 1992). In the end, the individual life tasks that serve the *optimum* of life were identified in two paradoxical virtues: *vulnerability* translates the task of reaching out to the compensatory antithesis that arises from the unconscious; *incorruptibility* translates the duty of understanding its meaning and putting it into perspective.

In the third section of the paper a gallery of concrete albeit fictitious moral characters were examined to look more closely into the complexity of these virtues. First, Bilbo Baggins and Stephen Fleming were used to reflect upon the correlative vices of 'in-vulnerability' and 'corruptibility', respectively. Then, faced with the problem of a *subject of centroversion* that could personify an optimal balance between the two virtues, the figure of Odysseus was examined. Yet, it was concluded that even the scene of his most famous 'askesis' achieved but an apparent synthesis.

Postscript

A great scholar once wrote:

> The psychologist who was preconized by Jung has not yet arisen, so aware of the relativistic limit imposed by his own typological perspective to begin his theoretical discourse by establishing – as a necessary premise – a connection between his own psychological type and his empirical or theoretical research.
> (Trevi, 1988, p. 14)

Neumann's NE first appeared to him in a dream (Jung and Neumann, 2015, pp. 324–325, 331). *Si parva licet componere magnis*, the model presented here clearly depends on the author being someone in the 'first half of his life' for whom the relationship with Anima has been a problem of the greatest importance. Do these connections diminish the validity of a theory? Or do they position it in its origin, from where it can still reach out to those who have gone through similar experiences?

References

Anscombe, G. E. M. (1958). 'Modern moral philosophy'. *Philosophy*, 33 (124), 1–19.
Aziz, R. (1999). 'Synchronicity and the transformation of the ethical in Jungian psychology'. In C. Becker (ed.), *Asian and Jungian views of ethics*. Westport, CT: Greenwood Press, pp. 65–83.
Barreto, M. H. (2007). '"It is something like antique philosophy": analytical psychology and philosophical practical wisdom'. *Spring*, 77 (*Philosophy and Psychology*), 79–98.
Barreto, M. H. (2018). 'The ethical dimension of analytical psychology'. *Journal of Analytical Psychology*, 63 (2), 241–254.
Beebe, J. (1992). *Integrity in depth*. College Station, TX: Texas A&M University Press.
Beebe, J. (2005). 'Foreword'. In D. Robinson (ed.), *Conscience and Jung's moral vision: from Id to Thou*. New York, NY: Paulist Press, pp. xi–xiii.
Bible. *The revised English Bible*. (1989 edn). Oxford/Cambridge: Oxford University Press.
Bion, W. R. (1965). 'Memory and desire'. In C. Mawson and F. Bion (eds.), *The complete works of W. R. Bion*, vol. 6. London: Karnac Books, pp. 1–19.
Borges, J. L. (1974). 'Fragments from an "Apocryphal Gospel"'. In N. T. Di Giovanni (trans.), *In praise of darkness*. New York, NY: Dutton.
Colacicchi, G. (2015). *Jung and ethics: a conceptual exploration* (unpublished doctoral dissertation), University of Essex, Colchester, UK.
Damage. (1992). [Motion picture] Directed by Louis Malle. Paris, France: StudioCanal.
Daniels, M. (1992). *Self-discovery the Jungian way: the watchword technique*. London/ New York, NY: Routledge.
Eliot, T. S. (1943). 'East Cocker' (pt. 3). In *Four quartets*. New York, NY: Harcourt, Brace and Company, p. 15.
Ellenberger, H. (1970). *The discovery of the unconscious: the history and evolution of dynamic psychiatry*. New York, NY: Basic Books.
Fawkes, J. (2010). 'The shadow of excellence: a Jungian approach to public relations ethics'. *Review of Communication*, 10 (3), 211–227.
Fichte, J. G. (1794–1795). 'Foundations of the entire science of knowledge'. In P. Heath and J. Lachs (trans. and ed.), *The science of knowledge*. Cambridge: Cambridge University Press, 1982, pp. 89–286.
Freud, S. (1912). 'Recommendations to physicians practising psychoanalysis'. In J. Strachey (trans. and ed.), *The standard edition of the complete psychological works of Sigmund Freud*, vol. 12. London: Hogarth Press, 1958, pp. 109–120.
Giegerich, W. (1975). 'Ontogeny = phylogeny? A fundamental critique of Erich Neumann's analytical psychology'. In G. Mogenson (ed.), *The neurosis of psychology: primary papers towards a critical psychology*. New Orleans, LA: Spring Journal Books, pp. 19–39.
Guggenbuhl-Craig, A. (1995). *From the wrong side: a paradoxical approach to psychology*. Woodstock, CT: Spring Publications.

Hart, J. (1991). *Damage*. London: Arrow Books.
Hillman, J. (1996). *The soul's code: in search of character and calling*. New York, NY: Random House.
Homer (8th century BCE). *The Odyssey*. Lucas Collins (trans.). Philadelphia, PA: J.B. Lippencott, 1875.
Horkheimer, M., and Adorno, T. W. (1944). *Dialectic of enlightenment*. Amsterdam: Querido, 1947.
Jacobi, J. (1942). *The psychology of C. G. Jung: an introduction with illustrations*. London: Routledge and Kegan Paul, 1951.
Jung, C. G. (1911–1912/1952a). 'The dual mother'. In *Collected works*, vol. 5, *Symbols of transformation* (2nd edn.). London: Routledge and Kegan Paul, 1967.
Jung, C. G. (1911–1912/1952b). 'The hymn of creation'. In *Collected works*, vol. 5, *Symbols of transformation* (2nd edn.). London: Routledge and Kegan Paul, 1967.
Jung, C. G. (1916a). 'The transcendent function'. In *Collected works*, vol. 8, *The structure and dynamics of the psyche* (2nd edn.). London: Routledge and Kegan Paul, 1969.
Jung, C. G. (1916b). 'The structure of the unconscious'. In *Collected works*, vol. 7, *Two Essays on Analytical Psychology* (2nd edn.). London: Routledge and Kegan Paul, 1966.
Jung, C. G. (1917). 'On the psychology of the unconscious'. In *Collected works*, vol. 7, *Two essays in analytical psychology* (2nd edn.). London: Routledge and Kegan Paul, 1966.
Jung, C. G. (1921a). 'Shiller's ideas on the type problem'. In *Collected works*, vol. 6, *Psychological types* (2nd edn.). London: Routledge and Kegan Paul, 1971.
Jung, C. G. (1921b). 'The type problem in poetry'. In *Collected works*, vol. 6, *Psychological types* (2nd edn.). London: Routledge and Kegan Paul, 1971.
Jung, C. G. (1925). 'Marriage as a psychological relationship'. In *Collected works*, vol. 17, *The development of personality* (2nd edn.). London: Routledge and Kegan Paul, 1954.
Jung, C. G. (1930–1931). 'The stages of life'. In *Collected works*, vol. 8 *The structure and dynamics of the psyche* (2nd edn.). London: Routledge and Kegan Paul, 1969.
Jung, C. G. (1934a). 'Archetypes of the collective unconscious'. In *Collective works*, vol. 9i, *The archetypes and the collective unconscious* (2nd edn.). London: Routledge and Kegan Paul, 1968.
Jung, C. G. (1934b). 'The development of personality'. In *Collected works*, vol. 17, *The development of personality* (2nd edn.). London: Routledge and Kegan Paul, 1954.
Jung, C. G. (1949). 'Foreword to Neumann: depth psychology and a New Ethic'. In *Collected Works*, vol. 18, *The symbolic life* (2nd edn.). London: Routledge and Kegan Paul, 1977.
Jung, C. G. (1951). 'The syzygy: anima and animus'. In *Collected works*, vol. 9ii, *Aion: researches into the phenomenology of the self* (2nd edn.). London: Routledge and Kegan Paul, 1959.
Jung, C. G. (1957). 'The undiscovered self (present and future)'. In *Collected works*, vol. 10, *Civilization in transition* (2nd edn.). London: Routledge and Kegan Paul, 1970.
Jung, C. G. (2009). *The red book: Liber Novus*. S. Shamdasani (ed.). M. Kyburz, J. Peck, and S. Shamdasani (trans.). New York, NY/London: W. W. Norton.
Jung, C. G., and Neumann, E. (2015). *Analytical psychology in exile: the correspondence of C. G. Jung and Erich Neumann*. M. Liebscher (ed. and intr.). H. McCartney (trans.). Princeton, NJ: Princeton University Press.
Kazantzakis, N. (1927). *The saviors of God: spiritual exercises*. Kimon Friar (trans.). New York, NY: Simon and Schuster, 1960, pp. 117–118.

Keats, J. (1817). 'Letter to George and Thomas Keats (22 December)'. In H. E. Scudde (ed.), *The complete poetical works and letters of John Keats*. Boston, MA: Houghton, Mifflin and Company, 1899.
Kris, E. (1952). *Psychoanalytic explorations in art*. New York, NY: International Universities Press.
Larmore, C. (1999). 'The idea of a life plan'. In J. Paul, F. Miller and E. Paul (eds.), *Human flourishing: Volume 16*. New York, NY: Cambridge University Press, pp. 96–112.
MacIntyre, A. (1999). *Dependent rational animals: why human beings need the virtues*. Chicago, IL: Open Court.
Madera, R. (2012). *La carta del senso: psicologia del profondo e vita filosofica*. Milan: Raffaello Cortina.
Mellard, J. M. (1998). 'Lacan and the new Lacanians: Josephine Hart's Damage, Lacanian tragedy, and the ethics of jouissance'. *Modern Language Association of America*, 113 (3), 395–407.
Merkur, D. (2017). *Jung's ethics: moral psychology and his cure of souls*. J. Mills (ed.), New York, NY: Routledge.
Mills, J. (2018). 'Critiquing Jung's ethics'. *International Journal of Jungian Studies*, 10 (2), 135–142.
Neumann, E. (1949a). *Depth psychology and a new ethic*. Boston, MA/London: Shambala Publications, 1990.
Neumann, E. (1949b). *The origins and history of consciousness*. Princeton, NJ: Princeton University Press, 1954.
Neumann, E. (1952). 'The psyche and the transformation of the reality planes: a metapsychological essay'. In H. Nagel, E. Rolfe, J. Van Heurck, and K. Winston (trans.), *The essays of Erich Neumann, Volume 3, The place of creation*. Princeton, NJ: Princeton University Press, 1989, pp. 3–62.
Neumann, E. (1953). 'The psychological stages of woman's development'. In B. Matthews, E. Doughty, E. Rolfe, and M. Cullingworth (trans.), *The essays of Erich Neumann, Volume 4, The fear of the feminine and other essays on feminine psychology*. Princeton, NJ: Princeton University Press, 1994, pp. 3–63.
Pieri, P. (1998). *Dizionario Junghiano*. Torino: Bollati Boringhieri.
Proulx, C. (1994). 'On Jung's theory of ethics'. *Journal of Analytical Psychology*, 39 (1), 101–119.
Robinson, D. (2005). *Conscience and Jung's moral vision: from Id to Thou*. New York, NY: Paulist Press.
Rocca, G. (2003). 'Vita attiva – mista – contemplativa'. In G. Rocca and G. Pelliccia (eds.), *Dizionario degli istituti di perfezione*, Vol. 10. Milano: Paoline, pp. 204–270.
Rozuel, C. (2016). 'Jung's insights on ethics in business and work organisations: examining the "moral nature of present-day man"'. *International Journal of Jungian Studies*, 8 (3), 141–158.
Samuels, A. (1985). *Jung and the post-Jungians*. London: Routledge.
Sanford, J. (1980). *The invisible partners: how the male and female in each of us affects our relationships*. New York, NY: Paulist Press.
Slote, M. (1997). 'Virtue ethics'. In M. Baron, P. Pettit and M. Slote (eds.), *Three methods of ethics: a debate*. Malden, MA: Blackwell, pp. 175–238.
Solomon, H. (1994). 'The transcendent function and Hegel's dialectical vision'. *Journal of Analytical Psychology*, 39 (1), 77–100.
Spinoza, B. (1677). *Ethics*. New York: Simon and Schuster, 1970.

Stein, M. (2006). *The principle of individuation: toward the development of human consciousness*. Wilmette, IL: Chiron publications.

Steiner, R. (1904, April 4). *The story of the green serpent and the beautiful lily* [Lecture given at Berlin on Goethe's Fairy Tale]. Rudolf Steiner Archive & e.Lib (number: S-0814).

Tolkien, J. R. R. (1937). *The Hobbit, or there and back again*. London: Harper Collins, 1996.

Trevi, M. (1988). *L'altra lettura di Jung*. Milano: Raffaello Cortina.

Vitolo, A. (2000). 'Introduction'. In Neumann, E. Il (ed.), *Il Sé, l'individuo, la realtà*. Milano: La Biblioteca di Vivarium, pp. 9–22.

Von Franz, M.-L. (1980). *Projection and recollection in Jungian psychology: reflections of the soul*. La Salle/London: Open Court.

Yourcenar, M. (1990). *Memoirs of Hadrian*. New York, NY: Noonday Press.

Zoja, L. (2007). *Ethics and analysis: philosophical perspectives and their application in therapy*. College Station, TX: Texas A&M University Press.

Index

AAD (Adversity-Activated Development) 32
abaissement du niveau mental 11
acculturation stress 33
adult third culture kid (ATCK) 33
Adversity-Activated Development (AAD) 32
Agamben, G. 39, 216
agency, identity 6
aggregation xxii
Ahn, P. 148
Aion 163
Aion, Researchers into the Phenomenology of the Self (Jung) 163–4
Akhtar, S. 64, 70, 158
Akinari, U. 162
Alarcón, N. 55
Alschuler, L. 53
AmkA (Office for Multicultural Affairs), Frankfurt am Main 82–3
Ammann, R. 100, 104
analytical psychology 211, 240; first half of life 241–3; identity 6–8, 11; virtue ethic 249–51
analytical work with children 98–9
ancestral spirits, *When Marnie Was There* (Robinson) 152–4
androgyny 98, 110
Anima 6–8, 178; male same-sex desire 138–9; Neumann, E. 244–5
anomalous, liminal stage xxii
anomie 234
Anscombe, G. E. M. 249
Anti-discrimination Office, Frankfurt am Main 83
anxiety 234
Anzaldua, G. 59
Anzieu, D. 8; bodies 10–11
Aphrodite 115, 117, 163

Apollo and Daphne (Bernini) 114, 116
appropriative identifications 140
Arán, M. 96
archeomythology 13
areas, European identity 16
Arendt, H. 30, 192; community 201; worldliness 39–40
ASD (autistic spectrum disorder) 211–14, 216–17
asignifying rupture 37
Asperger, H. 213
assimilation: Frankfurt am Main 82; Mexican-Americans 48–9
asylum seekers 19, 21–2, 31
ATCK (adult third culture kid) 33
Authentic Movement 198–9
autistic spectrum disorder (ASD) 211–14, 216–17
autistic spectrum syndrome 213
autobiographical self 4–5
average expectable environment 70
Aztlan 51–2

Bakebake-gakkô (1874) 170
barefoot, *Heart of Darkness* (Conrad) 184
Bartleby, the Scrivener (Melville, 1853) 215–16
Bartlett, N. 131
Bartlett, R. 14, 129
Basil-Morozow, H. 114
Bauman, Z. 28, 35; liquidity 225–6; philosophies compared to Jung 226–9
beauty 120
Beck, U.: individuation 223–4; philosophies compared to Jung 226–9
Beckett, S. 229
Beck-Gernsheim, E. 223–4
Beebe, J. 72, 138

bel composto 113, 120
belonging 201–2
Benjamin, J. 30
Berkeley, G. 235
Bernini, G. L. 108; Pont Sant' Angelo 118–21; *Salvator Mundi* 121–2; transcendental hermaphrodite 113–18; *When the Saint Teresa in Ecstacy* 119–21
Bernstein, R. J. 192
Bersani, Leo 140
betwixt and between xxii, 183
Bick, E. 8, 10
biographies 223–4
bodies, identity 10–12
Bolland, A. 116
Bollas, C. 136
border psychology xxiv
borders: *Heart of Darkness* (Conrad) 183–6; identity 10–12
Braidotti, R. 29
British psyche 65
Brodersen, E. 20
Brogan, C. 130–1
broken individualisation 221, 227
Bromberg, P. M. 5
Brooke, R. 121
Buddhism 217–18
Buriel, R. 49
Burke, E. 4, 14
Burke, P. J., self 5
Byington, C. A. B. 98

Calvino, I. 225
Campbell, J. 157–8
carp, 'Dream Carp' 170–3
case studies, European identity 12–22
Casement, A. 222
Cashford, J. 71
categorical fetishism 31
CBT (Cognitive Behaviour Therapy) 210–11
celebrations, Japan 167
centroversion 246–9, 253–4
charis (grace) 121
Chavez, C. 49
Chicanos 49
child development 98–9
children: analytical work with 98–9; gender identity issues (Sandplay therapy) 101–5; interventions 97; Sandplay therapy 99–101; symptoms of gender issues 96

Chodorow, J. 204
Chopin, T. 14
Christ, coincidentia oppositorum 122
Christianity, fish 163–4
Ciprut, J. V. xxi
citizenship of Frankfurt 80
Coelho, M. T. A. 96
cogito 6
cognitive ego 10
cognitive fluidity xxiii
Cognitve Behaviour Therapy (CBT) 210–11
coincidentia 112, 119, 121
coincidentia oppositorum 115, 122
collective cultural trauma 68–9
Colling, L. 95
Colman, W. 20
coming out, male same-sex desire 131–2
communality, male same-sex desire 139–41
coniunctio 116–18
coniunctio oppositorum 109
conjunction of opposites 51
Conrad, J., nekyia 176–7
consciousness 248–9
contact zones, between the ego and the other (European identity) 18–19
contingency 216
contrasting words, *Heart of Darkness* (Conrad) 179–80
coordination unit for LGBTIQ topics, Frankfurt am Main 83–5
coping with indeterminate state 217–18
core self 4
Cortez, H. 50–1, 56
cosmopolitan virtue 30, 40
creative regression 100
Critical Theory xix–xx
cultural complex of an unheroic heroine, European identity 17–22
cultural complexes 47, 64–5; Mexican-Americans 50–6; need to belong 201–2
Cultural Sensitivity in Psychosocial Services, AmkA (Office for Multicultural Affairs) 83
cultural unconscious 64

Damage (Hart), incorruptibility 252–3
Damasio, A. 4
dance therapy, Authentic Movement 198–9
darkness, *Heart of Darkness* (Conrad) 179–81
Dawson, C. 13

de Alba, A. G. 51–2
de Beauvoir, S. 229
default mode network (DMN) 211–12
Deleuze, G. 29, 36
Deleuzian philosophy 29–30
depression 234
desire, same-sex desire (male) 127–30
detachment 218
determinate state 209–10; shifting to indeterminate 212
determinism 210
de-territorialization 37
discrimination, Mexican-Americans 57–8
DMN (default mode network) 211–12
Doña Marina 50–1, 53–6
Doniger, W. 110
'Dream Carp' 161–2, 170–3
dreams 195–8
Dritte Option 91
duality of fish 161–5
Durkheim, E. 236n7

Earth Father 22
EBM (Evidence Based Medicine) 210
Ego 6, 18, 36–7; contact zones (European identity) 18–19; in *Heart of Darkness* (Conrad) 184–6
Eliade, M. 110
Ellenberger, H. F. 211
Elliot, T. S. 197
Ellis Island 63
embodied presence, transcendental hermaphrodite 118–21
emerging-mind theory 97
empire 71
Enns, C. Z. 109
environment 9
Eros 71, 110, 163
ethics, virtue ethic 249–51
ethnic specificity 66
ethnicity 63
European identity 3; cultural complex of an unheroic heroine 17–22; founding myth 12–13; past existence of 13–15; present existence of 15–16; territory 16; values 16–17
European Union 16–17
Europeanization of Europe 14
Evidence Base Medicine (EBM) 210
exclusion, male same-sex desire 130–3
expatriates 31–3
extremists 19–20

Eye of God, transcendent function 200–1
eye of the Heart 191–2, 197

Fanon, F. 54
Fassin, D. 32
Father, male same-sex desire 134–5
fathers 21–2
father-son relationships, terrorists 21
Feldman, B. 201
Felner, A. 192–5
Felner, G. 194
Fernández, J. R. 60n6
Filho, L. 96, 102
'First Diuno Elegy' (Rilke) 120
first half of life, analytical psychology 241–3
fish 161; 'Dream Carp' 170–3; duality of 162–5; significance in Japan 165–70
fishy 163
flexible ethnicity 58
fluidity 235
Foley, N. 48, 54
Fordham, M. 37–8
Foucault, M. 4, 30, 143
founding myth, of Europe 12–13
The Four Rivers Fountain 115
Frankfurt am Main xviii–xix; coordination unit for LGBTIQ topics 83–5; interculturality 80–2; Office for Multicultural Affairs (AmkA) 82–3
Frankfurt School of Critical Theory xix–xx
free association 209
free will xxi
Freud, S. 10
Fromm, Erich 227
Futbol Picante 60n6
fuzzy sets 34

Gadamer, H.-G. 120
Gastarbeiter (guestworker), Germany 82
gender 85; in-between (Germany) 91–2
gender identity 215
gender identity issues (Sandplay therapy) 101–5
Genderbread Person 87–8
genderqueer people, Germany 91–2
geneaological psychology 68
geographical dislocations 30
Germany: Frankfurt am Main *see* Frankfurt am Main; in-between (Germany) 91–2; international breakdown of population with migrant background 82; trans* people 73

Giaccardi, C. 227
Giddens, A. 235n1
Giegerich, W. 229–30
Gimbutas, M. 13
global citizenship 30, 38–41
global nomads 31–3; trauma 35
globalisation 28, 31
Goethe University xix
'good enough' mothering 56
Good Mother 22
Great Mother 22
group hero (terrorist), European identity 19
group skin 12
Guattari, F. 29, 36
Guyer, P. xxi

Habermas, J. xx, 15
Halperin, D. 140
Hardin, R. xxi
Hatanaka, C. 213, 216
Havel, V. 15–16, 227
Hayes, S. C. 203–4
Heart of Darkness (Conrad) 175–87
helping witnesses 205
Henderson, J. 64, 112
hermaphrodites 109–111; *Sleeping Hermaphoditos* 108–9; transcendent function 111–13; transcendental hermaphrodite 113–18
Hermaphroditos 110–11
Hermes 115, 139–40
Hernández, J. 60n6
heroes, European identity 18
heroine's journey, *When Marnie Was There* (2014) 157–8
heteronormativity 128
hikikomori 158
Hillman, J. xviii, 100, 117, 138–9, 181; hermaphrodites 110; individuation 222, 232, 235; nekyia 176
Hippolytus 198
Hirsch, M. 67
history of: Europe, founding myth 12–1; Mexican-Americans 48–50
The Hobbit (Tolkien, 1937) 251–2
holding environment 9
holding the tension of the opposites xxii
Homans, P. 131
home: Mexican-Americans 52; for people on the move 34
homelessness, trans* people 90–1
Honderich, T. xxi

Honneth, A. xx
Hopcke, R. 97
human environment, identity 8–9
Hungary 15
Huskinson, L. 9
hybridity 39
hyphens 39

'I' 36
identical self 4
identity 3–6; in analytical psychology 6–8; bodies and borders 10–12; European identity *see* European identity; space 8–9
identity development for people on the move 35–8
imaginary friends, *When Marnie Was There* (Robinson 1967) 152–4
imagination xxii
immigrants 31–2; intergenerational perspective 192–5
immunity to vertigo 226
in-between (Germany) 91–2
incorruptibility 250–53
indeterminacy xxi–xxii
indeterminate space 153
indeterminate state 209–10; background of 215–17; change of pathology 212–14; coping with 217–18; neuroscience and 210–12; shifting from determinate state 212–14
Indeterminate States xix, xxiv
indirect thinking xxii
individual hero (asylum seeker) 19, 21–2
individuation xx, 29, 38–41, 241; Beck, U. 223–4; Beck and Bauman versus Jung 226–9; clinical vignette 230–4; Jung, C. G. 222–3; re-visioning individuation 202–3; transcendental hermaphrodite 113–18
infancy 52–3
inner talk 229; clinical vignette 230–4
inner world, identity 3
interculturality, Frankfurt am Main 80–2
intergenerational perspective 192–5
inter-generational trauma 66–8
internally displaced persons 31
interventions, for children 97
interviews, Mexican-Americans 57–9
introversion 131
invisible magic circles 147; *When Marnie Was There* (2014) 155–7

in-vulnerability 251–2
ivory, Heart of Darkness (Conrad) 180–1
iwashi (sardine), significance in Japan 168–70

Jacobi, J. 243
Jacoby, M. 52–3, 56
James, W. 35
Japan: duality of fish symbol (Japan) 161; fish, significance of 165–70; indeterminate state 215
Joll, J. 14
Jung, C. G. xxi, xxiii, 65, 69, 212; Anima 178; creative fantasy 235; death 153; Ego 6; eye of God 200, 204; fish 161–5; gender identity 215; hermaphrodites 109–11; individuation 29, 38, 222–3; male same-sex desire, Anima 138–9; nekyia 176; non-human environment 9; paradise 53; participation mystique 11; philosophies compared to Beck and Bauman 226–9; relatedness between 'me' and 'us' 203; self 5, 36–7; splinter psyches 35; tree image 198; wholeness 202
Jungian model of the mind 243

Kalf, D. M. 103
kállos 120
kalós 120
Kalsched, D. 56
Kanner, L. 213
Kast, V. 222
Kasuga Gongen Kenki Emaki (Miraculous Stories of Kasuga Deity Picture Scroll) 169
Kawanabe, K. 169
Kerényi, K.110
Kimbles, S. 64, 66
Kingsnorth, P. 65
Kojiki 165
Konstan, D. 120
Koutonin, M. R. 31

Lacan, J. 216
Lapis 164
Laquer, T. 85
Larmore, C. 250
Lavin, I. 114, 118
Lexikon, H. 102
LGBTIQ (lesbian, gay, bisexual, transgender, intersex, and queer), Frankfurt am Main 83–5; suicide 89

light, *Heart of Darkness* (Conrad) 181
liminality xxii, 12, 205, 216; *When Marnie Was There* (Robinson) 153
liquid life 225
liquidity 35, 225–6, 234–5
Littlejohns, R. 13
logos 71
Lopez-Pedraza, E. 132, 139
lunar consciousness 205

M sound, Merlin 154–5
Maalouf, A. 73
Mackenzie, S. 97–8
Magatti, Mauro 227
male same-sex desire 127–30; Anima 138–9; communality 139–41; exclusion 130–3; Father 134–5; Pan 139–41; Persona 133–4; representations of 127–30; Senex/Puer 136–8; shadow 141–2; Trickster 139–41
malinche 55
Malintzin *see* Doña Marina
Mama lernt deutsch (Mum's learning German) 83
margin xxii
Marsman, M. A. 98
Martínez, E. C. 48
mastizaje 48–9
Maternal 52–3
Mather, J. M. 118
Maurette, P. 112
McMillan, C. 29
MDR (*Memories, Dreams, Reflections*) (Jung) 154
Mead, G. H. 5
meditation 228
Memories, Dreams, Reflections (MDR) (Jung) 154
mending the symbolic 128
Mercurius 111, 164
Merleau-Ponty, M. 206
Merlin 154–5
mestizaje 59
Mestizos 48
Mexican-Americans 47; depth-psychological perspective on cultural complex 50–6; history of 48–50; interviews 57–9; trauma 53, 56
migrants 31–3
migration xxiii–xxiv; Frankfurt am Main 82–3; trans* people 87
migration background 81–2

migration crisis, Europe 2015 31
migration psychology 32
migration trauma 64; personal migration trauma 69–72
Migrationshinstergrund 82
Miller, A. 205
Millot, C. 130
Mills, J. xx, xxi
mirroring 202
Mishima, Y. 130–1
Mitchell, S. A. 5
Mithen, S. xxiii
modernity 235n1
Monette, P. 132
monotheism 20
Montgomery, G. A. 200
Moore, J. W. 48
Moraga, C. 50
Mormando, F. 114
mothers 22; environment 9; fish 164
mother's touch 8
Movement-in-Depth 198–9
multiplicity 37–8
'Muo-no-Rigyo' 161–2
Murakami, H. 218
Murdock, M. 158
mythology, *Heart of Darkness* (Conrad) 182–3

namagusa 167
Naorai (Japan) 166
nationalism 31
nationalities, European identity 16
NE (new ethic) 241; centroversion 246–9
need to belong 201–2
nekyia 175–7
neue Ethik (Neumann) 241–5
Neumann, E. 18, 21–2, 103; anima/animus projections 244–5; first half of life 241–3; infancy 52; *neue Ethik* 241–5; night sea journey 245–6; self-perpetuating inertia 104; spiritual development 99
neuroscience, indeterminate state and 210–12
new ethic (NE) 241
night sea journey 176, 245–6
nomadic subject 29
nomadic thought 29–30
non-binary people, Germany 91–2
non-human environment, identity 8–9
nostalgic disorientation 35
nostalgic yearning, Mexican-Americans 52
nurturing environment 9

object relation theory 8
observing, versus witnessing 204–5
occupation, Mexican-Americans 48
Odajnyk, W. 54
Odyssey (Homer), centroversion 253–4
Office for Multicultural Affairs (AmkA), Frankfurt am Main 82–3
opposite direction 230
Orback, S. 226, 232
Osawa, M. 216
other xxiv, 201; ego and, contact zones (European identity) 18–19
otherness, trans teens 89
outer world, identity 3

Pan, male same-sex desire 139–41
Papadopoulos, R. 32, 52; nostalgic disorientation 35
paradisal 'primal unity' 52–3
Paradise 52–3, 56
parental images, Mexican-Americans 51–2
Paris, G. 115
participation mystique 11
Pasolini, P. P. 127–8, 130–1, 134–5, 139, 140–3
pathology, indeterminate state 212–14
Paz, Octavio 55
penis 85–6
people on the move: hierarchy of lexicon 30–3; home 34; identity development and sense of belonging 35–8; individuation and global citizenship 38–41; trauma 34–5; *see also* migrants
Pereira, H. C. 132
Persona 6–8; male same-sex desire 133–4
personal migration trauma, 69–72
phantom narratives, 64–65
phenotype, Mexican-Americans 50
pilgrims, *Heart of Darkness* (Conrad) 183–4
Pisces 163, 165
pluralism 41
Pont Sant' Angelo 118–21
Popper, K. xxi
positive-integral-ego 104
post-memory 67
present absence 68
primal relationships 52–3
primal scene 51
projection: Anima/Animus projections 244–5; *Heart of Darkness* (Conrad) 179
protoself 4

psyche 6–7, 36
psychic skin 12
psychoanalysis 209
psycho-généalogie 67–8
psychological development, centroversion 247
psychotherapy, neuroscience and indeterminate state 210–12
puberty, male same-sex desire 130
punctum 119–20

quantum indeterminacy xxi

race mixing 54
Rackete, C. 23n3
radiance 120–1
Ramirez, I. 55
Ramos, D. G. 100
Rape of Proserpina (Bernini) 116
realism 229–30
rebis 109–11
Rechtman, R. 32
recognition xx
Redfearn, J. W. T. 9, 36
refugees: defined 30–1; LGBTIQ people (Frankfurt) 84; trauma 32
relational fields, re-visioning individuation 202–3
relationships: father-son relationships, terrorists 21; primal relationships 52–3
religion, European identity 15
religious fanaticism 137
religious fundamentalism 20
representations of same-sex desire (male) 127–30
resistance 69
the return, *Heart of Darkness* (Conrad) 186
re-visioning individuation 202–3
rhizomatic identity 37–9
rhizome 29, 36–7
Rilke, R. M. 120
rites of passage xxii
Rizzo, F. 158
Robinson, J. G., *When Marnie Was There* 147–8
Rogers, C. 209
Russia 15

Saban, M. 202–3
sacrifice 20
Salvator Mundi (Bernini) 121–2

same-sex desire (male): exclusion 130–3; representations of 127–30; *When Marnie Was There* (2014) 148–50
Sampaio, C. 96
Samuels, A. 40–1, 51, 228; hermaphrodites 109
Sandplay therapy 99–101; gender identity issues 101–5
sardines (iwashi), significance in Japan 168–70
Schlatter, J. 197
schools, suicide in trans* teens 89–90
Schuman, R. 18
Sebastian complex 141–2
self 35–7, 196–7, 203; autobiographical self 4–5; identity and 4–5; society and 5
self-awareness 8
self-identity 4
self-knowledge 228–9
self-perpetuating inertia 104
self-realisation 29
self-regulation 100
self-responsibility 227
Senex/Puer, male same-sex desire 136–8
sense of belonging, for people on the move 35–8
separation xxii
Shadow 7, 54; *Heart of Darkness* (Conrad) 184–6; male same-sex desire 141–2; Neumann, E. 244–5
Shamdasani, S. 211; individuation 222, 232
shared skin 11–12
shared spaces, male same-sex desire 140
shojin (Japan) 166–7
Singer, T. xviii, 97, 201; cultural complexes 47; hermaphrodites 110
skin 10–12
skin ego 10
Sleeping Hermaphoditos 108–9, 111–13
Smith, W. 30, 40
snakes, *Heart of Darkness* (Conrad) 180
social indeterminacy xxi
society, self and 5
Sol Niger 181
solar consciousness 205
Soncini, S. 13
Sontag, S. 136
sould wounds 53
space, identity 8–9
spiritual development, children 99
splinter psyches 35
Spuybroek, L. 121

Stein, R. 19–20, 136; individuation 38
Steiner, R. 242
Stets, J. E. 4–5
structure, identity 6
Studio Ghibli 148
sub-personalities 37–8
suicidal terrorism 19–20
suicide, trans* people 89–90
Symbolic Interaction tradition 5
symbolisation, male same-sex desire 127–30
symbols xxiii; *Heart of Darkness* (Conrad) 182–3
Symposium (Plato) 109, 120
symptoms of gender issues, children 96

Tanabata festival, *When Marnie Was There* (2014) 155–7
TCKs (third culture kids) 33
teenagers, trans* people, suicide 89–90
temenos 103, 204
tenerreza (tenderness) 113–14
Tenochtitlan 55
tension between opposites 212
Terrible Father 22
terrible mother, Mexican-Americans 53–5
territory, European identity 16
terrorists, European identity 19–21
thinking ego 10
third culture kids (TCKs) 33
thirdness 30, 40
Thoreau, H. D. 202
touch 8
trans umbrella 87
trans* people: Genderbread Person 87–8; Germany 73; homelessness 90–1; interventions 97; migration 87; suicide 89–90
transcendent function xxiii, 39; Eye of God 200–1; hermaphrodites 111–13
transcendental hermaphrodite 112–18; embodied presence 118–21
transgender issues 85
transgender movement 96
transgenderism, Jungian perspective 97–8
trans-generational trauma 67
transitional object 9
transitional space 9
trauma 12; collective cultural trauma 68–9; inter-generational trauma 66–8; Mexican-Americans 53, 56; migration trauma 64; for people on the move 34–5; personal migration trauma 69–72; refugees 32
Treaty of Guadalupe Hidalgo 48
Treaty on European Union 16–17
Tree of Life 196–7
trees 195–8
Trevi, M. 255
Tricksters 114–15; male same-sex desire 139–41
Trump, Donald 68
Trump administration, Mexican-Americans 57–8
Trump era, racism 54
Turner, V. W. xxii–xxiii, 201, 205, 216

unconscious 211
unitary reality 52–3
United Kingdom 15
unthought knowns 64
'us' 203–4

vaginas 85–6
values, European identity 16–17
Van Gennep, A. xxii
Van Reken, R. 33
Vasquez, J. M. 49; flexible ethnicity 58
vertical mystical homoeros 20, 137
virtue ethic, analytical psychology 249–51
Visalius, A. 85
Volkan, V. D. xxiv
von Franz, M.-L. 155
von Zimmern, K. 191
Vulnera 250
vulnerability 250, 253–4

Warwick, G. 114
Watanabe, T. 218
Watkins, M. 228
Weil, M. S. 110
Western philosophy, identity 4
When Marnie Was There (2014) (film) 147–150; film synopsis 150–2; heroine's journey 157–8; Tanabata festival 155–7
When Marnie Was There (Robinson) 147, 152–5
When the Saint Teresa in Ecstasy (Bernini) 116–21
white Americans 54, 63
white racism 54
white supremacy 66
Whitehead, A. N. 34
Whitehouse, M. S. 199

whiteness-as-the-norm 65
whites: collective cultural trauma 68–9; inter-generational trauma 66–8; personal migration trauma 69–72
whole 39
wholeness 202
Wing, L. 213–14
Winnicott, D. 8–10; home 34
Wintle, M. 15
witness consciousness 202–3, 205
witnessing 191, 199, 202–3; Eye of God 200; mirroring 202; versus observing 204–205

world 30
World Wars, European identity 18
worldliness 30, 39–40

Yamanaka, S. 211
Yanagita, K. 167
Yonebayashi, H. 147–9

Zarathustra (Jung) 200
Zen Buddhism 217
Zoja, L. 17

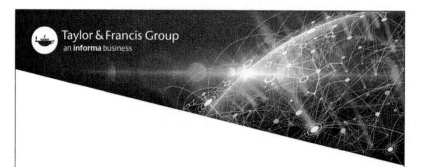